The Ultimate iPad®

Your Digital Life at Your Fingertips

James Floyd Kelly

800 East 96th Street,
Indianapolis, Indiana 46240 USA

The Ultimate iPad®: Your Digital Life at Your Fingertips

Copyright © 2015 by Pearson Education

ISBN-13: 978-0-7897-5289-5
ISBN-10: 0-7897-5289-1

Library of Congress Cataloging-in-Publication Data: 2014933220

Printed in the United States of America

First Printing: July 2014

Trademarks

All terms mentioned in this book that are known to be trademarks or service marks have been appropriately capitalized. Que Publishing cannot attest to the accuracy of this information. Use of a term in this book should not be regarded as affecting the validity of any trademark or service mark.

iPad is a registered trademark of Apple Inc.

Warning and Disclaimer

Bulk Sales

Que Publishing offers excellent discounts on this book when ordered in quantity for bulk purchases or special sales. For more information, please contact

U.S. Corporate and Government Sales
1-800-382-3419
corpsales@pearsontechgroup.com

For sales outside of the U.S., please contact

International Sales
international@pearsoned.com

Editor-in-Chief
Greg Wiegand

Executive Editor
Rick Kughen

Development Editor
Greg Kettell

Technical Editor
Karen Weinstein

Managing Editor
Kristy Hart

Project Editor
Elaine Wiley

Copy Editor
Bart Reed

Indexer
Erika Millen

Proofreader
Paula Lowell

Publishing Coordinator
Kristen Watterson

Book Designer
Mark Shirar

Compositor
Nonie Ratcliff

Contents at a Glance

Introduction   xi

CHAPTER 1   The Ultimate iPad   1

CHAPTER 2   Get Geek-Level Organized   17

CHAPTER 3   Additional iPad Storage Options   39

CHAPTER 4   Evernote: Your New Best Friend   59

CHAPTER 5   Cut the Clutter: Scan Everything   75

CHAPTER 6   Your Financials—Banking and Investment Apps   103

CHAPTER 7   Convert Your Collections: Reducing Book and Magazine Clutter   117

CHAPTER 8   Rip and Store: Your Movies and Shows on Demand   143

CHAPTER 9   Don't Forget Your Backup: Long-Term Deep Storage   163

CHAPTER 10   Automation: Video, Appliances, and More   181

CHAPTER 11   Build a Web Reference Library: Never Lose an Online Article   207

CHAPTER 12   "Plays Well with Others": Remote Control and an Extra Screen   241

CHAPTER 13   Scan and Use Again: Activity Books and More   265

APPENDIX A   Tips and Tricks   297

Index   303

Table of Contents

Introduction   xi

Chapter 1   The Ultimate iPad   1

What Will I Need?   2

iPad: $329–$929 (New)   3

Personal Scanner: $120–$500   4

External Hard Drive: $100–$200   7

A Dropbox Account: Free or Paid   8

The Evernote App and an Evernote Account   10

PDFpen/PDFpen Scan+ Apps ($14.99 and $4.99)   12

The GoodReader App: $4.99   13

Why Should I Do This?   15

Chapter 2   Get Geek-Level Organized   17

Dropbox and Evernote—Sign Up   18

Create a Dropbox Account   18

Create an Evernote Account   20

Dropbox and Evernote Apps—Configure   21

Install and Configure the Dropbox App   22

Install and Configure the Evernote App   24

Install and Configure the GoodReader App   25

A Simple Decluttering System   33

Some Thoughts About Security   36

Foundation Tasks Wrap-Up   37

Chapter 3   Additional iPad Storage Options   39

Cloud Hosting or Local Hosting?   40

Cloud Access Via Dropbox   41

Local Hosting Via Pogoplug   46

Your iPad's Extra Storage   57

Chapter 4   **Evernote: Your New Best Friend   59**

What Is Evernote?   60

Evernote Overview   61

Navigating in Evernote   63

Creating Notes in Evernote   68

The Power of Premium Evernote   71

Possible Uses for Evernote   72

   Send Emails Directly to Notebooks   72

   The Web Clipper   72

Don't Forget the Cleanup   74

Chapter 5   **Cut the Clutter: Scan Everything   75**

What Is a Scanner?   76

The App Scanner   78

The Portable Scanner   91

The Desktop Scanner   93

Summary   102

Chapter 6   **Your Financials—Banking and Investment Apps   103**

Banking Apps   104

Credit Card and Investment Apps   107

The Mint.com App   110

Be Careful!   113

Chapter 7   **Convert Your Collections: Reducing Book and Magazine Clutter   117**

Start with Digital Books and Magazines Now   118

The Cut-and-Scan Method   122

Use a Scanning Service   126

A Special Scanner for Books and Magazines   128

Risks and Legal Issues   140

Chapter 8   **Rip and Store: Your Movies and Shows On Demand   143**

Streaming Subscription Services   144

Digital Movies and TV Shows for Sale   147

Converting DVD/Blu-ray Discs   148

   Ripping with DVDShrink 3.2   150

   Ripping with MakeMKV   154

   Converting with HandBrake   157

The Legal Stuff   161

Chapter 9   Don't Forget Your Backup: Long-Term Deep Storage   163

Let's Talk About Backups   164

Unlimited Data Backup Made Easy   166

Online Backup Alternatives   174

It's Your Data; Guard It Carefully   178

Chapter 10   Automation: Video, Appliances, and More   181

Video Monitoring with Dropcam   181

Your iPad as Remote Control—WeMo   186

IFTTT—If This [Happens] Then [Do] That   191

Chapter 11   Build a Web Reference Library: Never Lose an Online Article   207

Don't Bookmark It, Pocket It   208

   Copy a URL to the Clipboard   215

   Email the URL to Pocket   215

Convert Online Content to PDF   219

   PrintFriendly.com   220

   PrintWhatYouLike.com   227

Notes and Sketches Straight into Evernote   233

Never. Lose. Anything.   240

Chapter 12   "Plays Well with Others": Remote Control and an Extra Screen   241

Remotely Control Computers and Laptops   242

Get Some Extra Screen Space   256

Chapter 13   Scan and Use Again: Activity Books and More   265

Kids Activity Books   266

Creating and Using Digital Activity Books   267

PDFpen for Filling Out Digital Documents   279

    Adding Text to a PDF Form   280

    Adding Your Signature to a PDF Form   286

Other Areas for Reuse   292

Your Ultimate iPad   295

Appendix A   Tips and Tricks   297

Online Instruction Manuals   297

LEGO Building Instructions   298

Backup Driving Directions   299

Cheap Password Manager   300

Index   303

About the Author

James Floyd Kelly is a writer from Atlanta, Georgia. He has degrees in Industrial Engineering and English and has written technology books on a number of subjects, including CNC machines, 3D printing, Open Software, LEGO robotics, and electronics.

Dedication

For Mom and Dad—1984, the first Mac, changed my life...thank you.

Acknowledgments

I remember pitching this idea to Rick Kughen at Pearson. For a few years, I'd been repeatedly explaining and demonstrating various iPad tricks and tasks to friends and family, and it just seemed like a good idea for a book. Thanks to Rick, the book you're holding in your hands is a reality and will hopefully give you even more reasons to love the iPad.

My technical editor, Karen Weinstein, did a great job of finding my errors and offering suggestions for improving the book. Even after years of using the iPad, I still sometimes explain things incorrectly—Karen kept me on my toes, and the book is better for it.

Every book has a variety of editors assigned to it, and they all have special duties that help to make a book great. I'd like to give a huge thank-you to the other editors involved in the book—development editors Greg Kettell and Todd Brakke, production editor Elaine Wiley, and copy editor Bart Reed. Thank you all for your confidence in this book and for your help in getting it completed.

A big thank-you goes to the entire crowd at Pearson and Que Publishing—I continue to enjoy writing for these folks, and they always do such a great job of spreading the word about their books (mine included) and making sure that all the cool topics are covered and ready for the world to learn.

Finally, I always thank my wife and two boys for their support. Deadlines are always stressful, but oftentimes the entire writing process can be that way, and they always give me the time I need to finish my writing, including the occasional weekend afternoon when I'd really rather be outside playing and spending time with them.

James Floyd Kelly
Atlanta, GA
April 2014

We Want to Hear from You!

As the reader of this book, *you* are our most important critic and commentator. We value your opinion and want to know what we're doing right, what we could do better, what areas you'd like to see us publish in, and any other words of wisdom you're willing to pass our way.

We welcome your comments. You can email or write to let us know what you did or didn't like about this book—as well as what we can do to make our books better.

Please note that we cannot help you with technical problems related to the topic of this book.

When you write, please be sure to include this book's title and author as well as your name and email address. We will carefully review your comments and share them with the author and editors who worked on the book.

Email: feedback@quepublishing.com

Mail: Que Publishing
          ATTN: Reader Feedback
          800 East 96th Street
          Indianapolis, IN 46240 USA

Reader Services

Visit our website and register this book at quepublishing.com/register for convenient access to any updates, downloads, or errata that might be available for this book.

Introduction

Your Ultimate iPad

Back in 2010, I remember watching Steve Jobs introduce the iPad. I was skeptical. No keyboard? No USB port? Same (or similar) operating system as the one I'd seen on the iPhone? (I wasn't convinced of the iPhone, either). I listened to the list of things this new tablet could do, comparing it to the various tasks I was already performing with my laptop. What was the big deal?

But as I sat there for a few hours, browsing the Internet, sending some emails, listening to my music, and collecting information for a book proposal I was writing, the battery on my laptop died. I'd gotten about three hours of work from the battery and was now looking at having to head to my office to finish what I was doing on the large, clunky desktop computer. Fighting the urge to get off the couch, I tried the onscreen keyboard on my mobile phone to send an email. It was frustrating. I'd been browsing a website with my phone's web browser and squinting to find some answer to a technical question my dad had pitched to me, and I kept tapping the wrong link and launching the wrong page.

Longer battery life, larger onscreen keyboard, larger screen, web browsing, email...all of a sudden, the iPad was starting to sound like a very good solution. I'm a bit impulsive at times about new technology (to my wife's dismay), so I placed my order and got one of the very first iPad tablets from the Apple Store (and still have it now, four years later). After just a few weeks, I was sold. The iPad was a game changer for me.

Jump forward four years and I cannot imagine getting through my daily activities without my iPad. I've continued to upgrade, and I've found new ways to use the additional processing power and iOS features to make my work and home life easier. Along the way, I've been forced by necessity to find new and interesting ways to get things done with my iPad—mainly because I try to resist turning to my MacBook Air laptop and Windows desktop computer. Wherever possible, I always try to reach for the iPad first.

This book's origin came about because of my intense desire to avoid using a laptop or desktop computer. If I find a task that cannot be performed by my iPad, something that forces me to reach for the laptop or head to my office for the completely immobile desktop computer, I will eventually begin a focused search for a workaround—a solution that will let me transition that task to the tablet. Although I have a few tasks that are yet to be solved by the iPad, almost every task I've historically performed on my laptop or desktop computer is now done with my iPad. Where there's a will, there's a way...and this book is all about the "way."

Friends, family members, and complete strangers...they've all stopped me over the years to ask me to show them some trick they've seen me do with my iPad. "How did you do that?" is a frequent question. "I didn't know you could do that!" is a frequent response to my demo.

The iPad is great. If you have one, you know how enjoyable the little device can be. But I have a strong suspicion you're not pushing your own iPad to its limits. There are likely some things you can do with that tablet that you're not doing...or might not know can be done!

I'm hoping to surprise you throughout this book by showing you some ways to make that iPad earn back its price. If you can find just one or two tricks in this book that save you a few minutes (or even hours) of work a day or week, my job is done. The iPad is supposed to make the online experience more fun, less stressful...easier. If your iPad isn't doing that, you're reading the right book. Stick with me, and learn just how your iPad can become an indispensible tool for home and work. By the book's end, it's my hope that you'll be looking at the tablet in your hands and calling it by a new name—Ultimate iPad.

The Ultimate iPad

In This Chapter

- Push your iPad to its limits
- Hardware and software (apps) you will need
- An example of an Ultimate iPad

Ask anyone who knows me, and they can confirm that I really do tend to carry my iPad with me no matter where I go. I'm not a gadget freak, honestly—and I'm totally over the iPad. But I use my iPad for everything. *Everything*. Over the last four years (starting with the first iPad in 2010), I've managed to figure out a lot of tricks and shortcuts and other ways to make the iPad really work for me. For me, it's not about the gadget; rather, it's about all what the gadget brings to my home and work life—reduced stress, saved time, improved efficiency, and much more. Suffice it to say, the iPad has become an indispensable tool for me—I spend more time using it than I do my Windows computer or my Mac laptop.

For the past few years, I have been asked one type of question over and over by friends and colleagues, and it pertains to my reliance on my Apple iPad: "How do you do _____?"

Sometimes the question takes a different format: "Can you show me how to _____?" or "I don't know how to make my tablet do _____." But ultimately what they're asking is for me to show them some particular task that they've seen me demonstrate or explain why I do something in a particular manner. Here are some examples:

- How did you get all your DVD movies onto your iPad?
- That book isn't available as an ebook—how did you get it on your iPad?
- Do you really keep your kids' mazes and activity books on your iPad?
- Why do you pay for a Dropbox account—isn't it free to use?
- Is your office really "paper free"? Really? Where does all the paper go?

- What is that Evernote app you have installed on every device you own?
- Would you show me that cool productivity app you use again?
- You safely monitor your investments from your iPad?
- Can you really monitor your home and turn on and off appliances with your iPad?

The questions don't stop—and neither does the training. I'm usually more than happy to demonstrate to someone (time permitting) how I use my tablet to make my life easier. And when I say "my life," I'm talking about my personal (home) life *and* my work life. Friends and family often catch a glimpse of me doing something productive with my iPad and wonder if it might work for them. And usually the answer is, yes!

I'm not going to tell you that your iPad (or other tablet) is the ultimate solution to all your problems. But I am going to tell you that with a few minor changes to how you do your day-to-day tasks, you can and will find that a tablet often makes your life easier. For the remainder of this book, I'm going to explain some of the tools and processes I use to make my "digital life" run smoothly.

These tools and processes aren't any big secrets; I make no claim to creating them. And unlike many authors who require you to read the entire book to get the complete list of apps and tools, I'm going to tell you everything I use in this first chapter—complete with pricing. I don't want to waste your time, and I'm sure you don't want your time wasted. But if you find yourself interested and wanting more details about how to use a particular piece of hardware or software, you can jump to the chapter in question. Feel free to skip any of my suggestions that don't apply to your needs.

The iPad isn't an inexpensive device, and when I first got one I really struggled to find a way to justify the expense. Now, four years after my first iPad (I've upgraded since then), I have finally reached a point where the cost of my iPad is a drop in the bucket compared to the time savings and conveniences it offers to me. My hope for this book is that you will walk away with a more solid understanding of just how far you can push your iPad as well as make your iPad earn back its price.

What Will I Need?

In this section, I want to briefly but accurately provide you with a list of most all the software and hardware I cover in this book. You will absolutely *not* need to purchase everything on this list, and in many instances some of the items (mainly software apps) will be free. I will do my best to provide you with a range of prices for hardware, apps, and services where these exist, along with a discussion of the price differences.

What I would recommend to you is this—examine the list, find those items that won't break your budget, and then read the respective chapters to understand what you're getting for the money and what the list item offers to you as an iPad user. I didn't start with all these items but instead gathered them over the last few years as I needed or discovered them. Feel free to do the same; this isn't a race. Purchase what you find useful, and ignore the rest.

NOTE

Some items covered in this book didn't make it into this initial list—these are mainly services and specialty hardware that I only want to introduce to you but aren't considered critical to turning your iPad into what I call an Ultimate Productivity Machine.

And what might you need to purchase? Glad you asked.

iPad: $329–$929 (New)

The most obvious item you will need is an iPad. Figure 1.1 shows the original 10" version and the iPad Mini (7"). Whether your iPad is a Wi-Fi-only version or you're paying a data carrier such as Verizon or AT&T for always-available Internet, this book won't be all that useful to you without one.

Does it need to be running the latest operating system (iOS 7 at the time I'm writing this chapter)? Absolutely not. However, in some instances a few apps might not work with the oldest versions (iOS 4, for example). With the exception of a small number of apps, most of this book will be useful to someone with the original iPad (1).

FIGURE 1.1 The iPad and iPad Mini.

The original iPad didn't come with a camera, but since the iPad 2, all iPad tablets (including the Mini) come with front- and rear-facing cameras. These can be important tools, as you'll soon discover, but don't sweat it if you own the original iPad.

Last but not least, one other concern for iPad owners relates to memory. iPads provide between 16GB and 128GB of storage, and every iPad owner will tell you that free space seems to go quickly. Don't worry about storage space right now—you'll learn about some options that will remove the fear of running out of space.

NOTE

Although I focus on the iPad in this book, I'm not saying the advice, apps, and hardware found in this book can't be used with another brand of tablet. In some instances, the apps I reference are only available for the iPad, but that doesn't mean the app developer hasn't made a version for other tablet operating systems. And many of the tricks and tasks you'll see in this book can easily be duplicated for any tablet, not just the iPad. You may have to do some digging to find compatible apps or services, but rest assured if an app is popular with iPad users, some enterprising individual or company is offering a similar app for other tablets.

Personal Scanner: $120–$500

A personal scanner is simply a piece of hardware that converts a photo or document to a digital file that can be viewed on your iPad (or computer). Think of a scanner as a photocopier that scans the item you give it, but instead of spitting out a duplicate copy on paper, it lets you open and view it (and in most instances modify it) on your iPad or computer screen.

Although a personal scanner is going to make your life so much easier, I should tell you right now that it's also one of those items that you can postpone purchasing indefinitely or until you do some research and examine your budget. I'm telling you this first so you'll understand just how noncritical it is to own a scanner—there are plenty of workarounds, such as using your iPad to scan (except the original iPad), as you'll soon see, and there are also scanning services for those who find they just don't have a lot of stuff to scan. (More on this in Chapter 5, "Cut the Clutter: Scan Everything.")

Personal scanners come in a wide range of sizes, shapes, and prices. The older flatbed-type scanners are really almost obsolete compared to the speed-demon scanners available today. You can find scanners that only scan in one black-and-white page (single sided) at a time as well as scanners that use a feeder to handle 100+ double-sided full-color pages at a time. What it comes down to is your budget.

Take a look at Figure 1.2, and you'll see an example of a simple scanner that can scan both sides of a page, and in color. It's called the Doxie Go, and for over a year this was the scanner that sat on my desk.

FIGURE 1.2 This Doxie Go scans in one page at a time.

The Doxie Go is convenient for a number of reasons—it's small and lightweight, making it easy to carry. It has a rechargeable battery, so you don't have to have it plugged into the wall. It also has a large internal memory, so you can scan in items without connecting it to your computer—simply download all the scans at your convenience! You can buy the Doxie Go for approximately $190, and it is without a doubt one of the most reliable little personal scanners you can find. (A lower-priced version called the Doxie One must be plugged into wall power, but it can be found for around $130 and offers the same quality in terms of scanning.)

Although I really enjoyed my Doxie Go, I upgraded a bit later to two different scanners from Fujitsu. The first was the ScanSnap 1300i, shown in Figure 1.3.

The 1300i is slightly larger in size than the Doxie Go, but rather than feed in a single sheet at a time, the 1300i holds up to 10 sheets of paper in a feeder in the back and the paper is pulled in one sheet at a time. As with the Doxie Go, scans can be set for single- or double-sided color pages. Although the 1300i is portable, it really is more of a desktop scanner, meaning you leave it attached to your computer (via a USB cable), and scans are stored on the computer's hard drive.

I loved the 1300i, but my scanning needs are quite constant month to month, and I began searching for a new scanner with more features and the ability to feed in more sheets. What I found and now use is the Fujitsu ScanSnap iX500, which can hold up to 50 sheets of paper in its paper chute (see Figure 1.4).

FIGURE 1.3   The Fujitsu ScanSnap 1300i is a great little desktop scanner.

FIGURE 1.4   The Fujitsu ScanSnap iX500 is my current choice for a personal scanner.

As with the other scanners, it can handle double-sided full-color pages. But the iX500 has a few capabilities that I absolutely love and will cover in more detail in Chapter 5. In addition to standard scanning to my desktop computer, I can also scan wirelessly and have scans sent directly to my iPad! (This feature is also available with the 1300i that runs around $250.) The iX500 comes with a heftier price tag—$420, but later in the book you'll get a better look at just how much scanning I do and hopefully understand my purchase decision.

There are a *lot* of personal scanners on the market, and you've likely seen them advertised on television or have maybe seen them in an office setting. Although I cannot imagine my life without a personal scanner, I will tell you that there are some inexpensive options to a personal scanner that will surprise you, so feel free to jump ahead to Chapter 5 for more details.

External Hard Drive: $100–$200

My third-generation iPad came with 32GB of hard drive storage space, of which only 12GB remains available as free storage. You might also be surprised to know that I have fewer than 30 apps installed on my iPad (only five of those are games). Still, storage space can be a real issue for users who love to install apps by the dozens. Luckily, I've discovered a number of methods for making storage space a nonissue, and I'll be sharing them with you later in the book. One of those methods involves using a dedicated external hard drive like the one shown in Figure 1.5.

FIGURE 1.5 A Seagate 3TB external (and portable) hard drive.

External hard drives available today run from 500GB (gigabytes) up to 5TB (terabytes). Remember, a terabyte is 1,000GB! My 3TB drive is 3,000GB, almost 100 times the amount of storage found on my iPad3. I bought this drive almost six months ago at $130, and today I went and found the same 3TB drive for $100.

These small and portable external hard drives connect to your computer via USB, providing more storage than you might possibly ever use. You can unplug them from one computer, move them to another, and have access to anything stored on them.

> **TIP**
>
> External hard drives (also called portable drives) can often by found with a catchy brand name, such as the Western Digital lines called My Book and My Passport, and My Cloud. Should you choose to buy one, check out customer reviews and warranty information. (I tend to stick to brand names I know because I trust their reliability.)

But the question remains—how does that 3TB external hard drive help my 32GB iPad3? Later in Chapter 3, "Additional iPad Storage Options," I will show you how to make all that wonderful storage space available to your iPad, thus freeing you from ever worrying about what must stay and what must be deleted from your tablet.

As with a scanner, an external hard drive isn't required, but as you'll discover in later chapters, having that extra storage space will go hand-in-hand with pushing your iPad to its productivity limits. When you're ready to buy one, you're going to be pleasantly surprised at the price—these things seem to be dropping in price by the week, and I have no doubt that the day is fast approaching where a 5TB drive will be under $100. (And rest assured, if you can find that much storage space or more for under $100, grab it.)

A Dropbox Account: Free or Paid

If you're not familiar with "the cloud," let me take a moment to explain. Your computer has a storage drive inside it that holds all your files; this drive is either the Hard Drive type referred to as HDD or a Solid State Drive (SSD). A traditional HDD has moving parts inside and writes data on a series of platters inside that can be easily damaged if dropped or hit with an electrical surge. SSDs are more expensive but are a bit more rugged (no moving parts inside), and much of the computing industry is slowing but surely moving away from HDD to SSD technology.

Similarly, your iPad has internal solid state flash storage to hold all of those apps and photos and songs you enjoy on your tablet. This kind of storage is also called "local" because it stays put—if you have a photo stored on your home computer's hard drive, that photo is going to be difficult to open and view when you're in a restaurant or even on the opposite side of the planet.

Now, imagine if you could place your files in a specific location so they could always be accessed no matter where you are at any given moment? (Of course, this mental exercise depends on Internet access, so let me just toss that in as a requirement.) Imagine a storage location holding your photos or music so that you can access them from your computer, your neighbor's computer, your cousin's mobile phone, your best friend's iPad, or even a free-access kiosk PC at your public library? Are you beginning to see the benefits of having your files stored somewhere they can be accessed (securely, requiring a password, of course) no matter what device you might have available?

Now you're beginning to see the benefits of "cloud" storage. In this case, the cloud is any Internet-based service that is willing to store your files for you and make them available via an Internet connection. Well, one of the most popular and well known is a service called Dropbox, and I cannot stop singing its praises. I've tried its competitors and always come back—Dropbox is king in my book. Dropbox makes an app for just about every device out there, including mobile phones, tablets, and computers of all operating systems. Because of this, Dropbox users are more likely to be able to access their files from any Internet-connected device.

NOTE

Some of you may be wondering about Apple's own iCloud service. I like it, I really do. You get free storage when you create an account, and it's a great way to synchronize photos and music between your iOS devices. You can certainly use it, and many of the apps I will introduce to you can take advantage of iCloud to move files back and forth between your iPad, but I've had nothing but good luck with Dropbox and it just plain works well.

You can register for a free Dropbox account and get 2GB of free storage with no strings attached. You can earn additional 500MB upgrades to your account by inviting friends and family to sign up for Dropbox, and I managed to raise my storage capacity from 2GB to 16GB before making the decision to pay Dropbox a yearly fee for some additional storage—more on that in Chapter 3.

Similar free services to Dropbox include Google Drive, Microsoft's SkyDrive, Box.com, and, of course, Apple's iCloud. Whatever you do, choose one (or more than one) and sign up. You'll get an initial amount of free storage space that you'll learn how to use later in the book, and accessing that free storage is as simple as opening the app on your iPad's home screen. Figure 1.6 shows the Dropbox icon.

FIGURE 1.6 Dropbox exists as an app on your iPad.

Just so you're aware, Dropbox provides an additional 100GB (added to your free space) for $10/month (or $8.25/month if you pay for a full year in advance), and that's the plan I use. Additional plans offer 200GB, 500GB, 1TB, and even more, but these are typically used by businesses, not individuals.

NOTE

If you're wondering why I pay for additional Dropbox storage space while also using a 3TB hard drive, my answer is a bit vague. In many instances, I use Dropbox to share folders and files with others, and it's much easier to share a single folder (with all the files inside) with a single user or multiple users than giving someone access to my external hard drive. This will become clearer later in the book.

The Evernote App and an Evernote Account

I find the service (and app) provided by Evernote to be so important that I've dedicated an entire chapter (Chapter 4, "Evernote: Your New Best Friend") to the topic and how to use it.

For just a moment, imagine you have a large bookshelf that can hold binders or notebooks dedicated to every imaginable topic, bill, receipt, recipe, or anything else you might need to keep as a record. One binder would hold recipes, another would hold How-To articles you've collected from magazines and websites, and yet another binder might contain all the chapters for your latest novel. You might group related binders on one particular shelf—for example, I might have one (or more) shelves that hold nothing but binders that contain the chapters for all the books I've written or am currently writing.

Over time, you might amass quite a large number of binders, but in theory you could use this system to store anything and everything that you might ever want to reference, now or in the future.

Of course, this system could easily outgrow a shelf or a room or even a house over time. A binder/notebook system like this could end up taking up a lot of physical space. And what happens with your Recipe binder should it become full? You'd start a new one (Recipes II) and fill that one up. But what happens when you want to dig out that recipe for lemon squares? Was it in Recipes I or Recipes II? Even if you know which binder it's in, you still have to thumb through that binder to find the recipe, which is buried in with all the other recipes.

Well, I'm here to tell you that the Evernote service solves these problems and many more. First, it's digital, so no physical space is needed to store actual binders or notebooks. Second, it's fully searchable. Just type in **lemon squares** with the Search tool and you'll get an immediate listing of all documents that make mention of those two words. You can continue to add notebooks as needed (there are limits, which I'll discuss in Chapter 4) and even combine them into special collections called "stacks." You can see an example of digital notebooks and stacks in Figure 1.7.

As you can probably tell, I'm very big on Evernote. I love Evernote. It is one of those tools I just cannot imagine ever giving up. And I'm going to show you exactly how useful it is and how you might integrate it into your home and work life with your iPad.

TIP

One last thing about Evernote—with a physical notebook, you're really limited to inserting paper, printed photos, and not much else. But with Evernote, you can store videos, PDFs, website text snippets, audio recordings, and much more. Jump to Chapter 4 if you just can't wait to see just how beneficial Evernote will be to you.

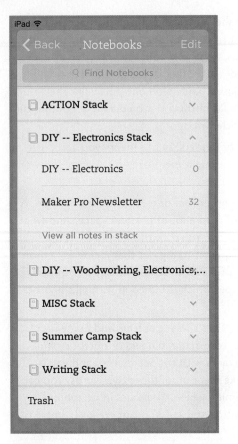

FIGURE 1.7 Evernote uses a system of notes, notebooks, and stacks.

PDFpen/PDFpen Scan+ Apps ($14.99 and $4.99)

In my line of work (writer), I deal with a lot of PDF files—contracts, chapter layouts, and other documents. PDFs are popular for good reason—you can see exactly how a document will look when it is printed, they're compatible with every operating system, and they're useful for sharing documents with others without worry about which word processing tool the other person uses.

One of my favorite apps for the iPad is PDFpen. It not only lets you open up and read PDFs, but you can also create them. You can highlight text, add graphics, and even apply a scan of your signature to PDF contracts, as shown in Figure 1.8. You'll see PDFpen in action later in Chapter 12, "'Plays Well with Others': Remote Control and an Extra Screen," where I'll show you some other interesting and useful ways to use this app.

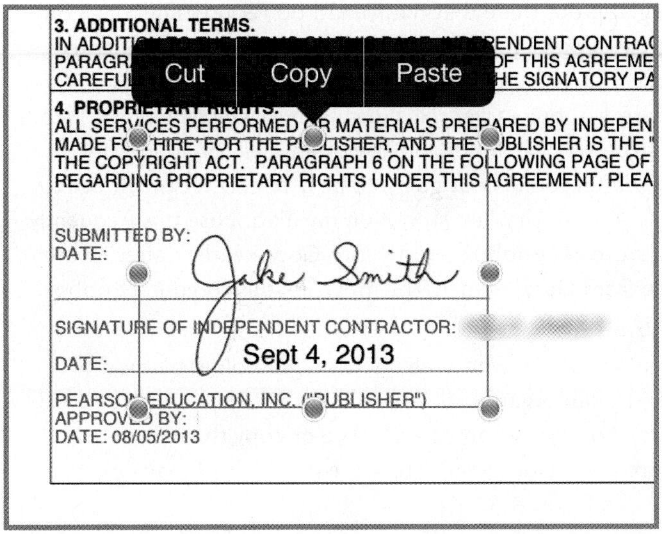

FIGURE 1.8 Fill out PDF signature lines with a digital scan of your signature.

Previously I mentioned that it's not necessary for you to go out and purchase a personal scanner, and now I'm going to explain that statement. A sister app called PDFpen Scan+ lets you use your iPad's camera to take photos of documents that are then converted into PDFs. Not only do you get a digital record of a paper document, but you can also apply what's called OCR, or Optical Character Recognition. OCR scans your photo and recognizes the words on the page, making the document instantly searchable.

For example, if you have a bill coming in each month for a service that doesn't offer online bill pay, you can take a photo of that bill for your records before sending it back with payment. With OCR applied, should you need to find that bill later (maybe it's stored in an Evernote notebook!), you could type in **Water Bill March 2013** and get instant access to the digital record without having to go searching through folders and subfolders. You'll see PDFpen Scan+ in action later in Chapter 5.

The GoodReader App: $4.99

The iPad comes with a variety of apps that are great for various types of media. You use the Music app to listen to your songs, the iBooks app to read ebooks purchased from Apple, and the Videos app to watch movies purchased from iTunes.

Over time, however, I've discovered that there are a number of files that cannot be opened by the standard iPad apps. Instead, should you need to open a Word document or a PNG file, for example, you'll usually end up having to download an app (either free or pay-to-use version) for each type of file you wish to open.

Fortunately, there is one amazing app out there that many iPad power users fall back on when it comes to opening a variety of files—GoodReader. Not only will GoodReader let me open PDF files, Word documents, PNG images, and much more, but it will also let me access that Dropbox account I wrote about earlier. This means most any type of file I store in Dropbox can be opened and accessed via GoodReader with an Internet connection. Even better, if I know an Internet connection is not going to be available, I can choose to download files directly to GoodReader so they are stored on my iPad. I use this frequently by downloading digital movies I store in Dropbox directly into GoodReader—after I watch the movie, I simply delete the file from GoodReader. The movie is still stored in Dropbox, but it isn't taking up space on my iPad.

GoodReader will also appeal to many of you who prefer a folder/subfolder method of storing files. With GoodReader, you can organize all your files into folders and even create folders within folders (subfolders). You can rename files, move or copy them from one folder to another, and much more. I use GoodReader to store the PDFs of many of my favorite magazines, as you can see in Figure 1.9.

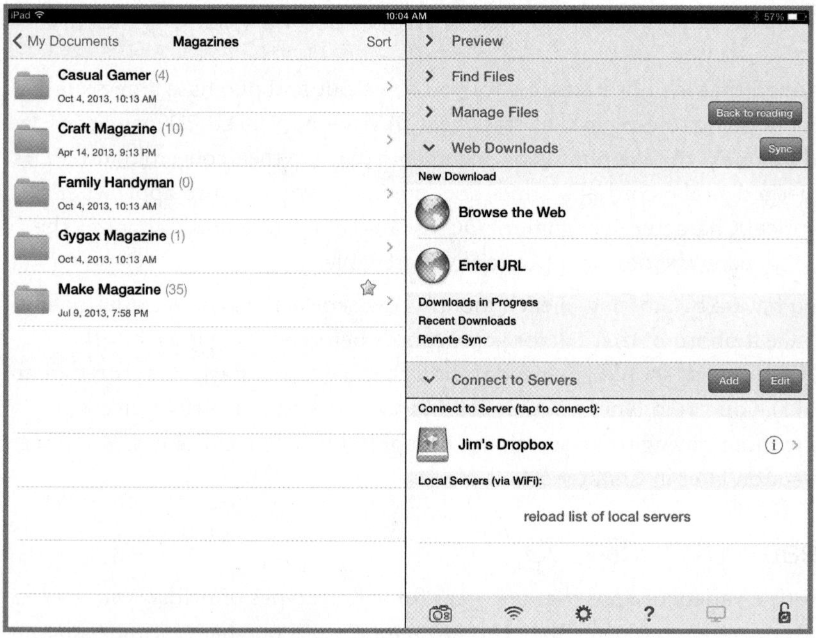

FIGURE 1.9   GoodReader is an amazing file multitool for every iPad user.

CAUTION

A number of apps out there compare themselves to GoodReader. I've not tested them, and I'm not really inclined to do so. I've had GoodReader installed since 2011 with my first iPad and have never been disappointed. That said, if you find something that works for you and you like it, then use it. A good file multitool app should be installed on every iPad.

Why Should I Do This?

I recently sat down and started listing all the things I do with my iPad that make my home and work life easier. "Easier" is a bit subjective, but I think you understand what I mean by it—things that reduce stress, save me some time, help me to stay organized, and provide me access to what I need when I need it. The list I came up with seems to grow regularly, and I thought I'd share it with you here in the hopes that you might find a new use for your iPad that you'd never considered before. (Or maybe even two or more new uses!)

Here are just a few examples from my list of Ultimate iPad tasks along with a brief description:

- **Watch any movie (in my collection) whenever I like**—I'm not talking about movies I can purchase from iTunes. I'm talking about my DVD collection that's been growing since around 1999-2000. Rather than repurchase a movie from iTunes, I simply rip these movies to a digital file so I can watch them on my iPad. I'll show you how to do this in Chapter 8, "Rip and Store: Your Movies and Shows On Demand."

- **Access my home's video security and turn on/off lights**—Not only can I view a live video feed of my home when I'm away, but I can also turn on any appliance that's plugged into a special device that I'll introduce to you in Chapter 10, "Automation: Video, Appliances, and More."

- **View banking and investment details securely**—Using special apps, I feel much more secure about monitoring my financial information on my iPad than logging in from a web browser—given so many web browser security issues of late. Chapter 6, "Your Financials—Banking and Investment Apps," will show you how you can securely monitor your finances with your iPad.

- **Go paperless**—This is no longer one of those future promises that we've all heard forever. My office is paperless with two exceptions—a Shred box and a Scan box. The stuff in the Scan box will get scanned and then moved to the Shred box. The stuff in the Shred box gets cleaned out once a month or so. Want to get rid of your clutter? Check out Chapter 5 for some advice on how to make it a reality.

■ **Reduce my library**—I've collected books for years and years. My library is simply too large, and I recently did a good purge with some large donations made to various libraries. The same goes for my magazines—I subscribe to a number of magazines that don't have digital versions. My solution? Reduce the magazine stacks by scanning it all in and use a special service to convert books I wish to keep into digital versions (thus avoiding having to purchase the book again in PDF or other digital format). You'll see how I do this in Chapter 7, "Convert Your Collections: Reducing Book and Magazine Clutter."

■ **Never worry about losing my data**—I used to be extremely stressed about losing my photos, documents, videos, and much more to a failed hard drive or theft. Fortunately, some great backup options are available out there (as low as $0.01 per gigabyte!), and I'll introduce you to a number of them so you never have to worry about losing the valuable photos, videos, and other important records in your life. These discussions are scattered throughout the book, but you'll find a good bit of details covered in Chapter 3 and Chapter 9, "Don't Forget Your Backup: Long-Term Deep Storage."

■ **Never lose an important piece of information**—Whether it's driving directions, a recipe, an online How-To article, or a digital photo, I've already told you how Evernote can provide you with a single point of storage and organization. Found a useful online article? I'll show you how to "clip it" quickly and send it to Evernote. Want to strip out all the images and advertisements? I'll show you how to quickly convert just the text or whatever you like from a web page to a PDF for quick storage (and searchable with OCR). Do you have an older child and a younger child who enjoy coloring books or other activity books? I'm going to show you how to convert the pages from those books into reusable files so you can have one copy per child. I'll also explain how to "erase" these pages so they can be used again and again. Chapter 11, "Build a Web Reference Library: Never Lose an Online Article," and Chapter 12 will show you all these tricks and more.

I hope what you're beginning to understand is just how valuable your iPad can be if you find the right apps, get set up with a simple system for organizing, and reduce the physical and digital clutter. Physical clutter consists of bills, photos, magazines, receipts, and much more. Digital clutter is all your digital photos, DVDs, PDFs, and other items that float around in various places on your computer or laptop and simply lack a single point of access.

Stick with me. By the end of this book, I think you're going to be a convert to the iPad lifestyle.

Get Geek-Level Organized

In This Chapter

- Sign up for Dropbox and Evernote
- Install three important apps: Dropbox, Evernote, and GoodReader
- Create a decluttering system
- Understand the importance of security

I'm certain there are numerous ways to build a house, but I'm betting there are only a few that would be considered logical and efficient and produce a safe place to live in. I've never built a house, but I have watched as one of my own was built, and I seem to recall that the foundation went in first, then the framework, then the roof and utilities (plumbing, electrical, heating/AC), and then the remaining elements, such as walls, cabinets, doors, and more. My memory may be a little faulty, but I hope you're seeing my point here—there is value in having a proper order to build a house, and it starts with the larger tasks (foundation and basic structures) before moving to the smaller and more detailed tasks.

The same can be said for getting yourself and your iPad prepared for what I call a geek-level of organization. If you truly wish to use your iPad to help you get control of your physical and digital clutter, you're going to need to perform some simple-yet-crucial tasks right now—these involve signing up for some services, purchasing a few inexpensive apps and configuring them properly, and creating a simple decluttering system. I'm going to walk you through all of these initial "foundation" tasks so you'll be ready for the more specific advice found later in the book.

Although you can perform these foundation tasks in any order, I'm going to recommend that you follow this roadmap because some tasks build on previous ones. Fortunately, these early tasks don't involve a large financial investment up front, so you won't need to make any decisions right now regarding the purchase of a personal scanner or whether or not to purchase a Premium account for services such as Dropbox and Evernote. (Rest assured, I'll introduce you to the concept of Premium services later in the book.)

So, here's where I'll be taking you in this chapter:

- Signing up for Dropbox and Evernote (both free)
- Downloading and installing the Dropbox and Evernote apps
- Purchasing and installing the GoodReader app
- Creating a system for clearing physical clutter
- Understanding the necessity of strong and unique passwords

I'm going to start you out by getting you set up to use the Dropbox and Evernote services, but feel free to skip ahead if you already have accounts.

Dropbox and Evernote—Sign Up

Because this book is all about maximizing your iPad's potential, most of the figures in this book will be taken directly from my iPad. That said, you can certainly sign up for Dropbox and Evernote on a PC or Mac or even on a mobile phone. The signup process is fairly simple and fast, too.

The order in which you sign up doesn't matter, but I'm going to start with Dropbox.

TIP

In this section, I walk you through downloading and installing the Dropbox and Evernote apps. Once both these apps are installed, they allow you to create an account from within them. However, I am not recommending that method. Why? Because when you visit the websites for these two services to sign up, you can watch some videos and take some tours to better understand the services. If you're already familiar with how they work and aren't interested in taking a tour of either service, feel free to skip to the next section, install the two apps, and create accounts using the apps.

Create a Dropbox Account

Open up a web browser on your iPad and point it to www.dropbox.com. You'll see a screen like the one shown in Figure 2.1.

Tap the blue Sign Up button—a simple registration screen will appear that asks for your first and last name, your email address, and a password. Tap the Dropbox Terms link to read the Terms of Service; if you agree to the terms, Tap the "I agree to Dropbox Terms" box and then tap the Sign Up button to create your account, as shown in Figure 2.2.

FIGURE 2.1 Sign up for a free Dropbox account.

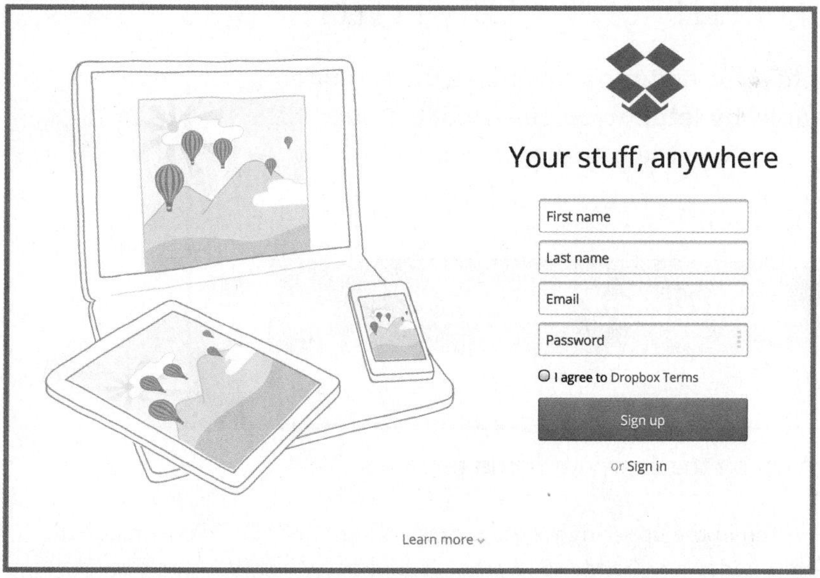

FIGURE 2.2 Provide the required information to create a Dropbox account.

After your account is created, you'll be given an opportunity to download the Dropbox app for the iPad as well as pick between a free or paid Dropbox account. I suggest you stick with the free plan for now and save yourself some money until you determine that you can benefit from a paid Dropbox account. If you do decide to go with a paid account, point a web browser to https://www.dropbox.com/pricing for more details on storage amounts and their respective prices.

Tap the Download for iPad button if you wish to go ahead and download and configure the app. The App Store will open, allowing you to download and install the app as you would any other iPad app. Feel free to install it now or skip to the installation section coverage on setting it up.

Create an Evernote Account

Next, point your web browser to www.evernote.com. The Evernote home page will open as shown in Figure 2.3.

FIGURE 2.3 Sign up on the Evernote home page.

Tap the Sign Up button in the upper-right corner of the screen and provide the required information, which includes email address, username, and password (but don't use the same password that you created for Dropbox). Be sure to tap the Terms of Service and

Privacy Policy links to read about Evernote's terms. Tap the Register button shown in Figure 2.4 to create your free Evernote account.

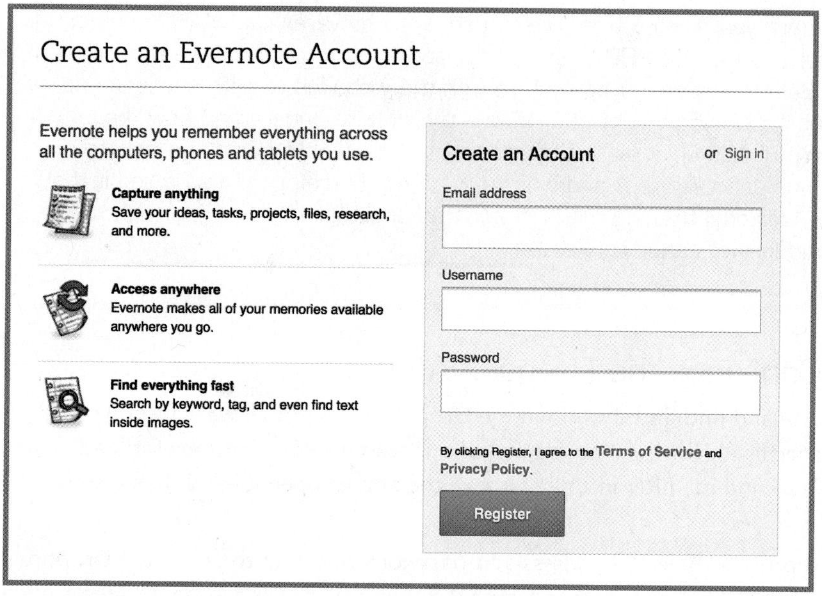

FIGURE 2.4 Provide the requested info to create your Evernote account.

The basic Evernote interface will open in the web browser, but close that down—you'll be wanting to use the Evernote app specifically designed for the iPad, which is much easier to navigate with the iPad's touchscreen. Up next, I'll show you how to install and configure the Dropbox and Evernote apps.

Dropbox and Evernote Apps—Configure

Using the App Store to find and download apps is one of those basic skills I must assume you already possess. If you are not familiar with the App Store and how to use it, let me simply point you to this FAQ on navigating your way around, browsing and searching, purchasing, and more:

http://support.apple.com/kb/HT2001

I'm going to walk you quickly through installing and configuring both the Dropbox and Evernote apps. Throughout the book, I'll also be showing you how to use these two services for various organizational tasks.

NOTE

These accounts are yours, so you're free to use them however you wish. Your new Dropbox account comes with 2GB of storage space for free, so feel free to use it for cloud storage. But I highly encourage you to visit the websites of both services and watch the videos and read through the various tutorials to understand how these services work. You'll pick up a lot just by reading this book, but I won't be able to cover each service and every bell and whistle it offers. Therefore, be sure to hit the Internet or find additional training material such as books or videos if you wish to become a power user of either service.

Install and Configure the Dropbox App

Open the App Store and find and download the Dropbox app. (You'll want to download the one created specifically for the iPad, so make your search term "Dropbox for iPad" and you're guaranteed to find it.) After installing it, tap the app to open it—and then tap the Start button.

You'll be asked to provide the email address and password you used to create the Dropbox account in the earlier section, as shown in Figure 2.5. Enter that information, tap the Sign In button, and you're almost done.

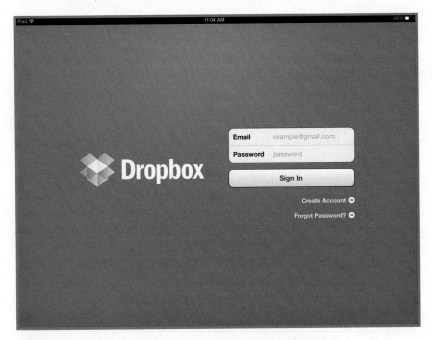

FIGURE 2.5 The Dropbox app successfully installed.

Dropbox will ask you if you wish to save photos taken with your iPad to Dropbox. I don't take a lot of photos with my iPad, but I do with my iPhone. The Dropbox app is also installed on my iPhone, so every time I take a photo a copy is placed in a folder called Camera Uploads. This folder is created by Dropbox if you choose to accept the offer shown in Figure 2.6.

FIGURE 2.6 Photos taken with your iPad can be backed up to Dropbox.

CAUTION

If you choose the "Wi-Fi + Cell" option, photos will be copied to Dropbox using your monthly cellular data allotment. Be careful with this option because taking a lot of high-resolution photos that copy to Dropbox can quickly add up to an expensive bill. I choose the "Only Wi-Fi" option and let my iPhone and iPad copy over photos whenever connected to the Internet via Wi-Fi—this doesn't use up my monthly data allotment.

When you're done, the Dropbox app will open. You can see in Figure 2.7 that I have a number of folders visible, but if this is the first time you've used Dropbox, you'll likely only have the Camera Uploads folder (if you chose to enable the option that places a copy of photos taken with your iPad or iPhone into Dropbox).

FIGURE 2.7 Dropbox folders and documents appear on the left.

I keep my Dropbox folders well organized, so you won't see any free-standing documents such as PDF files and JPG images. Instead, everything has its place—a folder or a subfolder holds all my individual files. As you progress through the book, I'll introduce you to some ways to use Dropbox using some folders created for very specific purposes. For now, go ahead and close down the Dropbox app and return to the App Store.

Install and Configure the Evernote App

With the App Store open, find and download the Evernote for iPad app. Once located, install it and then tap the app to open it—you'll see a screen like the one in Figure 2.8.

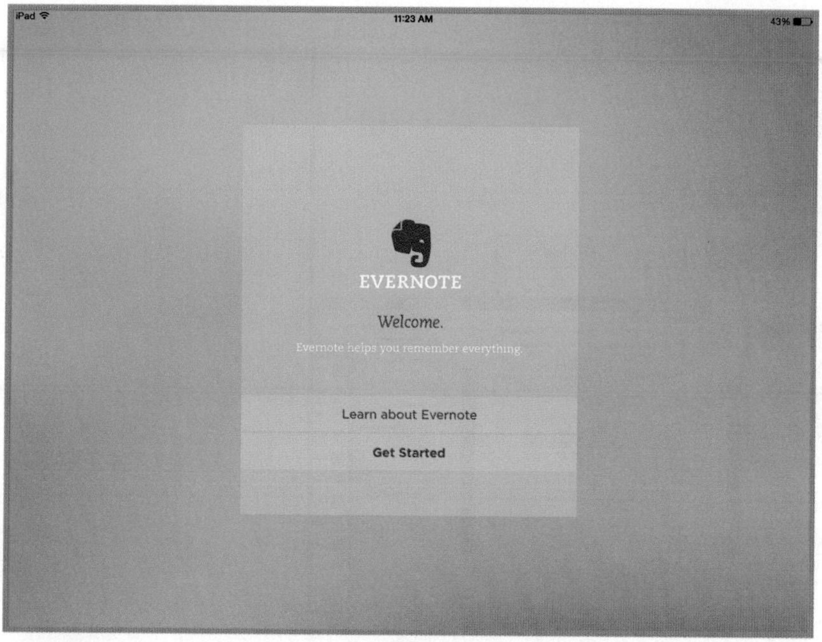

FIGURE 2.8 The Evernote app installed and ready for you to sign in.

Feel free to tap the Learn about Evernote button to view a short tour of the service or tap the Get Started button to log in. You'll once again need to provide your email address or username (Evernote will take either) and password that you used to create the Evernote account earlier.

The Evernote app will open and be ready for you to begin creating notebooks, notes, stacks, and much more. I'm devoting all of Chapter 4, "Evernote: Your New Best Friend," to using Evernote, so feel free to jump ahead if you just cannot wait to learn how to use Evernote.

After installing the Evernote app, there's one last app I'd like you to install for this chapter.

Install and Configure the GoodReader App

The GoodReader app isn't free (right now the app costs $4.99), but in my opinion, it's worth every penny of its inexpensive price. (But feel free to wait and purchase it later if you wish to see how I put it to use.)

For me, the GoodReader app is my primary tool for moving files on and off my iPad. Although there are a number of methods for connecting GoodReader to other services, the one I use most often is a direct connection with Dropbox, and I'll show you how this works in a moment. For now, however, go ahead and find the app in the App Store, purchase it, and download it to your iPad. Search specifically for "GoodReader for iPad" to get the tablet version and not the iPhone version. Figure 2.9 shows the app in the App Store.

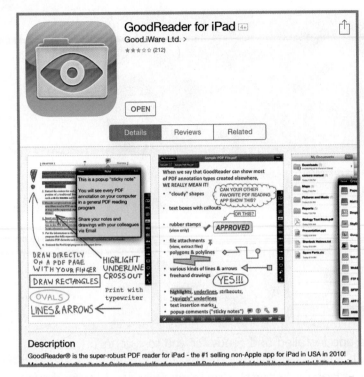

FIGURE 2.9 The GoodReader for iPad app in the App Store.

TIP

GoodReader offers a lot of services, and there is some overlap with other apps that I'll discuss later in the book (such as highlighting PDF files or adding notes and graphics to documents). Because of this, you may wish to hold off on purchasing GoodReader until you finish the book and see what other apps I use. You may discover that you don't need every app I recommend and can save a little money.

You'll see some examples of how I use GoodReader later in the book, but before I finish out this section I want to show you how to configure GoodReader to communicate with your Dropbox account. Start by opening the app. Figure 2.10 shows some folders I've created in GoodReader to organize my files, but you'll probably start out with an empty folder list on the left or possibly just the Downloads and iCloud folders.

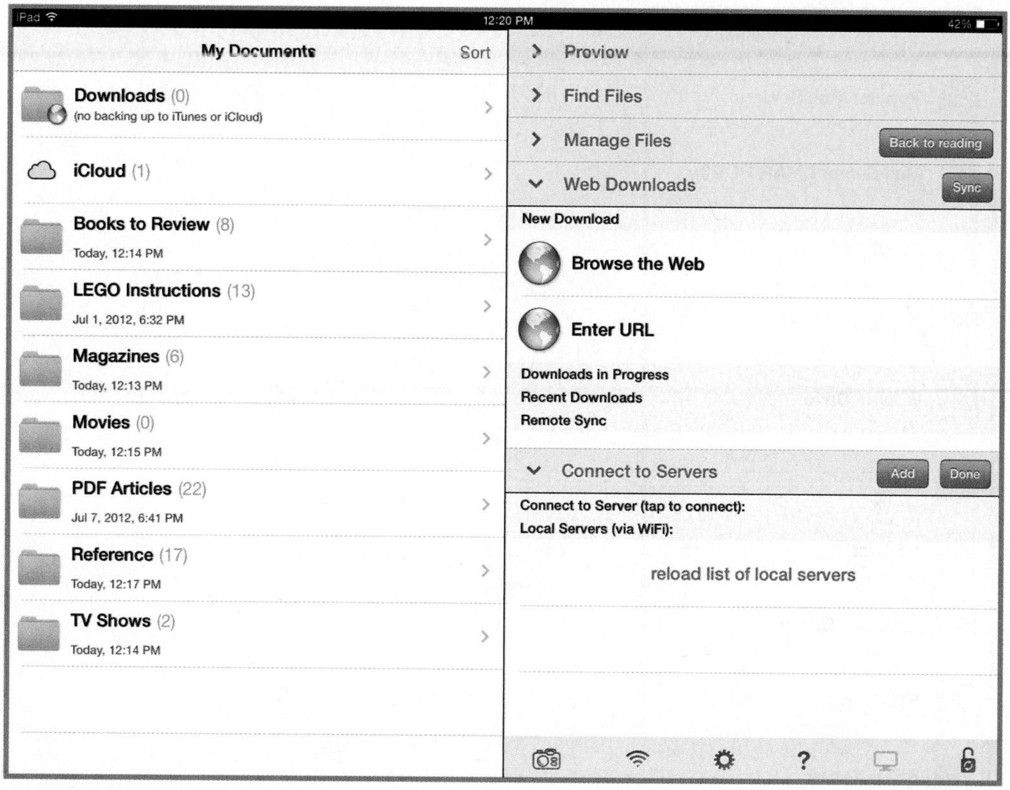

FIGURE 2.10 The GoodReader folder listing is on the left and tools on the right.

Just ignore the folders on the left side of the screen for now and focus on the tools on the right. Specifically, I want you to tap the "Connect to Servers" option. Tap the Add button (refer to Figure 2.10) and you'll be provided with a list of all the various services that "play well together" with GoodReader, as shown in Figure 2.11.

I'm going to tap the Dropbox option, but if you're a fan of Microsoft's SkyDrive or Google Drive, for example, feel free to tap one of those options. After selecting Dropbox, I'm asked to provide a name for the Dropbox connection—I've entered one into the Readable Title field, as shown in Figure 2.12, and then I click the Add button.

Cancel	**Create New Connection**
	Popular Mail Servers
	Mail Server (IMAP, POP3)
	Dropbox
	SkyDrive
	Google Drive
	SugarSync
box	box.net
	WebDAV Server
	FTP Server
	SFTP Server

FIGURE 2.11 Many services will work well with GoodReader.

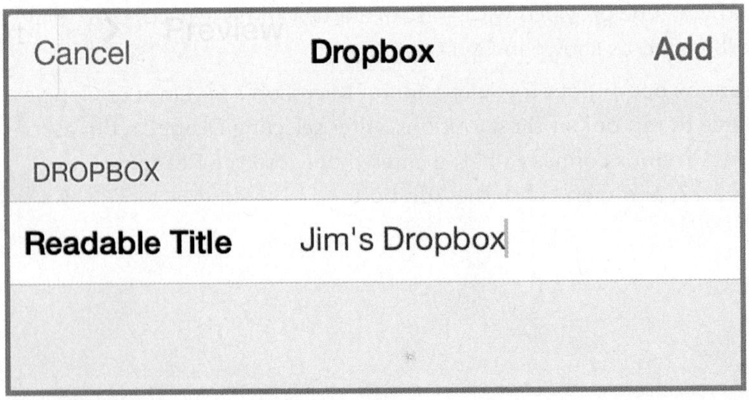

Cancel	**Dropbox**	Add
DROPBOX		
Readable Title	Jim's Dropbox	

FIGURE 2.12 Create a connection to Dropbox and give it a name.

You'll see the connection listed under the Connect to Servers tool, as shown in Figure 2.13.

FIGURE 2.13 The connection is created but lacks login credentials.

You've not yet provided GoodReader with your Dropbox login credentials, so tap the newly created connection and you'll see a screen appear like the one in Figure 2.14.

FIGURE 2.14 Provide GoodReader with your Dropbox email and password.

After the connection is made, any time you tap on the Dropbox connection in GoodReader (under the Connect to Servers tool), you'll be provided with a listing of your current Dropbox folder, as shown in Figure 2.15.

Jim's Dropbox		Close
Folders:		
Action Aug 14, 2012, 8:31 PM	ⓘ	>
Archive Feb 25, 2013, 9:26 AM	ⓘ	>
Camera Uploads May 6, 2012, 6:31 PM	ⓘ	>
Directions and Hours Nov 24, 2012, 9:10 PM	ⓘ	>
Gaming Today, 10:30 AM	ⓘ	>
Magazines Today, 10:28 AM	ⓘ	>
Miscellaneous Nov 29, 2011, 9:28 AM	ⓘ	>
Movies Today, 10:34 AM	ⓘ	>
My Books (PDF) Jun 1, 2012, 1:56 PM	ⓘ	>
My Documents		
↻		Upload

FIGURE 2.15 You can view your Dropbox contents from within GoodReader.

Now that the connection is made, what can you do with it? You may or may not have anything currently stored in your Dropbox folders (or subfolders), but if you did, you would tap the folder or file in the list that appears and then tap the Download button that appears at the bottom of the pop-up list, as shown in Figure 2.16.

In Figure 2.16, I've found a PDF file titled "PVC Size Guide" that I wish to store on my iPad. Although I can always tap this file in Dropbox to open and read it, by choosing to download it to my iPad, I can read the file any time I wish, especially if I lack Internet access. (After tapping the Download button, I'm asked to specify where in GoodReader to place it. I have an existing folder structure in GoodReader, so I simply tap the folder where I wish to place the file; otherwise, GoodReader will place the file in the listing on the left instead of inside a folder.)

FIGURE 2.16 Download a file from Dropbox to GoodReader.

This is the same method I use to transfer the digital files that contain the movies and TV shows I've converted from the physical DVDs I own (and I'll show you how to do this in Chapter 8, "Rip and Store: Your Movies and Shows On Demand"). I also use this connection with Dropbox to download images, Word documents, and many more items, all compatible and able to be viewed with GoodReader.

NOTE

There are ways to move digital files (especially movies and TV shows) to and from the iPad using iTunes software, but in my opinion the steps for doing this are overly complicated. By storing files in Dropbox and using the connection between GoodReader and Dropbox, you can move files back and forth between iPad and Dropbox fast and easy.

Just as you can download files from Dropbox to GoodReader, you can also move files from GoodReader into Dropbox. If you look carefully at Figure 2.17, you'll see that using the Manage Files tool on the right side of the screen, I select a file such as a PDF file by tapping it (a check mark appears to the left of the filename) and then tap the Upload button found in the Manage Files section.

Upload button

FIGURE 2.17 Upload a file from GoodReader to Dropbox.

After I tap the Upload button, a pop-up list like the one in Figure 2.18 appears showing my Dropbox, allowing me to select the folder where I wish to upload the file.

There's a lot more you can do with GoodReader, and I'll touch on some other cool tricks later in the book. For now, however, I want you to understand that this connection with Dropbox (or other cloud storage service) will be extremely useful to you as you begin to declutter your life. I use this partnership between GoodReader and Dropbox to provide me access to just about everything imaginable—books, magazines, online articles, movies, TV shows, Word documents, PDF files, and so much more.

But I'm getting ahead of myself—you're probably still wanting to know how to declutter your own life and make more of your own "stuff" accessible via your iPad. Much of that decluttering is going to be done by converting paper items to digital files. Chapter 5, "Cut the Clutter: Scan Everything," shows you the ins and outs of scanning paper items, and you can certainly begin right now by scanning anything and everything within reach. However, before you do that, let me make one additional suggestion for your "foundation" that I believe will make the decluttering tasks a bit easier and won't take long to set up.

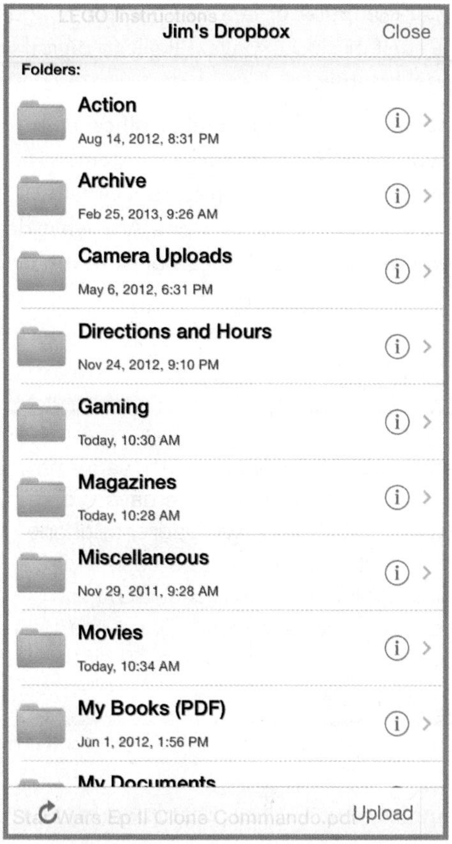

FIGURE 2.18 Select a Dropbox folder to store your uploaded file.

A Simple Decluttering System

I am not an organizational expert by any means. I know there are hundreds of books out there that talk about strategies for getting rid of kitchen clutter, cleaning out closets and garages, and eliminating the pack-rat mentality. This book isn't one of those. Yes, I can offer you some suggestions on reducing your paper clutter and a few other items (such as a DVD collection), but you're on your own when it comes to your kitchen, garage, and closets!

I break the kind of clutter that your iPad can help with into two categories—physical and digital. I explained back in Chapter 1, "The Ultimate iPad," that physical clutter can consist of bills, magazines, books, and other paper documents. Your digital clutter are the files, emails, and website bookmarks spread out across your computer or laptop's hard drive and all those DVDs and music CDs that take up valuable shelf or closet space. I'll get to digital clutter later, but right now I want to talk about physical clutter.

If you're truly wanting to eliminate as much of the paper in your home and/or office as possible, you're really going to need a system. Sure, you could go from room to room, picking up pieces of paper and running back to your scanner (or taking pictures of them with your iPad's camera), but this is not only tiresome, but also quite random. And what do you do with the paper after you've scanned it? Do you toss it in the trashcan or does it need to be shredded?

NOTE

I didn't include a shredder in Chapter 1 because I think it's simply one of those items that every person should already own given the risk of identity theft these days. Your rule should be as follows: If it has your name, physical address, email address, phone number, account number or any other piece of information that could be used to find you, it needs to be shredded. What you'll find if you apply this filter is that 90% or more of the stuff that comes to you in the mailbox should be shredded. Of course, not everyone goes to these extremes, but a shredder is most assuredly a required and valuable tool for the organized person.

I'm not going to say that my system is perfect or complete, but I will say that it works well for me and has allowed me to continue to have a paper-free office. The best part is it doesn't even have to cost you a dime if you can get your hands on two small cardboard boxes that are large enough to hold stacks of paper inside.

Figure 2.19 shows my system—two clear boxes. One is labeled Shred and the other is labeled Scan. Any paper that doesn't find a place in one of those two boxes goes into the garbage can. I have two boxes in my office, and I have two boxes in my kitchen (where the mail and other random paperwork inevitably finds itself).

Once a month or so, I take all the paper from the Shred box and hit the shredder. Mine can handle about 8-10 pages at once without jamming, so it usually takes me about 15-20 minutes to shred my monthly stack.

FIGURE 2.19 A simple Scan box and Shred box for organizing paper items.

The Scan box is a little different. Sometimes I scan weekly; other times monthly. It just depends on my free time or how important it is that a document be scanned and available to me on my iPad. I'll show you my scanning method in Chapter 5, but for now all you need to know is how my Scan box often fills up:

- I read a magazine once. If I find an article I wish to keep, I rip it out and put it in the Scan box.

- The few paper bills I still receive used to jump to the top of the Scan box and get scanned almost immediately. Now, I just take a photo with my iPad's camera and use the PDFpen Scan+ app so I can immediately write a check and put the bill in the mail.

- My 6-year-old son comes home from school every day with at least half a dozen drawings, completed math and spelling sheets, handouts, and the occasional form or information sheet. I don't keep it all, but I do like to keep scans of some of my son's work so one day he can look back at how far he's come with his education.

- I don't know about you, but I am completely inundated with paperwork regarding my investments and retirement accounts. Most of this stuff can be tossed or shredded, but every now and then a report or statement comes in the mail that needs to be kept long term. Into the Scan box it goes.

- I do sometimes find the occasional recipe on the side or back of a box of rice or other food item. If I'm not in a hurry, I'll tear around the recipe and toss the item into the Scan box in the kitchen. If I'm in a hurry, I'll take a photo.

- I enjoy woodworking, and I've got a number of tools I've collected over the years that come with a small paper manual that explains some aspect about the tool that I'll never remember. The same goes for kitchen appliances, new electronics, and some toys. All those instruction manuals (some of them often nothing more than a single sheet of paper) go in the Scan box.

- When I travel with my family, I often pick up the tourist brochures found in hotel lobbies and restaurants. These frequently have a map on the background along with address, phone number, and other valuable information. Because these brochures often have folds in them, they can be a bit annoying to photograph because they refuse to stay flat. Nothing a scanner can't handle... into the Scan box they go.

- I do keep the actual receipts for many items I purchase (especially electronics), but I also scan these. I've been saved by a scanned receipt more than once after losing the original. (Many stores are also starting to email you a receipt immediately after you make a purchase, and I'll show you later in the book how to send emails directly into services such as Dropbox and Evernote.)

There are plenty of other things I scan for one reason or the other—old photos, circuit diagrams from How-To magazines, business cards, membership cards, and even once a square of wrapping paper with a pattern I wanted to use for a wallpaper background.

When I started reducing my paper clutter a few years ago, it took me about three weeks to get it under control. Notice I didn't say "get it done." The decluttering really never ends—it just gets a bit easier once you have it under control because you'll then only be scanning periodically (weekly or monthly, perhaps) and shredding when the Shred box starts getting full. But once you get to that point, you'll most likely have developed a habit of putting the paper in the respective boxes (or trashcan) and scanning and shredding at regular intervals.

Some Thoughts About Security

You're likely to hear all sorts of horror stories and warnings about using the cloud. And you'd be right to pay attention! Storing your valuable data in the cloud with services such as Dropbox and Evernote definitely comes with risks. You don't want someone accessing your data or possibly even deleting it. For that reason, this book also discusses options related to backups in Chapters 3, "Additional iPad Storage Options," and 9, "Don't Forget Your Backup: Long-Term Deep Storage."

Ultimately, your decision to use the information in this book, to sign up and store your data with Dropbox, Evernote, or another service, and to access it all with your iPad over an Internet connection is just that—your decision. You'll need to balance your comfort and trust of the various services you sign up to use with your understanding of the risks involved.

The only recommendation I'm going to provide here as I wrap up Chapter 2 is related to passwords. As you saw with creating Dropbox and Evernote accounts, you are given the opportunity to create a unique password for both of your accounts. You've probably heard about how easy it is for the bad guys to crack accounts using passwords such as 12345, password, and special dates such as birthdays and anniversaries. Because both Dropbox and Evernote use your email address as your username, it really comes down to creating a strong and unique password for each of these accounts since your email address is often available with nothing more than a Google search, a visit to your Facebook page, or maybe even your bio page on your company's website.

Strong and unique passwords are most definitely a key to giving you peace of mind. By "unique," I mean don't use the same password across a variety of accounts and services. I know people who use the same password for Facebook, Gmail, banking, Dropbox, and other services. Yes, it's easy to remember one password, but if someone gets your Gmail address and password, they might think to try logging in to other websites with your Gmail address and password. If you're using the same password, you've given them the key to open up every door in your house, so to speak. (Later in the book in Chapter 10, "Automation: Video, Appliances, and More," and Appendix A, "Tips and Tricks," I will show you a couple of options for helping you manage your user accounts and password.)

Let me close by talking about strong passwords. Some services force you into using a certain number of characters (eight, for example), and others require you to use a mix of numbers, uppercase letters, lowercase letters, and special characters (such as ! and #). I'm no security expert, so I'm simply going to point you to three websites related to password security and ask you to create a strong and unique password for both Dropbox and Evernote, because if you follow my lead in this book, you'll be using those two services to store every bit of valuable information you wish to make easily available to you on your iPad.

Take a moment and check out these websites and consider changing your Dropbox and Evernote passwords if you feel your existing passwords aren't good enough for protecting your data:

http://en.wikipedia.org/wiki/Password_strength

http://strongpasswordgenerator.com

http://www.passwordmeter.com

Foundation Tasks Wrap-Up

Let's recap where your iPad current stands if you've installed and configured the apps described in this chapter:

- Your iPad now has access to your Dropbox account via the Dropbox app. You start with a minimum of 2GB of free storage space.

- Your iPad now has the Evernote app installed, which will be useful to you for storing information in the cloud in an organized manner (using notes, notebooks, and stacks—more on this in Chapter 4).

- GoodReader is now installed and allows you to move files to and from your iPad using the Upload and Download tools and connecting to Dropbox or another cloud service.

- Although not an iPad app or feature, you also have two boxes (clear, cardboard, or whatever you find useful) labeled Scan and Shred that will help you organize your paper clutter by changing it from a physical item in your home or office to a digital file stored in Dropbox, in Evernote, or on an external hard drive.

As I stated earlier in the chapter, these actions create the foundation for you to become more organized. Combine these foundation tasks and apps with the discussions that follow in later chapters to move your iPad from simply an Internet, email, and/or gaming tablet to something you'll truly be able to label as an Ultimate iPad.

My Ultimate iPad uses these foundation apps to support the more useful and creative tasks I've handed over to my tablet. My iPad acts as my single source of information, giving me access to pretty much anything I need from day to day. And because of the foundation I've created for my iPad with Dropbox, GoodReader, and a few other tricks, I rarely encounter a situation where some bit of information isn't available to me. (But should I find something that's not accessible to me, it doesn't take long for me to develop a method to make it accessible.)

Up next, you're going to learn about the various methods available to you for information transfer, storage, and backup. You've already created a Dropbox account (or have access to another cloud service), but there are a few other options you should know about that you might choose to use that go hand-in-hand with using your own Ultimate iPad.

3

Additional iPad Storage Options

In This Chapter

- Cloud Hosting or Local Hosting?
- Cloud Access Via Dropbox
- Local Hosting Via Pogoplug
- Your iPad's Extra Storage

If you truly intend to begin using your iPad to access as much of your data as possible, you're going to have to also come to grips with the fact that the iPad is a "locked" device when it comes to internal storage—there is simply no way to upgrade your iPad's storage.

The first iPad released in 2010 had three options when it came to internal memory—16GB, 32GB, and 64GB. In 2013 Apple bumped up the maximum memory by offering a 128GB option, but iPad power users have certainly reached that limit already. It's difficult to say whether Apple will increase this again in the near future, but given the high price of the flash storage found inside iPads, don't anticipate great leaps in storage capacity in the near future.

If you've used your iPad for any length of time, then you've probably reached the limit of internal storage. The remedy for this is typically to begin uninstalling unimportant apps and deleting pictures and videos (but first copying them to a computer or CD/DVD). There really isn't much else you can do to free up storage space. So what can you do when it comes to accessing the large volume of data that is created when you begin scanning documents to digital files, ripping DVDs (converting the movies to digital files), and digitizing your books and magazines for reading on your tablet?

The answer is quite simple: You need to find an external storage solution that works well with your iPad when you're out and about. There are storage solutions that work via Wi-Fi when you're at home; your iPad connects to them the same as it would a home Wi-Fi connection, but the device has its own SSID and typically requires a password to access any files stored on it. For purposes of this chapter, however, we'll be talking about options that give you access to your data from any location where you have an Internet connection.

In this chapter, I provide you with two tried-and-tested methods for ensuring that you'll always be able to access your movies, music, books, and every other file you'll ever want access to—and it all starts with a simple choice.

Cloud Hosting or Local Hosting?

When it comes to increasing your iPad's storage potential, what I'm really referring to is external storage. You can't crack open your iPad and add more storage, but you can find ways to make external storage available to your iPad.

When I use the term "external storage," I'm referring to a host of options—cloud storage such as that offered by Dropbox (with competitors being Box.com, Google Drive, and Microsoft SkyDrive, among others), external hard drives, and "micro" solutions such as USB drives or SD memory cards such as the ones you find inserted into digital cameras.

You can choose to implement one, two, or all of these options to guarantee you always have enough storage for all the various types of data you need to access with your tablet. But let me just assume for the moment that you wish to find just one solution—and the best one for your needs. To do that, you need to first answer a question: Are you willing to pay a monthly or yearly fee for cloud hosting (where a copy of your files are being stored on someone else's hardware) or would you prefer to have all your files stored on a device you own (from here on out I'll call it "local hosting")?

Before you answer, there are some pros and cons for you to consider:

- **Cloud hosting (such as Dropbox)**—Pros: reliable "always on" service, faster downloads to the iPad, compatible with many iPad apps such as GoodReader and PDFpen Scan+ (I briefly covered these in Chapter 2, "Get Geek-Level Organized"), data syncs to any or all devices you choose. Cons: higher price per gigabyte of storage, risks/concerns of data theft, data cannot be accessed if Wi-Fi is not present and your iPad doesn't have cellular service, and data is stored on hardware you don't own.

- **Local hosting**—Pros: lower cost to implement, lower price per gigabyte, maintain control of your own data, and can be "taken with you" as a portable device. Cons: storage device could be lost/misplaced, risk of fire/theft if not backed up, slower downloads to the iPad (in my testing experience), and more difficult to sync the data with multiple devices.

What I'm going to do in the remainder of this chapter is show you how both methods work. I'm going to show you how to use Dropbox as your primary external data storage solution and then cover a hardware solution offered by Pogoplug to do the same.

TIP

Keep in mind that that $120 3TB drive you buy today will be $100 next week and $80 next month. My point is that prices change, so be certain to do a cost analysis at the time you are considering implementing any solution. Price changes do not occur as often with the various cloud hosting services, but they are not unheard of, so check those prices too.

Here's one final thought before I show you an example of each type of hosting: These are not the only solutions to providing additional storage to your iPad. Just as Dropbox isn't the only cloud hosting service out there, neither is the PogoPlug service I'll be introducing to you for local hosting—one such "local" solution is the Western Digital My Cloud drive. These are just two solutions I use and enjoy and can recommend. However, if you google "Dropbox competitors" or "Pogoplug competitors," you'll probably find a good list of alternatives.

Cloud Access Via Dropbox

I'm going to start with cloud hosting first because it's also the shortest and fastest to implement, especially if you've installed GoodReader and the Dropbox app from the instructions in Chapter 2.

Dropbox offers new users 2GB of "free" storage—no additional purchases are necessary. Why is free in quotes? Because for free accounts, the Dropbox Terms and Conditions state that they can change pricing at any time, plus Dropbox does not guarantee access to your files after 90 days of inactivity. (If you're using a free Dropbox account to access files with your iPad, just be sure to login once a month or so and you should be okay.)

If you choose to do nothing else with Dropbox you'll be able to make a connection between Dropbox and your iPad that essentially makes 2GB of extra storage space available to your tablet.

TIP

Dropbox allows you to invite up to 32 friends to join and begin using the Dropbox service. For each friend who signs up you'll get 500MB of bonus storage. Invite 32 friends who each begin to use Dropbox and you'll have 18GB (2GB you start with plus 16GB for the invites) of free, non-expiring external storage. For Dropbox users with paid accounts, the bonus storage amounts double—1GB per invited friend for an extra 32GB of storage.

Dropbox offers an app for just about every device and operating system out there; this means you can have access to your Dropbox storage not only on your iPad but also your mobile phone, your home and work computer, and even a friend's devices—you simply log in to Dropbox.com from any web browser and you'll be able to view, open, and even download any files stored in your Dropbox account.

One of the many features that Dropbox offers is the ability to upgrade your storage, as shown in Figure 3.1. Starting at $9.99 per month (or $99.00 per year, if prepaying for an entire year), you can get an extra 100GB of Dropbox storage on top of any free storage you've collected, such as the 2GB of free space or the extra 5GB you got when your 10 friends began using Dropbox.

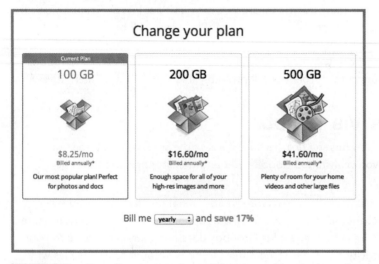

FIGURE 3.1 Dropbox has a few different subscription plans.

Whether you have the 2GB of free storage space or you're a yearly subscriber with 100GB+, you'll be able to use any app on your iPad that can "link" to Dropbox to open, view, and save files. Many apps can move files to and from Dropbox, but my favorite is GoodReader. Using GoodReader, I can view TV shows, movies, Word documents, PDFs, and so many more types of files.

I showed you back in Chapter 2 how to make a connection with GoodReader to Dropbox, so refer to those instructions if you need help creating that link between your cloud hosting and your iPad.

But even if you don't have the GoodReader app, you'll find that you can still access almost all of your files directly from the Dropbox app by simply tapping a file.

But why would you choose to download files from Dropbox into GoodReader when you can simply open them in Dropbox with a single tap? Here are a few reasons:

- **No Internet connection**—If you're in a location where Wi-Fi isn't available, and your iPad does not have cellular service, you're out of luck. There is a way to force files to save themselves locally to your iPad, but it's a slower download via Wi-Fi (in my tests).

- **No basic file management**—If you wish to change the filename of a photo from 0328392.jpg to vacation2013.jpg, the Dropbox app won't allow it. And the Dropbox app won't let you move files from one folder to another.

- **Faster download to iPad**—In my testing, downloading a movie from Dropbox into GoodReader was significantly faster than downloading it by "favoriting" the movie with a star (as you'll learn about next).

Should you choose to leave a file in Dropbox and not download to GoodReader, there is still a method for making sure a copy of a file is placed on your iPad if you anticipate a lack of Wi-Fi. That file will be stored locally, on your iPad, and can be opened even if an Internet connection doesn't exist. Here's how.

Open up the Dropbox app on your iPad and browse to a file's location. As you can see in Figure 3.2, I've opened up a folder containing all the digital versions of *Make:* magazine I keep stored in Dropbox.

FIGURE 3.2 Open the Dropbox app and find a file you wish to store locally.

Drag your finger from left to right on a file, and a small menu will appear in the place of the file's name, as shown in Figure 3.3.

FIGURE 3.3 Open a Dropbox submenu by dragging left to right on a file.

Tap the hollow Star icon to indicate you wish for a copy of the file to be stored locally on your iPad. The star will become solid to let you know the file is being copied to your iPad as a "Favorite." You can tap the Star icon at the bottom of the screen, as indicated in Figure 3.4, to view all files you've elected to have copied from Dropbox to local storage on your tablet.

If you want to free up some space, simply go back to the file that you starred and click on the Star icon again. When it turns hollow, you'll know the file has been removed from local storage.

One final warning: Look carefully at Figure 3.4 and you'll see that I've starred a movie file (2.0GB) that is now downloading. This is certainly one way to transfer movies and TV shows to your iPad...but it's slooooooow. Again, I've found that downloading video files from Dropbox while inside the GoodReader app goes much faster. Still, if you don't wish to purchase the GoodReader app, this is a perfectly acceptable method for saving video files to your iPad for later viewing.

Star icon

FIGURE 3.4 View all your locally stored Dropbox files.

Using Dropbox (or any cloud hosting service) is most definitely a useful and convenient way to access your files...but it does come at a cost. Although 2GB of free storage sounds like a lot, it's really not—one or two large movie files will easily wipe out that storage space. I pay for the extra 100GB of storage each year because I also use Dropbox for my business. I find Dropbox to be reliable—it just works. But GoodReader will also link to Google Drive, Microsoft SkyDrive, Box.com, and a few others. If you have a favorite cloud service you already use, you may find that it will work just fine with GoodReader or even have its own method for copying files to your iPad similar to the Dropbox Favorite method that uses the Star icon. (At the time I'm writing this, GoodReader has a built-in connectivity tool to communicate with Dropbox, SkyDrive, Google Drive, SugarSync, box.com, a WebDAV server, ftp servers, sftp servers, AFP servers, and SMB servers.)

But what if you're not comfortable with a cloud hosting service? What if you either don't wish to pay a monthly or yearly fee or you just don't like the idea of some third party maintaining control of your personal data? In that case, you're going to have to create your own local hosting service to make your files available to your iPad. There are plenty of methods for doing this, and they are super-easy, as you will see in the next section.

Local Hosting Via Pogoplug

Before I explain how to set up and use Pogoplug, let me briefly explain that there are actually two different services for your consideration. The first is a 100%-software solution that can be installed on your home computer (Windows or Mac) and allows you to select folders, hard drives, and even USB and SD cards that will be available over the Internet to your iPad running the free Pogoplug app. This software is $29.95 per computer and is a one-time fee.

The second option is a 100%-hardware solution (it doesn't even require a computer, only an Internet router) that involves connecting a small Pogoplug device to a free port on your Internet router. You then connect an external hard drive or an SD card (or both) to the Pogoplug device. Any storage device attached to the Pogoplug device can then be accessed with your iPad running the free Pogoplug app. This device costs about $18 for the Pogoplug device (plus the cost of any external hard drive you choose to connect to the device).

Which service should you use? Let me offer up some thoughts on both before I show you how they work.

I've tested both, and I've chosen the $29.95 software solution because I can connect that 3TB external hard drive to my home computer that's running the Pogoplug software and make it available to my iPad. Nothing else on my home computer is visible. My home computer also has eight USB slots in all, and five of them are still unused. This means I could add another five 3TB hard drives for a total of 18TB of data storage. Or I could insert five USB drives into those five USB slots; a recent visit to Costo showed me that I can buy a 32GB USB drive for $20. I could buy five of these and dedicate each of them to holding one category of files: Movies, Photos, TV Shows, PDFs, and Books/Magazines. For $100 (about the same price as only one year of 100GB of Dropbox storage), I could have over 150GB of storage space that remains in my control and can be disconnected from the Internet any time I choose.

Some of you might now be wondering why you would ever consider purchasing the Pogoplug device. Well, not every home computer has free USB slots. And not everyone chooses to leave their home computer turned on (like mine) 24/7—when the computer is off, storage devices connected to that computer are unavailable to the Pogoplug app. And some users might not like the idea of their home or work computer even running the Pogoplug software initially just to set up the visible folder system that you'll learn about shortly. All great reasons to consider using the Pogoplug device shown in Figure 3.5. (It's just a little larger than a pack of playing cards.)

FIGURE 3.5 Connect an external hard drive to the Pogoplug device.

NOTE

Another option available from Pogoplug (for $49.95 per year) works like Dropbox and basically allows you to use Pogoplug as a cloud hosting service. One thing to consider—that $49.95 per year is for unlimited storage. Yes, you read that correctly—unlimited. It's certainly worth testing out if you're comfortable with cloud hosting but need more storage than the 100GB for $99/year that Dropbox offers.

Whether you choose to install the 100%-software solution called Pogoplug PC or use a Pogoplug device connected to your Internet router, you'll be required to create an account that consists of an email address and password.

I cannot stress enough how important it is to create a *strong* password. Your email address may be out there for anyone to find, so feel free to create a new and unique email address just for use with Pogoplug. But do not skimp on a strong password.

NOTE

Want to test a password to see how strong it really is? Point a web browser to passwordmeter.com and type in your potential password to get a score (from 0 to 100% secure) and see where it might be considered weak (such as not enough unique characters or no mix of upper and lowercase).

If you choose to use the Pogoplug device, simply follow the instructions that come in the box. In a nutshell, you'll connect the power cord to the device and then connect the device to your Internet router with the included Ethernet cable. Next, you'll connect an external hard drive to the Pogoplug device with a USB cable (or insert an SD card into the memory card slot). Once that's all done, you don't even need a computer to finish the installation. Simply open a web browser on your iPad, point it to my.pogoplug.com/activate, and follow the instructions that will allow the Pogoplug device to be found (over the Internet). After the device is located, you'll then use the Pogoplug app on your iPad to access files—I'll show you how to do that in the next section, but first let me walk you through using the Pogoplug PC software if you're considering that option.

The Pogoplug PC service has a 30-day free trial, so I highly encourage you to download the software and try it out before you buy. After downloading the software, double-click it to begin the installation. An installation wizard will do most of the work, but when you reach the account creation screen shown in Figure 3.6, stop and create your account if you haven't already done so. (You can also click the Sign In link if you already have an account.)

FIGURE 3.6 Create a Pogoplug account or sign in with an existing one.

After creating an account and signing in, you'll next be asked if you wish to make certain folders visible over the Internet. As you can see in Figure 3.7, Pogoplug picks a few familiar ones, such as Photos and Documents.

Place a checkmark in any box if you wish, or click on the End Tour link to skip this step. You can undo these selections (or enable them if you change your mind) later if you like.

When the software finishes installing, you will see the Pogoplug configuration screen, like the one in Figure 3.8. If you've never used Pogoplug services before, the configuration screen will appear blank.

FIGURE 3.7 Pogoplug offers up some standard folders to select for local cloud access.

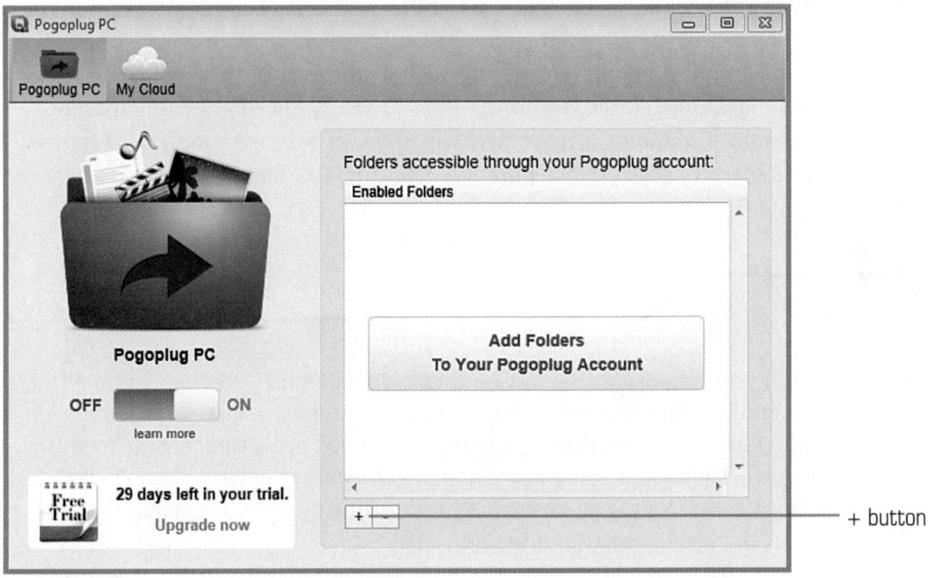

FIGURE 3.8 The basic Pogoplug configuration screen

I chose to leave my computer and its files completely unavailable to my iPad—only the 3TB external hard drive that I have connected to my computer will be made available. To make that hard drive (or USB drives or SD cards) available to the Pogoplug app on my iPad, I need to select them. To do this, I click on the + button indicated in Figure 3.8. After clicking the + button, a new window appears like the one in Figure 3.9.

FIGURE 3.9 Select a drive or folder from the list.

From this screen you can select entire hard drives (such as the J: drive that represents my Seagate 3TB external hard drive) or expand those hard drives by clicking the tiny triangle to the left of their names. Expanding a hard drive will allow you to select individual folders such as the Movies folder I've selected in Figure 3.9. Click the OK button to select an entire drive or a specific folder.

NOTE

Even though you can use the Pogoplug device and a connected hard drive without ever turning on a computer, you will need a computer to create a series of folders on that hard drive to store your files. Just disconnect the hard drive temporarily from the Pogoplug device, plug it into your computer, and create your folders and subfolders. Disconnect the hard drive from your computer, reconnect it to the Pogoplug device, and you'll now have a folder structure available.

You'll need to perform this task (clicking the + button and then selecting a drive or folder) for each drive or folder you wish to have visible in the Pogoplug app. As you can see in Figure 3.10, I've selected three different folders—Movies, TV Shows, and Photos—that will be used with the Pogoplug app to access those kinds of files stored on the 3TB external hard drive.

FIGURE 3.10 Selected folders to be made visible to the Pogoplug app.

When you're done, simply close the Pogoplug PC application (on your Windows or Mac computer). You can open the Pogoplug PC application again at any time to add additional hard drives or folders or remove them. (Highlight a folder or drive name in the list and click the – sign to remove it.)

And now, you either have an external hard drive connected to a Pogoplug device that's available to your iPad as additional storage *or* you have a home computer running Pogoplug PC and sharing a drive or folders (or both) with your iPad as additional storage. Either way, the best part is the additional storage!

But how do you access that storage from your iPad? Easy! Open up the App Store and find the Pogoplug app shown in Figure 3.11.

When the app finishes its installation, tap it to open it, and you'll be greeted by a sign-in screen like the one in Figure 3.12. Enter your email and password, and tap the Sign In button.

FIGURE 3.11 The Pogoplug app is a free download for your iPad.

FIGURE 3.12 Sign in to your Pogoplug account.

You'll be given a short tour of the app—feel free to skip it if you like. When the tour is over, you'll see a screen like the one in Figure 3.13 that lists either your Pogoplug PC connection or your Pogoplug device.

FIGURE 3.13   Your Pogoplug PC or device connection will be visible.

Tap the connection to open it. As you can see in Figure 3.14, I've opened my Pogoplug PC connection (called Jim-PC) and I can now see those three folders I selected to be visible over the Internet. (If I had selected an entire drive such as J:, shown back in Figure 3.9, it would also be visible.)

Now it's starting to all come together. When I tap the Movies folder shown in Figure 3.14, that folder opens and I can view all files inside it. I've placed a single digital movie in the Movies folder on the 3TB hard drive as a test, as shown in Figure 3.15.

All I have to do is tap the movie's name and then tap the big Play button in the center of the screen to begin playing the movie on my iPad.

I can tap the Expand button in the lower-right corner of the screen to force the movie (or any other file) to grow and fill the screen. I can even rotate my iPad 90 degrees to view the movie in landscape mode!

FIGURE 3.14 View all drives and folders that were made visible.

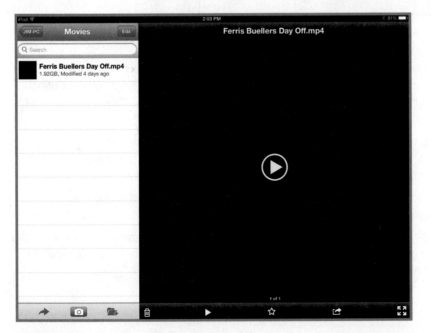

FIGURE 3.15 Tap a photo, video, or document to open and view it.

TIP

Got an AppleTV device? Any iPad (version 2 or higher) can use AirPlay to send anything on the iPad's screen to your TV screen if you have an AppleTV connected. This means you can stream movies from Pogoplug to your iPad to your TV!

Playing movies using the Pogoplug app on your iPad is great, but there is one really big problem—you can only play or pause the movie. There are no Rewind and Fast Forward controls! This means no jumping back to a missed scene or skipping ahead over a boring portion of a film.

This isn't an issue for viewing photos or reading PDF files, but it's definitely a problem for Pogoplug users who are also movie fans.

I did tell you earlier that GoodReader is one of my favorite iPad apps, and for good reason. The GoodReader app can do a *lot* of things, including allowing me to rewind or fast forward through any digital movie I may be watching using the app. But you may have already discovered that there is no way to "link" GoodReader to your Pogoplug account—if you don't believe me, open up GoodReader and follow the instructions I offered back in Chapter 2 for adding a service such as Dropbox—you won't find Pogoplug in that list of connections you can create. That means either watching a film, start to finish, using the Pogoplug app, or finding a way to get a video file from Pogoplug to GoodReader.

Just because I said there isn't a way to create a link from Pogoplug to GoodReader from within the GoodReader app doesn't mean you should give up. "Where there's a will, there's a way" is my motto.

So, here's my workaround solution for getting files from Pogoplug into GoodReader.

Open up your movie or other file in the Pogoplug app by tapping the file's name. Once you've opened the file, tap the Share button indicated in Figure 3.16.

After you tap the Share button, the file will begin to download. A progress circle will begin to fill like the one in Figure 3.16. (In my tests, a 2GB movie took about 7–8 minutes to completely download over Wi-Fi.) When the download is complete, a pop-up menu will appear like the one in Figure 3.17. Do you see a certain favorite app's icon in that list?

If you have installed the GoodReader app, it will appear in the pop-up menu. Simply tap it and wait a minute or so for the file to completely copy itself into the GoodReader app. Once that's done, you can open and view the movie (or other file) inside GoodReader and use the built-in Pause, Rewind, and Fast Forward features to your heart's content.

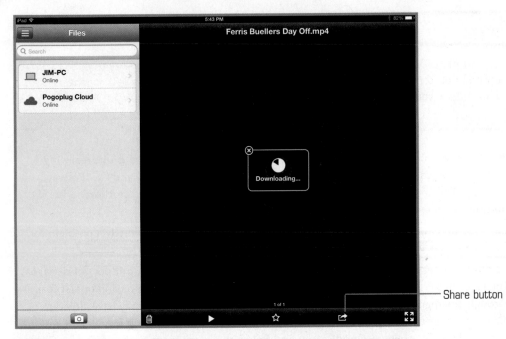

Share button

FIGURE 3.16 Tap the Share button to begin downloading the file.

GoodReader app

FIGURE 3.17 Choose the app where you wish to send the download.

Your iPad's Extra Storage

Your iPad will most likely run out of storage room at some point in the future. If you love to install apps, there will come a time when you just can't install any additional apps without deleting older ones. Apps must be installed on your iPad—they simply won't run from an external hard drive or cloud hosting service like the ones I showed you in this chapter.

Although I can't help you with your app collection, I hope I've given you at least one possible solution to provide your iPad with additional storage space.

There are pros and cons to both local hosting and cloud hosting, and only you can make the decision as to which option you will choose. Cost, trust, Internet availability, and technical skills are just a few of the factors you'll need to weigh when comparing cloud to local hosting options.

For me, I use both. I am a Dropbox customer and I absolutely love the 3TB of external hard drive storage I purchased and can access via Pogoplug PC. I use Dropbox to store my work files and other documents that I wish to have backed up by Dropbox and available to me from any mobile device or computer in the world from which I have Internet access. And I use my 3TB drive to hold all those movies, TV shows, home videos, and photos that require lots of storage space. All in all, I have a storage system in place that offers me access to anything and everything I have in digital form.

NOTE

I may store all my files on that 3TB drive, but that drive is kept in my home. Should it be lost or stolen or the files somehow deleted, how easy would it be to replace all the files stored on it? Fortunately, some super-inexpensive options are available for ensuring that you never lose your valuable data. I'll discuss backups and your options in Chapter 9, "Don't Forget Your Backup: Long-Term Deep Storage."

If you're going to implement any or all of the solutions I offer in this book for decluttering your life, you're going to discover the importance of digital storage. Having a storage system in place that your iPad can access is crucial, so be thinking about everything you've learned in this chapter as you continue reading the book. In later chapters, you'll begin to see how having those "foundation" tasks completed and an in-place external storage solution will turn your iPad into that Ultimate iPad I keep hinting at.

4

Evernote: Your New Best Friend

In This Chapter

- What Is Evernote?
- Evernote Overview
- Navigating in Evernote
- Creating Notes in Evernote
- The Power of Premium Evernote
- Possible Uses for Evernote
- Don't Forget the Cleanup

With the additional storage (discussed previously in Chapter 3, "Additional iPad Storage Options") available to your iPad, I hope you're beginning to see how you could take just about any file, document, movie, or photo and make it immediately available. Whether you go with a cloud-based storage service such as Dropbox or choose to use a Pogoplug service to create a home-based, local storage system, you'll have in place a storage solution for your iPad that will help ensure you always have access to anything and everything you choose to store digitally.

But let's talk for a moment about file organization. Although it's great to have a 1TB hard drive available to your iPad, you're only creating more work for yourself if you throw every file—song, movie, PDF, Word doc, and so on—into a single folder labeled Documents (or My Documents), for example. If you've worked with computers at all, you know that there's value in creating folders for storing and dividing up your files to make them easier to find. For example, on my 3TB external hard drive I have a number of folders I've created: Movies, Music, Photos, PDF Articles... you get the idea.

And inside each folder are subfolders. For example, my PDF Articles folder contains five folders: Woodworking, Health, Recipes, Technology, and Electronics. I store scanned articles from woodworking magazines in the Woodworking folder and scanned recipes in the Recipes folder. (And these subfolders don't just contain scanned pages that I've turned into PDFs—later in Chapter 12, "'Plays Well with Others': Remote Control and an Extra Screen," I'll show you how to convert online articles you find into PDFs.)

Although I use my 3TB hard drive to organize similar files (only MP3 music files go into the Music folder), I use another tool when I need to collect a variety of file types into one central location. I write technology books, so there are times when I want to have all my research files in one location and not scattered over a number of folders. For example, in my research for this book I collected (and scanned) brochures on hardware, online reference articles, photos of products, screenshots of software, and even videos and voice recordings. This mix of different types of files are kept in a single location that I can access on my iPad at any time.

The tool I use to do this is called Evernote, and it's not just for writers. Evernote users have discovered that Evernote is a crucial tool for staying organized, collecting vast amounts of information easily, and synching that information with a central cloud storage system that then makes their information available on any device—phone, computer, or tablet.

In this chapter, I introduce you to Evernote and show you some of the useful tools and features that make it a worthy app and service for your own Ultimate iPad.

What Is Evernote?

Evernote is many things, but I would describe it as a tool for collecting and accessing your important information from all your digital devices—phone, computer, and tablet. In a way, it's a cloud service because the data you choose to store in Evernote is backed up on the Evernote organization's own storage service. But it's also a local storage service because all of that data is synchronized and stored on any devices you install the Evernote software. If you make a change to a document on your phone (running the Evernote app), that change will be pushed out to any other devices you have running the Evernote software.

Evernote will run on Mac and Windows computers, and the app is available for iOS and Android phones and tablets. For each version, however, the app looks a little different. Although I have Evernote installed on my iPhone, iPad, MacBook Air laptop, and Windows 7 desktop computer, I tend to only create data in Evernote on my laptop and iPad (and occasionally my phone). The Windows version looks and operates differently from my Mac and iOS versions, and I really only access Evernote on my desktop when I need to print something (my printer is only connected to the Windows PC), which is rare. Very rare.

Evernote is free to use, but it does have a Premium service that runs $45 per year (or $5 per month). I encourage you to try out the Free version first, of course. Not everyone will need all the advanced features that the Premium account offers (and I'll cover some of those later in this chapter), so check out Evernote and learn how it works and whether or not it is useful to you before committing to the Premium version.

Entire books have been written about Evernote, so there is simply no possible way I can cover every feature, tool, and use that Evernote brings to the table. Instead, I want to provide you with just a quick overview to get you started using Evernote and then show you some of the useful tools that will go hand-in-hand with using your iPad.

Evernote Overview

As I mentioned previously, Evernote is not only available for a variety of platforms and operating systems, but it also offers users a Free version and a Premium version. I think it's important for users to understand how the Free and Premium accounts work with respect to using the service on an iPad.

To do that, let me offer up a sample scenario of how Evernote might work for a couple who have the app installed on their mobile phones, her iPad, and his work computer.

> Janell and Jack are going to be remodeling their guest room, and Janell has decided to collect ideas and images and How-To articles in an Evernote notebook titled Guest Room. She is sitting in the dentist office reading a magazine and finds an advertisement for a bed and dresser set that she thinks would be perfect for the room. She opens up the Evernote app and uses the Camera feature to take a photo of the advertisement with her phone's camera. The photo is now stored, safe and secure, with her Evernote account, and it also begins to synchronize (via Janell's data service provided by her mobile phone carrier) with the Evernote servers.
>
> Walking back to work, she reads an email on her phone from Jack that contains a link to a local artist's website. Jack likes this artist's style and asks Janell to take a look at the paintings he has available for sale. Janell doesn't have time to browse the site right now, so she quickly saves the link to the Guest Room notebook.
>
> During a conversation at lunch about the room remodel, a co-worker tells Jack about a great handyman they used a few months back. He doesn't have the phone number, but the co-worker remembers the handyman's name was John Hasbright. Jack opens up the Evernote app on his computer and adds a note to the Guest Room notebook that contains a short audio clip—"Google John Hasbright handyman and get phone number."
>
> At home that night, Janell and Jack sit down with her iPad and open up the Evernote application. They browse the Guest Room notebook that contains all the various items they've collected— How-To articles, photos of various paint options for the walls, and more. They also find today's new additions—the photo of the bed and dresser, the link to the artist's website, and Jack's voice recording.

Even if you're not familiar with how Evernote works (and I'm going to get to that next), I hope you're beginning to see how this tool is used to collect a mixture of content (photos, recordings, websites, PDFs, Word documents, and much more) and organize it in such a way that it's easier for you to find what you need.

In addition to what Jack and Janell have done in the preceding example, here are some other things they could do with Evernote:

- Store quotes from various contractors for the wall knockdown and rebuild—these could be text files, PDF files, Word documents, or even photos of printed documents.
- While browsing paint colors at the hardware store, they not only can take photos of the paint cards, but they can also add a text note to each photo so they will know the color

name (Sunset Breeze) and the color number (M23325), which aren't always the easiest to remember.

■ Jack and Janell could hire an interior decorator and share the Guest Room notebook with her so she can view all of the content stored there.

■ Janell took over 30 photos on her phone of various rugs. She could send those to an Evernote note any time she wishes—photos do not have to be taken with the Evernote app. She can then delete the photos from her phone.

■ When the interior decorator finds a brochure showing a variety of wood floor colors, she could scan it and then upload it to the Guest Room notebook for Jack and Janell to examine.

Where Evernote really shines is when you use it to store information you need now or in the immediate future. Although it can be used as an archive service, you'll be much better off sending information and files you no longer need to an archive solution (and I cover this in Chapter 9, "Don't Forget Your Backup: Long-Term Deep Storage"). Evernote has limits on how much content you can upload—the Free account limits you to 60MB per month and the Premium service has a 1GB upload limit per month. Consider that some high-resolution photos can be 3MB–5MB in size, and the Free account will be maxed out at around 15–20 photos!

CAUTION

In addition to the monthly upload limit of 60MB, you should also be aware that the Free account also requires you to have an Internet connection to access your Evernote notes and notebooks. This means if you're on an airplane or climbing a mountain or are in any other location where you lack a data or Wi-Fi signal, you won't be able to access Evernote (with the Free account). The Premium account doesn't have this restriction, and it allows you to access notebooks offline when an Internet connection isn't available. (You specify these notebooks as available offline.)

Even if you have a Premium account and aren't facing the upload limit and the Internet-connection requirement, I still encourage you to only use Evernote for information that you need on a regular basis or for an upcoming project. Although Evernote will allow for up to 250 notebooks for both Free and Premium users, you'll really be pushing the limits of your iPad's internal storage (or your phone's) if you choose to have that many notebooks synchronizing between phone, iPad, and computer. Instead, try to create notebooks that can serve your immediate needs until you can move something from Evernote to a personal archive (covered in Chapter 9). Here are some ideas for notebooks you can create:

- **Receipts**—Create a notebook called Receipts and place photos or scans of any receipts you need to keep inside. When you no longer need access to a receipt, archive it. You can either use the tagging system built into Evernote (where you type in keywords for items that are searchable within Evernote) to tag a receipt as a tax-related item, a charitable donation, a business expense, or other type *or* you could create notebooks for each of these types to separate your receipts by type.

- **Recipes**—A notebook that contains your favorite recipes (or new ones you've just discovered) is great for those moments when you're in the grocery store and need to know which ingredients to purchase.

- **User Manuals**—Scan in the guides for your tools and electronics and especially toys that often have unusual requirements for opening to install batteries.

- **Book/Novel**—This notebook is a great place to collect your chapters, photos of locations (or character inspirations), and other bits and pieces that you just don't want to lose. (I create a notebook for each of my technology books and use them to store websites, photos, user manuals, and so much more.)

- **School**—Consider using this notebook to store records, permission forms, contact info, class schedules, and anything else that pertains to your education (or your child's). It's also useful for high school seniors to collect applications (PDF files) and paperwork related to applying for colleges, scholarships, and financial aid.

Navigating in Evernote

All of this talk about notes and notebooks probably has you wondering exactly how it all works. Keep in mind that the Evernote app looks a bit different on each platform. And Evernote doesn't sit still either—the company's cadre of programmers seems to update the look of the service a few times each year, so keep this in mind as you view this chapter's figures. What you see may not be exactly what you get.

Because this book focuses on the iPad, that's the version of the app you're seeing in Figure 4.1.

Figure 4.1 shows the basic control panel for Evernote, and if you look carefully you'll see a few sections—Notes, Notebooks, Tags, Places, and Market. Each of these has a small number to the right of its name—I have 27 notebooks, for example, and 197 notes.

Each of the sections can be opened by simply tapping its name or number. Figure 4.2 shows that the Notebooks section has been opened and is now displaying the various notebooks I've created to store my notes.

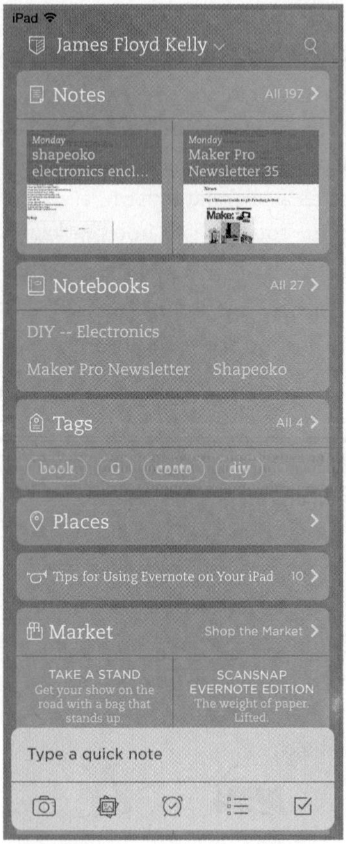

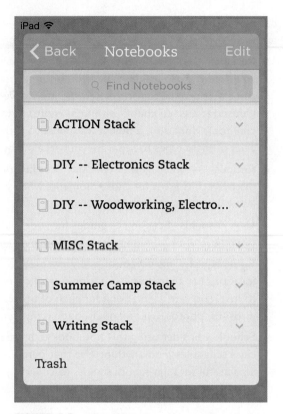

FIGURE 4.1 The iOS version of Evernote for the iPad.

FIGURE 4.2 The Notebooks section lists your Evernote notebooks.

A Notebook can contain many sub-notebooks (but it stops there—no sub-sub-notebooks), and when you perform this kind of action, you're creating what Evernote calls "stacks." Tapping the DIY – Electronics Stack expands it to show the subnotebooks I've placed inside (see Figure 4.3). One of them is currently empty (DIY – Electronics has 0 notes) but the Maker Pro Newsletter has 38 notes tucked inside.

Notebooks are all about storing notes. Notes are the building blocks of Evernote, and as I mentioned earlier in the book, notes can contain text, audio, photos, videos, and more. After I tap the Maker Pro Newsletter notebook (shown in Figure 4.3), it opens and shows me all the newsletters that I've dragged and dropped into this Evernote notebook. Figure 4.4 shows that this list of notes is displayed with the most recent at top. Swiping from the bottom scrolls the list so all notes can be viewed.

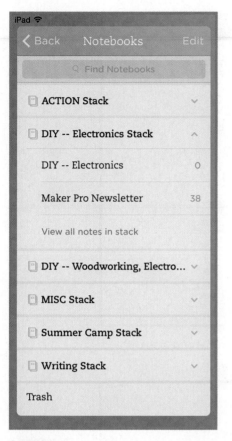

FIGURE 4.3 Expand a stack to see all notebooks contained inside.

Evernote does not store every note on your iPad (or iPhone)—if this were the default setting, many iPad users with large Evernote collections of notes and notebooks would find themselves running out of space. This is why Evernote works best with an Internet connection. If you have an Internet connection and tap on a note that contains anything other than text and try to open it, you'll see a screen like the one in Figure 4.5.

As you can see, there is a button labeled "Tap to Download" that will grab your note from the cloud and allow you to view it on your iPad. Depending on your connection speed, this may take less than a second or up to a minute or more for video or audio. Figure 4.5 contains a PDF file, so it's not stored on my iPad until I need it.

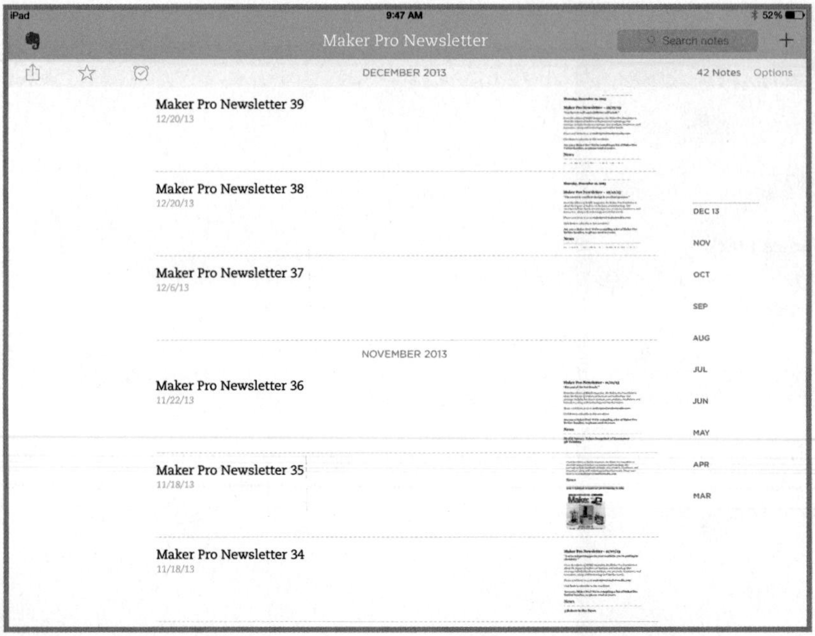

FIGURE 4.4 The individual notes stored in a single notebook.

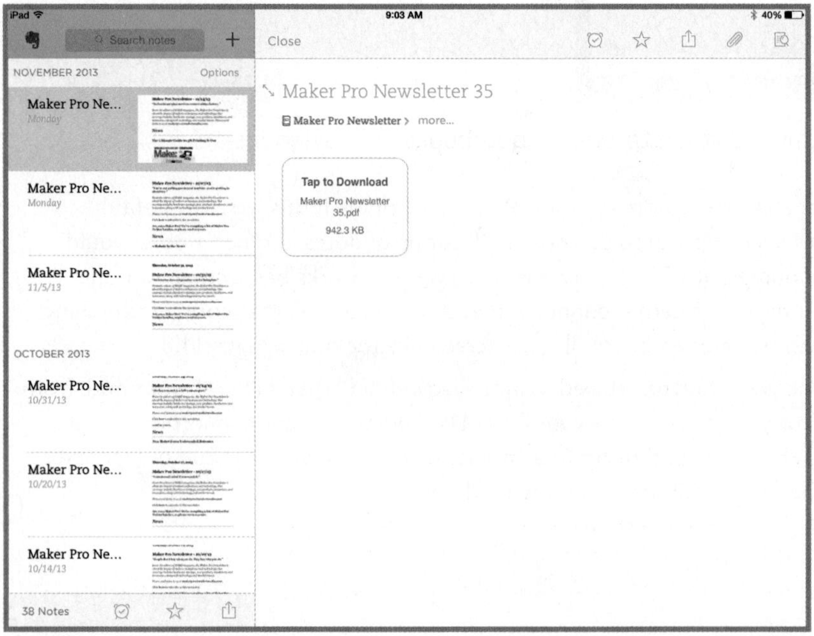

FIGURE 4.5 You'll have to download the note to view it.

After the note has been downloaded, it will open full screen for you to examine. Figure 4.6 shows that the PDF file is open and contains seven pages that can be navigated using the thumbnails at the bottom of the screen. Swiping left and right will also move you back and forth between pages.

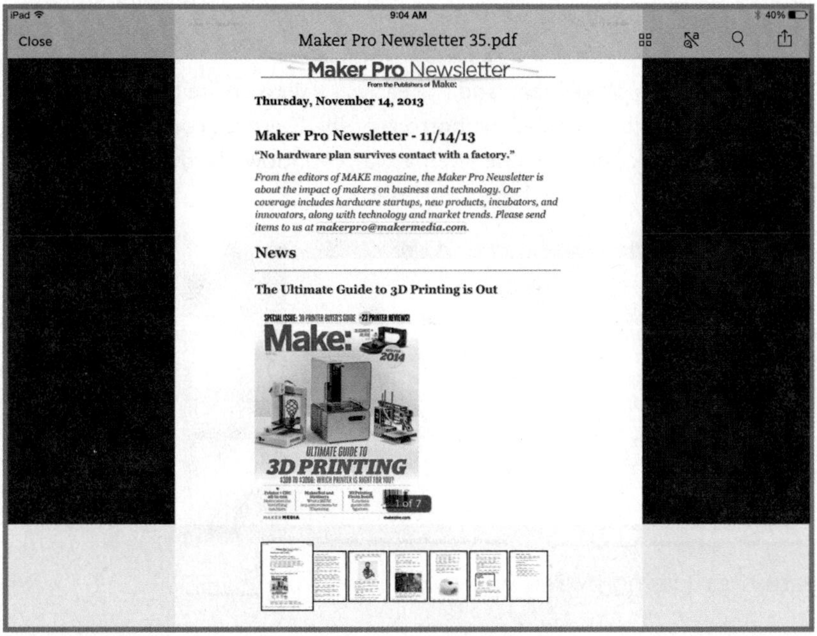

FIGURE 4.6 Open a note to read it full screen.

TIP

If you upgrade to a Premium Evernote account, you'll find that you can specify certain notebooks to be downloaded and stored on your iPad for access anytime. This is called "offline notebook" access. Should you lose Internet connection with your iPad, you'd still be able to open Evernote and read those selected notebooks and their notes.

To return to a previous screen, tap the Close button (when reading a note) in the upper-left corner of the screen or tap the small Elephant icon or the Back button in the upper-left corner to move backward from notes to notebooks to the original control panel shown back in Figure 4.1.

Creating Notes in Evernote

There is simply no way for me to cover every bell and whistle that Evernote provides, so you're going to have to do some exploring on your own. At the end of the chapter I'll point you to some videos and tutorials that can really get you trained up in Evernote, but before moving on to Chapter 5, "Cut the Clutter: Scan Everything," you need to know how to create notes and notebooks.

The easiest note you can create is simple text, and the easiest way to create this text-based note is to tap the "Type a quick note" link at the bottom of the Evernote control panel (refer to Figure 4.1). Tap that link and you'll be given a blank window like the one in Figure 4.7.

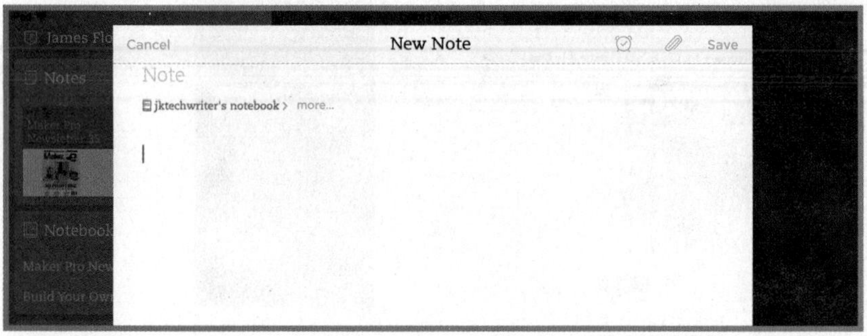

FIGURE 4.7 Create a simple note filled with text.

You'll use the keyboard to type your note. Notice that the default location is the general-purpose notebook that is created when you sign up for Evernote. If you wish to send your new note to a different notebook, tap the default notebook's name and a drop-down menu appears listing all your notebooks, as shown in Figure 4.8. (Notebooks inside stacks will appear in this list, so you won't need to drill down any further—just scroll through the list to find your desired notebook.)

FIGURE 4.8 Select a notebook to store your new note.

If you look in the upper-right corner of the screen, you'll see a small paperclip icon. Tap it to add an attachment. When using the iOS version of Evernote, you can attach a photo, audio recording, or a document. (If you wish to attach a video to a note, you'll need to use a PC or Mac version of Evernote.) Figure 4.9 shows an image attached to the note—the full image is visible in the actual note itself, and additional text can be added above or below.

FIGURE 4.9 An attachment can be added to a note.

The last thing to do is to rename the note. Tap the "Note" title at the top, type in a more descriptive title, and click the Save button in the upper-right corner. And you've just created a note.

But what about creating a notebook? Easy!

Return to the Evernote control panel and tap the Notebooks section to open and expand it. Tap the Edit button shown in the upper-right corner of the notebook list and then tap the New Notebook button shown in Figure 4.10.

Enter the name of your notebook using the keyboard and then tap Done. Your new notebook will be added to the list. Figure 4.11 shows the new "Evernote Novice Tips" notebook added to the list. Notice that it has the numeral 0 next to it to indicate it is currently empty of notes. (It also lacks the small icon to the left of its name to indicate it's a stack and contains subnotebooks.)

New Notebook button

New Notebook

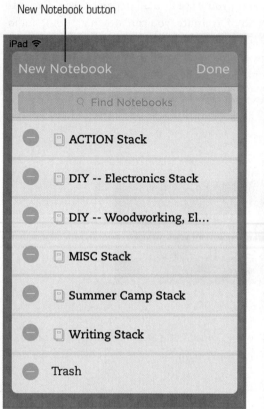

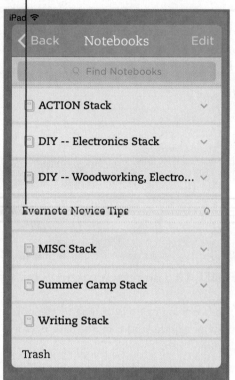

FIGURE 4.10 Use the New Notebook button to create a new notebook.

FIGURE 4.11 A new notebook added to Evernote.

> ## TIP
>
> If you wish to add a new notebook to an existing stack, simply tap the Edit button. A small square with an arrow pointing upward will appear to the right of any standalone notebooks (notebooks not contained in a stack). Tap that button and select Add to Stack. All existing stacks will be listed, and you tap one to move your notebook into that stack (or type the name of a new stack for the selected notebook to be added). After clicking the Edit button, you can also delete a stack or notebook by tapping the minus sign (–) to the left of the stack or notebook's name.

You'll want to investigate Tags and Places on the Evernote control panel. These options let you assign keywords to notes and notebooks as well as specific locations (such as where on the planet a note was created). There's also a Market section that contains free and pay-to-use upgrades to Evernote options that you might find of interest.

The Power of Premium Evernote

Now that you've been given a brief introduction to Evernote, you're probably wondering why a Premium account is so beneficial to the concept of the Ultimate iPad. Evernote certainly doesn't add any additional storage space to your iPad—it's even a consumer of storage space if you're a Premium user and wish to use offline notebooks.

In the previous chapter, you saw how easy it is to collect all your files—documents, photos, videos, and so on—and make them available over the Internet using a cloud-based service or a device such as Pogoplug. If you can always access all your files (with an Internet connection), then where's the benefit of storing your notes and attachments inside Evernote notes and notebooks? Consider the example earlier in this chapter where Jack and Janell were collecting information related to the remodeling of a room in their house.

Where Evernote shines is in its ability to collect dissimilar files—three photos, one audio recording, one video, two web URLs, a couple PDF brochures, and a simple text file containing a list of professional painters is one example of a collection found tucked away inside Jack and Janell's Guest Room notebook. You can certainly store a mixed collection of files in Dropbox or in a folder on an external hard drive, but if you lose Internet access, those options are gone. A Premium user account combined with offline notebook access means you can store files that are important to you on your iPad and always have access to them.

And there are so many more benefits for Premium account users:

- **Sharing notes and notebooks with other users**—You can give others access to add, edit, and delete notes and notebooks. (Free account users can invite others to view notes, but not edit them.)

- **PDF search**—PDFs added to notes and stored in Evernote are scanned so you can search all your notebooks using keywords.

- **Increased note size**—One note can be up to 100MB in size, as opposed to 25MB for Free accounts.

- **Emails forwarded into Notes**—Free users can send up to 50 emails per day right into notebooks, but Premium users can forward up to 250 emails per day. (More on this in a moment.)

- **Huge monthly upload quota**—Premium users can upload up to 1GB of data versus only 60MB for free users. Over 15 times the upload quota means you won't have to worry about uploading videos, audio clips, and photos to your heart's content.

Install Evernote on your computer, your mobile phone, and your iPad and you'll always have access to those important files you wish to keep at hand.

Possible Uses for Evernote

Installing the Evernote app on your iPad truly pushes your tablet closer to the Ultimate Tablet status. The Ultimate iPad is all about putting everything you need at your fingertips *and* making it easy and fast to find. Evernote is one of those tools that will continue to surprise you and have you saying, "I didn't know it could do that!"

Here are just a couple of Evernote features that might help convince you to sign up.

Send Emails Directly to Notebooks

This is one of my absolute favorite features of Evernote. When you sign up for Evernote (Free or Premium), you get an Evernote email address in the form of name@m.evernote. com. If you forward an email message (including any attachments) to this address, that message will be placed inside a new note. The subject line of the email becomes the new title of the note.

You can go one step further and specify the notebook you wish the email message to be added to by adding **@notebook_name** to the subject line. For example, "Map to Dan's House @Action" in the Subject line would place the email with directions to Dan's house in the Action notebook.

To find your unique Evernote email address, open up the Evernote app, tap your account name in the top-left corner, and scroll down the Account listing until you find Evernote Email Address, as shown in Figure 4.12. Tap there, and you can view your Evernote email address—create a new contact with that email address and you'll always be able to quickly forward any email received and store it in Evernote.

The Web Clipper

Because Evernote can be installed on all devices, you'll probably want to have the service running on your mobile phone as well as a work or home computer. If you choose to install the Evernote application on a computer, you'll definitely want to investigate the Web Clipper add-on that works with the Chrome, Firefox, Safari, Internet Explorer, and Opera web browsers.

Point your computer's web browser to http://evernote.com/webclipper/ and download and install the Web Clipper tool for your particular browser. Once it's installed, you can use it to "clip" an entire web page's contents or a smaller portion of it.

It looks and works a bit differently from browser to browser, but in a nutshell you'll see a small button (with an Elephant head icon) added to your web browser like the one in Figure 4.13. Click it (and sign in to Evernote with your login credentials if it asks for them) and then select whether to clip the entire web page, a screenshot (of only what's being displayed currently), or maybe just the bookmark URL.

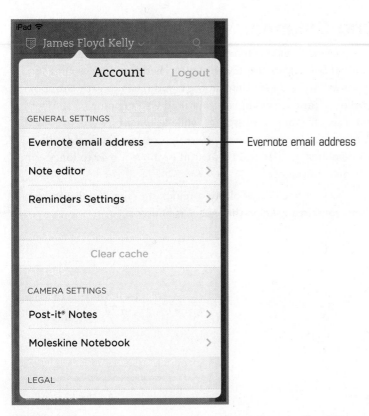
Evernote email address

FIGURE 4.12 Send emails to your Evernote email address.

Evernote Web Clipper icon

FIGURE 4.13 Use the Web Clipper tool to save a web page's content or URL.

The clip will be uploaded to your Evernote account and stored in the default notebook. (Look through the settings for the Web Clipper tool if you wish to specify a different default storage location.)

Evernote users use the Web Clipper to grab all kinds of things from the Web and pull them into Evernote—a map of an upcoming destination, the text of a recipe and photo of the final dish, and an online purchase receipt (instead of printing it on paper) are just a few ways that the Web Clipper makes it easy for you to grab some information and store it away for later use.

Don't Forget the Cleanup

You'll find your own uses for Evernote, but one thing is for certain—you're going to want to do an occasional purge of old content to keep Evernote lean and fast. You've already seen how to store just about anything and everything in the cloud (such as with Dropbox) or on your own external hard drive (and accessible on your iPad via Pogoplug or another similar device), so move stuff there for long-term storage while keeping Evernote filled with the projects and information you need access to now. When a project is finished (such as Jack and Janell's guest room remodeling), delete all that stuff or move it over to long-term storage, but definitely take it out of Evernote.

And if you're a Premium user, keep offline notebooks to a minimum. They'll only eat into your iPad's storage space, and you already know that space is limited.

5

Cut the Clutter: Scan Everything

In This Chapter

- What Is a Scanner?
- The App Scanner
- The Portable Scanner
- The Desktop Scanner

Of all the things you can do, perhaps nothing does more to turn your mild-mannered iPad into the Ultimate iPad than converting anything and everything you can into a compatible digital file. Many files are already in a compatible format, and just require available storage—music and video files come to mind. But for most folks, clutter typically comes in the form of paper—letters, personal documents, recipes, old photos, magazines, permission forms, bills, and so much more. These are all items that can and should be converted to digital files to reduce physical clutter.

Of course, many items are best kept in their physical form—car titles, marriage licenses, stock certificates, and wills—but having a digital backup is still always a good idea. However, for everything else, you need to ask yourself if something can be converted to a digital file and then the original tossed in the garbage or shredded. If you've set up a storage solution that can be easily accessed with your iPad, then by converting documents to digital you're ensuring that just about everything you'll ever need is just a tap away on your iPad. (And you'll see shortly just how easy it is to locate *everything* using keyword/tag searches.)

For me personally, my office is 98% paper free. I do have a few folders or boxes that contain paper items that I either must keep (for legal reasons) or want to keep (for personal reasons). These include business documents that I'm forced to keep a copy of for tax purposes and sentimental items such as a number of my children's sketches, paintings, and report cards.

But everything else? Digital. PDF, JPEG, DOC, and a dozen more formats are all available using an app or two. How did I get all of my paper clutter into these digital formats, and how will you do it? The answer is simple—you're going to scan them with a scanner.

What Is a Scanner?

In its simplest form, a scanner converts a single document or a photo from its physical form into a digital file. That file can be one of many formats—PDF, JPEG, PNG, and even Word or Excel files with the proper software.

Scanners come in many sizes—from large, refrigerator-sized machines that are typically used in commercial settings where large quantities of documents and high speed are required, to scanners that exist only as apps that run on your iPhone or iPad. In between are devices that are often referred to as "personal scanners." These scanners typically fall between the size of a shoebox and an office laser printer. Some are portable in the sense that you can unplug them from a computer and take them with you, whereas others are just large enough that you'll want to plug them into a computer and leave them be.

Not only do scanners come in a variety of sizes and shapes, they also rely on varying methods for converting photos and documents to digital files. Some act like a camera, taking a photo of the entire document at once. Others use a more expensive image sensor, capable of detecting colors, grayscale, and the difference between black and white.

Some scanners can only handle a single document or photo at a time, whereas more advanced scanners often come with a tray that allows a user to insert 10, 20, or even 100 pages at once. The scanner uses a feeding system to pull in a page, scan it, and then pull in another page. Older scanners like the flat-bed scanners shown in Figure 5.1 require you to open a lid, place a document, close the lid, and then scan—a very slow process.

FIGURE 5.1 An older flatbed scanner with its lid open.

Although flatbed scanners will work just fine for short scanning jobs, they've really been replaced by the more modern scanner. Today's modern scanners, even the ones that only handle a single item at a time, often skip the lid and let you simply feed the document into the top of the scanner. And there are even more features available with today's modern scanners, such as the following:

- **Higher resolution scanning**—Many inexpensive flatbed scanners just couldn't offer the resolution required to scan photos, for example. If you enlarged a scanned photo on your computer screen, the image would appear grainy and with blemishes.

- **Multiple file types supported**—Older scanners could scan to JPG and possibly PDF or PNG, but today's scanners can save scans as Word documents, Excel spreadsheets, and much more. (You'll see an example of just how many different types are available to one scanner model later in the chapter.)

- **Flexible speeds**—Older scanners had one speed—slow. Today's scanners offer much higher scan speeds, even at high resolution. If you're willing to sacrifice some scan resolution (for black-and-white documents, for example), you can even increase the scan speed by dropping the scan resolution from 600DPI to 300DPI (dots per inch). You'll gain even more speed if you elect to scan color documents and photos to grayscale files.

- **Smaller footprint**—The old flatbed scanners were huge, taking up a large chunk of a desktop. Modern scanners free up desktop space by growing up, not out. This means they have a slot at the top to feed in documents, and the scanned item comes out the bottom.

- **Portable means portable**—Some new scanners are so small they'll fit in a purse or briefcase with plenty of room to spare. These mini-scanners are mostly single-page scanners, but they often come with rechargeable batteries and internal memory, meaning you can scan something wherever you are and have the scan saved in the device until you have time to plug it into a computer and download the scans.

Less desk space, lower price, and faster scans means that today's scanners are all about efficiency and ease of use. And that's exactly what you need if you decide you want to move toward a paperless home or office (or both). And it's also absolutely required for anyone choosing to turn an iPad into an Ultimate iPad—if you wish to access anything and everything from your iPad, some sort of scanner is going to be necessary.

In the next few sections, you'll see some of the options available when it comes to personal scanners. This chapter is going to avoid the large, expensive scanners you might find in an office setting and instead offer you three different scanner formats to consider, each with pros and cons, but all helpful in getting you moving toward your own Ultimate iPad.

The App Scanner

If you own an iPad 2 or higher with a built-in camera, you're halfway to owning the simplest and least expensive type of scanner possible. With nothing more than a free or inexpensive app, you can turn your iPad into a portable scanner that uses the built-in camera to take photos of documents. This type of app isn't great for scanning photos (you're basically taking a photo of a photo, and the results are never great), but when it comes to text on a page, the right app not only can provide you with a PDF of the scanned document but even convert the scanned text into an editable document that you can open in a text editor or even Word. Let's take a look at a few options.

NOTE

In a sense, taking a photo with your iPad's camera app is performing a kind of scan. You can take photos of receipts, tax documentation, and other important items that you wish to keep a digital record of but don't want to keep the paper original. The photo exists as a JPG and doesn't take up much space, so there's nothing wrong with snapping a photo of a piece of mail and then shredding the original if you don't need it. Just keep in mind that a photo may lose some of its details if enlarged, depending on the quality of your iPad's camera.

A simple search of Apple's App Store using "PDF scanner" provides over 300 results. A favorite free PDF scanner for your iPhone and iPad is called Genius Scan (also available for Android and Windows phones). After installing the app and opening it, you tap the orange button (with a camera icon on it) and point it at a document, as shown in Figure 5.2.

Press the shutter button to take a photo and then Genius Scan will attempt to find the borders of a scanned document, such as a receipt sitting on a desk, as shown in Figure 5.3. You can use your finger to redraw the border if it cuts off any part of the document you wish to have included.

You can tap the Use button to accept the image or the Cancel button to go back and reshoot. If you choose to use the image, you'll find a few controls at the bottom of the screen, as shown in Figure 5.4. The Image Controls button (lower-left corner) allows you to convert a color photo to black and white (and back again), rotate the image, and turn off the image enhancement made by the app. The Share button (lower-right corner) lets you email the photo, save it to the iPhone's Camera Roll, or post it to Facebook.

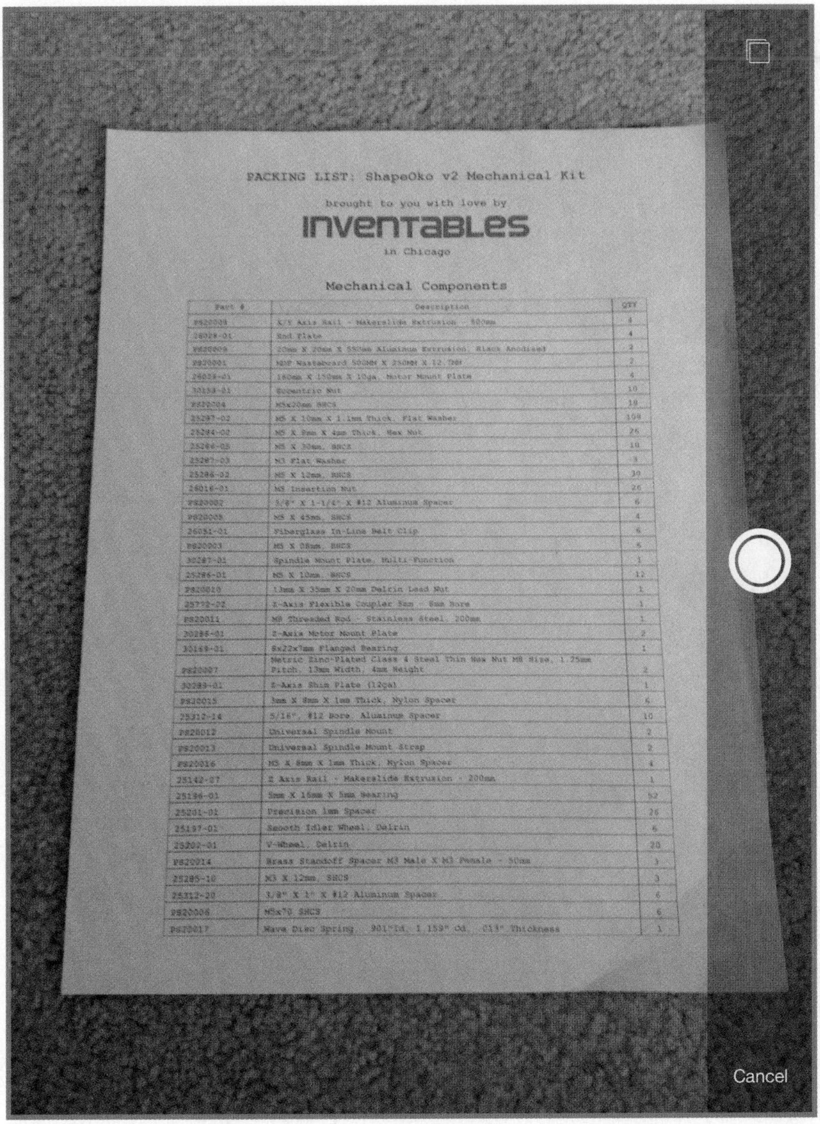

FIGURE 5.2   The Genius Scan app lets you use your iPad as a scanner.

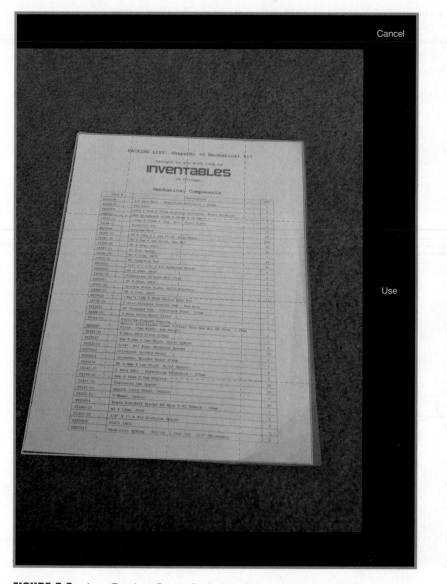

FIGURE 5.3   Let Genius Scan find the document's borders.

iPad 🛜   12:37 PM   99% 🔋

Cancel   **Scan**   Save

PACKING LIST: ShapeOko v2 Mechanical Kit

brought to you with love by

INVENTABLES

in Chicago

Mechanical Components

Part #	Description	QTY
P820008	X/Y Axis Rail - Makerslide Extrusion - 500mm	4
26020-01	End Plate	4
P820009	20mm X 20mm X 550mm Aluminum Extrusion, Black Anodized	2
P820001	MDF Wasteboard 500MM X 250MM X 12.7MM	2
26029-01	160mm X 150mm X 10ga. Motor Mount Plate	4
30158-01	Eccentric Nut	10
P820004	M5x20mm BHCS	18
25287-02	M5 X 10mm X 1.1mm Thick, Flat Washer	108
25284-02	M5 X 8mm X 4mm Thick, Hex Nut	26
25286-05	M5 X 30mm, BHCS	10
25287-03	M3 Flat Washer	3
25286-02	M5 X 12mm, BHCS	30
26016-01	M5 Insertion Nut	26
P820002	3/8" X 1-1/4" X #12 Aluminum Spacer	6
P820005	M5 X 45mm, BHCS	4
26051-01	Fiberglass In-Line Belt Clip	6
P820003	M5 X 08mm, BHCS	6
30287-01	Spindle Mount Plate, Multi-Function	1
25286-01	M5 X 10mm, BHCS	12
P820010	13mm X 35mm X 20mm Delrin Lead Nut	1
25772-02	Z-Axis Flexible Coupler 5mm - 8mm Bore	1
P820011	M8 Threaded Rod - Stainless Steel, 200mm	1
30288-01	Z-Axis Motor Mount Plate	2
30169-01	8x22x7mm Flanged Bearing	1
P820007	Metric Zinc-Plated Class 4 Steel Thin Hex Nut M8 Size, 1.25mm Pitch, 13mm Width, 4mm Height	2
30289-01	Z-Axis Shim Plate (12ga)	1
P820015	3mm X 8mm X 1mm Thick, Nylon Spacer	6
25312-14	5/16", #12 Bore, Aluminum Spacer	10
P820012	Universal Spindle Mount	2
P820013	Universal Spindle Mount Strap	2
P820016	M5 X 8mm X 1mm Thick, Nylon Spacer	4
25142-07	Z Axis Rail - Makerslide Extrusion - 200mm	1
25196-01	5mm X 16mm X 5mm Bearing	52
25201-01	Precision 1mm Spacer	26
25197-01	Smooth Idler Wheel, Delrin	6
25202-01	V-Wheel, Delrin	20
P820014	Brass Standoff Spacer M3 Male X M3 Female - 50mm	3
25285-10	M3 X 12mm, SHCS	3
25312-20	3/8" X 1" X #12 Aluminum Spacer	6
P820006	M5x70 SHCS	6
P820017	Wave Disc Spring, .901"Id, 1.159" Od, .013" Thickness	1

⫴   ↶ ↷   ⬆️

Image Controls button   Rotate buttons   Share button

FIGURE 5.4 Share your scan as well as change from color to black and white.

NOTE

Genius Scan also comes in a paid version for $6.99 that offers you the ability to save your scans to a cloud service such as Dropbox, Twitter, box.com, Google Drive, SkyDrive, Evernote, and a few more. These options are shown as gray icons (versus orange icons for available options) in the free version when you tap the Share button. Tapping on a gray icon will open a new screen that offers the upgrade.

Although Genius Scan is a great free app that does a good job of converting images to PDF files, there's one more app for your consideration. If you'll remember back to the discussion of Evernote in Chapter 4, "Evernote: Your New Best Friend," you'll recall that Evernote offers both free and paid accounts, with the paid account offering a few upgrades to the service, such as a higher monthly upload quota.

One interesting feature that Evernote also offers paid users is a PDF scanning service—when you upload a PDF as a note to a paid account, that PDF is scanned so that it becomes a searchable document by keyword. Why is this important?

If you scan a receipt of a recent purchase with Genius Scan, the app can convert the document to a PDF, but that PDF is not keyword searchable. Let's say you took a photo of a receipt for your new Sony LCD television that clearly states the brand, model name, and price paid, and you've uploaded the newly created PDF file to Evernote. If you have hundreds of PDFs stored in a free Evernote account and wish to find one that has the word "Sony" on it, unless you renamed the PDF with a filename that easily identifies that receipt, you may find yourself having to open up a lot of PDFs as you search for that one receipt scan.

If you have a paid Evernote account, this is done for you when you upload your PDF files as notes. Go into Evernote, type **Sony** in the search box, and every document stored in your Evernote notes and notebooks will be searched for any occurrences of that keyword.

But what if you're using a free Evernote account? How can you make certain your PDF files are also searchable with keywords? To do this will require a slightly different scanning app, one that can scan a file, save it as a PDF, but also scan the original item and convert words to text. This is called OCR, or Optical Character Recognition, and not only do more advanced scanners offer this ability, as you'll soon see, but there are even iPhone/iPad apps that offer this feature. One of them is PDFpen Scan+.

PDFpen Scan+ costs $4.99 (and you can install on both an iPhone and iPad for the single purchase), but if you're using a free Evernote account, this is one inexpensive way to have your PDF notes made searchable.

After purchasing, installing, and opening PDFpen Scan+ on your iPad, you'll see a screen similar to the one in Figure 5.5.

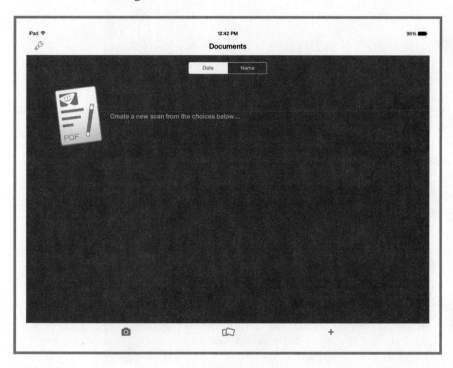

FIGURE 5.5 PDFpen Scan+ for iPad is an OCR-capable scanning application.

To create a new scan, tap the camera icon in the lower-left corner and line up your document as shown in Figure 5.6.

After taking the photo, tap the Accept button to keep the photo or the Retake button to reshoot. If you choose to accept the scan, you'll next be asked to help the app determine the edges of the document, as shown in Figure 5.7.

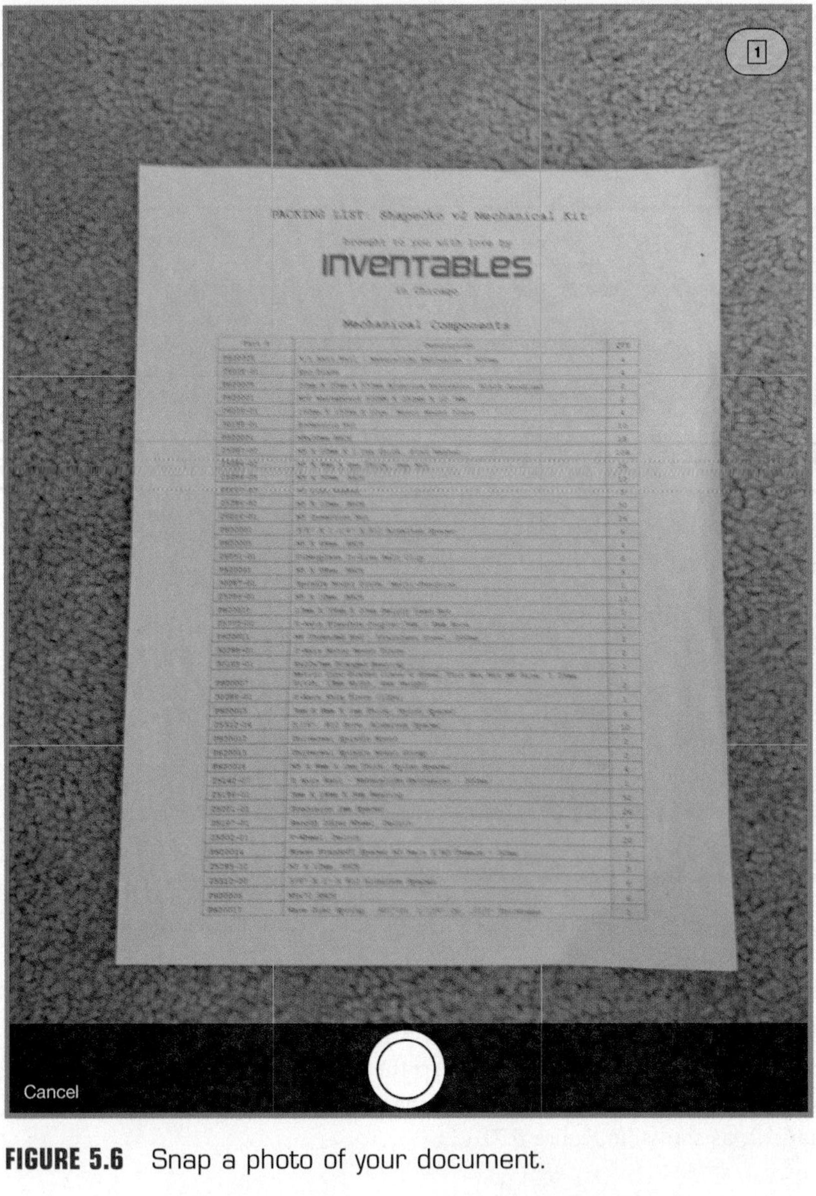

FIGURE 5.6 Snap a photo of your document.

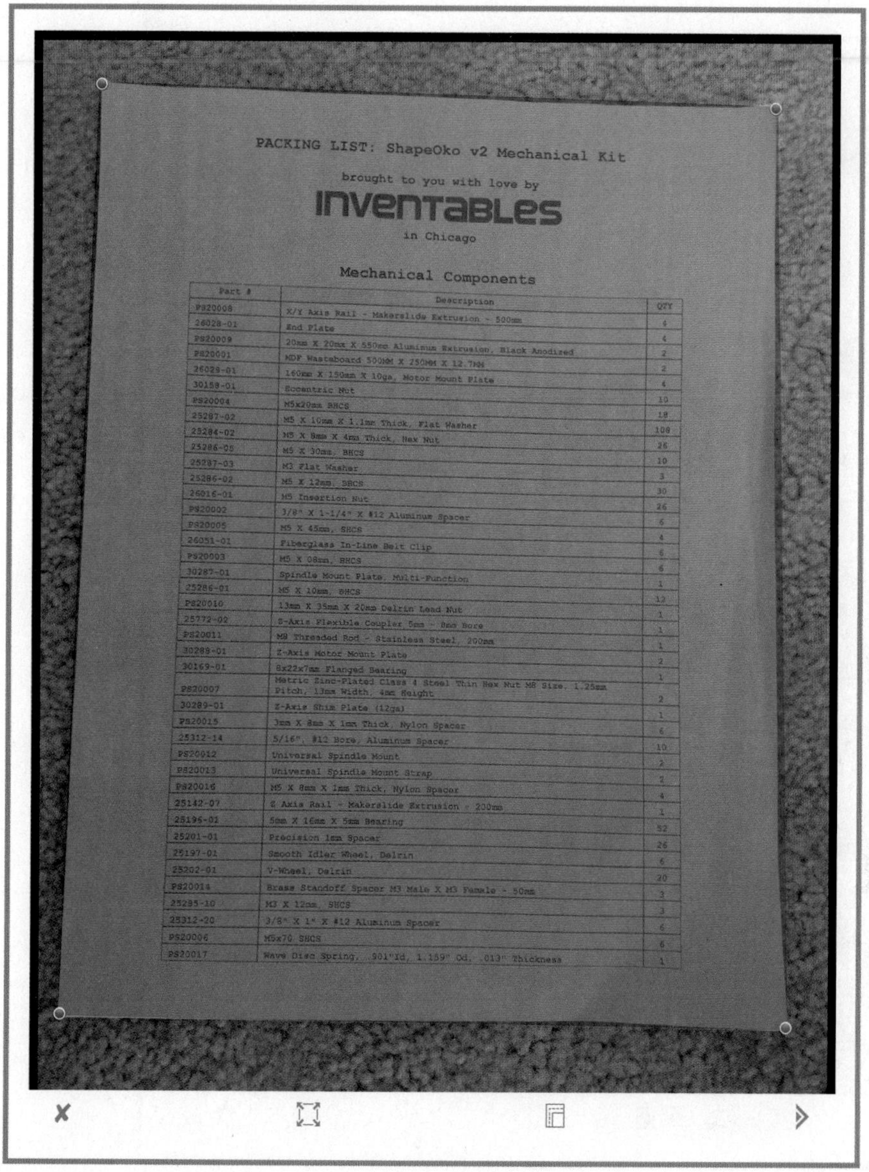

FIGURE 5.7 Make certain the edges of the scanned document are correct.

You'll need to drag the dots to the corners of the document if they aren't already there. It doesn't have to be perfect, and the purple shading really only needs to cover the text you wish to convert. Tap the small arrow (lower-right corner) to have your document cropped. You can remove the carpet surrounding the document you see in Figure 5.7, as you can see in Figure 5.8.

PACKING LIST: ShapeOko v2 Mechanical Kit

brought to you with love by

INVENTABLES

in Chicago

Mechanical Components

Part #	Description	QTY
PS20008	X/Y Axis Rail - Makerslide Extrusion - 500mm	4
26028-01	End Plate	4
PS20009	20mm X 20mm X 550mm Aluminum Extrusion, Black Anodized	2
PS20001	MDF Wasteboard 500MM X 250MM X 12.7MM	2
26029-01	160mm X 150mm X 10ga, Motor Mount Plate	4
30158-01	Eccentric Nut	10
PS20004	M5x20mm BHCS	18
25287-02	M5 X 10mm X 1.1mm Thick, Flat Washer	108
25284-02	M5 X 8mm X 4mm Thick, Hex Nut	28
25286-05	M5 X 30mm, BHCS	10
25287-03	M3 Flat Washer	3
25286-02	M5 X 12mm, BHCS	30
26016-01	M5 Insertion Nut	26
PS20002	3/8" X 1-1/4" X #12 Aluminum Spacer	6
PS20005	M5 X 45mm, SHCS	4
26051-01	Fiberglass In-Line Belt Clip	6
PS20003	M5 X 08mm, BHCS	6
30287-01	Spindle Mount Plate, Multi-Function	1
25286-01	M5 X 10mm, BHCS	12
PS20010	13mm X 35mm X 20mm Delrin Lead Nut	1
25772-02	Z-Axis Flexible Coupler 5mm - 8mm Bore	1
PS20011	M8 Threaded Rod - Stainless Steel, 200mm	1
30288-01	Z-Axis Motor Mount Plate	2
30169-01	8x22x7mm Flanged Bearing	1
PS20007	Metric Zinc-Plated Class 4 Steel Thin Hex Nut M8 Size, 1.25mm Pitch, 13mm Width, 4mm Height	2
30289-01	Z-Axis Shim Plate (12ga)	1
PS20015	3mm X 8mm X 1mm Thick, Nylon Spacer	6
25312-14	5/16", #12 Bore, Aluminum Spacer	10
PS20012	Universal Spindle Mount	2
PS20013	Universal Spindle Mount Strap	2
PS20016	M5 X 8mm X 1mm Thick, Nylon Spacer	4
25142-07	Z Axis Rail - Makerslide Extrusion - 200mm	1
25196-01	5mm X 16mm X 5mm Bearing	52
25201-01	Precision 1mm Spacer	26
25197-01	Smooth Idler Wheel, Delrin	6
25202-01	V-Wheel, Delrin	20
PS20014	Brass Standoff Spacer M3 Male X M3 Female - 50mm	3
25285-10	M3 X 12mm, SHCS	3
25312-20	3/8" X 1" X #12 Aluminum Spacer	6
PS20006	M5x70 SHCS	6
PS20017	Wave Disc Spring, .901"Id, 1.159" Od, .013" Thickness	1

FIGURE 5.8 Make certain the edges of the scanned document are correct.

You can tap the arrow in the lower-left corner to go back if you're unhappy with the cropping process. If you are satisfied, once again tap the arrow in the lower-right corner to finalize the scan. As you can see in Figure 5.9, you can choose to change a color scan to a black and white or grayscale scan with the touch of a button.

PACKING LIST: ShapeOko v2 Mechanical Kit

brought to you with love by

INVENTABLES

in Chicago

Mechanical Components

Part #	Description	QTY
PS20008	X/Y Axis Rail - Makerslide Extrusion - 500mm	4
26028-01	End Plate	4
PS20009	20mm X 20mm X 550mm Aluminum Extrusion, Black Anodized	2
PS20001	MDF Wasteboard 500MM X 250MM X 12.7MM	2
26029-01	160mm X 150mm X 10ga, Motor Mount Plate	4
30158-01	Eccentric Nut	10
PS20004	M5x20mm BHCS	18
25287-02	M5 X 10mm X 1.1mm Thick, Flat Washer	108
25284-02	M5 X 8mm X 4mm Thick, Hex Nut	26
25286-05	M5 X 30mm, BHCS	10
25287-03	M3 Flat Washer	3
25286-02	M5 X 12mm, BHCS	30
26016-01	M5 Insertion Nut	26
PS20002	3/8" X 1-1/4" X #12 Aluminum Spacer	6
PS20005	M5 X 45mm, SHCS	4
26051-01	Fiberglass In-Line Belt Clip	6
PS20003	M5 X 08mm, BHCS	6
30287-01	Spindle Mount Plate, Multi-Function	1
25286-01	M5 X 10mm, BHCS	12
PS20010	13mm X 35mm X 20mm Delrin Lead Nut	1
25772-02	Z-Axis Flexible Coupler 5mm - 8mm Bore	1
PS20011	M8 Threaded Rod - Stainless Steel, 200mm	1
30288-01	Z-Axis Motor Mount Plate	2
30169-01	8x22x7mm Flanged Bearing	1
PS20007	Metric Zinc-Plated Class 4 Steel Thin Hex Nut M8 Size, 1.25mm Pitch, 13mm Width, 4mm Height	2
30289-01	Z-Axis Shim Plate (12ga)	1
PS20015	3mm X 8mm X 1mm Thick, Nylon Spacer	6
25312-14	5/16", #12 Bore, Aluminum Spacer	10
PS20012	Universal Spindle Mount	2
PS20013	Universal Spindle Mount Strap	2
PS20016	M5 X 8mm X 1mm Thick, Nylon Spacer	4
25142-07	Z Axis Rail - Makerslide Extrusion - 200mm	1
25196-01	5mm X 16mm X 5mm Bearing	52
25201-01	Precision 1mm Spacer	26
25197-01	Smooth Idler Wheel, Delrin	6
25202-01	V-Wheel, Delrin	20
PS20014	Brass Standoff Spacer M3 Male X M3 Female - 50mm	3
25285-10	M3 X 12mm, SHCS	3
25312-20	3/8" X 1" X #12 Aluminum Spacer	6
PS20006	M5x70 SHCS	6
PS20017	Wave Disc Spring, .901"Id, 1.159" Od, .013" Thickness	1

Save

FIGURE 5.9 Your document is converted to a digital PDF version.

If you're unhappy with a grayscale conversion, you can always tap back on the Color button to return the scan to its original color version. Tap the Save button when you're done and the document will appear on the app's desktop, as shown in Figure 5.10.

FIGURE 5.10 Your scanned documents are stored in the Scan+ app initially.

If you tap and hold a moment on the name of the file (Untitled is the default), you can rename the document and give it a more descriptive title.

Although the scan is complete, the PDF hasn't yet been converted to a searchable document. You still need to run the file through the OCR process, so tap the document to select it and you'll notice an OCR button in the upper-right corner of the screen, as shown in Figure 5.11. Select OCR Document from the pop-up menu. (The other option is OCR Document Text, which will remove graphics such as letterhead logos and signatures, leaving only plain text.)

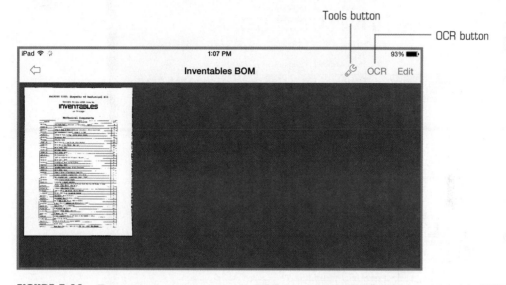

FIGURE 5.11 Preparing to convert the PDF to a searchable document with OCR.

Once the OCR conversion process begins, you'll see the screen start to turn yellow as the text is scanned. Figure 5.12 shows the OCR process almost complete.

After the document is converted to a searchable PDF, I can tap the Tools button (it's the wrench icon shown in the upper-right corner in Figure 5.11) and select Share to Evernote. The PDF is pushed to my Evernote account (and I'm asked to select the notebook where I wish it to be stored). As you can see in Figure 5.13, if I search for the term "Universal Spindle," the PDF I just converted in Evernote is found. A single tap on the document opens it so I can examine it in more detail.

All this power and functionality is available to you from a simple app or two. If you are a paid Evernote user, you could go with the free Genius Scan app and let Evernote handle the PDF scanning operation. And if you use a free Evernote account, the PDFpen Scan+ app may require a few extra steps on your part to make the final PDF searchable, but it's well worth the small price of the app and the time to run OCR on important documents.

FIGURE 5.12 The OCR process highlights the image as it converts to text.

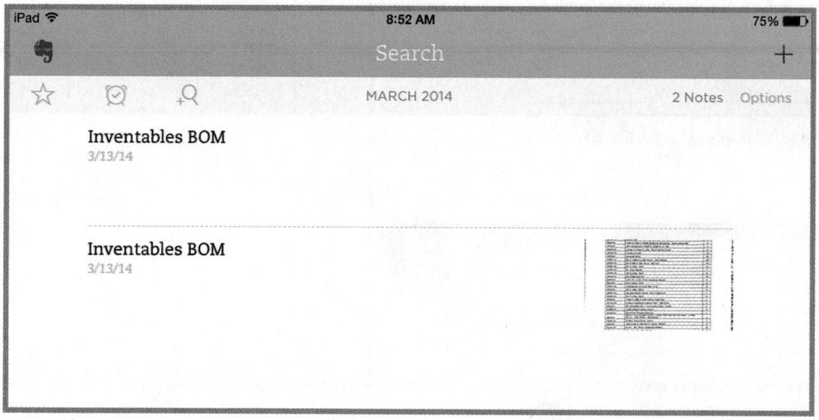

FIGURE 5.13 Evernote contains the PDF document that is keyword searchable.

The Portable Scanner

One of the benefits to going with a non–app-based scanner is often found in the software that comes bundled with the scanner. This special software often contains features that allow you to save scans in different formats other than PDF or JPG. Other features will let you scan special items such as business cards and have all the details automatically filled in to a contact database. Some scanners even have software that lets you edit scans on the fly, letting you fix a word or letter in a document, for example, or even combine two scans into a single page (such as when scanning a two-page article from a magazine).

The software is often shared by various models of scanner from a manufacturer, so if you've identified a scanner manufacturer you're interested in, often your only real choice is to decide on the particular model you wish to purchase. Not all manufacturers offer a range of scanning models, but those that do will often have what are called "portable scanners." Portable scanners typically can only scan a single item at a time—you feed the photo or document in on one side and out it comes on the other. Portable scanners are small, light, and often run on a rechargeable battery, making them easy to tote around.

As I mentioned in Chapter 1, "The Ultimate iPad," one of my favorite portable scanners is the $199 Doxie Go shown in Figure 5.14.

The Doxie Go scans in a single item at a time—insert it into the front and it comes out the back. Its particular size does mean it has a limitation on the size of items you can scan—8.5"×15" is the maximum size sheet that can be inserted.

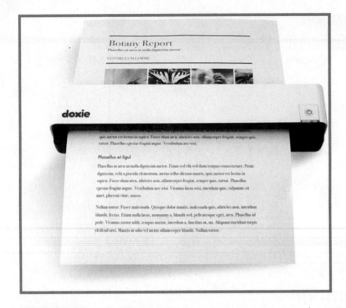

FIGURE 5.14 The Doxie Go is a battery-powered portable scanner.

It can handle resolutions up to 600DPI (and can be dropped down for faster speeds and smaller file size), and its built-in memory means you can scan and scan (up to around 100 scans on one charge) without the need to have it connected to a computer. The specs say it can hold about 450 single-sided pages or 1,800 scanned photos.

I have one in my kitchen where my wife and I can scan in important documents that we get in the mail. (I also have a shredder in the kitchen, meaning after we scan a document, it goes into the shredder and reduces clutter). After a month or so of scanning, I simply connect the Doxie Go to my home computer with a USB cable and upload all the scans, placing them either in Dropbox or Evernote, depending on the content.

But connecting the Doxie Go to a computer isn't even necessary now. For an extra $30, the Doxie Go + Wi-Fi version will allow for scans to be uploaded to your computer over a Wi-Fi network or even directly to your iPad. That's right—an app you install on your iPad allows you to scan directly from the Doxie Go + Wi-Fi device to your iPad and straight into a cloud service such as Dropbox or Evernote. Oh, and the software that comes with the Doxie Go (and the Doxie Go + Wi-Fi) model offers OCR for your scans, just like PDFpen Scan+, so scan comfortably knowing your scans will be keyword searchable from your Ultimate iPad.

A portable scanner like the Doxie Go is a great way to get rid of your clutter, allowing you to take your piles of documents to a coffee shop, the living room, or even the outdoor deck (provided it's not gusting!) to get comfortable and start scanning. If you have an initial manageable amount of documents to scan and a small amount of weekly or monthly items (financial documents, for example) that are coming in, the portable scanner is likely all you'll ever need.

But even the portable scanner has some limitations. If you have boxes and boxes of documents to scan, oversized photos you wish to convert, and maybe some documents that need to be scanned into files other than PDF or JPG file types, you may find that your scanning needs can only be satisfied with a desktop scanner.

The Desktop Scanner

Desktop scanners are the slightly larger brother to the portable scanners. They're not really meant to be ported from place to place, but instead are linked to a computer (usually with a USB cable) that has special software installed allowing users to preview, edit, and save scans in a variety of ways. (Some desktop scanners, as you'll soon see, also support Wi-Fi scanning, requiring no connection to a computer.)

> **NOTE**
>
> You may be familiar with the All-in-One type devices that include a scanner, printer, and fax machine. These are certainly an option, but often the built-in scanner does not offer as many options as a dedicated scanner, such as saving as a PDF (most of these scanners only scan as JPEG images). There are also dedicated photo scanners that offer super-high resolution scanning of photos if that's the main source of your scanning needs.

There are simply too many scanners and too many variations of software to review, but most of them have a few things in common. Most desktop scanners, for example, can hold 10 or more pages at a time, so you don't have to feed single sheets, one at a time, as you do with the portable versions. (If you've got books and magazines that you want to scan, be sure to check out the specialty scanner I cover in Chapter 7, "Convert Your Collections: Reducing Book and Magazine Clutter," that will keep you from having to cut up your books and magazines to scan them in.)

Desktop scanners typically allow for larger original documents and photos, and they usually scan at a much faster rate than the smaller scanners. That said, there are always exceptions to the rule.

In this chapter, I'm going to introduce you to my go-to scanner for almost all of my scanning needs. Why have I chosen a desktop version over the portable version? Mainly because every week I have a small pile of documents to scan—contracts, financial paperwork, kids' artwork and spelling tests, and so much more. I also frequently find myself needing to combine two pages together into either a single PDF file or one single graphic that would normally span two pages. Either way, I've found over the last few years that a desktop scanner works best for me, and the one I'm looking at right now that has served me well is the Fujitsu ScanSnap iX500, shown in Figure 5.15.

FIGURE 5.15   The ScanSnap iX500 desktop scanner closed up.

The scanner in Figure 5.15 is in what I call Sleep Mode—it has its top and bottom panels closed up to save desk space. When everything is opened up, the iX500 looks like the one in Figure 5.16.

FIGURE 5.16   The iX500 desktop scanner opened up and ready to scan.

The iX500 has a single button on the front labeled Scan. In normal operation it's lit up blue and all that's required of me is to insert anywhere from one to 50 pages in the rear of the scanner. The iX500 is also a double-sided scanner—it can scan the front and back of a page at the same time if required. (I'll show you a bit more about this in a moment.)

When I press the Scan button, the first sheet is pulled down into the scanner and comes out the front. Onscreen, the software will automatically open and I'm greeted with what you see in Figure 5.17.

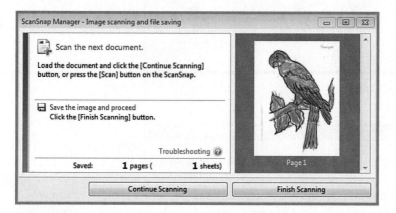

FIGURE 5.17 The iX500 automatically launches the software after a scan.

I'm scanning in some of my young son's artwork, and I'd like to store them all in a single PDF. To do that, I can place another piece of paper in the tray and click the Continue Scanning button. When I'm done scanning, I click the Finish Scanning button.

After finishing a scanning operation, the ScanSnap software puts up a window like the one in Figure 5.18 that lets me choose how I wish to save the scan.

TIP

Windows and Mac versions of the software are available. They look a little different, but the functionality is the same. Some of the nontraditional file types do require optional software to be installed as well.

As you can see in Figure 5.18, I can save the scan as a photo, send it to the printer, save it to Evernote or Dropbox, and even send it directly to an email message as an attachment. The software offers up the ability to scan a text document and have it saved as a Word file that can be edited, and there's even an option for scanning a spreadsheet and saving it to Excel.

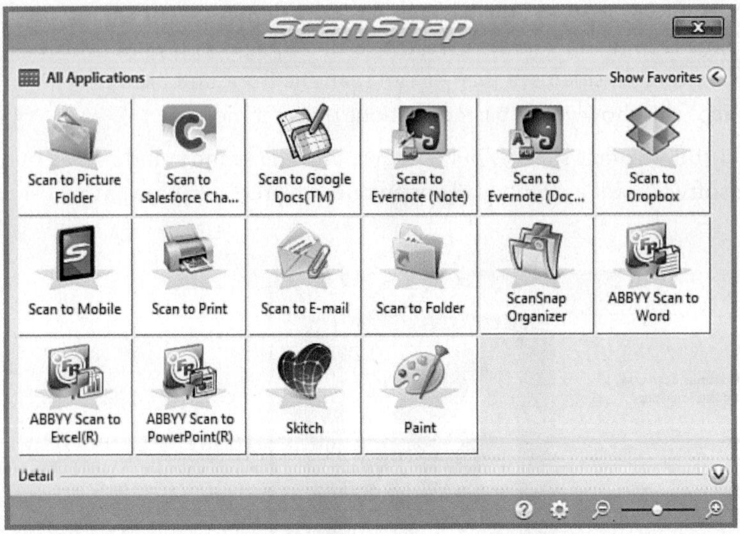

FIGURE 5.18 Select how the scan is to be saved and where.

If you wish to save the scan to your desktop, simply choose the Scan to Folder option, type in a name for the file, and select the folder where the file is to be placed, as shown in Figure 5.19. (For me, I usually scan directly into Dropbox or Evernote, depending on the item scanned.)

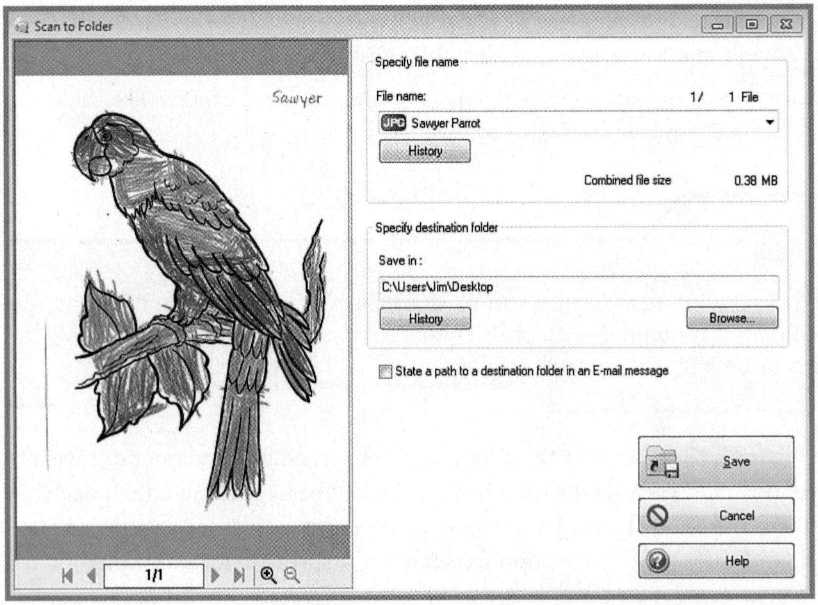

FIGURE 5.19 Rename your file and choose where to save it.

By default, a scan is initially saved either as a JPG or a PDF, and you select which option you prefer using the ScanSnap control panel, shown in Figure 5.20.

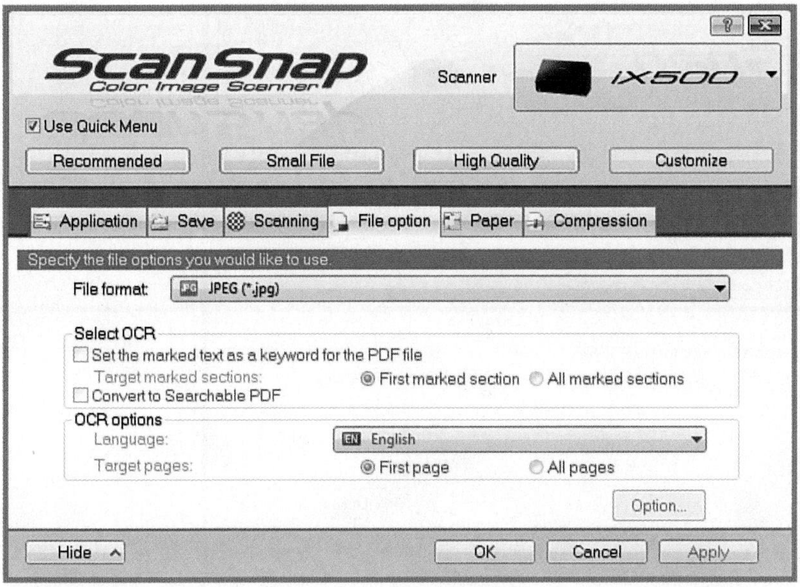

FIGURE 5.20 The ScanSnap control panel.

The control panel offers you a single place to make scanning configuration settings that include the following:

- **Default save location**—You can specify the default folder as well as a name format using the Save tab.

- **Color versus B/W or grayscale**—Use the Scanning tab to choose whether you want color to be the default scanning option. (Choosing B/W or grayscale will speed up scans.)

- **Single or dual-side scans**—The Scanning tab also allows you to set whether the iX500 always scans both sides or a single side. (You can manually override this default setting at any time.)

- **PDF or JPG**—The File Option tab lets you choose between PDF or JPG as the default file type.

Other tabs allow you to configure paper size, compression (to save on storage space), and a few other options.

If you'll recall, the PDFpen Scan+ app for the iPad allows you to scan a document and run it through OCR conversion. Just as you can choose to not run a file through OCR if you don't need it keyword searchable, the ScanSnap software also allows you to turn on or off the OCR feature by default.

Figure 5.21 shows the File Option tab from the control panel. Notice that the first check box and the Convert to Searchable PDF check box are both checked.

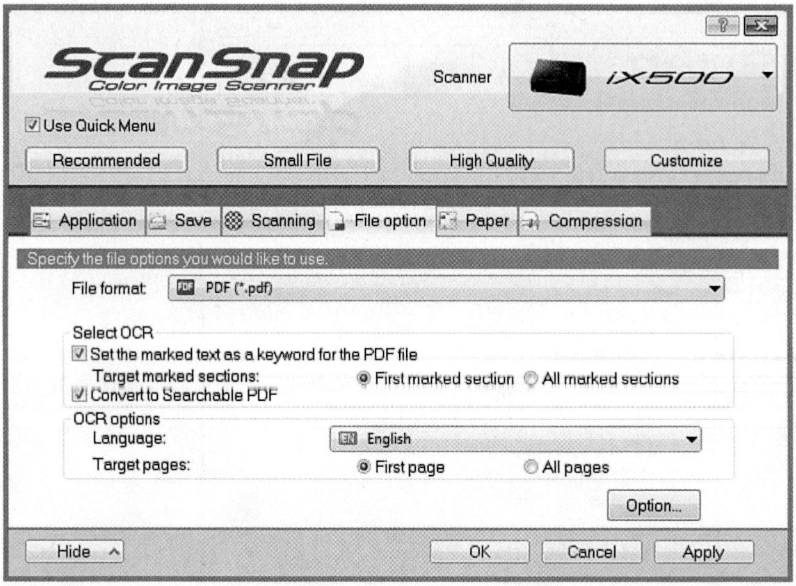

FIGURE 5.21 You can turn on and off the iX500's OCR capability.

The OCR process does slow the scanning process just a little a bit (one to two seconds extra per page), so keep in mind you can always go in and disable it temporarily if you're going to be scanning photos and other non-text items or documents that you don't necessarily need to be keyword searchable. (Notice also that the First Page option is selected versus the All Pages option—sometimes all you need to do is make the first page of a document searchable for keywords to be helpful.)

Most desktop scanners and their respective software work in a similar manner to the iX500. You scan an item, save it as a PDF or JPG, and then export it or save it to a location you specify. Some scanners will hold more sheets in the tray; some will hold fewer.

Before I close out this chapter, I'd like to show you one final feature that works so well with my iPad. As mentioned earlier, the iX500 can communicate via Wi-Fi, so with the special app from ScanSnap, I can send scans directly to my iPad's screen instead of to my computer. Figure 5.22 shows the app running on my iPad.

After loading a document (or documents) into the tray, instead of tapping the Scan button on the iX500, I tap the Scan button on my iPad and the scanned document appears in the list, as shown in Figure 5.23. (A message also appears on the computer screen telling me the iX500 has switched over to mobile scanning.)

FIGURE 5.22 The ScanSnap app running on the iPad.

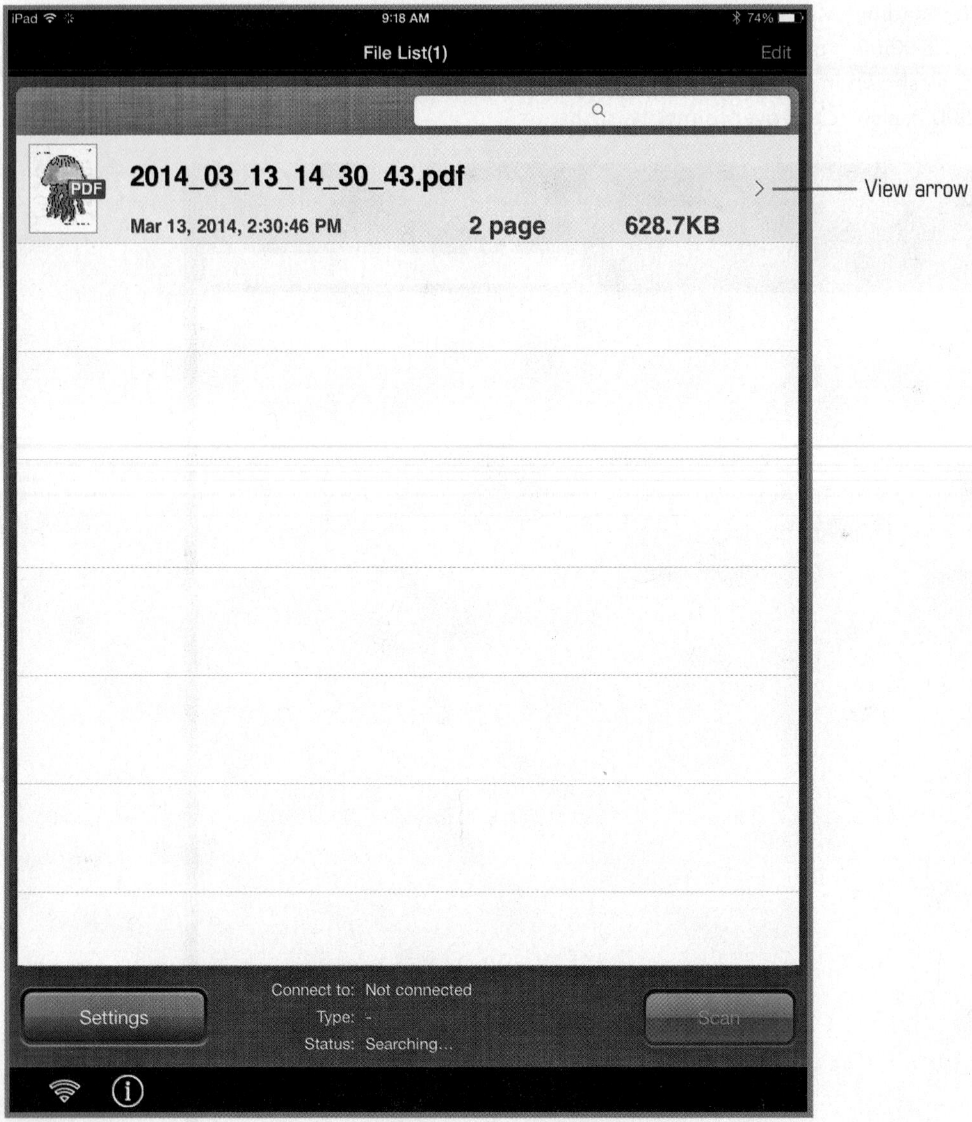
iPad
9:18 AM
74%
File List(1)
Edit
2014_03_13_14_30_43.pdf
Mar 13, 2014, 2:30:46 PM
2 page
628.7KB
View arrow
Settings
Connect to: Not connected
Type: -
Status: Searching...
Scan

FIGURE 5.23 The scan is saved to the iPad, not the computer.

By tapping the View arrow on the right, I can view my scanned item on my iPad. But tapping anywhere else on the file opens a small menu like the one in Figure 5.24, allowing me to select where I wish to send the scan—Evernote, Dropbox, Pogoplug, or somewhere else.

FIGURE 5.24 Choose what service will import the scan.

As you can see, the iX500 desktop scanner does offer me quite a few more capabilities than an app scanner or a portable scanner. When I'm done, I close up the iX500 panels and it sits patiently for our next scanning session, typically when my Scan box gets about halfway filled or I receive a document that's important enough to justify an immediate scan.

Summary

When shopping for a scanner, take what you have learned in this chapter and identify what's important to you when it comes to scanning. Do you need speed because you have lots of weekly or monthly scanning to do? If so, the desktop scanner will likely serve you well. Can you be satisfied with a simple photo taken of receipts and other documents? If that's the case, save some money and use either your iPad's Camera app or find a free or inexpensive scanner app. Or maybe all you need is a portable scanner that you can take with you to the coffee shop or to a client's office where you expect you might want to capture some documents as digital files for viewing on your iPad. Whatever your need, there's probably a scanner technology that matches your lifestyle.

Ultimately, one of the steps toward turning your ordinary iPad into an Ultimate iPad is to find a way to turn as many paper documents into digital ones and then storing them in Dropbox or Evernote or on Pogoplug-connected hard drive, where you'll be able to find them with a few keyword searches. By doing this, you've made your iPad into a single source for finding anything you need, when you need it. And having access to all your documents from the iPad means you're more than halfway home to owning an Ultimate iPad.

6

Your Financials—Banking and Investment Apps

In This Chapter

- Managing accounts with banking apps
- Monitoring your money with credit cards and investment apps
- Using the Mint.com app
- Security issues with financial apps

For a long time, I tried to manage my banking and investment accounts using my iPhone, but I finally gave it up. I'm not in my twenties any longer, so I recognize that my eyes aren't as sharp as they used to be, but if I have to do a reverse-pinch on the screen to enlarge a website's text so much that only a few dozen or so words are visible on the screen... then that is one website that won't work for me on a mobile phone.

Thankfully the iPad's screen has more than enough room to spare for displaying websites. Now, depending on your browser app of choice, you may find that some browsers automatically format a website to display the mobile version—a slimmed down version of the full website. This is extremely annoying to me, so I switched from using the iPad's default Safari browser to the Perfect Web browser app that lets me select whether to display websites in their original format or default to their mobile versions. (Other browsers may offer this feature, but I've yet to find any reason over the last four years to leave Perfect Web.)

For a while I used my iPad's web app to check in with my banking and investment accounts, and I still do this when I need to do some behind-the-scenes account management. Today, however, with the popularity of apps, I can easily bypass using a web browser and simply use the specialty apps that have become available from a number of financial institutions.

In this chapter, I'm going to talk about how the iPad can be used to help you stay informed when it comes to your money—checking and savings accounts, bills, finances, investments, and so on. Remember, the goal of this book is to have access to as much of your information from one source—your iPad—as possible. Let's take a look at some of the tools that are available to help you keep a finger on your bank account, your bills, and your investments.

Banking Apps

Banks are smart. Not only do they know how to make money, they also know how to keep it in their vaults. I don't know many people who are extremely happy with their current bank's fees and other rules, but I do know that the process to change banks is just annoying enough that it takes some major hassles from a bank to get a person to jump to another bank.

While banks vary in their services, one thing they all seem to have in common these days is the ability to conduct online banking. Figure 6.1 shows my banking institution's homepage as viewed on the iPad.

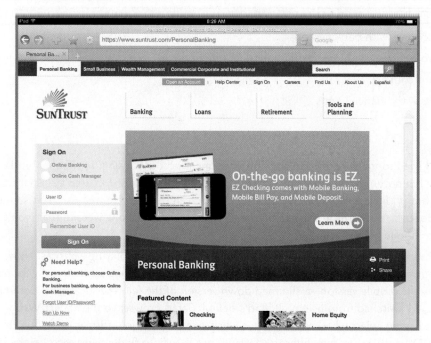

FIGURE 6.1 Online banking via a web browser.

Online banking from the iPad varies from bank to bank, but most banks offer the ability to view balances on checking, savings, and money market accounts as well as the ability to transfer funds from one account to another. Some banks offer the ability to wire funds to another bank or individual online, and a surprisingly large number of banks even offer automobile and home financing, as well as personal loans. In many cases, there's no need to get on your nicest suit and drive in to talk with a loan officer—everything can be done from the comfort of your home or office, including filling out forms and getting a fast "Yes" or "No" answer.

Website online banking is still quite popular, but banks have been developing and improving their own apps for customers that allow them to do an amazing number of things all from a mobile device.

Again, I don't like using these apps from my iPhone because the buttons, menus, and text are so small, and it's too easy to tap something incorrectly. But I do like to use these apps on my iPad. In Figure 6.2, you can see my bank's app open and ready for me to log in.

FIGURE 6.2 Many banks offer apps for mobile devices.

As you can see in Figure 6.3, I can view my checking account and money market balances, as well as recent pending transactions. Buttons along the bottom let me make online payments to billers I have previously set up, transfer funds between my accounts, and even make deposits (see Figure 6.4) by taking photos of the front and back of a check (and then destroying the check after 10 days). Very convenient!

A quick search in the App Store using your bank's name is the easiest way to find out if your bank offers a mobile app, but some apps might have obscure names, so check with your bank's website or a teller and ask if an app is available. The biggest banks all have them, of course, but credit unions and other smaller banks might not yet be onboard with a mobile banking app of their own.

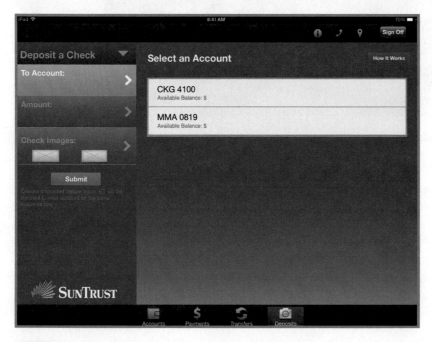

FIGURE 6.3   My bank's app lets me transfer funds and view account details.

FIGURE 6.4   Make a deposit by taking photos of a check with the iPad's camera.

Credit Card and Investment Apps

Credit card, banking, and investment apps are great for staying on top of your financials. What many consider to be the Big 10 Banks all offer their own apps for keeping an eye on checking, savings, and investment accounts—Bank of America, Wells Fargo, Chase, Citi, Bank of New York Mellon, US Bancorp, HSBC, PNC, Capital One, and TD Bank all have apps for iPhone/iPad. Small banks and credit unions are slowly starting to offer their own apps—a quick search of the App Store will tell you if one exists.

The same goes for investments you may wish to monitor—various specialty apps exist for a number of investment companies such as Charles Schwab, TD Ameritrade, and Edward Jones. These are just a few of the apps available for accessing investment info, issuing trades, and other services.

Many banks also offer credit cards, so if you have a credit card account with your bank, you may find that the bank's mobile app also offers you the ability to view your credit card balance and make payment transfers.

Figure 6.5 shows the Bank of America mobile app—this is one of those apps that offers banking and credit card account management all in one. (It'll even let you open an account from within the app!)

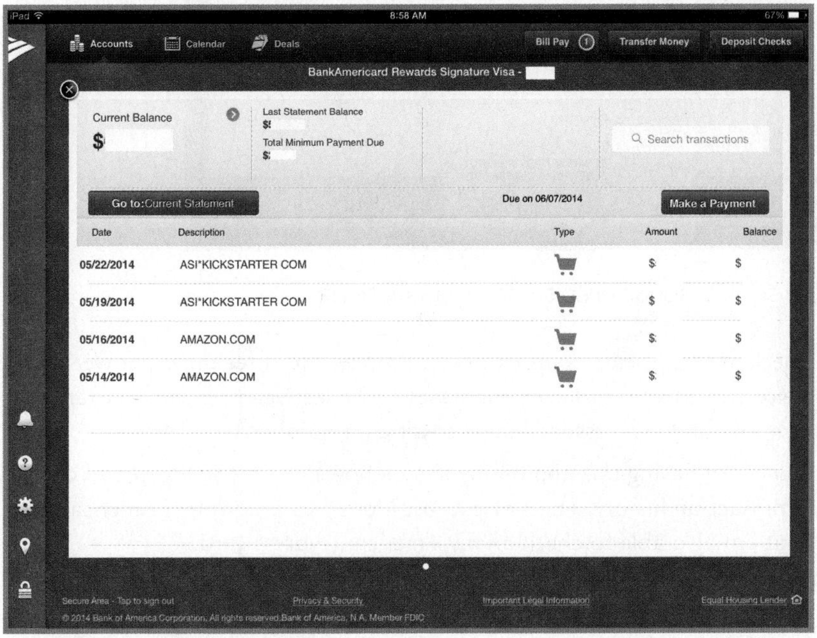

FIGURE 6.5 Use a credit card app to monitor your account.

Notice that this app will not only let me view my credit card details, but I can also pay the bill and view my current statement. (If I were a Bank of America banking customer, I could also transfer funds and deposit checks.)

Tapping a charge pulls up more details about the charge, including the date, the name of the merchant, and even a phone number if I have questions. This little feature shown in Figure 6.6 may not sound like a big deal, but think about just how many times you've heard about fraudulent charges in the news these days.

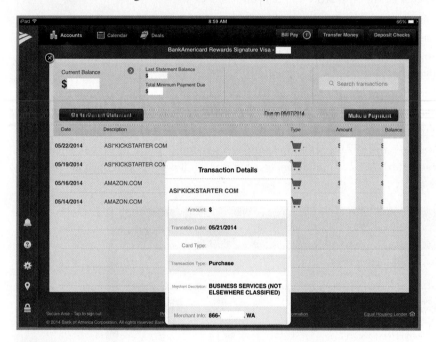

FIGURE 6.6 View details about credit card transactions.

As a rule, I try to check my credit card transactions at least two or three times per week, and this has allowed me to catch two fraudulent purchases in the last year. (In those instances, the charges were removed and I was issued a new credit card number.)

One of the conveniences of having this app on my iPad is how easy it is to log in and check my statement and transaction history. And I'm not just limited to my Bank of America card. Figure 6.7 shows that I'm also able to check on my American Express card.

Just as with the Bank of America app, the American Express app lets me view balances, check transactions, and even make a payment. I can save a statement as a PDF (for viewing on GoodReader, for example) and manage my Membership Awards.

Finally, if you're an investor with any of the big investment firms, you'll likely find that these organizations have apps that let you buy and trade stocks and bonds, view accounts, and transfer funds. Figure 6.8 shows the Edward Jones app that I use to track my investments.

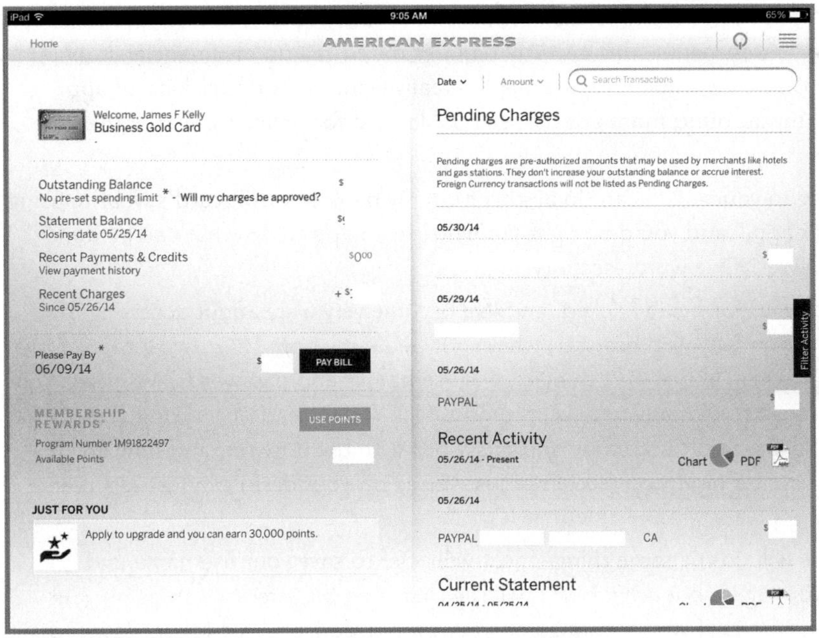

FIGURE 6.7 American Express offers even more services with its app.

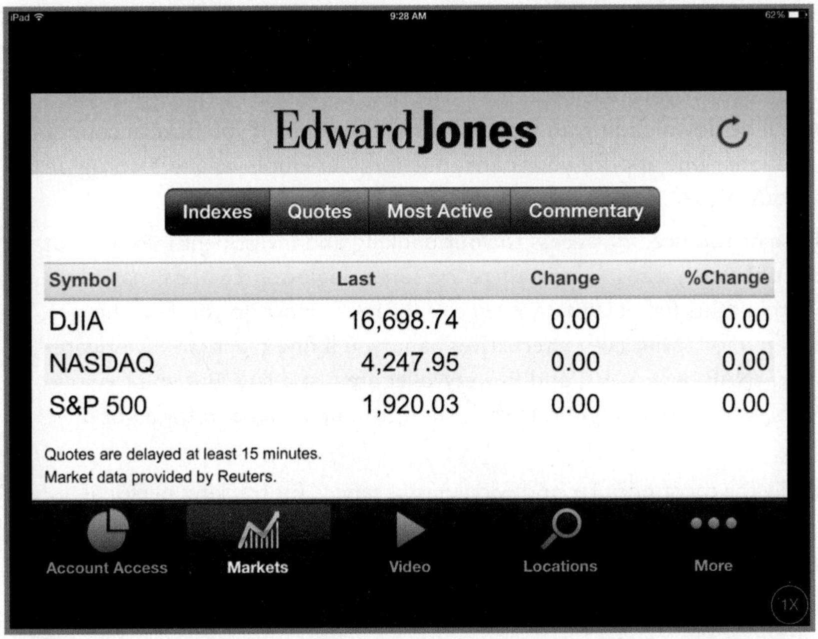

FIGURE 6.8 The Edward Jones market and investment app.

With this simple app, I can keep an eye on stocks and mutual funds that interest me, as well as monitor my investments. This app still requires me to call up my financial planner, but I'm fine with that... my trades are rare. All I'm really wanting from this kind of app is a quick view of my account; more advanced apps do exist for online trading, if that's your thing.

You may be saying to yourself, "I can do all this from my bank or credit card's website using my iPad's browser app," and you'd be right. So why use an app to do what can be done from within a browser? One word—security.

Browsers are notorious for being hacked, and I've become very wary about accessing my financial accounts from any web browser, whether it be on my home PC, my laptop, or my iPhone or iPad. Browsers like to save things... like usernames and passwords. Many ask your permission to do so, but so many people often just click YES instead of thinking about what they're really doing. Save that username and password with the browser, and now anyone who uses your computer or laptop (stolen or just sitting on your desk) can just log in and view your details.

Now, mobile apps will do the same thing—most will offer to save your username and password when you log in, but *don't do it!* I will say that it's a bit safer to do this on your iPhone or iPad, but ONLY if you've configured your mobile device with a login password.

The Mint.com App

If you're needing to conduct banking and investment transacations from your iPad, you've got two options—find out if a financial institution offers an app that will allow it OR log in to its website and conduct your business there. The only downside to either of these methods is that you'll be downloading and installing multiple apps if you have accounts with different institutions—one app for your bank, one for your employer's 401k program, another for your spouse's IRA... it can get out of hand.

Fortunately for those of you needing access to your banking and investment info without any need to conduct business transactions, there are some single-source apps that can provide you access to all this financial data from one location. How do you find them? Just do a Google search for "Mint.com alternatives" and you'll find plenty to investigate—MoneyDance, iBank, YNAB, LearnVest, and PowerWallet are just a few. But you'll notice that it's searching for Mint.com competitors that I'm recommending, and for a good reason.

Mint.com is probably the most popular and widely-used service for tracking personal banking and investment data. It provides budgeting help and plenty of reports for finding out where your money is going. It also doesn't hurt that Mint.com is completely free to use. Simply visit Mint.com and create an account.

Mint.com will lead you through linking your banking, credit cards, mortgate, car loan, and investments accounts so that all this information is visible from a web browser, as shown in Figure 6.9.

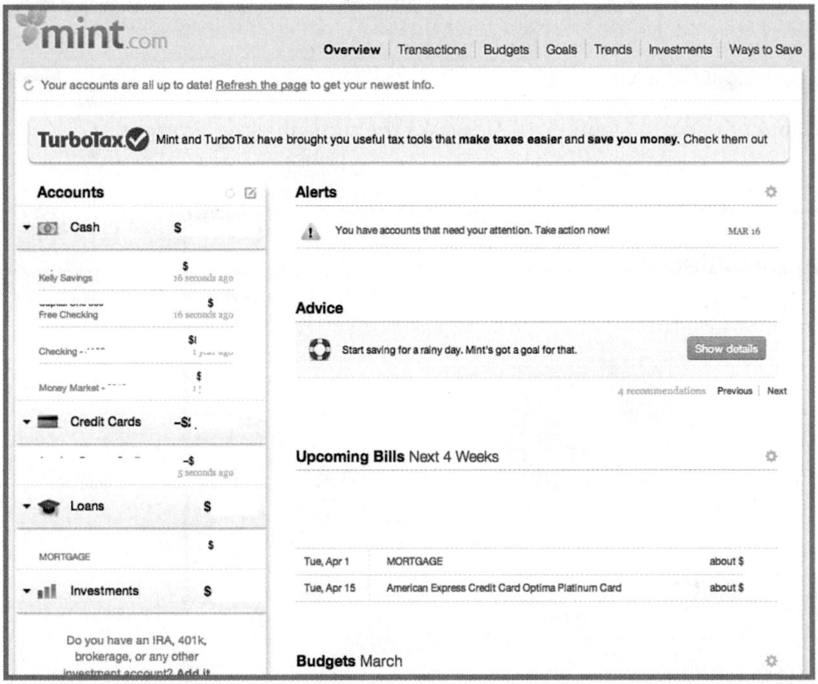

FIGURE 6.9 Mint.com provides access to all your financial details.

Of course, Mint.com also has a great (and still free) app to download for your Ultimate iPad. While logged in, you can view all the financial details to any accounts you've linked to Mint.com—view, not make changes. That's important, because Mint.com does not allow you to conduct transacations like transferring funds from a savings account to a checking account or paying a credit card bill or mortgage payment. Mint.com is all about data viewing, and for this reason, it's a very secure way to track your financials without worrying that someone gaining access to your iPad could start transferring funds and making credit card charges. Every account that Mint.com accesses is done with an encrypted password to download the most up-to-date data, ensuring that even if a bad guy gets your iPad and opens the Mint.com app, all he or she can do is view your current financial situation, not make it worse.

> **TIP**
>
> The Mint.com app can be set with a passcode any time you leave the app. Even when switching between currently opened apps on your iPad by double-tapping the Home button, returning to the Mint.com app will require you to re-enter the passcode.

You can see the Mint.com app in Figure 6.10—it works the same in either Portrait or Landscape view.

FIGURE 6.10 The Mint.com app loaded on an iPad.

The Settings tool is in the lower-left corner and allows you to set up a 4-digit passcode to lock the Mint.com app. You can also view details on all of the various accounts that are configured for viewing with the app.

It's still going to be easier for you to add new accounts and do basic maintenance on your Mint.com account from a computer and web browser than using the iPad's app, but there's no arguing that the Mint.com app is an outstanding way to get an immediate summary of your loans, bank accounts, and investments from a single screen. Tapping any of those accounts will open to a more detailed screen such as viewing checks that have cleared, automatic payroll deposits made, or stock and mutual fund trades conducted. You can go as deep into the details as you like or just view the quick summary of your financial situation as shown in Figure 6.10.

Be Careful!

Even though the Mint.com app can be secured with a passcode, let's not forget that when you're dealing with your financial information, it never hurts to be over-cautious. If you're running the app on your iPad, now might be the best time to consider adding a password or passcode that's required whenever you turn on your iPad.

This is so simple to do, and yet I constantly encounter friends and family who have not secured their iPads (and iPhones) with a simple code that can keep unwanted visitors out of their devices.

If you haven't done it, *do it now*. Open up the Settings app, tap the General listing on the left, and scroll down to the section that starts with Auto-Lock, as shown in Figure 6.11.

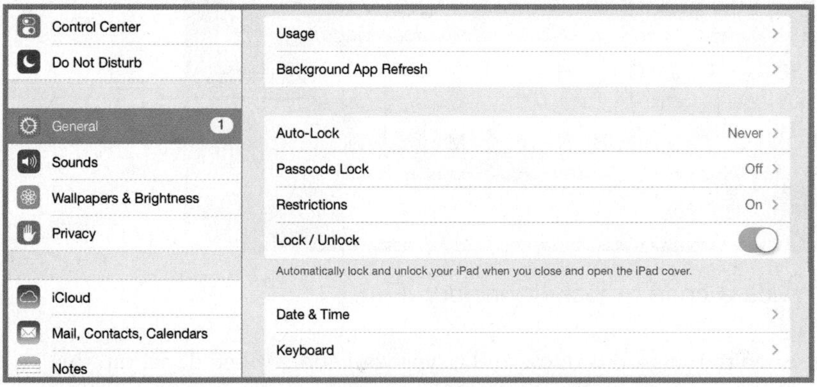

Control Center	Usage >
Do Not Disturb	Background App Refresh >
General ①	Auto-Lock Never >
Sounds	Passcode Lock Off >
Wallpapers & Brightness	Restrictions On >
Privacy	Lock / Unlock ⬤
	Automatically lock and unlock your iPad when you close and open the iPad cover.
iCloud	Date & Time >
Mail, Contacts, Calendars	Keyboard >
Notes	

FIGURE 6.11 Add some security to your Ultimate iPad.

Tap the Passcode Lock option, and you'll be taken to a new screen like the one in Figure 6.12.

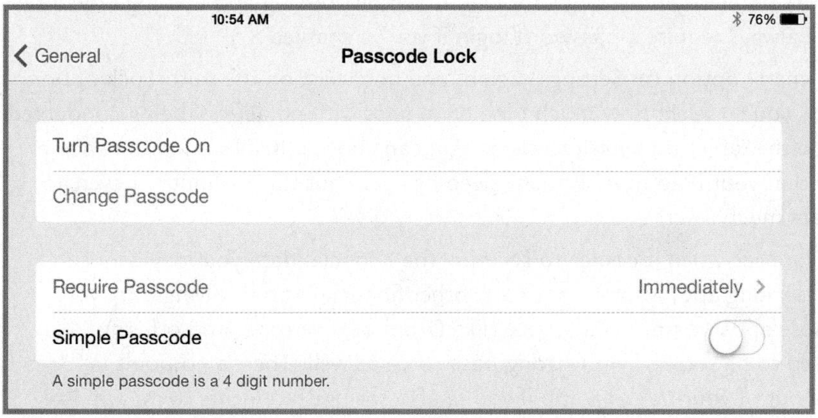

10:54 AM   ❋ 76% ▮▮

‹ General   **Passcode Lock**

Turn Passcode On

Change Passcode

Require Passcode   Immediately >

Simple Passcode   ⬤

A simple passcode is a 4 digit number.

FIGURE 6.12 It's time to turn on the passcode option.

Tap the "Turn Passcode On" option (at the very top) and and enter a simple 4-digit code (turn on the Simple Passcode button to enable this), a text password, or a mix of characters in the pop-up window that appears, as shown in Figure 6.13.

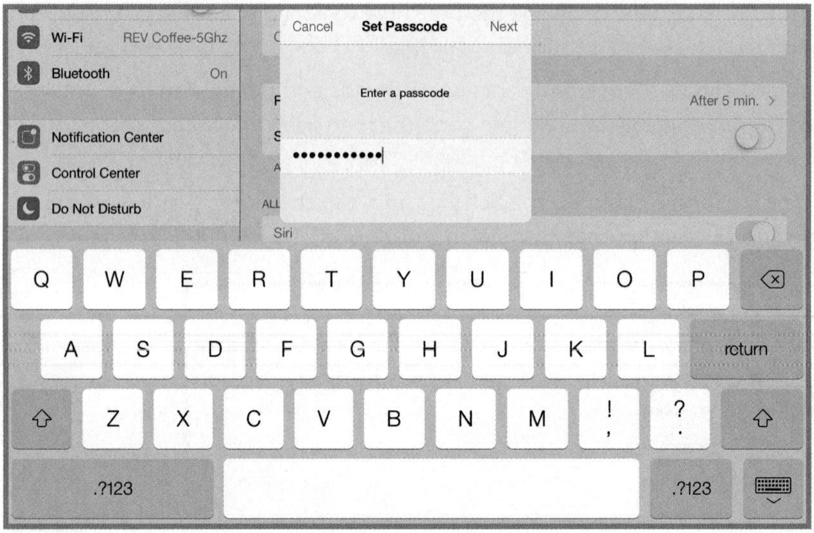

FIGURE 6.13 Provide a code to lock down your iPad.

Tap the Next button on the pop-up window and retype your code. When done, tap the "Require Passcode" option (shown in Figure 6.12) and make a selection. If you tend to frequently turn your iPad on and off with the Sleep button, consider selecting the "After 5 minutes" option. If you put your iPad to sleep and then turn it back on within 5 minutes, you won't be required to type in your passcode again. The "Immediately" option will force you to always enter the passcode, no matter how little time has passed after you last put the iPad to sleep. (Completely powering your iPad down by pressing and holding down the Power button will always require a password login if you've enabled it.)

Finally, tap the General option (in Settings) again, and now click on the Auto-Lock option. This option allows you to select how much time must pass with no activity being conducted on the iPad before the tablet puts itself to sleep. You can choose the Never option shown in Figure 6.14 so that your iPad never goes to sleep by itself, but the 5 Minute or even 15 Minute options are much safer.

One final word of advice when it comes to securing the financial data you may choose to access from a banking app, Mint.com, or any other financial app involving data you may pull from those apps to store in a service (like Dropbox, Evernote, and others): Those services need to be secured with strong passwords as well. There's no point in keeping someone out of your banking app if you're also saving statements to an app like GoodReader, Mail, or Message that doesn't have password security itself.

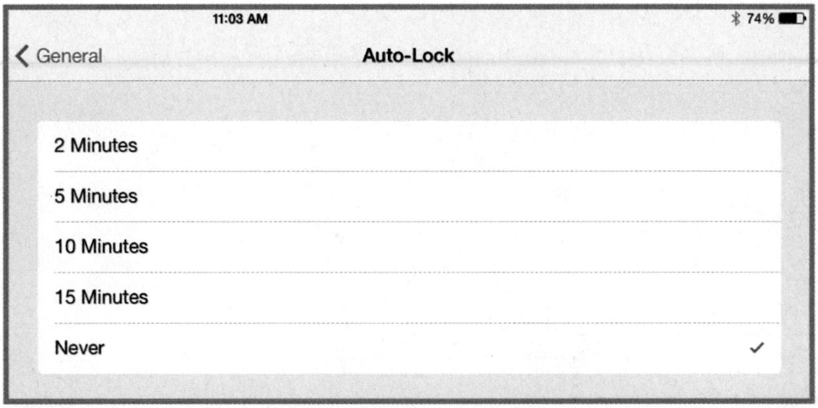

FIGURE 6.14 Enable your iPad to go to sleep on its own after inactivity.

Put all these security measures in place and you'll have peace of mind as you use your Ultimate iPad to monitor your bank accounts, investments, credit cards, and much more.

Convert Your Collections: Reducing Book and Magazine Clutter

In This Chapter

- Buy digital books and subscribe to digital magazines
- Use the (slow-but-works) Cut-and-Scan method
- Use a book/magazine scanning service
- Use a specialized book/magazine scanner
- Risks of converting paper to digital

One of the most common requests I get from friends and family about my Ultimate iPad has to do with all the books and magazines that I have available from my Dropbox and Pogoplug accounts. I've been a book collector for decades (especially reference books) and I've subscribed to half a dozen magazines over the years that I keep for reference (many of these are related to my woodworking hobby). As you can imagine, after a certain point the space requirements began to be too much and I was forced to put a lot of my collection in a storage unit. The annoyance with not keeping my books and magazines on a bookshelf and instead tucked away in protective boxes comes when it's time to retrieve one in storage.

I knew there had to be a better way, but it wasn't until I started using the iPad that I realized the tablet could hold a substantially large amount of books and magazines in digital form. And even if my iPad ran of out of storage space, it would be a simple manner to transfer these digital files back and forth between either Dropbox or my Pogoplug-connected hard drive. I began to think how enjoyable it might be if I had a digital copy of every book and magazine I owned...and then I began to look for solutions.

Any solution (or solutions) I might find would need to allow for the fact that I already owned a lot of nondigital books and magazines. I had no desire to re-buy these items in digital format if they were even available, and in many cases some of the older books (such as my engineering textbooks from years ago) were no longer available in print or digital! And even if a book was available in digital format, I buy a lot of reference books on sale in the bargain bins—frequently I could buy a print version of a book cheaper than the digital version. My solution(s) would also need to make certain that my digital books and magazines would be searchable with keywords to make finding what I need fast and easy.

Solutions were found, and the chapter you're about to read is going to show you all of the various methods that I've used over the last few years to convert about 80% of my book and magazine collection to digital files (the remaining 20% are books that I want to keep in print form for one reason or another). These converted books and magazines don't exist in any proprietary format such as ePUB or Mobi—I save it all as searchable PDF files so I can read any book or magazine I own with the GoodReader app or even directly from Dropbox or Pogoplug. (I frequent the GoodReader app covered in Chapter 1, "The Ultimate iPad," so I can add notes, highlight text, and perform other unique tasks.)

One of the goals of the Ultimate iPad is to make all your data available to you when you need it. This should include your books and magazines. Keep reading to learn about three different methods for bringing your entire book and magazine collection with you wherever you may travel.

Start with Digital Books and Magazines Now

If you're truly wanting to lose the book and magazine stacks and push your iPad closer to Ultimate iPad status, one of the easiest solutions to implement immediately is to simply start buying your books in digital format from the beginning (if they are available as ebooks). The same goes for magazines.

If you've purchased ebooks from either Apple, Amazon.com, or BarnesandNoble.com, you may already be aware that apps are available for the iPad that allow you to read your digital purchases on your iPad. Figure 7.1 shows these three apps (iBooks, Nook, Kindle, respectively) installed on my iPad.

FIGURE 7.1 Three digital book reader apps.

Purchases from Apple's bookstore are opened in the iBooks app, purchases from Amazon are read on the Kindle app, and Barnes & Noble purchases can be read using the Nook app. (You may run into the occasional need to download a special reader of some sort;

the Bluefire Reader shown in Figure 7.1 is one of those apps that I rarely use, but I do have some digital books that will only open with that app.)

All three of the aforementioned apps will display your books on a virtual bookshelf with miniature versions of the covers to help you find a particular title. Figure 7.2 shows the iBooks bookshelf with a handful of digital books.

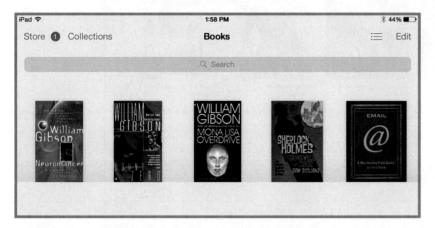

FIGURE 7.2 Apple's iBooks app displays covers of the digital books.

Magazines are also enjoying a growth in popularity when it comes to their digital versions, called "ezines." When it comes to the iPad, there are numerous options for subscribing to ezines, and three popular ones are Zinio, NextIssue, and Apple's own Newsstand. Each of these installs an app on your iPad so you can access both paid and free periodicals. Browse for magazines, as shown in Figure 7.3, and tap a cover to purchase a single issue or subscribe.

NOTE

Be aware that some magazines are only available by subscribing and not as single-issue purchases. Also, some digital subscriptions come free with a paid print subscription—if you have a subscription to a print magazine, check to see if digital copies of those issues you've received are still available for download.

Users of apps for accessing digital books and magazines often have a lot of questions related to digital books and magazines. Is it better to buy ebooks from Amazon or Barnes & Noble? Should I subscribe to magazines using the Newsstand app or maybe Zinio? What happens if an app or company goes out of business—will I still have access to my books/magazines?

FIGURE 7.3 Apple's Newsstand app has a store for purchasing or subscribing to magazines.

These are all good questions, and unfortunately there's not very many good answers. Many digital book buyers will simply stick to the app they've used from the beginning and buy books from that source; others will buy an ebook from whichever source is selling it for the lowest price. And other ebook/ezine readers will only buy digital content if it's available as a downloadable file that can be backed up in case a company goes out of business or an app is no longer available for a future tablet purchase.

In my case, I try to always buy ebooks as PDF files first, followed by ePub files next, and then Mobi if one of the previous two formats isn't available. If I want a PDF file, this often means buying an ebook directly from the author (if the author has a website that offers PDF-formatted books for sale) so that I have a file that can be saved to Dropbox or my Pogoplug hard drive and will always be available to me if I have an app that can open PDF documents.

CAUTION

There are methods available for backing up books that are purchased from sites such as BarnesandNoble.com (for the Nook app) and Amazon.com (for the Kindle app), but what you're backing up are files that are typically formatted for the specific app and won't work with any other app. What this means is that if you choose to use a different app to read your ebooks, you may find that some ebooks won't open or are not the correct format. It's a true buyer beware situation.

Unfortunately, most ebooks these days don't come in PDF format, and many ebooks are formatted or saved in such a way that they'll only work with one particular app. Because of this, ebooks you buy from Amazon.com can only be read on your iPad with the Kindle app. The same goes for ebooks purchased from BarnesandNoble.com—those ebooks will require the Nook app. And you may find yourself purchasing an ebook directly from an author or website that requires a completely different app reader. It's a mess out there when it comes to ebook standards, and it's not looking like a solution will be coming from any of the players in the ebook game.

TIP

One of my favorite technology book publishers, O'Reilly (www.oreilly.com), actually makes its books available as PDF files as well as ePub, Mobi, and DAISY.

Still, if you don't have a large library of books and don't wish to grow one, buying ebooks and ezines only (while avoiding print versions) is one good way to keep the clutter down. If you can stick with one source for purchases (such as Amazon.com), over time you'll end up with a single app that contains almost all of your digital books and magazines. You'll never have any guarantee that your ebooks and ezines will always be available to you in the future unless you find a method to back them up, but the odds of Amazon.com going out of business are slim to none. (Can you tell that I lean a bit toward the Kindle app when it comes to my ebook purchases?)

But what's a person to do if they want their ebooks to be in the PDF format, searchable by keywords, and available for storage on the Ultimate iPad or easily stored off in the cloud somewhere until needed? And what's a person to do if they already own a substantial library of printed books and magazines and don't want to re-buy them in digital format but want to be able to access them from their iPad?

These are two good questions, and I've got two possible solutions for your consideration.

The Cut-and-Scan Method

You learned back in Chapter 5, "Cut the Clutter: Scan Everything," about the value of scanners for converting sheets of paper such as bills, sketches, and other loose items into digital files, but desktop scanners aren't really designed for books and magazines...unless those books and magazines are reduced to stacks of loose sheets of paper.

Yes, I'm referring to removing the cover and spine (and any glue that remains) on books and scanning in the separated pages, one at a time or in batches of 10–20 pages (if your scanner has a tray that can autofeed a bunch of pages). If you wish to include the cover of the book, you can either find a digital image of the cover (images.google.com is a great place to start), take a photo of it (with the Camera app or a mobile device scanning app), or actually scan the cover if it's from a paperback book. For magazines, you'll have fewer pages to scan than a book, but you'll also likely want to keep the cover and scan it as well.

It's a destructive method, to be sure (although I cover a non-destructive book and magazine scanner later in this chapter). Your book or magazine will never be the same again, and unless you also list bookbinding as a hobby, you're unlikely to want to pay someone to put the book or magazine back together. So, if you're okay with ripping a book or magazine apart for scanning and can handle the loss of the original, this is definitely a method that will work for converting your books and magazines to a digital format.

What's the best way to perform a cut-and-scan on a book or magazine? Carefully pull or cut off the cover of the book or magazine, cut the binding or scrape off the glue, and hopefully you'll end up with a free-standing stack of pages. You can certainly do this all by hand, but it's frustrating. Trust me...I've done it. But there is a better, safer, and faster way.

What you're going to need to find is a company in your area that has a very special machine. Where I live, there's a FedEx/Kinkos office that has this machine—they call it a paper guillotine because it can cut down and through 300 pages or more at a time. If you give them a paperback book, this machine will cleanly and accurately cut in between 1/8-inch to 1/4-inch (you specify) from the spine, separating the front and back cover and the spine from the pages inside.

TIP

If you don't have a FedEx/Kinkos or similar business in your area, call a few print shops and politely inquire if they have a machine that can cut magazine and book spines off and if they'd be willing to do so for you for a small fee.

It's even better for magazines. Because FedEx/Kinkos charges $1.50 per cut, I typically hand them 6-8 issues of a magazine and they perform a single cut down through all the issues. Figure 7.4 shows a stack of recently cut magazines (*Family Handyman*) that I had converted to loose sheets.

FIGURE 7.4 Cut off the spine from magazines and then scan them in.

Look closely at the magazine on the far right in Figure 7.4 and you'll notice that the spine is gone and the pages under the cover have been spread out to show you that the magazine is now a simple stack of pages that are ready to be scanned.

You can refer back to Chapter 5 for more discussions on the various types of scanners, but the one that works best for this kind of method is the desktop scanner with a tray to hold 10 or more pages at a time. Remember to set your scanner for duplex scanning (front and back), to save as PDF, and then start scanning. Figure 7.5 shows that I've scanned in 44 pages of a 90-page magazine (22 sheets, front and back).

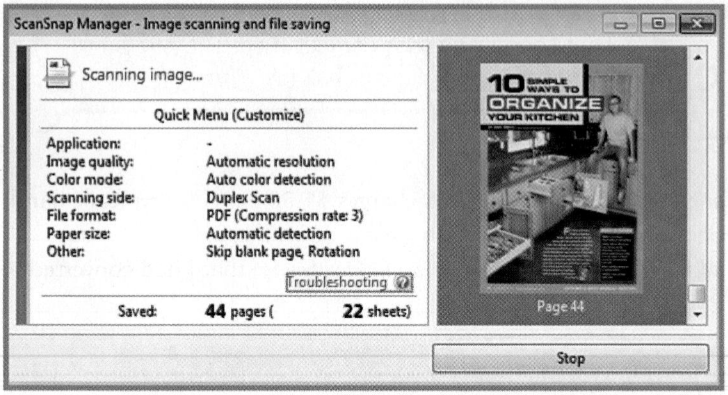

FIGURE 7.5   Start scanning a loose batch of magazine pages.

MyScanSnap iX500 can hold up to 50 pages, so these 80–100 page magazines only take one reload of the tray when the first 50 pages have been run through.

You may also remember from Chapter 5 that OCR (Optical Character Recognition) can be performed on these scans. This means that once I've converted a magazine to a PDF file and stored it on my iPad or in Dropbox, a search of "window repair" will return me a list of scanned magazines (or any other documents) that have to do with window repair or at least contain that word *repair*.

This method works the same for hardback and paperback books that have had their spines removed. Grab 10–50 pages at a time, stick them in the tray, press Scan, and when the tray is empty put another stack in.

When you're done, save the file with a useful, descriptive name and put it in your favorite cloud service (such as Dropbox) or on your own hosting hard drive (such as Pogoplug) or download it directly to your iPad with an app such as GoodReader. This particular scan created a file only 60MB in size. To put that into perspective, it would take about 17 similar-sized magazines to equal 1GB (gigabyte). This was a full-color scan, so it takes more space than a black-and-white book scan—a 300-page text only book comes in at only 27MB, meaning an iPad with 27GB of storage space left could hold 1,000 books of similar size! And if you're using Dropbox or Pogoplug or some other service to store digital files off your Ultimate iPad until you need them, you won't ever have to worry about having access to a book or magazine when you need it.

Figure 7.6 shows my magazine with my iPad's GoodReader app; the loose pages are going in the recycle bin for pickup.

FIGURE 7.6 That magazine is now a digital file available on the iPad.

Just to show you how the OCR can help once you start getting lots of magazines and books scanned, take a look at Figure 7.7 to see a search result for "kitchen remodel Handyman" and you'll notice that not only did the recently scanned magazine show up, but two other magazines have one or all of those words found inside their pages.

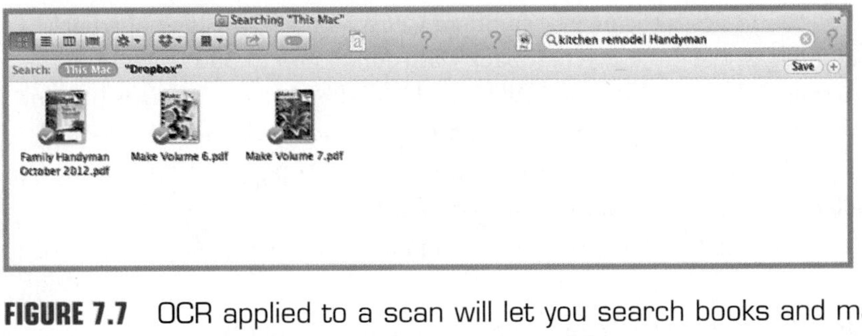

FIGURE 7.7 OCR applied to a scan will let you search books and magazines.

The cut-and-scan method works, but it is definitely slow if you have to do the separation of the cover and pages on your own. If you're comfortable destroying a book or magazine by yourself or by paying a company with the proper machine to do it for you, this method can save you some money, although it won't save you a lot of time because you'll be doing the scanning yourself. If this isn't the option for you, you still have two more possibilities to consider.

Use a Scanning Service

Believe it or not, there are companies out there that will scan your documents for you—for a price, of course. Many of these services only scan loose sheets, so their frequent customers are most often businesses looking to scan a lot of paperwork for long-term storage and then shred the originals. Most of these services will not scan books or magazines, even if you cut off the spines.

One company that will help you with converting your books and magazines to digital documents is 1DollarScan.com. They have a very reasonable pricing scheme based on $1 per 100 pages of a book or magazine; 100 pages is called a set (and pricing for scanning and special features is all based on sets). One catch is that they do not return your books or magazines after they've scanned them; instead, they shred the originals, leaving you with one digital copy.

1DollarScan.com handles the removal of the covers and spines on any book or magazine, but they do not scan hardcover book covers. Paperback books will have the covers scanned, however.

Besides the basic $1 per 100-pages scan, 1DollarScan also offers a number of additional paid services that include OCR conversion (making your books/magazines searchable), a DVD with your files (versus an online download you initiate from an email that is sent out when your conversion job is completed), and conversion to different file types such as Word and ePub.

Figure 7.8 shows three different items I shipped to 1DollarScan. One was a hardback book, another a paperback, and finally a magazine (with spine intact).

1DollarScan has you round up to the nearest hundred value, so the 478-page paperback was rounded to 500 pages, the 247-page hardback was rounded up to 300 pages, and the 84-page magazine rounded up to 100 pages. All in all, I was submitting 900 pages (or nine sets) for $9.00 in scanning. Not bad at all, but I wanted some additional services applied.

A high-resolution scan is priced out at $2 per set (and includes OCR), but I didn't want this for the books, only the magazine. Because my magazine is only one set, $2 is added and my total is now $11.00 or about $3.75 per item. Why am I mentioning per-item pricing? For two reasons:

- **Shipping costs**—You still have to figure in the cost of shipping your books. You can save money by shipping them slow to 1DollarScan. I didn't have time for slow shipping, so I ended up paying shipping costs of $15. Now my total is $26.00 for three items, or approximately $8.66 per item. That's more than the cost of the magazine!

- **Quantity of scanning**—If you've only got a few dozen or more books you want scan, you're still likely to save money versus purchasing a desktop scanner. Let's say you have

50 books, each 300 pages in length to scan. That's $150 in just scanning fees (three sets per book × 50 books = 150 sets), and now you're in the portable scanner price range—but at one page per scan with no tray/feeder, you'd be spending a lot of time scanning pages one at a time.

FIGURE 7.8 Send 1DollarScan your books and magazines for scanning.

What you really must do is ask yourself if you have now and in the future enough scanning needs to warrant the cost of your own desktop scanner. (And remember that a desktop scanner isn't just for books and magazines.)

Keep in mind that 1DollarScan does have special pricing for its members. The company offers a membership for those who have large quantities of scanning needed or regular scanning (on a monthly basis). For $100 per month, members get 100 sets of scanning, but that price also gets you many of the extra services for free (such as OCR and Express Service that gets you your scans in 5–10 business days, instead of $2/set for nonmembers).

Membership can go month to month with no contracts, so it's very possible you might save money and avoid the need to purchase a scanner with a membership plan. You'll need to do an inventory of your books and magazines and crunch the numbers to determine if 1DollarScan.com will end up saving you money to convert your library to digital or if you'll ultimately be better off purchasing a portable or desktop scanner that you'll always have for any future scanning needs.

Whether you go with the cut-and-scan method or 1DollarScan.com (or a similar scanning service), however, the end result is that your book/magazine collection will shrink as you convert paper to digital. If this is unacceptable to you and you would prefer to keep all or some of your print books and magazines while at the same time having access to a digital copy on your iPad, then there's one more option for you to examine that lets you have the best of both worlds.

A Special Scanner for Books and Magazines

I've been using Fujitsu's ScanSnap products for years, all starting back with my original 1100, then a move to the larger 1300, and then on to the iX500. My wife likes the Doxie line of scanners, and I've got one in the kitchen that we use quite often for scanning bills and other items so the originals can go straight to the shredder instead of sitting on our countertops.

But of all these scanners we use, none of them is designed to scan large items such as 12×15 photos or for two-page book and magazine spreads. A book or magazine cannot be fed into the scanners unless those pages are removed using the cut-and-scan method. I have a number of books that I'd love to have in digital format but I'm unwilling to spend more money on a digital copy and I'm most certainly not willing to cut apart the print copy. So what to do?

Thankfully, Fujitsu released a new product last year called the ScanSnap SV600 Contactless Scanner (MSRP is around $800) that's shown in Figure 7.9.

FIGURE 7.9 The ScanSnap SV600 scans without ever touching an item.

Although this is a specialty scanner, it still functions great as a single-sheet scanner. The only difference in scanning with the SV600 versus most other types of scanners is that the user doesn't feed in sheets by hand and there's no tray to hold multiple sheets. The SV600 scans one item at a time; if you need the front and back of a page scanned, you scan the front, flip it over, and then scan the back.

Although the SV600 can be used as a standard scanner, it's real strength lies in its ability to scan multiple items at once as well as the complete contents of an open book or magazine placed in front of the scanner.

If you place a collection of items in front of the SV600, the software can distinguish between each item and will allow you to save each as an individual JPG or as separate pages in one PDF file. Figure 7.10 shows that I've placed a handful of cards on the soft mat that comes with the scanner. (The mat is nonreflective and has lines on it to define the maximum scannable area.)

Notice that the cards do not have to be perfectly lined up on the mat. The software will find text and graphics and edges of items you place on the mat, and after scanning the items, the software will attempt to place a selection box around each item, as shown in Figure 7.11.

You can drag the selection boxes if they're not properly surrounding an item, or just enlarge the selection boxes if you'd prefer to capture a bit of the surrounding black mat in each image. If for some reason a scanned item is upside down or rotated 90 degrees, control buttons allow you to rotate the item before saving the scan.

When done, if you selected to scan images as JPGs, you'll see one JPG file for each scanned item. If you had elected to save the scan as a PDF, all four items (in this instance) would be saved in a single four-page PDF with one item viewable on each page. Figure 7.12 shows all four cards that were scanned.

Scanning multiple items at once is useful and can save you plenty of time, but it's the ability to scan open books and magazines that really puts the SV600 in a different category of scanner.

FIGURE 7.10 Place multiple items in front of the SV600 scanner.

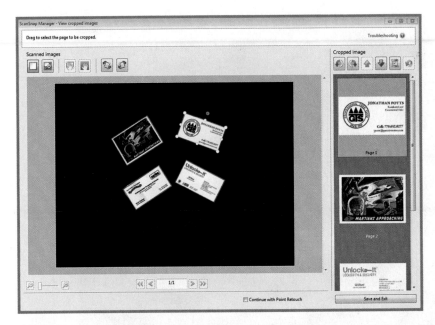

FIGURE 7.11 The SV600 can identify unique items, even if they're askew.

FIGURE 7.12 Each item is saved as an individual JPG file.

If you place an open book in front of the scanner, as shown in Figure 7.13, you may notice that there's a slight curve to both pages and think to yourself that it will surely look strange reading a PDF file where text and figures aren't laying flat.

FIGURE 7.13 An open book will have curved pages prior to scanning.

If this open book's pages are scanned as is, the software will display what is shown in Figure 7.14, confirming your suspicions that the curve of the open pages will look a bit strange in a final scan.

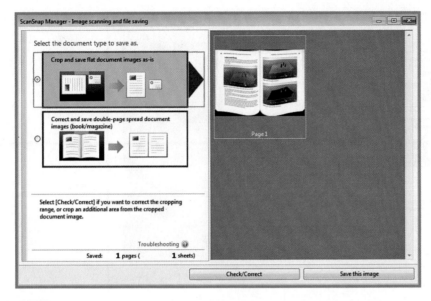

FIGURE 7.14   The curve of the open book is picked up by the scanner.

Scanning a book or magazine is interpreted differently by the SV600's software, so what you're seeing in Figure 7.14 is the scanner attempting to identify flat items on the mat. The curve in the book is retained because there is no break in the white of the pages, and the software interprets this as a single item, not multiple items (like business cards).

Look closely again at Figure 7.14 and you'll notice that on this window the first option is selected; this is the option for scanning a flat item or multiple flat items. It's the second option just below it that will reveal the magic behind using the SV600 to scan books and magazines.

In Figure 7.15, the second option is selected; notice that the thumbnail on the right now shows the book's two pages flattened.

The software is able to take text or images on the curve of a scanned page and "flatten" it out so that it looks like the original page.

As it stands, if you saved this scan as it is, you'd end up with a single page PDF file that would display two pages of the book. This isn't what you want if you're planning on scanning books and magazines to PDF for reading on your Ultimate iPad.

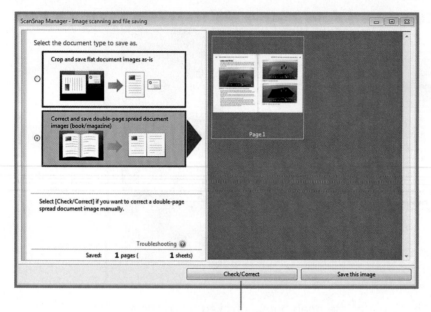

Check/Correct button

FIGURE 7.15 Books and magazines can be "flattened" with the software.

Tap the Check/Correct button at the bottom of the screen (in Figure 7.15) and an editing window will open like the one in Figure 7.16.

First, notice in Figure 7.16 that the book wasn't even lined up straight (with respect to the front edge of the SV600). The software was still able to find the two pages and place a dotted selection window around them; you may also notice that the selection window has a vertical line that runs down between both pages and marks the spine of the book.

The thumbnail on the right still shows the flattened pages, but it's a single image (or PDF page), not two. To fix this, you tap on the 1|2 button to indicate that the order of the pages should be maintained as a normal book, with the first page on the left and the following page on the right.

1|2 button

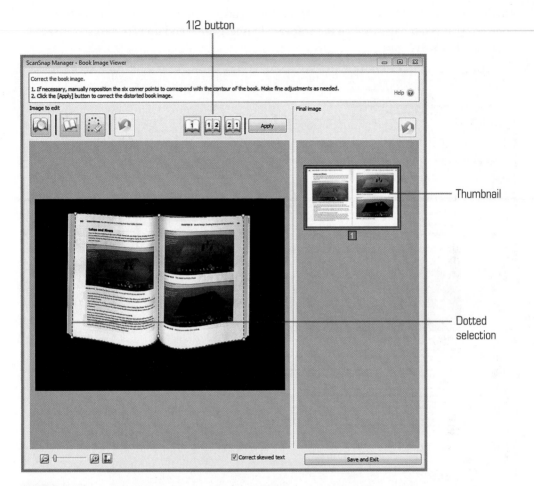

Thumbnail

Dotted
selection

FIGURE 7.16   Editing your book scans will allow you to split pages.

NOTE

When might you ever need the 2|1 button? Some books from around the world are actually read back to front, so the last page in the book is actually the first page. Japanese Manga (comic) books are one example of this, so not only would you be scanning the book back to front, but you'd also have to remember to use the 2|1 button to keep the order of the final PDF book the same.

After tapping the 1|2 button, tap the Apply button and confirm that the action is to be done on all selected pages. When the software finishes, you'll end up with two separated pages, as shown in Figure 7.17.

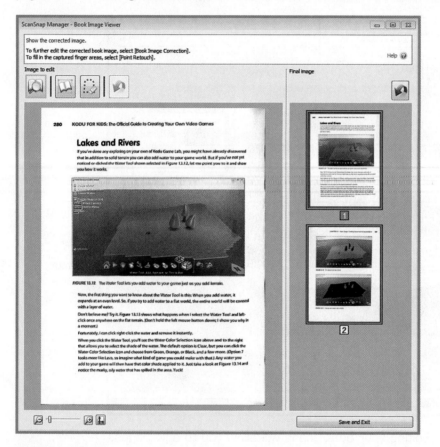

FIGURE 7.17 Split a single scan into two separate pages.

In the previous figures, I scanned only two pages of an entire book. In reality, you'll be doing all the scanning first and then perform the split action at the end. If you have a 300-page book, for example, when scanning is done you'll have 150 single image scans displayed in the software. If you're confident in your page flipping, hold down the Shift key and select all 150 single scans. Next, tap the 1|2 button and then the Apply button, and the split will be performed instantly on all 150 single pages, leaving you with 300 pages that are ready to be saved by tapping the Save and Exit button in the bottom-right corner, as shown in Figure 7.17.

TIP

The SV600 is fully capable of scanning both the front and back covers of a book, so don't forget to scan those if you need them. They won't need the "flattening" effect to be applied, but they'll still be displayed in the collection of scans in the software and will be included in the final PDF file.

You'll be surprised at how good a job the SV600 and its matching software does at flattening pages in both books and magazines, even thick books with a much more noticeable curve when opened. Still, for thicker books like the one in Figure 7.18, you'll often find that they won't stay open on the mat unless you're holding the pages down.

FIGURE 7.18
Scanning thicker books is sometimes a bit difficult.

You could come up with some sort of clear plastic holders to hold a book open as the SV600 scans the pages, but before you go that route, take a look at Figure 7.19, which shows the flattened scan of a page from this thick book and a bit of fingertip on the right side.

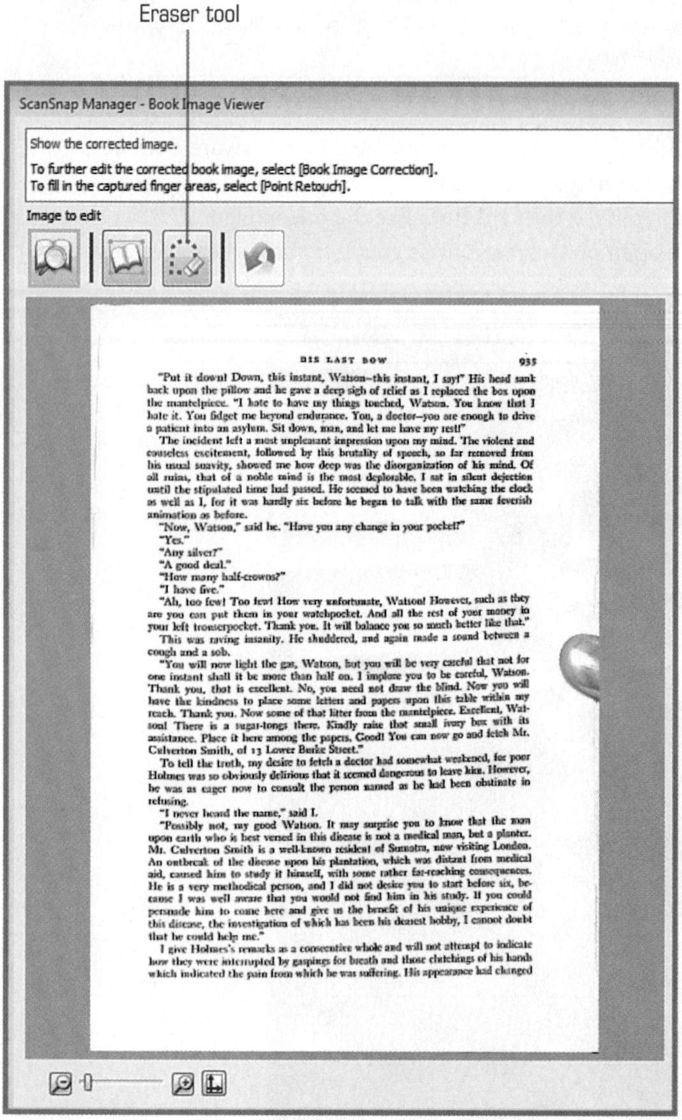

FIGURE 7.19 Fingertips don't magically disappear from a scan.

To remove a fingertip, simply tap the Eraser tool and then tap the fingertip. You can drag the small white dots so that the fingertip is completely surrounded by the selection tool, as shown in Figure 7.20.

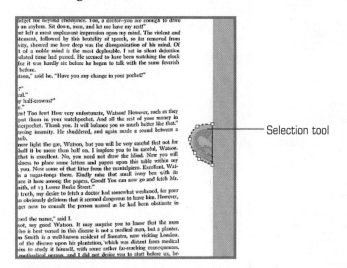

Selection tool

FIGURE 7.20 Use the Eraser tool to erase a fingertip from a scan.

Tap the Apply button and say goodbye to the offending digit. Figure 7.21 shows the final results: Page 1, Fingertip 0.

As with the iX500 scanner, the SV600 software allows you to turn OCR on and off, depending on whether you want a PDF file that is searchable. The software will also allow you to save the final book (or magazine) scan as a Word document, save it directly into Dropbox or Evernote, and a few more options.

With the SV600, you can scan your books and magazines (and anything else that will fit within its 11.7×16.5-inch A3 size limitation) without damaging the original. It's the best of both worlds for those who want to keep their print books and have digital copies for their iPads or just a backup in case of loss due to fire or theft.

NOTE

Homemade versions of book scanners like the SV600 have been created and the plans shared on the Internet. Most of these versions use a digital camera to take a photo of a book's pages and lack the ability to "flatten" a page like the SV600's software possesses. Visit www.instructables.com and search for "book scanner" for instructions on creating one if you're interested.

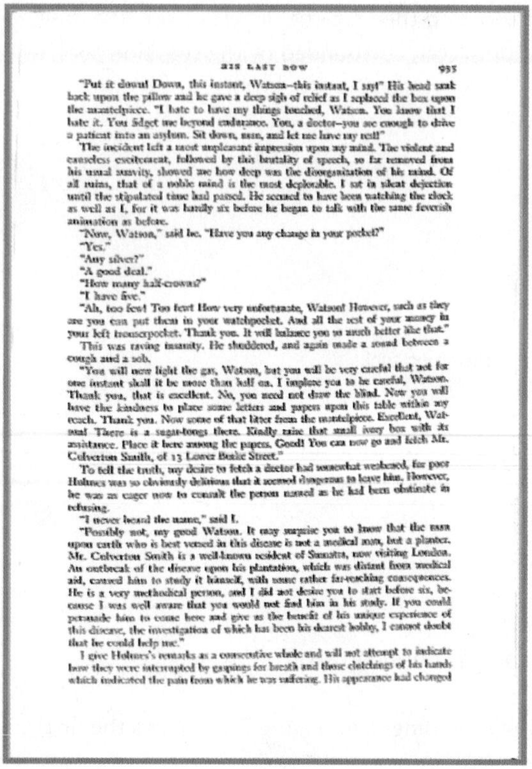

FIGURE 7.21 The fingertip is gone, leaving a pristine scanned page.

Risks and Legal Issues

Besides being asked how I got all my books into digital form for reading on my Ultimate iPad, I also get questions related to the legality of scanning books as well as questions about what I will do if my Pogoplug hard drive dies or my Dropbox account suddenly disappears with all my PDF books. I also hear concerns about new ebook standards and how well my PDF collection will hold up to time and technology's forward progress.

I'm going to show you in Chapter 9, "Don't Forget Your Backups: Long-Term Deep Storage," how I go about ensuring that my PDF books and magazines are protected and will always be available to me. (Believe it or not, it's my paper books and magazines that are at greater risk than any of the digital files I own, and not just the books and magazines.)

The concern about what will happen when the PDF file format becomes an ancient standard is a valid one, but I honestly don't see the PDF standard going away any time soon, and I imagine that for decades to come there will be readers and apps that can open PDF files. A worst-case scenario might be that one day I'll have to find a special piece of software that can convert PDF files into whatever new standard is required for reading on tablets...or in the holographic displays provided by my cornea implants.

The legal issue, however, is definitely a topic worth a discussion, but I'm not a lawyer. I'm not really qualified to make any grand statements on the right or wrong of book scanning. With book scanning, I think the question to be asked is whether or not a publisher is losing any money with a particular action. In the case of scanning a book I already own, the publisher got their fee that I paid for the book. Is making a copy of the book (for my own use) stealing money from the publisher's pocket? I don't believe so. Is scanning the book so I can read it on my iPad stealing money from the publisher's pocket. Again, I don't see it that way. I own the material already; all I've done is change the format of what I purchased.

But again, I'm not a lawyer. All that can really be said on the topic of book scanning is that it's somewhat new territory given that scanners are only now dropping to prices that are affordable outside of the corporate world and educational institutions. It remains to be seen if publishers attempt to make it illegal for book owners to scan their print books for conversion to digital files. Time will tell.

Rip and Store: Your Movies and Shows On Demand

In This Chapter

- Netflix and similar streaming services
- Purchasing digital movies and TV shows
- Ripping DVD and Blu-ray discs
- The legal mumbo-jumbo

In Chapter 7, "Convert Your Collections: Reducing Book and Magazine Clutter," I told you that one of the most common requests I get concerning my Ultimate iPad was about converting books and magazines so they could be read on a tablet. The other most common question I get also has to do with a conversion process and viewing something on a tablet, and it involves movies and television shows that one owns on DVD or Blu-ray discs.

If you're not familiar with subscription services such as Netflix and Hulu that allow you to watch movies and TV shows on most any Internet-connected device, you will be by the time you finish this chapter. These services offer up thousands of titles when you want them, turning your iPad into a great source for video entertainment, whether you're on a couch, a boat, a plane, or even at a ballgame.

But your iPad isn't just limited to watching the movies and TV shows that these subscription services offer. Not every TV show and movie is available over the Internet, and many iPad owners already have their own movie and TV show collections that exist on DVD and/or Blu-ray discs. You're also going to learn in this chapter what's involved in converting a library you already own into digital files that can be viewed not just on your iPad, but other devices as well.

You've seen how easy it is to get your books and magazines converted for viewing on your Ultimate iPad, so now let's take a look at what's involved in viewing movies and television shows on your tablet.

Streaming Subscription Services

A number of services offer up movies, TV shows, how-to videos, sporting events, and much more to your iPad. Some are free (such as YouTube), and others are not (such as Netflix). What most of these video services offer to you on your iPad is called "streaming video." And if they charge you a monthly or yearly fee (as opposed to a per-video charge), then you're talking about a subscription service.

When it comes to watching video on your iPad, the term "streaming video" simply means that the file isn't loaded (or being loaded) on your tablet, but is instead hosted elsewhere (similar to a cloud service like Dropbox) and is being downloaded via an Internet connection in real time. You can pause, rewind, and even fast forward, but all your iPad is doing is continually downloading bits of the video at a time (instead of downloading the entire video, for example, before you can view it). The parts of the video file that have downloaded are put on the screen and then forgotten; the file continues to download as it plays so there's no interruption (hopefully), and you end up with a continuous movie, for example. One key benefit here is that streaming video doesn't use up your iPad's valuable internal storage space.

One of the most popular services out there right now for viewing movies and TV shows is Netflix. Netflix works on just about every operating system and device you can imagine—phones, tablets, and computers can all have the Netflix app installed. Even televisions and video game consoles come preloaded with the app, as you can see in Figure 8.1. (Can you tell I have children?)

When you subscribe to Netflix (currently $8 per month for digital streaming or $16 per month for streaming and DVDs in the mail), you choose to either receive DVDs in the mail or to access streaming movies through your high-speed Internet (DSL or cable, for example).

NOTE

Dial-up Internet doesn't offer the download speeds necessary to view streaming movies; if you attempt to do this, you'll end up watching 10 seconds of a movie and then the movie will pause for 10–30 seconds before the next 10 seconds of the movie plays and then pauses again...over and over. Streaming services such as Netflix absolutely require high-speed Internet.

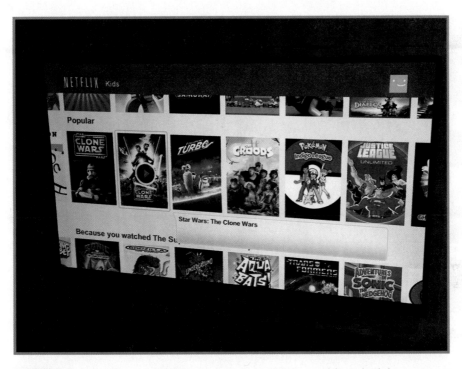

FIGURE 8.1 Netflix came installed as a service on this television.

The focus of this section is on the streaming service offered by Netflix, not the disc delivery service. When you sign up with Netflix and install the Netflix app on your iPad, you're presented with an almost overwhelming collection of movies and TV shows, all displayed with an icon on a virtual shelf, as shown in Figure 8.2.

All that's required to view a movie is to tap its icon and then tap the Play button that appears on that movie's information screen. For TV shows, you can scroll through the various seasons and episode numbers/titles and tap the Play button to play a specific episode, as shown in Figure 8.3.

CAUTION

There's a toggle button labeled "KIDS" in the Netflix app that lets you flip over to displaying only kid-friendly movies and TV shows. Unfortunately, there's currently no way to lock this feature or to put a password on the adult account to prevent a child from opening the app and viewing inappropriate content.

FIGURE 8.2 The Netflix app offers access to thousands of movies and TV shows.

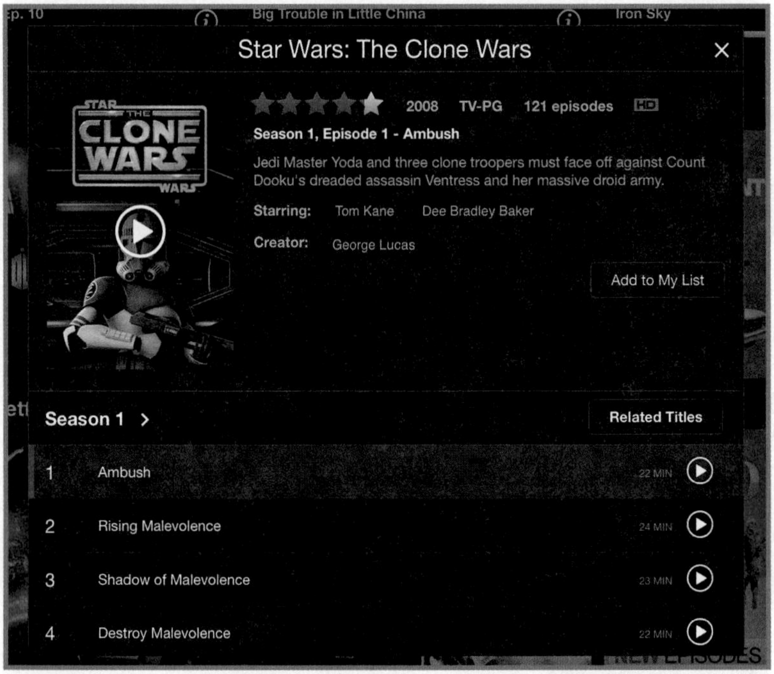

FIGURE 8.3 TV shows let you select a season and episode to view.

Netflix offers you the ability to search using the Search tool in the upper-right corner of the screen, and the service offers up recommendations based on any movies or TV shows you have watched. The service even saves your viewing progress, so if you need to stop halfway through a movie, when you return to that movie in Netflix later, you can pick right up where you left off.

Netflix isn't the only subscription service in town, however. Other popular services include Hulu Plus (Hulu Plus offers HD streaming as well as support on streaming devices; regular Hulu can only be viewed from a computer) and Amazon Prime, both paid services that can be streamed on a range of mobile devices. You'll want to do some investigations to see which service is best for you (almost all of them offer a free trial period) and compare prices and movie/TV offerings. If you choose to subscribe to Netflix or other service, you'll be able to enjoy a seemingly endless supply of movies and TV shows all from your Ultimate iPad.

Digital Movies and TV Shows for Sale

Although services like Netflix are great, they aren't comprehensive. There are tons of movies and TV shows that Netflix doesn't offer. Fortunately, today's movie and TV fans have the ability to purchase or rent their entertainment from a variety of sources.

Apple's own iTunes, for example, sells and rents movies and TV shows that are downloaded as digital files to a computer and can be displayed on an iPad with the Video app shown running in Figure 8.4.

FIGURE 8.4   The iPad Video app allows users to watch purchased movies.

As you can see in Figure 8.4, these movies are stored "in the cloud" on Apple's hardware until you wish to view one—the small cloud icon in the lower-right corner of each movie icon indicates that the movie is not currently stored on the iPad's own internal storage. Although movies purchased from iTunes can be streamed to save storage space, users can also choose to download a movie directly to the iPad. This is useful for those times when you want to watch a movie but suspect there will be no Internet access (such as on an airplane).

TIP

When you purchase a TV show or movie from iTunes, you are given a choice between a high-definition version and a standard version (if you purchase the Hi-Def version, however, you are allowed to download the standard version for mobile devices). The lo-def version takes up less storage space, so keep that in mind if you're low on iPad storage space or wish to download a small number of movies.

Apple's iTunes offers movies and TV shows for purchase (including individual episodes of a TV show or an entire season), but it's always best to shop around when buying digital content. If you're serious about converting over to digital content, however, keep in mind that buying movies from a variety of sources does mean you'll be watching those items from a variety of apps as well. A TV show season or episode purchased from Apple can only be watched with an Apple app such as iTunes or Videos. Likewise, a movie purchased on Amazon.com can only be watched with the Amazon Instant Video app. And, in most instances, those files are of a proprietary format that's not suitable for watching on any other video players.

Buying your video content in digital format is a great way to have access to your favorite movies and shows without stealing shelf space to store all those disc cases. As with digital books and magazines, you can immediately reduce the amount of DVDs and Blu-ray discs you have in your home or office by purchasing movies and shows already in digital format.

But what are Ultimate iPad owners to do if they already have a collection (small or large) of existing movies and TV shows in DVD and/or Blu-ray format? If they wish to watch these on their iPads, must they purchase the items again in a digital format? Maybe not....

Converting DVD/Blu-ray Discs

Prior to being able to purchase digital movies and TV shows online or subscribe to a service like Netflix, fans of certain movies and TV shows would have to rent or purchase a disc (DVD or Blu-ray) if they wished to watch a favorite movie or show that was no longer in the theaters or broadcast on TV.

Movies and TV shows have been available on DVD for years, and many iPad owners are likely to have small or large collections of DVDs that they enjoy watching from the comfort of their favorite couch or chair. And that's the problem with DVDs (and the newer Blu-ray discs)—they require a disc player connected to a TV to enjoy.

The iPad doesn't come with a built-in disc player (thankfully); it doesn't even have a USB port for plugging in an external DVD/Blu-ray drive. So iPad owners are forced to buy digital movies (or rent them) online or subscribe to a streaming service. Or are they?

For many years now, DVD and Blu-ray owners have been performing an action called "ripping" on their movie and TV show collections. Ripping is taking a disc's content and converting it to a digital file (or files) that can then be viewed on a computer, tablet, phone, or any other device that can play one of the few popular file types that exist—MOV, MP4, and MPEG.

How is a disc ripped? The ripping is done with special software that can examine the disc, find the main content plus other stuff (such as behind-the-scenes extras as well as the previews/advertisements that play when you insert a disc into a player), and allow you to select what content is converted and what format will be used.

There are plenty of applications out there, and many of them cost anywhere from $10 to $100, but you really don't have to spend money. There are a handful of free applications you'll see in this chapter that can get you started on ripping your digital movies and TV shows and converting them to a format you can watch on your iPad (or anywhere else you wish). Not all the software is required, however, so depending on your computer's operating system (Windows or Mac) and the type of disc (DVD or Blu-ray), you'll want to collect any or all of the following and install them on your computer of choice:

- **DVDShrink 3.2 (http://dvdshrink.org)**—This is absolutely required for Windows, but not for Macs. The DVD-ripping software is no longer supported, so 3.2 is the last version ever released—but it's still available as a free download. Also, you should be aware that some DVDs just won't work with DVDShrink 3.2—in those instances, you may have to resort to a paid DVD-ripping application.

- **HandBrake (http://handbrake.fr)**—Handbrake will take the ripped files from DVDShrink 3.2 and convert them into a format suitable for viewing on the iPad. Mac owners can skip DVDShrink 3.2 and go straight to Handbrake. At the time of this writing, Handbrake 0.9.9 is the current version for Mac (OS X 10.6 and later) and Windows (XP and later).

- **MakeMKV (http://makemkv.com)**—MakeMKV is an application for ripping Blu-ray discs. It is currently a beta application and is a free download as it's being developed. Eventually, however, MakeMKV will become a paid application. (MakeMKV can rip DVDs as well, but I've found DVDShrink 3.2 to be a more stable and reliable application for ripping DVDs on Windows.)

Next you'll find a walkthrough for ripping a DVD with DVDShrink 3.2 and ripping a Blu-ray with MakeMKV. Following the ripping walkthroughs, you'll also find an example of converting the ripped files into an iPad-compatible file with HandBrake.

Ripping with DVDShrink 3.2

On a Windows computer, insert a DVD movie; if the movie attempts to auto-play, stop it and close down the video player. Open the DVDShrink 3.2 application, click the Re-Author button, and you'll see a screen similar to the one in Figure 8.5.

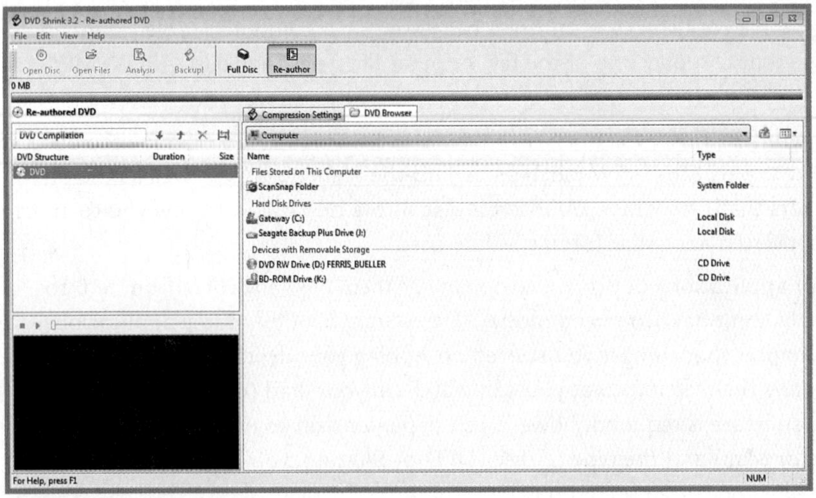

FIGURE 8.5 DVDShrink 3.2 will scan all drives looking for a DVD.

Double-click the drive letter that corresponds to your DVD drive. (In Figure 8.5, it is the D: drive.) The software will open the disc and attempt to identify the main movie (typically the longest continuous bit of video on a disc). Figure 8.6 shows that it has identified the main movie and it's 1 hour and 42 minutes in length.

For TV shows, you'll often find a listing of almost identical-length titles that should correspond to the number of episodes found on a disc. (For example, a 24-episode television show split over four DVDs will most likely have six episodes per disc.)

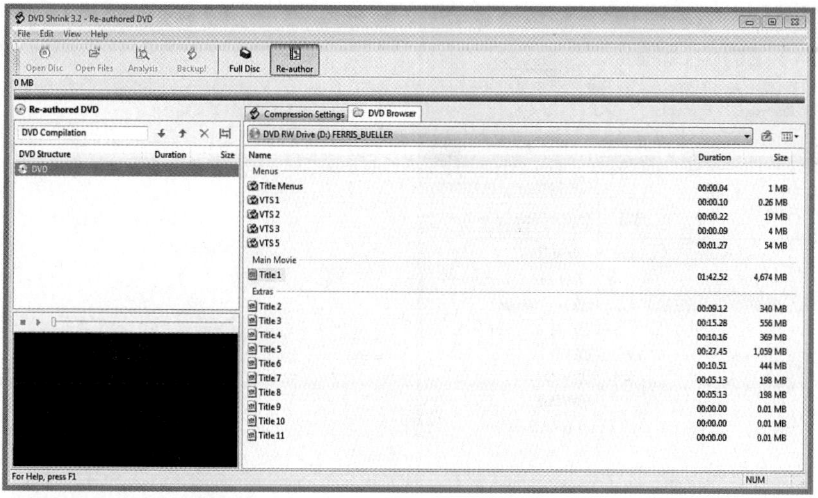

FIGURE 8.6 Let DVDShrink try to identify the main movie.

You'll want to perform the following steps once per movie or once per episode. (If you perform these steps for all episodes on a disc, the final file containing the episodes will be quite large and continuous—six one-hour episodes, for example, would create one six-hour long video.)

1. Drag the title you wish to rip from the right side to the left side into the section labeled DVD Structure. When this is done, the software will scan the file, as shown in the analysis stage in Figure 8.7.

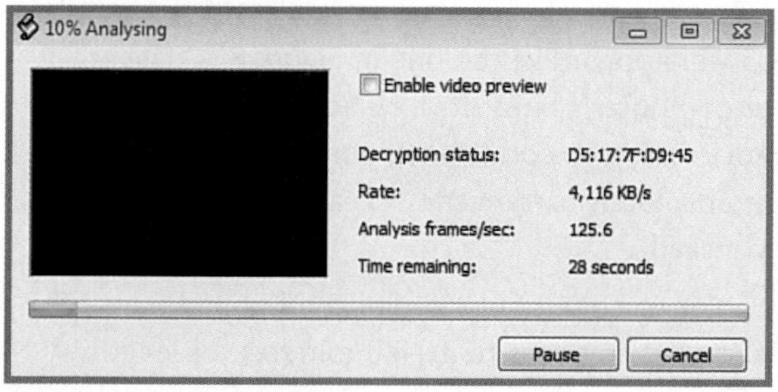

FIGURE 8.7 The video to be ripped must be analyzed by the software.

After the title (main movie or an episode) is analyzed, it will appear in the DVD Structure listing, as shown in Figure 8.8.

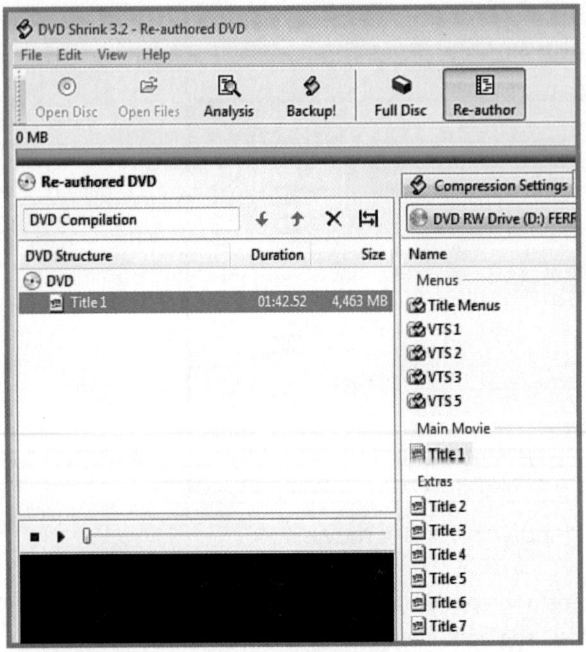

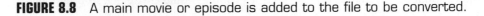

FIGURE 8.8 A main movie or episode is added to the file to be converted.

2. For a movie rip, this is the only analysis that must be performed. For a TV show, you can drag additional titles (episodes) to the left, one at a time. All titles listed in the DVD Structure section of DVDShrink 3.2 will be lumped together into the final video that you will watch on your iPad.

3. Click the Backup! button and a screen will appear like the one in Figure 8.9. This is where you will specify a folder on your computer's hard drive to hold the ripped files. Feel free to create a folder with the movie or TV episode name/number. Use the Browse button to locate that folder and make absolutely certain the "Create VIDEO_TS and AUDIO_TS subfolders" check box is checked.

Click the OK button and the selected movie or episode(s) will begin to be ripped. This can take anywhere from a minute or less for short TV episodes to 10–20 minutes for lengthy movies. You'll see a screen like the one in Figure 8.10 that will provide you a progress bar on the ripping (Encoding) process.

When the ripping process is done, open the folder you specified in Figure 8.9 and you should see two folders—VIDEO_TS and AUDIO_TS—as shown in Figure 8.11.

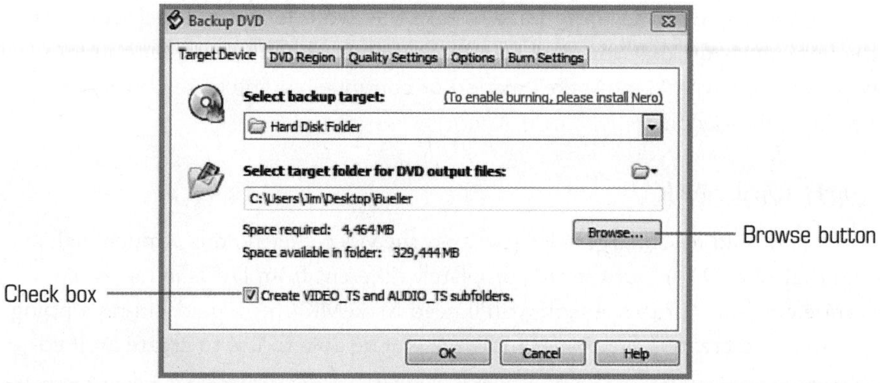

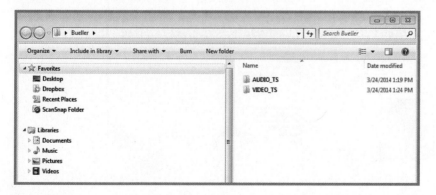

FIGURE 8.9 Back up the selected title(s) to a folder on your hard drive.

FIGURE 8.10 The ripping process begins for your movie or TV show.

FIGURE 8.11 You'll need these two folders to convert a disc to digital.

You can return to DVDShrink 3.2 and rip more TV episodes or movies, but be sure to create a custom folder to hold the special folders for each movie or episode.

Your next step is going to be to use HandBrake to take the two folders (and their contents) and create the final movie file that you'll be able to view on your iPad. Feel free to jump ahead to the "Converting with HandBrake" section or continue reading to see the steps involved in ripping a Blu-ray disc.

Ripping with MakeMKV

Blu-ray discs not only hold much larger files (because the video they hold is a much higher resolution than that of a DVD), but they're completely different from DVDs in how they hold and organize content. For this reason, you'll need MakeMKV (or a paid Blu-ray ripping software application) to create a file that HandBrake will be able to use to create an iPad-compatible movie.

Insert a Blu-ray movie or TV show disc into a Blu-ray drive and close down the movie if it attempts to autoplay. Open up the MakeMKV application and you should see your movie listed, as shown in Figure 8.12.

TIP

Blu-ray discs will not work on a DVD drive in your computer—fortunately Blu-ray drives can be purchased for around $30–$40 and plug into a USB port on your computer. (DVDs will, however, work just fine in a Blu-ray player.)

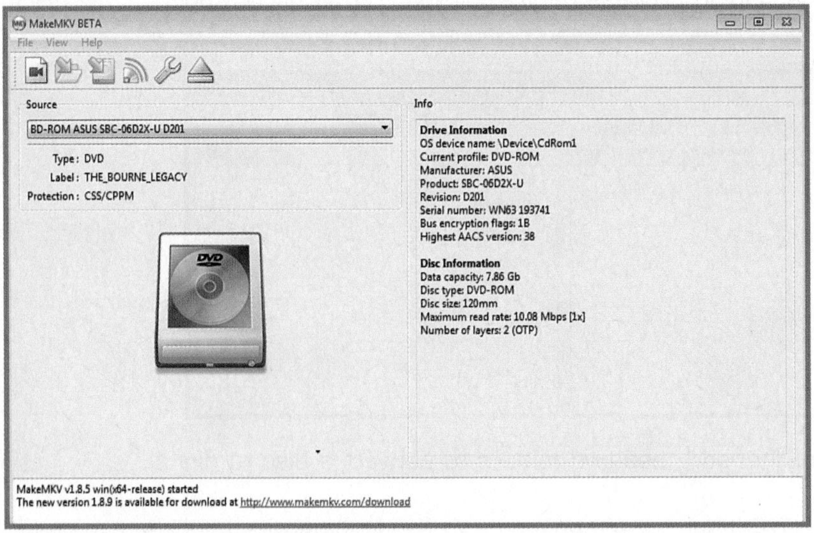

FIGURE 8.12 Use MakeMKV to rip Blu-ray movies and TV shows.

As with DVDShrink 3.2, you'll want to create a folder on your computer to hold the ripped files as MakeMKV processes the disc. Create this folder first and then click the big disc icon shown in Figure 8.12. MakeMKV will begin scanning the Blu-ray disc to look for the movie or episodes, as shown in Figure 8.13. This can take a couple of minutes, so be patient.

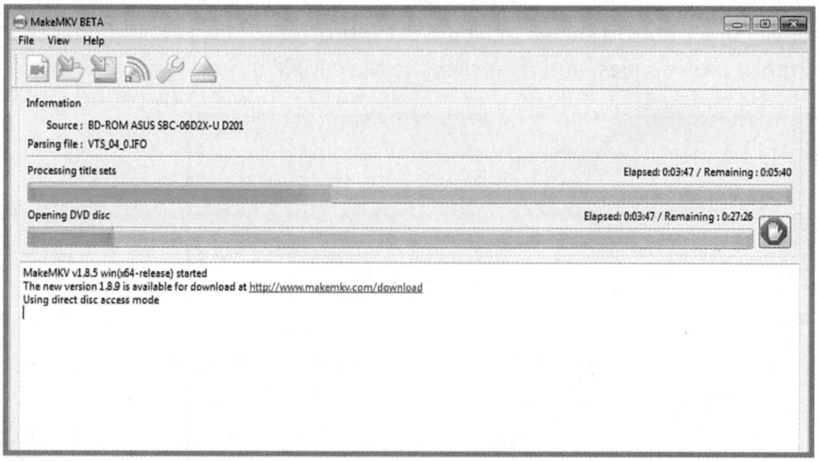

FIGURE 8.13 The disc is scanned as MakeMKV looks for the files.

When the scan is done, you'll see a list of Titles like the one in Figure 8.14.

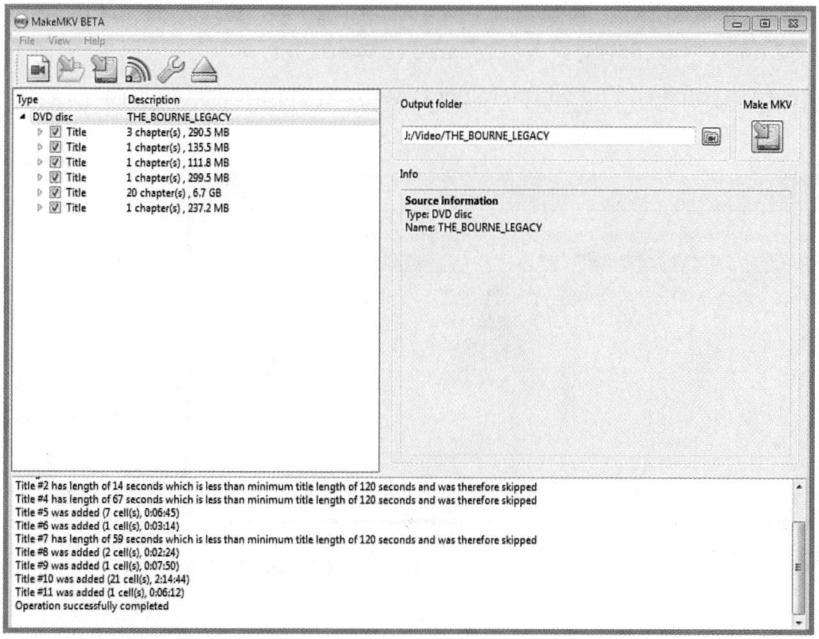

FIGURE 8.14 Movie and TV episodes will exist as Titles.

For movies, the one you're most likely going to be using will also tend to be the largest. In the case of the Titles shown in Figure 8.14, uncheck all but the fifth check box down the list, which holds the 6.7GB main movie. (The remaining items are the extra "exclusives" that frequently come on a disc with behind-the-scene interviews, director commentary, and so on—leave them checked if you like to include these features in the final movie conversion.)

Next, click the Change Folder button shown in Figure 8.15, browse to the custom folder you made to hold the ripped movie's files, and then click the MakeMKV button.

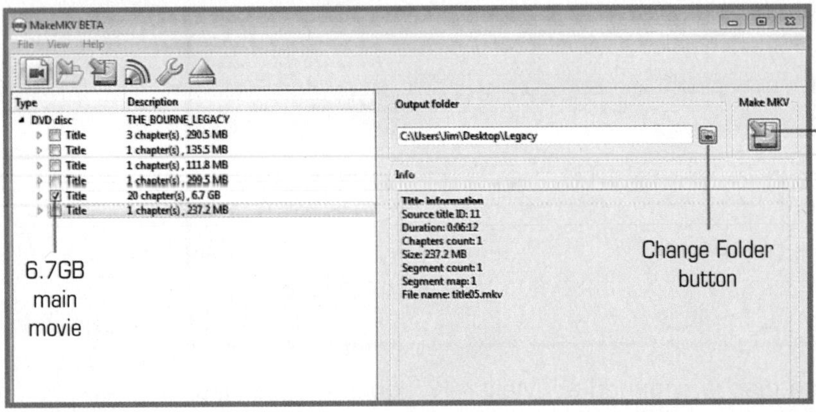

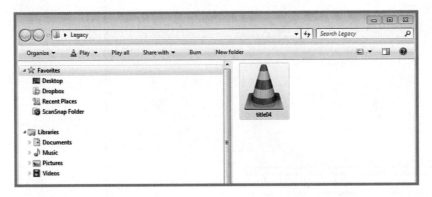

FIGURE 8.15 Select the movie or episode you want to rip; uncheck the rest.

Ripping a Blu-ray typically takes a lot longer than ripping a standard DVD. This two-hour movie took about 32 minutes to finish, so be prepared to wait a bit.

When it's done, however, you'll end up with a folder that holds the special .MKV file like the one in Figure 8.16.

FIGURE 8.16 This special file is needed by Handbrake to convert a Blu-ray.

And that's how you rip a Blu-ray. But you're only halfway done with the process. Next, you'll learn how HandBrake takes the special folders created by DVDShrink 3.2 and the special .MKV file created by MakeMKV and uses them to create a custom video file that will play on your Ultimate iPad.

NOTE

Both DVDShrink 3.2 and MakeMKV have additional features I've not covered in this chapter. You'll want to consult the help files and/or the websites devoted to these two applications if you have additional questions or wish to learn about more advanced features.

Converting with HandBrake

Now that you have either a DVD or Blu-ray ripped, it's time to take the ripped files and do something useful with them. You'll use the HandBrake application to take either the VIDEO_TS and AUDIO_TS folders (and files inside) created by DVDShrink 3.2 or the .MKV file created by MakeMKV and create a special file that can be saved to any hard drive or cloud service (such as Dropbox or Pogoplug) and viewed on your iPad.

To get started, after downloading the HandBrake app, open it and you'll see a screen like the one in Figure 8.17.

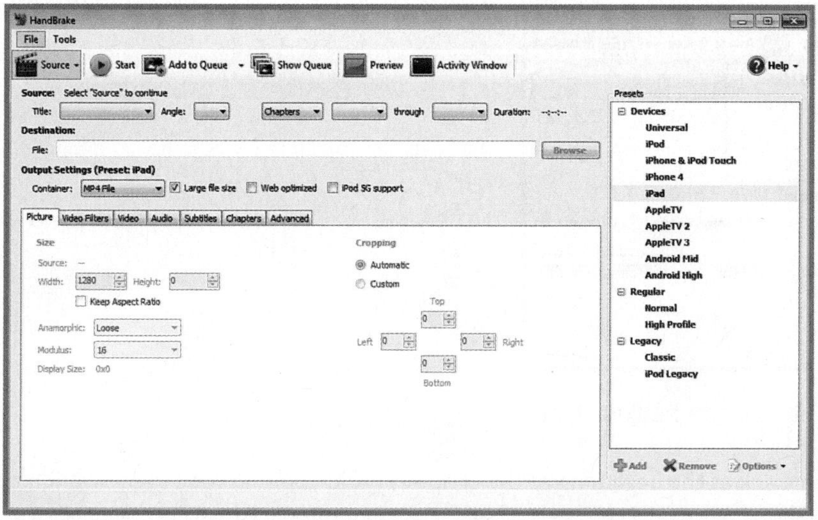

FIGURE 8.17 The HandBrake app is used to convert discs to digital.

The HandBrake app has dozens and dozens of features and special abilities that I cannot cover in this chapter. You'll want to consult the Help menu for many more features than I'll be showing you here. For purposes of this chapter, I'm only going to show you how to convert movies specifically for viewing on iPad. What this means is that the movie or TV show will be formatted for the iPad's screen and resolution—watching it on a mobile phone or a larger TV might not provide the highest resolution you're used to viewing.

TIP

If you want to rip movies and have them saved in a viewing format to match their original resolution and video quality, you're going to want to invest in a lot of hard drive storage or a lot of cloud storage. HandBrake can definitely save your videos in their original format, but one or two movies will be enough to use up all your iPad's internal storage.

To begin with, look on the right side of the screen shown in Figure 8.17 and make certain the iPad option is selected. If it isn't, click it. (If you don't see it, click the Add button and select it from the list that appears.)

After the iPad option is selected, click the Source button in the upper-left corner of HandBrake and you'll see a small list of options appear, as shown in Figure 8.18.

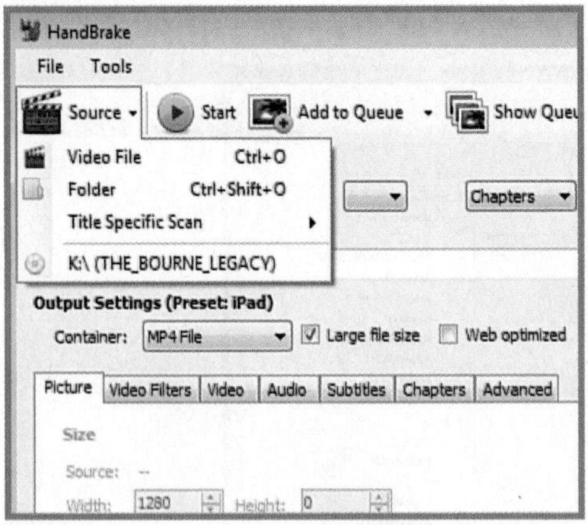

FIGURE 8.18 The Source button options.

If you'll remember back at the beginning of the chapter, I told you that Mac users wouldn't need to use DVDShrink 3.2 to rip DVDs—that's because HandBrake can access a Mac's DVD drive directly and create the iPad-compatible video file directly from the DVD. That's the option shown at the bottom of the pop-up menu in Figure 8.18. You would select that option to avoid creating the VIDEO_TS and AUDIO_TS folders created by DVDShrink 3.2.

Click the Folder option in the drop-down menu and browse to the folder you created with DVDShrink 3.2 or MakeMKV and then click the Select Folder button shown in Figure 8.19. You do not have to click either the AUDIO_TS or VIDEO_TS folder—you just need to be able to see them before clicking the Select Folder button.

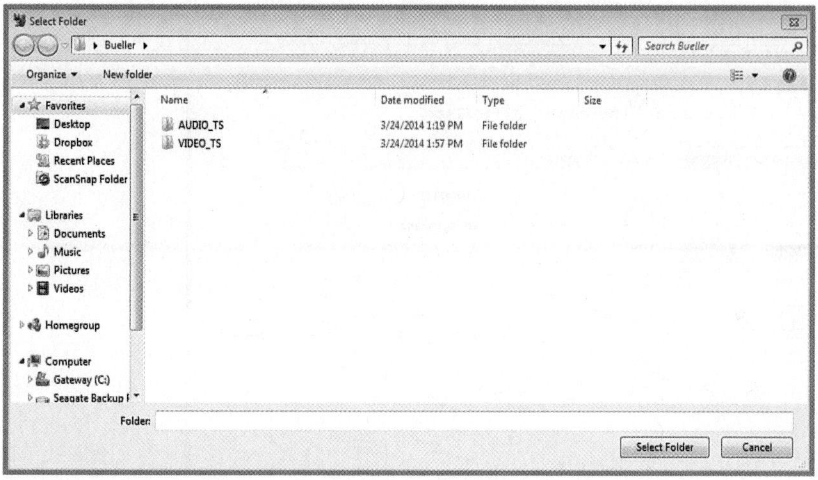

FIGURE 8.19 Select the folder you created for the DVDShrink 3.2 rip.

The movie or TV episode will appear in the Source listing along with the length of the video. Below that, in the Destination section, click the Browse button and select the same folder that contains the VIDEO_TS and AUDIO_TS folders, as shown in Figure 8.20.

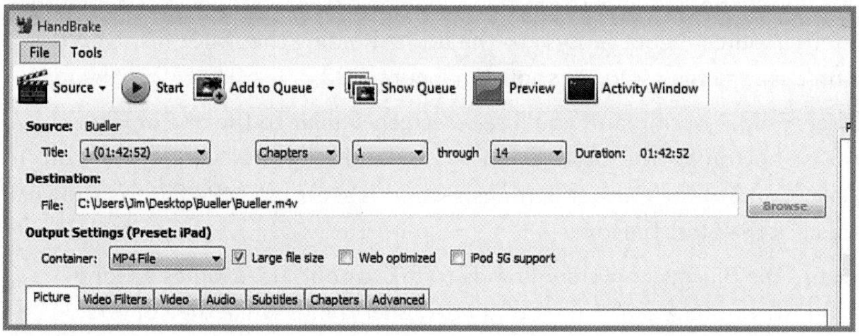

FIGURE 8.20 Make sure Source and Destination are correct.

Confirm that the MP4 file type is selected in the Output Settings section (below the Destination section) and then click the Start button. The converting process begins, as shown in Figure 8.21, with a progress bar near the bottom of the screen. This can take anywhere from five minutes for short, 30-minute long TV episodes, to an hour or more for 2+ hour-long movies.

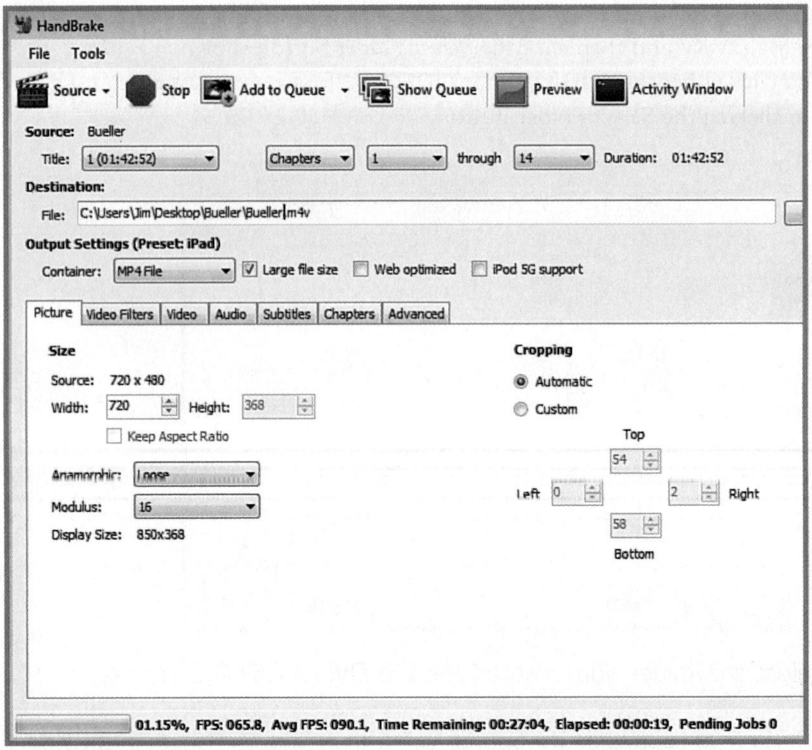

FIGURE 8.21 The conversion process begins to turn disc to digital.

For your MakeMKV Blu-ray rip, you'll perform the same basic steps, but when selecting the Folder option from the Source menu, browse to the folder holding the .MKV file. Don't panic when you don't see the file listed, as shown in Figure 8.22.

Simply click the Select Folder option and you'll see a screen similar to the one in Figure 8.20. Click the Browse button for the Destination section and select the same folder containing the .MKV file. Confirm the Output Settings section is set to an MP4 File, as shown in Figure 8.23, and click the Start button.

Once again, you wait. The Blu-ray conversion tends to take about 1.5–2 times as long as a DVD conversion, so you have some time to go do other things while the conversion completes.

When the conversions are completed, you can delete the AUDIO_TS and VIDEO_TS folders or the .MKV file—they're not needed anymore. What's left over is an .MP4 file that can be placed in Dropbox or a Pogoplug-connected hard drive or even copied to your iPad directly with iTunes or the GoodReader app.

And that's how you convert a DVD or Blu-ray disc to a digital file that can be viewed on your Ultimate iPad. Enjoy!

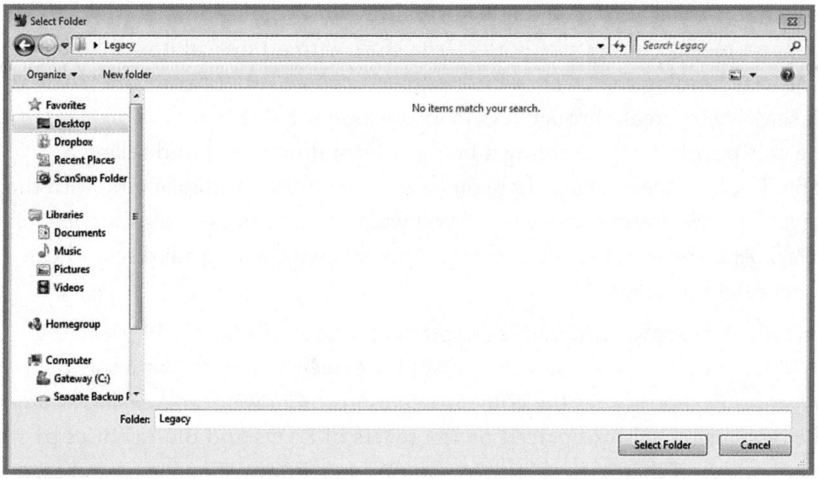

FIGURE 8.22 Select the .MKV folder for a Blu-ray conversion.

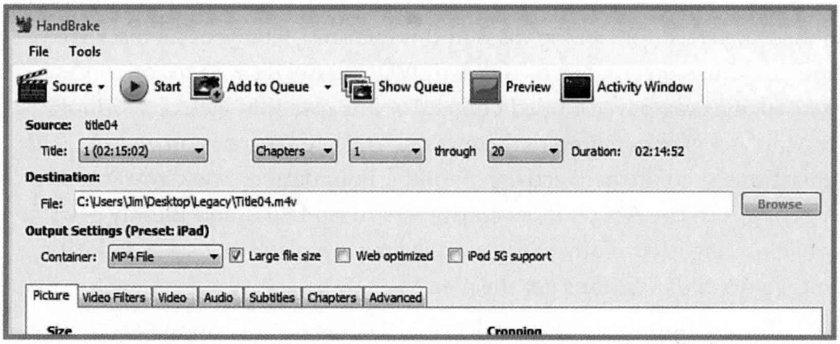

FIGURE 8.23 Converting the Blu-ray file to an iPad-compatible video begins.

The Legal Stuff

In the last chapter, I told you that the law is a bit vague right now when it comes to scanning books and magazines for your own personal use. That's not the case when it comes to your DVD and Blu-ray discs, unfortunately.

Thanks to the Digital Millennium Copyright Act (DMCA) Act. 17 U.S.C. 1201, it is currently illegal for owners of DVDs and Blu-rays that contain DRM (Digital Rights Management, also known as encryption or copy-protection) to use any method to change that content to another format (called format shifting). You can read much more detail about DMCA by visiting http://en.wikipedia.org/wiki/DMCA.

What this means is that it's illegal to take a DVD or Blu-ray that you legitimately own (you paid money, got a receipt, and walked out of the store with a physical item in your hands—namely, the case holding the DVD or Blu-ray) and use any kind of software (such as DVDShrink or MakeMKV) to break through a copy-protection scheme that is implemented on the disc for the sole purpose of preventing a bad guy from duplicating and selling a copy of it for profit. The law doesn't care that you have no intention of duplicating with the purpose of selling it. The law doesn't care that all you want to do is make a digital copy for viewing on your iPad. And the law doesn't care that you still own the original disc and can prove that you purchased it legally.

In a nutshell, everything I've shown you in this chapter is probably illegal for 99.9% of the DVDs and Blu-ray discs that you own; almost all discs have been sold with some sort of copy-protection. It doesn't matter that the copy-protection is often weak and easily circumvented, either—the responsibility is not placed on the sellers of DVDs and Blu-ray discs to develop stronger encryption if they wish to prevent bootleggers from selling illegal copies. Consumers are caught between a rock and a hard place when it comes to the decision to convert their legally owned discs into a format they can enjoy somewhere other than on their television.

So why have I included the steps for ripping discs in this chapter? First, not all discs are copy-protected; you could use these steps to convert DVD/Blu-ray discs that contain public/non-private items such as tax-payer funded content or any disc that lacks encryption protection. Second, this Act is revisited every three years, and the last revision was in 2012. A number of organizations such as the Electronic Frontier Foundation (www.eff.org) are trying to lobby for changes to the Act to allow consumers to rip DVDs and Blu-ray discs for personal use, so while ripping is currently considered illegal, it may not be so in 2015 if a number of consumer rights organizations get their way.

Yes, ripping is illegal, but the ripping software still exists. People rip their movies every day. Why aren't the media companies going after all the people out there who are ripping their legally owned discs and storing the files on their own hard drives for viewing on a TV or mobile device? I don't know, but I suspect that even these media companies recognize that it's a bit over-reaching to tell someone they can't convert a legally owned disc for their own use. Certainly they're watching websites that traffic in the illegal trade and download of music and movies and television shows, but if you're ripping your movies and not giving them away or sharing them over the Internet, you're probably small fish to the these companies. (It probably also doesn't hurt that there's really no way for the media companies to know you've ripped your movies and are viewing them in the privacy of your own home or on your tablet unless you're also sharing them illegally.)

Still, ripping is illegal. My recommendation for now is to adhere to the DMCA and refrain from ripping until the law is changed. It would be nice if there existed a way to trade in your discs for a digital copy, but so far that solution isn't available (probably because the media companies would much rather you buy a movie or TV show again, generating more revenue).

Don't Forget Your Backup: Long-Term Deep Storage

In This Chapter

- Your data and risks to its well-being
- Pros and cons of standard backup methods
- Unlimited online backup services
- Options for unlimited backup
- Guard your data

If you've never lost a digital file before, consider yourself lucky. Years ago, I lost three chapters of a book I was writing; fortunately, I had emailed one of them to my editor, so I only had to rewrite two of them. It could have been a lot worse. I've had friends lose all their digital photos when the hard drive in their computers crashed, and I know one gentleman who lost a year's worth of research data when his laptop was stolen.

Technology has made it so easy to store files that we tend to forget just how easy it is for those files to disappear. Those of us who own homes have insurance (and hopefully those of you who rent have renter's insurance) to cover fire, theft, and other risks to our physical property, but what kinds of insurance do we have in place for our digital property?

Why is data backup part of this book? Owning an Ultimate iPad means you'll also own a lot of digital data—web articles, ebooks an ezines, movies and TV shows, financial documents, photos, home videos, and so much more. The goal of the Ultimate iPad is to be that single source for accessing all your data. But not all of your digital data will be stored on the iPad (and nor should it be). This means storing it elsewhere. And this means putting it at risk of theft, fire, deletion, and other unpredictable losses.

In this chapter, I'm going to introduce you to one of the lowest priced insurance plans around, and I'm going to show you how to use it. Along the way, you'll learn about some of the basic backup methods used that work great, but may not always be the best option for you. By chapter's end, you should be thinking long and hard about how you plan on backing up all the data you'll be creating and collecting as your Ultimate iPad becomes a reality.

Let's Talk About Backups

I have no idea what kinds of files you'll be collecting and organizing and creating as you take the various techniques in this book and implement them. But here's a short list of some of the more popular file types:

- **Photos**—Photos taken with a digital camera or your mobile phone will run anywhere from 2MB (megabytes) in size up to 12MB or more, depending on the quality of the camera and other factors. And this doesn't count the paper photos you've collected over the years and are maybe now beginning to scan in and save as digital photos.

- **Home videos**—From baby's first steps to graduation to vacation to retirement, people love shooting videos of their special moments. Videos take up huge amounts of storage, and it's not unheard of for simple home videos taken with a mobile phone to be 1GB or more in size. Shoot a hundred or more short, 30-second videos with your mobile phone in a year and you've got over 50GB of video that has to be stored somewhere.

- **Movies and TV shows**—If you're downloading digital movies (or ripping them—see Chapter 8, "Rip and Store: Your Movies and Shows On Demand"), you're going to quickly discover that any one-to-two-hour movie is going to take between 500MB and 5GB or storage.

- **Scanned financial documents**—If you're scanning in all your financial files (and maybe shredding the originals), the size of these files is negligible but probably not their informational value. Imagine losing these digital files and then the amount of time and energy it would take to call and email businesses to request replacement copies.

- **Kids drawings, reports cards, and so on**—If you have kids and you've been scanning in their artwork, homework sheets, report cards, and other keepsakes, storage space is also going to be minor. These items may not have a dollar-value associated with them, but we all know how difficult it is to put a price on memories. Losing these kinds of files is as almost as bad as losing family photos. Some may think it worse.

- **Ebooks and ezines**—If you've used a scanning service to convert your books and magazines to digital files, you probably no longer have the originals. Imagine losing all your ebooks and then having to buy them again. And many magazines (and ezines) may not have back issues available. Your digital library does have a financial value, and it could take years and thousands of dollars to duplicate the collection you own now.

■ **Music**—Music lovers are likely to have a large collection of digital music files. Between digital music purchased from iTunes or Amazon.com, ripped CDs, and even collectible vinyl records, there's a lot to lose should a music collection be damaged, stolen, or deleted.

When it comes to your digital data, there's a storage value, a replacement value, and a personal value. Storage needs will likely never decrease—as you collect more photos, more eBooks, and more music, your storage needs will climb. So, too, will the replacement value of your data. Although some files such as digital movies and music can be replaced if the originals are deleted (you simply log in and download them again), this isn't always the case. And photos, home videos, and other items, if there's no backup, will have a personal value that cannot have a number assigned to it.

For all these reasons, many people do turn to creating backups of their data. There are a number of simple backup methods that people use, but they often have their drawbacks:

■ **An extra hard drive**—Copying files from one hard drive to another is one form of backup, but if that hard drive isn't immediately stored elsewhere, it's subject to fire, flood, and theft just like the other hard drive. And then there's the issue of hardware failure—hard drives die, just like any other electronic device.

■ **CD/DVD/Blu-ray discs**—Writing your data to discs is a reliable backup method, but discs are subject to breaking, scratches, the elements, and even loss of data over time. Plus, discs don't hold a lot of data. A basic single-sided Blu-ray disc can hold 25GB, but if you have 1TB of just photos (not counting videos, music, and so on), it'll take 40 Blu-ray discs to hold all those images.

■ **Tape drive**—Businesses tend to use this technology more than homeowners, but tape drives are capable of storing a lot of data. The downside to tape drives is they have a higher cost, they're slower in terms of backing up and retrieving data, and the tapes are much more susceptible to heat and cold and degradation of data over time.

■ **Dropbox and other cloud services**—Cloud services such as Dropbox are not meant to serve as backup options, and they're definitely not priced for it, but if your data demands aren't high, it is an option. Dropbox, for example, costs $100 per year for 100GB of storage—that can get eaten up with about 10–12 home movies and a few thousand family photos.

Extra hard drives, discs, tape drives, and cloud services are certainly capable of providing you with backups of your data, but they're not ideal. Some of them require time on your part (such as backing up data to discs) to maintain and others just get more and more expensive as your data needs increase (such as buying more cloud storage space).

So, what's the solution? How can you ensure that all the data you're creating and collecting is available to your Ultimate iPad as well as securely backed up?

The answer is pairing a portable USB hard drive with an unlimited online backup service.

Unlimited Data Backup Made Easy

A number of services today offer unlimited data backup over the Internet. Most of these services charge a monthly or yearly fee and provide an application that is installed on your computer that allows you to select all files and folders you wish to back up (or in some cases allows you to elect to back up everything and choose files and folders you wish to exclude). The software communicates between your computer and the service's storage over the Internet, so a high-speed connection is preferred (versus a dial-up connection) and often required.

With most unlimited backup services, however, the drawback is that if you delete a file from your computer, the special software installed on your computer picks up that deletion and requests that the file also be deleted from the online backup. This may or may not be a problem for some users, but if you're going to be using your Ultimate iPad to access just about every bit of digital data you own, that means keeping a copy of all this data on your home or work computer.

Back in Chapter 3, "Additional iPad Storage Options," I showed you how to use Dropbox to make some data available to your iPad. These files (stored on Dropbox) do not have to reside on your computer's hard drive, but that also means they won't get backed up to your online backup service. The same holds true for any cloud service you use that holds files that aren't also found on your computer's hard drive.

You might think that all you need to do is copy the Dropbox data to your hard drive, let it be backed up to the online backup service, and then delete it again. Unfortunately, most online backup services remove any file not found on your computer's hard drive after 30 days have passed. So unless you're going to copy everything over once a month, let it back up, and then delete it, this will get annoying fast.

No, the solution here is to first purchase and connect a dedicated external hard drive to your computer like the one shown in Figure 9.1.

External hard drives are an amazing buy. Years ago, an external hard drive with 100GB of storage space would have cost you $250 or more. Today, you can't hardly find an external hard drive that holds less than 1TB (1 terabyte, or 1,000GB). And prices have plummeted. Today, a 3TB external hard drive can be purchased for less than $100. Think about that— 3,000GB for $100. I've been converting books and magazines and other items to digital files for years, and I'm only now passing 1.5TB for my photos, home videos, and other digital file storage.

I have a dedicated 3TB external hard drive connected to my computer and I put everything on it. Everything. This is the same 3TB drive connected to my Pogoplug device (refer back to Chapter 3), and it also functions as my Deep Storage drive. As you can see in Figure 9.2, when viewing the hard drive from the Pogoplug app on my iPad, I see all the various folders I use to organize my digital files, including Archive.

FIGURE 9.1 Your Ultimate iPad Backup Solution starts with an external drive.

FIGURE 9.2 The Archive folder is visible from the Pogoplug app.

NOTE

"Deep Storage" is typically used to refer to archived storage that you put files into but rarely access. A Deep Storage drive usually has one job—hold files and hold them indefinitely. Should you run out of space, buy a bigger drive, copy everything over, and keep going. But there's nothing wrong with dedicating a sufficiently large hard drive to both Archive and Pogoplug service, and you'll certainly save some money.

With a 1TB, 2TB, or even a 5TB Deep Storage external hard drive, you have a single place to drop every digital file you own. You can still work from this drive, copying files and opening documents on it, but you might still consider purchasing a dedicated Deep Storage drive— one you put files into and never access them again (unless you need to recover them). If you have Word documents and PDF files that you open and close and edit, it's best to store these on your computer or in a cloud service such as Dropbox.

Once you have your Deep Storage/Archive hard drive purchased and set up, it's time to connect it to an online storage service.

When it comes to online storage services (OSS), what you're looking for is an OSS that will not only back up your computer's hard drive but also any external hard drives connected to it. Bingo! That means your Pogoplug-connected drive and your Deep Storage drive can be backed up. (In my case, a single drive serves both purposes.)

A number of online storage services support external hard drives, and the one I'm going to walk you through in this chapter is the service offered by Backblaze. It works for both Windows and Mac computers, and offers unlimited backups of one computer (plus all connected external hard drives) for only $5 per month. No, that's not a typo. For $5/month (even less if you pay for a one- or two-year contract in advance), Backblaze's software will copy over all files (minus a few exceptions) and folders on your computer's hard drive (as well as a Deep Storage external hard drive).

Peace of mind. And it all starts by signing up for Backblaze. Point your web browser to www.backblaze.com and create an account, as shown in Figure 9.3.

NOTE

Do not skimp on a strong password for your online backup. This is the password that you will use to retrieve your files should something catastrophic happen to the original Deep Storage hard drive (or your computer's hard drive), so don't lose it either.

FIGURE 9.3 Create an account with Backblaze.

After you provide an email address and password, the Backblaze software will be downloaded. After the installation file is downloaded, double-click it to install. Figure 9.4 shows that the software is ready to be installed on a Windows computer. Click the Install Now button to begin.

FIGURE 9.4 Install the Backblaze software on your computer.

CAUTION

Keep in mind that the $5/month service is for backing up one computer and any external drives connected to it. For the remainder of this section, I'll be using my Windows computer, but the software installation and operation for Mac is almost identical.

As the software is installed, it is looking for drives connected to your computer, as shown in Figure 9.5.

FIGURE 9.5   Drives are scanned on the computer as the software installs.

When the installation is finished, the backup will begin in the background, with your data files being sent over your Internet connection to Backblaze.

NOTE

Depending on how much data you have to back up, the initial backup process can take days...maybe even weeks. The good news is you can use your computer normally; everything involved in the backup is being handled in the background—just don't turn off your computer. You can visit www.backblaze.com/speedtest to get an estimate on your own data and the backup storage time required; Backblaze states that two weeks is the average.

Keep in mind that Backblaze will be constantly monitoring the files and folders on your computer and its connected external drives. If Backblaze detects a missing file, it will keep that file stored as a backup for 30 days, no more. After that, it removes that file as it determines you've either deleted it or moved it to a folder or other computer that doesn't require a backup.

You also need to understand that although it's okay for you to turn off your computer, don't leave it off for more than 29 days or Backblaze will interpret that as moved or deleted files—even though your computer is simply powered down. The same goes for a backed up external hard drive; if you unplug it, that's fine. But you need to make certain that it's powered up and connected to your computer at least once every 30 days or Backblaze will think you've deleted all the content off that drive and do the same with your backup!

Once the software is installed, you can use the Backblaze Control Panel that's installed on your computer to customize what you wish to back up. Notice in Figure 9.6 that the software will let you pause any backup that is occurring, and there's a Restore Options button that you'll use just in case you need to recover accidentally deleted files.

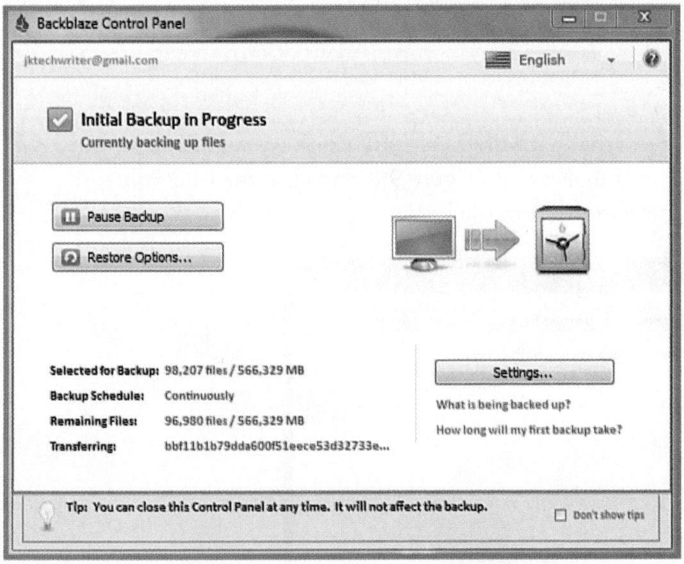

FIGURE 9.6 The Backblaze Control Panel.

Click the Settings button and examine the Hard Drives section where drives are selected for backup. My Windows computer has an internal hard drive (C: drive), and the external drive (J: drive) is powered on and connected via USB. Both boxes are checked, as you can see in Figure 9.7.

Notice also in Figure 9.7 that I've configured the software to alert me if seven days have passed without a backup operation or at least the software verifying that all is well.

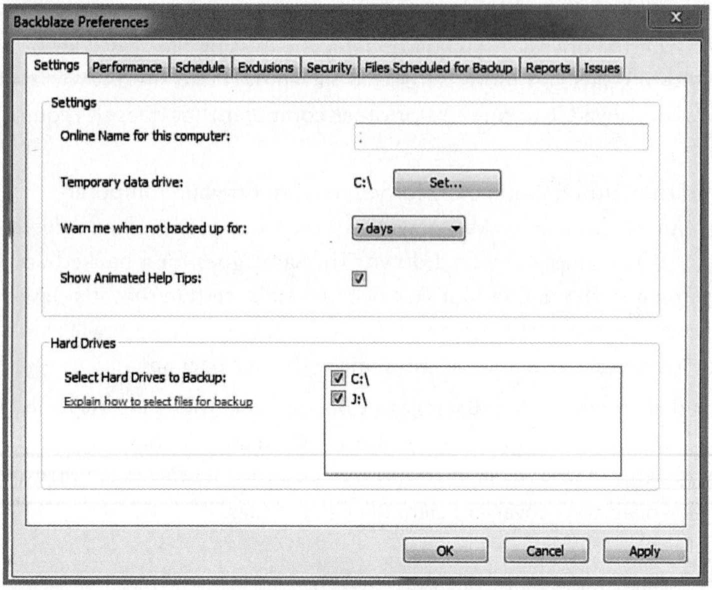

FIGURE 9.7 Verify all drives are selected that you wish to back up.

Are there some folders on your external hard drive that you don't want included in the backup? If so, click the Exclusions tab shown in Figure 9.8 and click the Add Folder to browse to the folder you wish to remove from the backup operation.

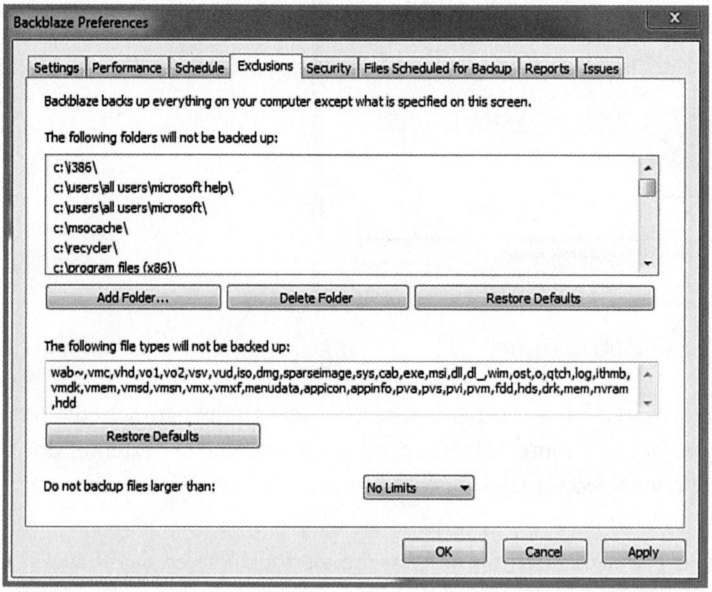

FIGURE 9.8 The Exclusions tab lets you specify folders not to backed up.

After your files are backed up with Backblaze, you'll be happy to know that you can install the free Backblaze app on your iPad and use it to view your backed up files as well as share them. As you can see in Figure 9.9, you browse to the drive (or drives) that holds a file, tap the file to open and view it, and then click the Share button (upper-right corner) and select the iPad app you want to use to share the file.

FIGURE 9.9 Use the Backblaze app to view and share backed up files.

Backblaze offers a 15-day free trial of the software, so there's no risk in downloading it and trying it out. It took Backblaze just over one week to back up over 560GB of data files, and 300GB of that was my Archive folder.

Over time, my Archive folder will grow and grow; I rarely delete any files these days because it's too easy and inexpensive to just archive files and have Backblaze store them as a backup. Two year, five years, even 10 years from now, should I discover I need a copy of that contract from 2012 or am looking for the phone number and address of the company that stained my fence back in 2009, that contract and invoice will still exist. It may take me a few minutes or more to find them, but probably not because I use subfolders to organize my files, I use descriptive filenames, and I convert PDFs to OCR for keyword searches. And I don't even have to search for them from my computer—my Ultimate iPad connects to the Archive folder through the Pogoplug app, letting me verify the Archive folder is still safe and sound on the external hard drive as well as being backed up to Backblaze. I sleep soundly at night for many reasons, and one of those is knowing that my digital life has a copy that costs me $60 per year and is always turned on.

Online Backup Alternatives

Backblaze isn't the only online backup service in town, so you'll definitely want to look around, check some prices, kick some tires, and see what solutions are available for you out there.

Do you have multiple computers? Backblaze has its flat-rate $5/month per computer, but here are a few other unlimited online backup options:

- **Carbonite.com**—For $60/year, one computer and all its files can be backed up. This does not include external hard drives, however—that's the $99/year plan, and it comes with some additional services over Backblaze, such as backing up your operating system and applications if you want that level of protection.

- **CrashPlan**—This is an option for families with multiple computers. For $14/month, you get unlimited backup of two or more computers. The basic $6/month unlimited plan does not cover backing up your external hard drives, only the computer's internal/local hard drive.

- **SOS Online Backup**—Although $60/year does get you unlimited backup of one computer and any external drives connected to it, SOS Online Backup software does not run continually. But if you don't need real-time backups as you work, this is a comparable option to Backblaze.

NOTE

There's a great online resource that summarizes a lot of the online backup solutions available, including the unlimited plans. The resource does appear to be updated periodically, so you should be able to find updated and relevant information by browsing http://abt.cm/1djnfhb.

One service I've been asked about by my friends and family is the Deep Storage solution offered by Amazon.com called Glacier. The Glacier service offers backups for $0.01 per gigabyte per month. Yep, one penny per gigabyte per month. The idea, however, is that although it costs almost nothing to store files with Amazon.com, it will cost you money to retrieve those files, and the final cost depends on how much you pull out of the storage and how fast you need it.

Need 100GB over the next few hours? Expect to pay a bundle. Need 2GB by tomorrow? You should be okay.

Glacier is intended to be used as true Deep Storage; put something in and forget about it. It's long-term, hands-off storage that's intended for the most dire of situations—a complete and utter loss of major data.

For a while I was a fan of Glacier, but I've since changed my mind, especially with the increase in unlimited online backup services like Backblaze.

For sheer storage, not retrieval, let's look at the price of backing up 200GB+ of data, and for this exercise I'll be using the unofficial Amazon Glacier Calculator (http://liangzan.net/aws-glacier-calculator/) shown in Figure 9.10.

Let's start with just 200GB of data that you wish to back up. As you can see in Figure 9.11, I've uploaded the 200GB and I've kept it in there for a month (30 days).

As expected, I'm going to be billed almost $2 per month for that 200GB. Not bad. But let's say 20GB of that data is a mix of photos and documents I need for my job and I need that data out today. Figure 9.12 shows that if I request that 20GB be provided to me within eight hours, I'll have to pay $20.28.

Unofficial Amazon AWS Glacier Calculator

A single page angular js app for calculating the rates for AWS glacier

View the Project on GitHub
liangzan/aws-glacier-calculator

Download ZIP File	Download TAR Ball	View On GitHub

Assumptions

1. 1 month equals 30 days
2. Request costs are assumed to be zero
3. Data transfer rate beyond 350TB is assumed to be the the same as the 350TB tier
4. You are making a single set of retrieval job requests, evenly spread over the retrieval time

This project is maintained by liangzan

Hosted on GitHub Pages – Theme by orderedlist

Should you discover any mistakes, please let me know at @liangzan or my email. Thanks!

Select your region

- ⊙ US East (N. Virginia)
- ○ US West (Oregon)
- ○ US West (N. California)
- ○ EU (Ireland)
- ○ Asia (Tokyo)

Storage information

Amount of data stored (GB)
Duration that data was kept (days)

Retrieval information

Amount of data to retrieve (GB)
Length of time for retrieval (hours, min 4)

Early deletion information

Amount of data to be deleted (GB)
Duration that data was kept (days)

Estimated cost breakdown

Storage Cost	$0.00
Retrieval Cost	$0.00
Deletion Cost	$0.00
Transfer Cost	($0.12)
Total Cost	($0.12)

FIGURE 9.10 This calculator determines storage and retrieval costs for Glacier.

Select your region

- ⊙ US East (N. Virginia)
- ○ US West (Oregon)
- ○ US West (N. California)
- ○ EU (Ireland)
- ○ Asia (Tokyo)

Storage information

Amount of data stored (GB) `200`
Duration that data was kept (days) `30`

Retrieval information

Amount of data to retrieve (GB)
Length of time for retrieval (hours, min 4)

Early deletion information

Amount of data to be deleted (GB)
Duration that data was kept (days)

Estimated cost breakdown

Storage Cost	$2.00
Retrieval Cost	$0.00
Deletion Cost	$0.00
Transfer Cost	($0.12)
Total Cost	$1.88

FIGURE 9.11 Calculate monthly storage charge for Glacier.

Retrieval information

Amount of data to retrieve (GB)	20
Length of time for retrieval (hours, min 4)	8

Early deletion information

Amount of data to be deleted (GB)	
Duration that data was kept (days)	

Estimated cost breakdown

Storage Cost	$0.00
Retrieval Cost	$18.00
Deletion Cost	$0.00
Transfer Cost	$2.28
Total Cost	$20.28

FIGURE 9.12 Retrieval costs depend on speed and quantity of data.

Now let's jump the numbers up a bit. Let's assume that I backed up 480GB of data just days before my computer crashed. I don't need all that data back the same day, but I do need it all back...let's say in one business day (eight hours). Look at what happens to the retrieval costs in Figure 9.13. That's right—almost $500 to get all my data back in less than eight hours.

Retrieval information

Amount of data to retrieve (GB)	480
Length of time for retrieval (hours, min 4)	8

Early deletion information

Amount of data to be deleted (GB)	
Duration that data was kept (days)	

Estimated cost breakdown

Storage Cost	$0.00
Retrieval Cost	$432.00
Deletion Cost	$0.00
Transfer Cost	$57.48
Total Cost	$489.48

FIGURE 9.13 A pricey retrieval for a lot of data in a short time period.

Obviously if you can download all 480GB over a weekend or, even better, a full five days, your costs go down, as shown in Figure 9.14.

Retrieval information

Amount of data to retrieve (GB)	480
Length of time for retrieval (hours, min 4)	120

Early deletion information

Amount of data to be deleted (GB)	
Duration that data was kept (days)	

Estimated cost breakdown

Storage Cost	$0.00
Retrieval Cost	$28.80
Deletion Cost	$0.00
Transfer Cost	$57.48
Total Cost	$86.28

FIGURE 9.14 Retrieving all data during a business week.

To back up 480GB will cost $4.80 per month. That's very close to the $5 per month charged by Backblaze, and Backblaze doesn't charge me to retrieve my data like Amazon's Glacier service.

The magic number is 500GB. If you have more than 500GB of data to back up, you're almost better going with a service such as Backblaze. If you have 1TB of data to back up, Amazon will charge you $10 per month, but Backblaze charges you the same $5 per month. Unlimited backups, remember?

So Glacier is definitely a service to consider. You'll certainly save money if you're backing up less than 500GB per month and not ever retrieving it. But with Backblaze (and similar services), not only can you back up an unlimited amount of data, but you won't get dinged when it comes time to retrieve a file or an entire archive.

It's Your Data; Guard It Carefully

Owning an Ultimate iPad means having access to everything—movies, music, books, financial, personal, work, photos...the list goes on. Most of us take our data access for granted, expecting it to just "be there" when we need it. But part of "being there" also means being able to quickly and reliably replace anything that's missing.

It's just as easy to delete files from your iPad as it is from a computer—especially if you have kids that know your iPad password. One accidental tap or pressing the wrong button (Delete instead of Save) and work is gone. A photo deleted. A song purged.

Data storage is just too cheap to take chances. Whether you trust an external hard drive to keep your files where you can see them (well, see the drive, that is) or whether you trust an online backup service to care for your valuable data, the key is to trust something. Make a copy of your files on a backup hard drive, burn them to a DVD or Blu-ray disc, put them in a safe deposit box, give them to a co-worker or family member, or...pay someone else to play caretaker for your information. Either way, you're doing something to help ensure that your Ultimate iPad will remain an Ultimate iPad and offer you access to anything and everything you need—today, tomorrow, and in the years to come.

10

Automation: Video, Appliances, and More

In This Chapter

- Using DropCam for remote live video from your iPad
- Letting WeMo remotely control your home and office
- Automate tasks from your iPad using IFTTT

Many of the tools and services you've learned about in this book will also work on an iPhone. In a pinch, I can use my iPhone to read a book or watch a movie or a dozen other tasks that I normally perform on my iPad. But given a choice between the two, I typically reach for my tablet with its larger screen (and larger onscreen keyboard) and save my iPhone (and its charged battery) for phone calls, texting, and quick checks of emails, among other things.

Over the years I've found more and more tools and tricks I can do with my iPad that have made my work and home life more efficient and even a little more secure. Some of the tools and tricks I'm going to introduce to you in this chapter are a bit difficult to categorize, but I've learned to lump them together under the loose title of "Automation." As you're about to learn, your iPad can do some even more amazing things with the right amount (but not a lot) of setup and testing.

Let's start by seeing what your Ultimate iPad can do for you when it comes to monitoring your home or office.

Video Monitoring with Dropcam

I first discovered Dropcam two years ago at a very popular Consumer Electronics Show (CES). Little did I know that this little camera was going to offer me a number of uses besides the traditional video surveillance.

Take a look at Figure 10.1 and you'll see the basic Dropcam on the left and the Dropcam Pro on the right.

FIGURE 10.1   The Dropcam is a Wi-Fi camera for remote viewing.

NOTE

The basic Dropcam is $150 and the Dropcam Pro is $200, and you'll want to visit www.dropcam.com to compare the technical specs of both if you're interested making a purchase. For the examples in this chapter, I'm using the basic Dropcam.

In a nutshell, the Dropcam uses a Wi-Fi connection to stream live video to an app (for your iPhone or iPad) or to your computer (if you log in to dropcam.com). The Dropcam does require power, so it's not completely wire free. However, as long as it can pick up your home or office's Wi-Fi signal and you have a convenient wall plug, you can place the Dropcam anywhere you like and have a live video stream.

Take a look at Figure 10.2 and you'll see that the Dropcam app is running on my iPad and is capable of displaying video from up to four cameras.

Tap one of the four video streams and the video expands to fill the iPad's screen, as shown in Figure 10.3.

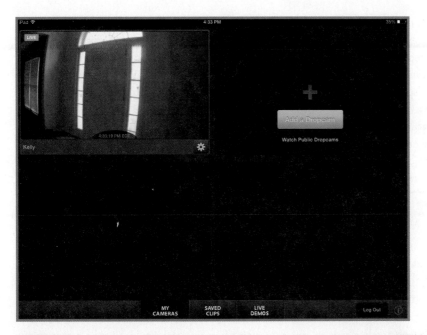

FIGURE 10.2 The iPad app lets you view up to four Dropcam video streams.

Microphone button

Share Photo button

Settings button

FIGURE 10.3 View a Dropcam video stream full screen on your iPad.

The camera has a microphone and speaker, both of which can be turned on or off. If you wish to hear conversations or any other sounds in the area the camera is monitoring, you can increase or decrease the volume or completely turn it off for no-sound viewing. Likewise, the app (or the viewer on your computer's web browser) allows you to turn the microphone on if you wish to speak to someone in the room through the Dropcam's speaker—just tap the Microphone icon shown at the bottom of the screen in Figure 10.3. (My kids both love and hate this feature because I like to set the camera up downstairs where they're playing—hearing Dad's voice telling one of them to stop jumping on the couch and seeing their reaction never gets old.)

NOTE

You can also schedule the Dropcam to turn on and off by itself using a built-in scheduling feature. Multiple schedules can be created, such as Monday–Friday 9 a.m. to 5 p.m., Saturday 10 a.m. to 1 p.m., and Sunday 1 p.m. to 4 p.m.

In addition to viewing the live stream, the app also offers you the ability to take a picture that can be emailed, posted to Facebook, or saved to your iPad's Photo Gallery. Just tap the Share Photo button at the bottom of the screen in Figure 10.3.

The Settings button (the little gear icon) allows you to remotely turn the camera on and off (as long as its plugged into power and has maintained its Wi-Fi connection). Other options in Settings allow you to edit the name of a camera (such as "Room 2B"), enroll in Dropcam's CVR (Cloud Video Recording) service, and enable alerts.

The CVR capability is a subscription service that Dropcam offers that saves the video stream so that it can be reviewed at a later time. Options for this include 7-Day recording (168 hours) with a monthly or annual payment plan ($9.95 for monthly and $99 for yearly) or 30-Day recording (720 hours for $29.95 monthly/$299 yearly). If you've been looking for a video surveillance plan for your home or office, this is definitely one of those options to look at—you won't be saving the video feed to a device in your home or office that could be destroyed or stolen because the recording is kept safely offsite.

One other great feature with the Dropcam is its built-in Alert system. Using the Settings controls, you can configure Dropcam to email you if the camera detects motion, sound, or even is going offline (unplugged or lost Wi-Fi signal), as shown in Figure 10.4.

You configure how you wish to get the alert notifications by logging in to Dropcam.com. (The method for receiving alerts cannot be set from the iPad app.) Options include email and text message on your computer(s) as well as the mobile devices where you install the Dropcam app.

Figure 10.5 shows an example of an alert I received on my iPad when motion was detected by the Dropcam.

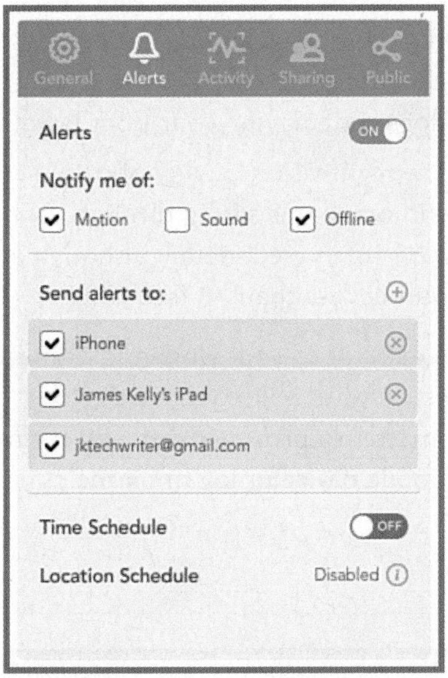

FIGURE 10.4   The Alerts feature will have Dropcam contact you with problems.

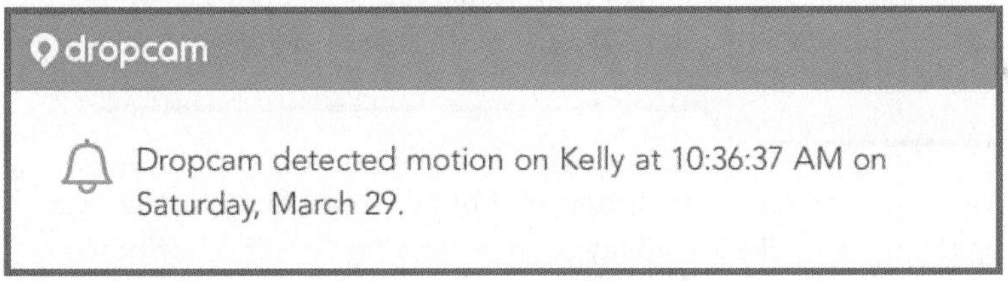

Dropcam detected motion on Kelly at 10:36:37 AM on Saturday, March 29.

FIGURE 10.5   A motion alert sent to my iPad from Dropcam.

Dropcam is a great video surveillance system, but there are a number of useful ways you can use the system from your iPad (or computer or mobile phone):

- **Troubleshooting**—Instead of having my parents try and describe over the phone the error message they're getting on their computer, I have them point their Dropcam at the screen and show me what's going on.

- **Package delivery**—Point the camera out a window at the front lawn and set the Alerts to motion. If you're expecting a delivery, the alert can let you know when someone (most likely the delivery man) approaches your front door. Unfortunately, Dropcam won't sign for packages that require a signature.

- **Nanny cam**—Another traditional use for the Dropcam. The Dropcam isn't disguised as a teddy bear or book, but you can turn off the power light on front (from within Settings) to draw attention away from the camera.

- **Bird (animal) watching**—The Dropcam isn't weatherproof, but you can buy enclosures if you want to mount one outside. You could use this thing to watch the activities in a bird's nest, or maybe to see which of your neighbors' dogs is damaging your front lawn.

- **Nighttime monitoring**—I'm not 100% impressed with the night vision quality of the Dropcam, but it is an option if you want to find out who or what is sifting through your garbage cans during the night. Don't expect faces to show up in great detail, although a baby in a crib shows up perfectly if the Dropcam is mounted less than 10 feet away.

There are so many other uses for the Dropcam that will be relevant to your work and home lifestyle. I have two young boys with grandparents who aren't always able to make the long-distance drives for birthday parties and such. It's a simple matter to provide them with login credentials so they can install the Dropcam app on their mobile device or log in on their computer's web browser and watch the action.

CAUTION

When using the Dropcam to stream any kind of activity, it's often a good idea to alert anyone covered by the video coverage that they're being watched. It's easy to explain to friends and family that someone else is enjoying the gathering and have them all wave and say hi. But definitely let them know—people don't like it when they discover they've unknowingly been on camera.

There are many other Wi-Fi cameras similar to Dropcam, but I've yet to find one that is as easy to set up and configure. If you'd like the ability to monitor a home, office, or other locale and watch the video stream from your iPad, the Dropcam and its app couldn't make it any easier.

But viewing a live video stream is only the start for maintaining control of a home or office setting. As you're about to see, your iPad can be one amazing remote control for a variety of items.

Your iPad as Remote Control—WeMo

Are you one of those people who when they go on vacation they set timers on various lights around the house to make it appear as if someone is home? Or are you the person who arrives first at the office and must get the coffee maker going for that first cup of Go-Juice? Have you ever been driving somewhere and wondered if you left the iron on?

You can probably think of dozens of examples where having the ability to remotely turn an electrical appliance on or off would be nice. I cannot count the number of times that my peace of mind has been maintained because I didn't have to turn the car around to go back when my wife stresses over whether she turned her curling iron off.

How do I do this? Easy. I use a Belkin WeMo device like the one shown in Figure 10.6.

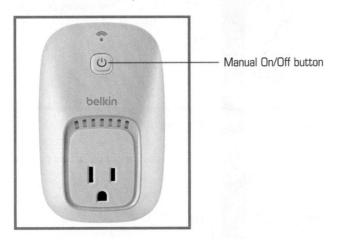

Manual On/Off button

FIGURE 10.6   The Belkin WeMo Switch.

WeMo is a line of products that all communicate with a mobile app via a Wi-Fi connection. Basically, you join a WeMo device to your home or office's Wi-Fi network and then toggle the devices between an On or Off position. Some of the WeMo devices, such as the WeMo Switch, allow you to plug in a simple device—toaster, coffee maker, or lamp—and then supply power to it by toggling the On/Off button from the app shown in Figure 10.7.

NOTE

The WeMo app is an iPhone app, but it will run on an iPad. Although I have it installed on both my iPhone and my iPad, I'm one of those people who always has the iPad handy but not always my iPhone (otherwise I'd most likely just use the WeMo app on the phone).

With the app, a virtual On/Off button appears grayed out if power is not being supplied to a device plugged into the WeMo. If the button is green, power is being supplied. By plugging in my wife's curling iron to a WeMo switch, I can open the app and tell immediately if the curling iron is on or off because the virtual On/Off button for that WeMo Switch will be gray (Off) or green (On). If it is on, I tap the button to turn it off; no need to turn the car around and head back to the house.

Power button. Green means On, gray means Off.

FIGURE 10.7   The WeMo app communicates with WeMo devices.

NOTE

On top of the WeMo Switch is a manual On/Off power button. To properly use an attached appliance, you first turn on its own power switch and then plug it into the WeMo Switch. From that point forward, use the manual On/Off button at the top to turn on the device manually or use the WeMo app. If someone presses the WeMo manual On/Off button and leaves it turned on, when you open the WeMo app, you'll see the WeMo Switch button lit green.

If you have multiple WeMo devices, each device will show up in the app, and you can customize the name of the WeMo device depending on its function. I have two WeMo switches, and I frequently move their location depending on how I wish to use them. Figure 10.7 shows that one is configured to control a living room lamp and another is for my wife's curling iron.

In addition to the simple On/Off functionality, you can also program the devices with a schedule or when certain conditions are met. For example, I could program the living room lamp to turn on every night at 8 p.m. and turn off at 1 a.m. Not only can I continue to turn the lamp on and off with the app, but with the WeMo Switch+Motion shown in Figure 10.8, I can also plug in a motion sensor near the top of the stairs and have it trigger the lamp to turn on so that anyone heading down the stairs at night won't have to fumble in the dark for a light switch.

FIGURE 10.8 The motion sensor comes with the WeMo Switch+Motion product.

Speaking of light switches, you'll want to visit www.belkin.com and browse the complete line of WeMo devices. Believe it or not, the company sells special LED light bulbs with the WeMo hardware built right in—you can see these in Figure 10.9.

That's right—from the WeMo app, you can toggle an LED light bulb on and off. It even has built-in dimmer capability. And just like the WeMo Switch, you can also program the Smart LED Bulb with a timed schedule.

FIGURE 10.9 The WeMo Smart LED Bulb.

The WeMo Smart LED Bulbs are $40 each, so they're probably not an affordable option for every bulb in your house. Fortunately, the WeMo Light Switch shown in Figure 10.10 is another great option to consider.

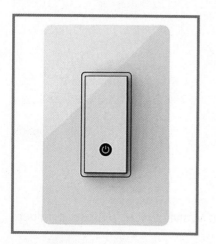

FIGURE 10.10 The WeMo Light Switch.

The WeMo Light Switch replaces an existing wall-mounted light switch and offers you the ability to turn on and off a room's lights from the app. It can also be programmed with a schedule from the WeMo app. (Oh, and it also functions just like a traditional light switch that you can press to turn on and off the lights.)

NOTE

Do you have a room in the house that always has the lights on? You could install a motion-detecting light switch that turns off the lights after a certain amount of time passes. However, the problem is that sometimes it will turn off the lights when someone is in the room and sitting still reading a book, for example. The WeMo Light Switch won't have this problem. I'm going to install one on my son's room (he always leaves his room's lights on) and program it to turn on every day at 6:30 a.m. (wake up) and off at 8 a.m. when I know he's in school.

I've gotten more enjoyment out of the WeMo devices than I ever imagined possible from such a small device. Just knowing when something is turned on and off offers a nice sense of security. I'm slowly but surely adding more WeMo devices to my household and enjoying the ability to both program them with a schedule as well as remotely toggle them with the app.

The Dropcam and the WeMo devices have really made my life easier in many ways, but I'm not done yet. In the next section, I'm going to introduce you to one of my favorite software tools for automating certain activities that saves me time and headache. This tool even works with the WeMo devices, believe it or not, giving me some additional fun and interesting controls as you're about to see.

IFTTT—If This [Happens] Then [Do] That

I absolutely love introducing people to IFTTT. It's short for *If This Then That*, a simple (and free) online service that helps you create automated tasks using the various popular apps you probably already have installed on your iPad. Before you can use IFTTT, however, you'll need to visit www.ifttt.com and create a free account, as shown in Figure 10.11—just click the big blue Join IFTTT button and follow the instructions.

IFTTT   Learn more   Sign in

Put the internet to work for you.

Join IFTTT

FIGURE 10.11 Create a free account with IFTTT.

Before you can understand just how fun and cool IFTTT can be, you need to understand it's four basic concepts:

- **Trigger**—With IFTTT, a Trigger is a condition that is being monitored. Did you get a new email? Did John post a photo on Facebook? Did the temperature in my area drop below 60 degrees Fahrenheit? Did a file get added to Dropbox? Did my WeMo motion sensor get triggered while I was away on vacation? These are all conditions that can be tested for a Yes/No answer or a measurable value (such as the temperature) and can be used to trigger an Action.

- **Action**—IFTTT defines an Action as a single task that will be performed when a Trigger's condition is satisfied. Actions can include sending you an email or turning on a WeMo device or even making a copy of a file and moving it to a particular folder.

- **Recipe**—In IFTTT terminology, a Recipe consists of a Trigger paired with an Action, thus the name: If This [Trigger] Then This [Action]. You can create hundreds of Recipes as well as browse thousands of custom Recipes created by other IFTTT users.

- **Channel**—A Channel is an app or service. With some Channels, you must provide some credentials such as your Gmail address (for the Gmail Channel) or your phone number (for the Phone Number Channel). Other Channels are services such as a temperature/weather-monitoring service (which needs your ZIP code) or even your iPhone's current location (using iOS Location Services.) All this information is kept confidential and is secured by your IFTTT username and password. (So make it a strong password.)

Recipes are associated with your IFTTT account and exist as colorful Channel icons, as you're about to see (along with a helpful title description that you'll provide). Let's take a look at a few examples (created by other IFTTT users) before you learn how to create your own. Figure 10.12 shows a simple Recipe.

FIGURE 10.12   Find a hiding phone with a simple email.

My phone gets left all over the house (and this isn't counting my young son who sometimes picks it up and moves it) and sometimes I just can't find it. This Recipe is simple and breaks down as follows:

If [Trigger – when I search Gmail for X] Then [Action – call my phone]

On the left of the Recipe is the Gmail Channel. On the right is the Phone Call Channel. Channels have one or more possible Triggers that can be turned on. Figure 10.13 shows the Gmail Channel's Trigger and the Phone Call Channel's Action.

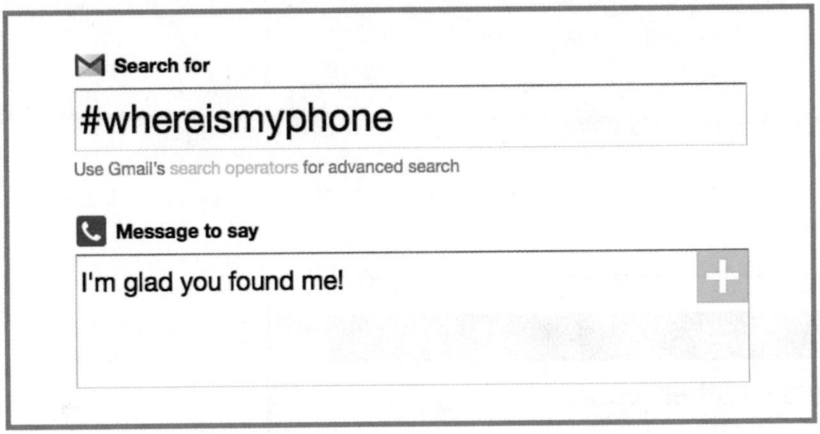

Search for

#whereismyphone

Use Gmail's search operators for advanced search

Message to say

I'm glad you found me!   +

FIGURE 10.13   The Trigger and Action for this Recipe.

> **NOTE**
>
> Click the Phone Call Channel to save your phone number with IFTTT. Likewise, the Gmail Channel will need your Gmail address, and the Facebook Channel will need info on your Facebook account.

As you can see in Figure 10.13, the Gmail Channel has a single Trigger—IFTTT monitors to see if I perform a search of my Gmail account for #whereismyphone. The Phone Call Trigger has a single Action—call my phone so I'll hear it ringing (and say "I'm glad you found me" when I answer it).

Another useful Recipe is shown in Figure 10.14.

I never catch the weather report on TV, and I never really think to check my phone's Weather app until it's too late. Well, with this Recipe I can get tomorrow's weather forecast as a text message at a time I specify.

FIGURE 10.14 Get tomorrow's weather forecast as a text message.

On the left is the Weather Channel and the right is the SMS Channel. A closer look at the Trigger and Action for these Channels is shown in Figure 10.15.

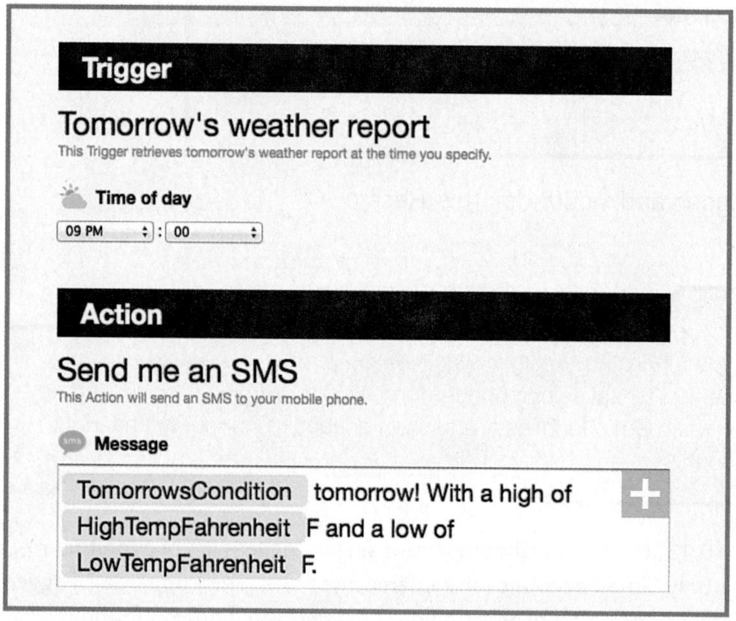

FIGURE 10.15 Trigger and Action for the Text Me Tomorrow's Weather Recipe.

Some channels only offer one Trigger whereas others offer half a dozen or more. (You'll see in a moment how to open a Channel to view all of its available Triggers and Actions.) The same goes for Actions. In this instance, the only Trigger for the Weather Channel is a check for the time. This one checks to see if it's 9 p.m.

If the time is 9 p.m., then the SMS Channel has its Action completed. That Action consists of an SMS message (text message) with some placeholders that will report the High and Low as well as the Condition (rainy, sunny, and so on). The SMS Channel will receive the values for the High, Low, and Condition from the Weather Channel and pass those along in the text message.

If you visit www.ifttt.com and click the Browse button near the top of the screen, you can view thousands of Recipes created by IFTTT users, including Recipes that are trending (popular), recommended (based on Channels you have enabled), and newly added.

But the real power of IFTTT comes when you start to create your own Recipes, and that all starts by clicking the Create button (right next to the Browse button). Do this and you'll see a simple screen guide like the one in Figure 10.16.

FIGURE 10.16 Create your own Recipe by following the IFTTT guide.

This guide is used every time you create a custom Recipe, and it starts by tapping the big blue "this" on the screen. When you tap "this," the screen changes to offer you a scrolling window of Channels (currently at 85, but constantly growing), as shown in Figure 10.17.

It helps if you have an idea of what kind of automated task you wish to create, but if you don't have one, a brief look over all the Channels will often give you an idea.

Let's create two recipes—one will be very simple and the other will involve one of the WeMo devices you learned about in the previous section. For the first recipe, let's see how easy it is to get a text message alert when a particular stock drops below a certain value.

It all begins by tapping the Stocks Channel, and this opens up the screen shown in Figure 10.18.

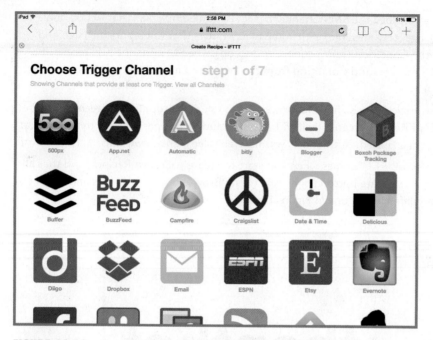

FIGURE 10.17 Scroll down the list to browse all Channels.

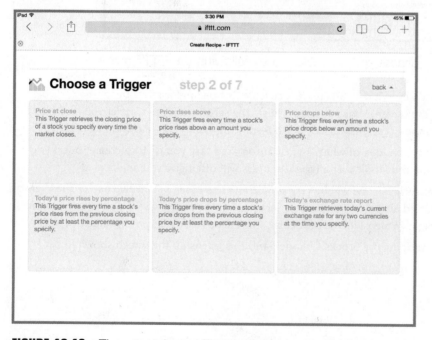

FIGURE 10.18 Time to select a Trigger for my new Recipe.

Six Triggers are available for the Stocks Channel. If we want to know when Apple's stock drops below $500 per share, we'll want to select the "Price drops below" trigger. After tapping on that Trigger, I'm shown a new screen like the one in Figure 10.19.

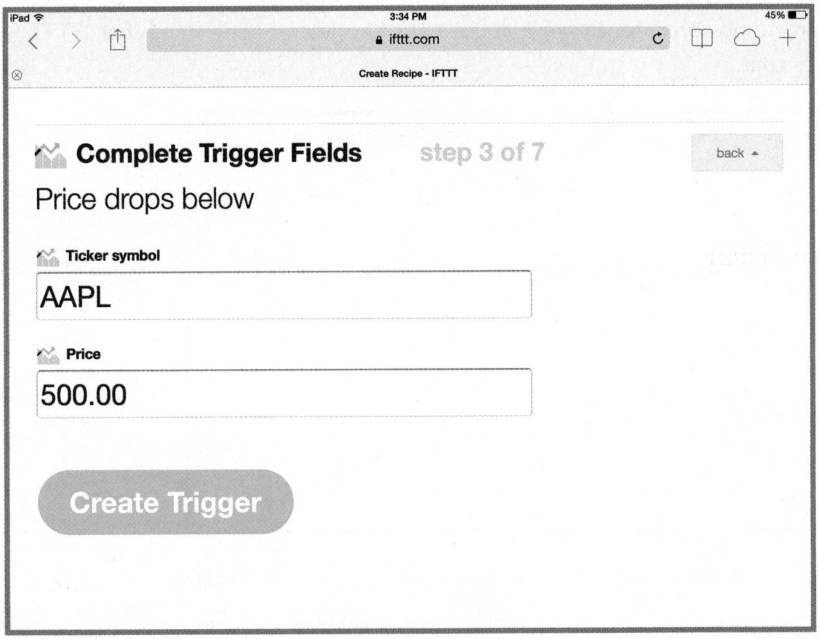

FIGURE 10.19 Select a Trigger and configure it if necessary.

This particular trigger requires the stock symbol for Apple and the price I wish to set for a text message alert. After entering the required details (shown in Figure 10.19), I click the Create Trigger button (step 3 of 7) and then tap the big blue "that" shown in Figure 10.20.

FIGURE 10.20 Half done with creating a new Recipe with IFTTT.

After tapping the "that" link, you're once again given a list of all Channels that will work with the Gmail Channel selected for the Trigger. I want to receive a text message alert, so I'll simply scroll down the list, select the SMS Channel, and I'm given only one possible Action, as shown in Figure 10.21. (If this is your first time using the SMS Channel, you'll be asked to activate it by providing some information about your phone and confirming that IFTTT can send messages to it.)

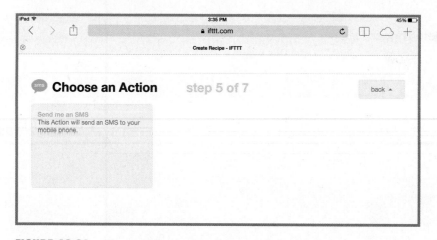

FIGURE 10.21 Choose an Action to associate with your new Recipe.

After you tap the Action, a new screen appears, as shown in Figure 10.22.

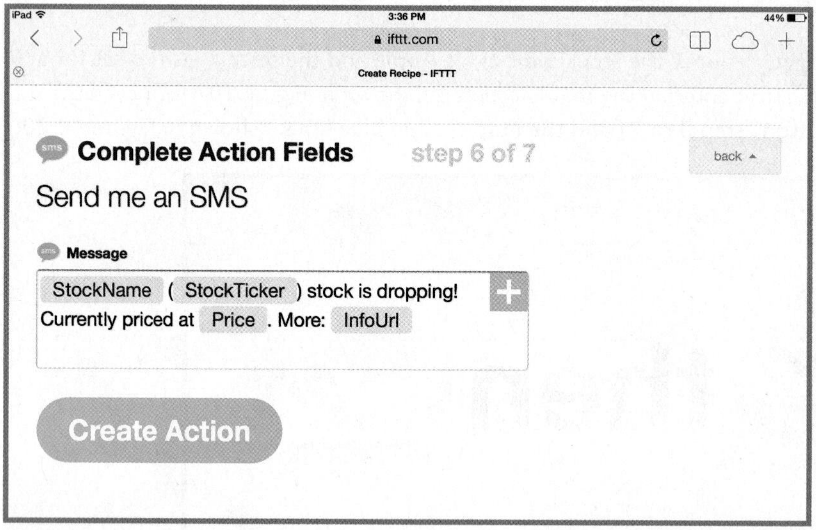

FIGURE 10.22 Configure the Action of your Recipe if necessary.

Each gray button indicates a bit of information that will be provided by another channel. (In this instance, Gmail will provide details such as the Price and SubjectName.)

Next, I tap the Create Action button (for step 6 of 7) and I'm taken to the final screen shown in Figure 10.23, where I can modify the short description if I like.

FIGURE 10.23 Provide a title/description and you're ready to go.

All that's left is to tap the Create Recipe button to create the Recipe, and I'm done.

My new Recipe will be listed on the screen, as shown in Figure 10.24.

I even know it's active and ready to go because the Channel icons are in full color. (If they are grayed out, you have to turn the Recipe on by tapping its Power button.)

Let's do one more just for fun. Let's say my wife goes to the office and then worries she has left the curling iron on. She calls me, but I'm not available. How about a recipe that will allow her to turn off the WeMo Switch (controlling the curling iron) by just sending an email to me with a subject line of "Turn Off Curling Iron"—is that possible? Let's see.

Basically I want to create a recipe that says:

If [email to me from wife with "turn off curling iron" in subject line]

Then [turn WeMo Switch "Curling Iron" off]

FIGURE 10.24 The Recipe is created and ready to go.

I start by tapping the Create button again, tapping the blue "this" to get started, and choosing the Gmail Channel from the scrolling list of Channels. I'm presented with six possible Triggers, as shown in Figure 10.25. (As with the SMS Channel, if this is your first time using the Gmail Channel you'll have to follow the on-screen steps to link your Gmail account to IFTTT.)

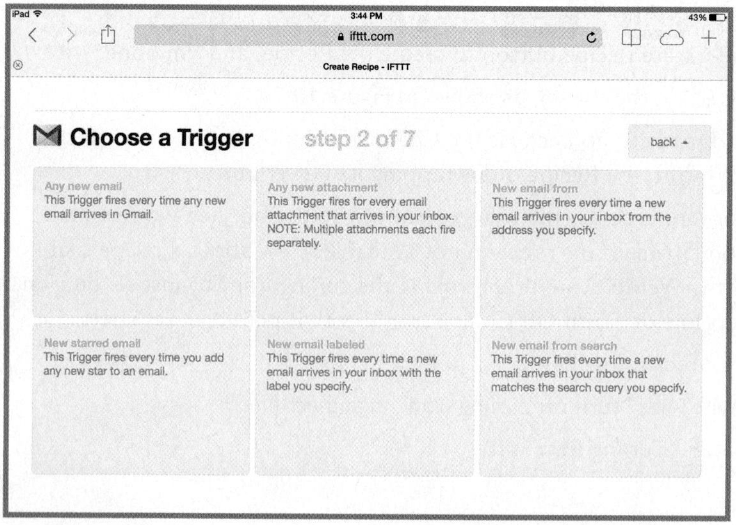

FIGURE 10.25 Select the Gmail Channel for the new Recipe.

There isn't a trigger that works with the Subject line of an email, but there is one that will trigger when a specific Gmail label is detected. That might work, so I'll tap it and I get the screen shown in Figure 10.26.

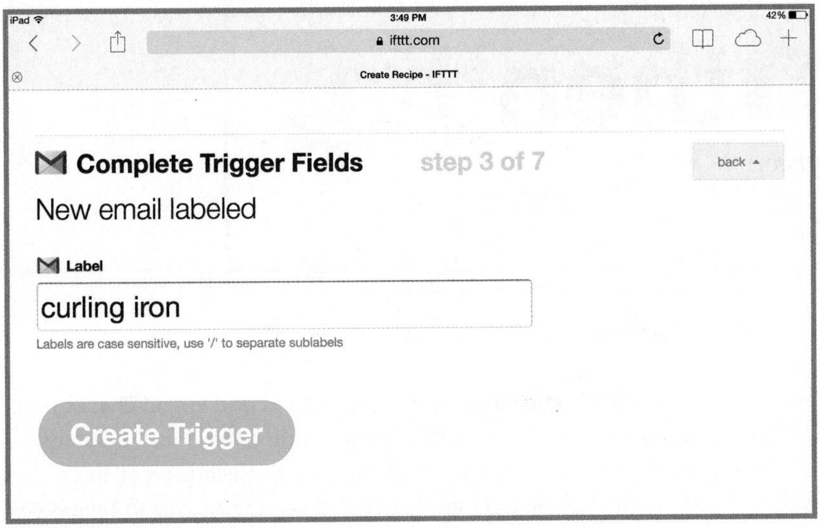

FIGURE 10.26 Specify a label in Gmail for this Trigger.

CAUTION

I've created a label called "curling iron" in Gmail. This required me to also create a rule that checks every incoming email for "curling iron" in the Subject line. Further, I limit it to just checking if the email comes from my wife AND has the "curling iron" words in the Subject line. As you can tell, this particular recipe requires a knowledge of Gmail's labels. If you're not familiar with labels, why not? They're a great way to sort emails. Also, this feature adds a nice color-coded label to each email in your Inbox and other folders. Unfortunately, I don't have the room here to cover labels in detail, so visit https://support.google.com/mail for more information.

After entering the words **curling iron** into the text box, I tap the Create Trigger button and I'm halfway done, as shown in Figure 10.27.

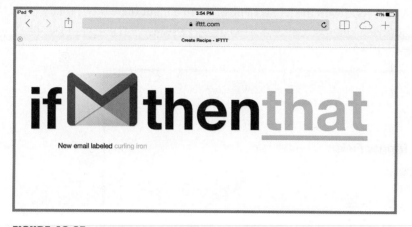

FIGURE 10.27   Half of the "curling iron" Recipe is completed.

Now it's time to create the Action. After the email comes into Gmail and Gmail checks that (1) it's from my wife's email address and (2) it has the words "curling iron" in the Subject line, Gmail automatically adds the "curling iron" label to the email, which is what this IFTTT Recipe is watching and waiting to see happen. When it does, the Action to take is to turn off the WeMo controlling the actual curling iron in our house.

So, I tap the "that" link (shown in Figure 10.27) and scroll down the list and tap the WeMo Switch Channel shown in Figure 10.28.

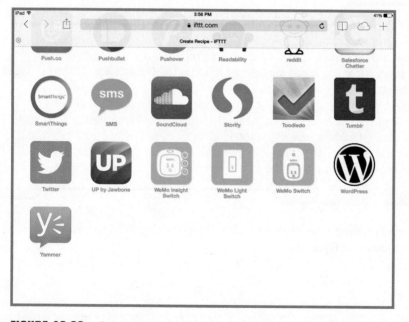

FIGURE 10.28   Select the WeMo Switch Channel to configure the Action.

NOTE

IFTTT requires a PIN from the WeMo app to link to your WeMo devices. The first time you choose a WeMo Channel, you'll be asked to enter this PIN in a special pop-up field on the screen. The PIN can be obtained by opening the WeMo app, tapping the More button (near the bottom of the screen), and tapping the Generate IFTTT PIN. Write down the PIN and enter it in the requested pop-up field.

The WeMo has six actions, as you can see in Figure 10.29.

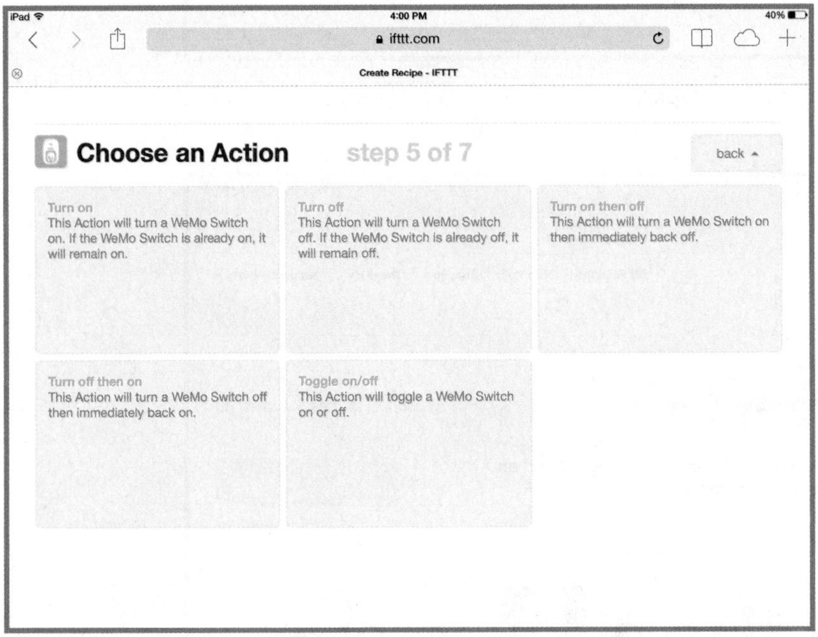

FIGURE 10.29 Choose an Action for your WeMo Switch.

I want my wife to be able to turn off the curling iron if it's turned on. For that reason, I'll select the "Turn off" Action shown in Figure 10.29. If the WeMo providing power to the curling iron is already turned off, her email to me won't accidentally turn it back on. The selected Action will *only* turn off the WeMo.

After tapping the "Turn off" option, I'm asked to specify which of the two WeMo Switch devices to control, as shown in Figure 10.30.

I pick the Curling Iron option from the drop-down menu and tap the Create Action button followed by the Create Recipe button. The Recipe is listed in the My Recipes list, as shown in Figure 10.31.

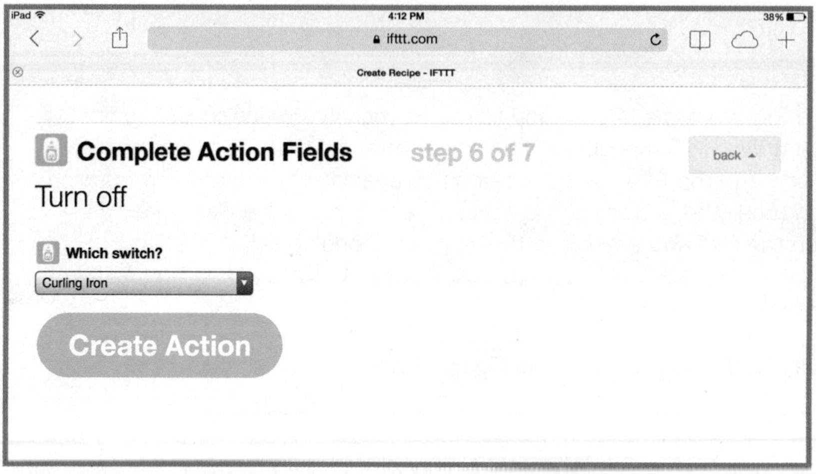

FIGURE 10.30   Select a WeMo Switch or device if you have more than one.

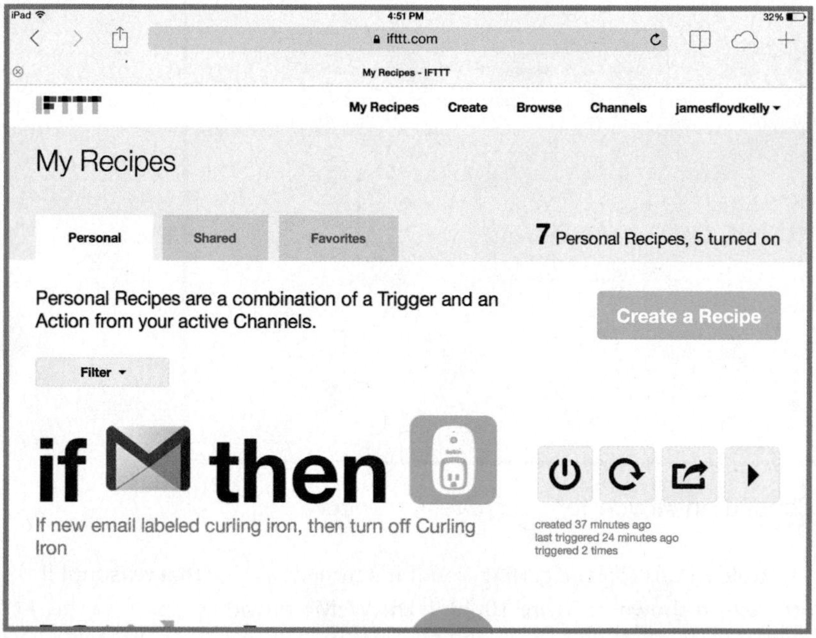

FIGURE 10.31   Control a curling iron with email—amazing.

And guess what? It worked correctly on the first try. Below in Figure 10.32 you'll see the filter (rule) I created to add the "curling iron" label to my wife's incoming message and the actual label applied to the email in my Inbox. (This is also a useful way for me to track how many times she almost burns our house down...not that I would ever mention the grand total in a conversation.)

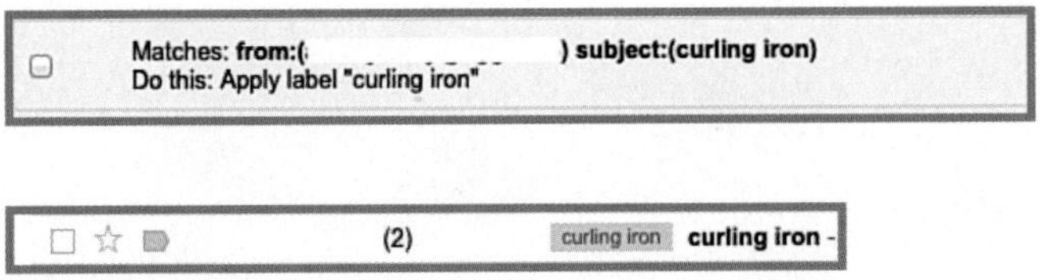

FIGURE 10.32 The filter and the actual email that arrived.

As you can see, IFTTT can do some amazing things. With 85 channels that include many of the services I cover in this book—Dropbox, Evernote, box.com, Google Drive, and Pocket (covered in Chapter 11, "Build a Web Reference Library: Never Lose an Online Article")—you're sure to come up with a few recipes of your own that can help automate some aspect of your home and work life.

If you're coming up short on ideas, click the Browse button to see what other IFTTT users are creating. And the IFTTT blog is always offering up tutorials and notices of new channels that have been added.

Build a Web Reference Library: Never Lose an Online Article

In This Chapter

- Using the Pocket service and app
- Using PrintFriendly.com and PrintWhatYouLike.com
- Using an Evernote Smart Notebook

My Ultimate iPad is my go-to source for accessing just about everything—books, magazines, movies, TV shows, work files, home files, email, personal calendar, Dropbox, book proposals for my publishers (and book chapters for my editors), photos, medical records, and so much more. Over the last few years, I've developed good habits that allow me to make certain that almost anything I might need to access can be reached through my iPad. It has required a bit of planning—creating storage solutions, logical folder structures to hold files, and using OCR as much as possible so that I can quickly search through everything are just a few of the tasks I've had to perform to turn my iPad into what is basically a digital 24/7 personal assistant.

Think about that for a moment—with a living, breathing 24/7 personal assistant (that you trusted, of course), you would expect this person to help you maintain your schedule, check your messages, and perform dozens, maybe even hundreds, of additional tasks. A perfect assistant would help you to never forget an appointment, to never lose an important document, and to never be unprepared.

If you're lucky enough to have a personal assistant, he or she is probably the one who should be reading this book. But if you don't have one (like me), you should always be on the lookout for ways to push your Ultimate iPad to take on more responsibilities.

In this chapter, I want to share with you three work- and home-related obstacles I've encountered since becoming an iPad user and show you how I've used the iPad to get me around them. You're also going to learn about the three tools I've found that have helped me to solve these problems—as a matter of fact, I've already used two of them this morning prior to writing this chapter!

Don't Bookmark It, Pocket It

I do a lot of research online for my book projects as well as my hobbies. I frequently discover online articles or even entire websites that I really need to examine in detail, but I might not have the time at the moment. My typical solution was to just bookmark the website or article and come back to it when I had the time. Sometimes I would discover an online item that I knew wasn't relevant right at the moment, but might be useful months or even a year or more down the road—and I'd bookmark it. I use subfolders to organize my bookmarks, but many users don't; this just creates one long list of bookmarks (sometimes listed in alphabetical order and other times in the order you've added them) that eventually turns into the needle-in-a-haystack conundrum.

Organizing my bookmarks into folders (three examples are Woodworking, Kids Activities, and Book Projects) has helped me to navigate the thousands of URLs I've collected over the years. Yes, I said thousands. I don't like to delete bookmarks, okay? (I found a nice tutorial on creating dovetail joints with my band saw years ago that I swear I'll one day use.) I even created a READ LATER folder to hold bookmarks for me to, well...read later. It works, but I often forget it's tucked into the Bookmarks folder. What I really want is something that's easy to use, fun to use, and that I won't forget about.

NOTE

Some of you may be saying, "But Apple's Safari web browser has that really cool Reading List feature for saving websites to read later." Yes, and it works well...if you use the Safari app. I frequently use a Windows computer and a Chrome or Firefox browser to save bookmarks. I also don't use the Safari browser app on my iPad, favoring another one called Perfect Browser. But if you only use Safari, the Reading List feature is one way to always keep URLs organized for later viewing.

I've already told you I found a solution, so I won't keep you in suspense any longer. It's called Pocket, and it's a really great way to flag websites for later viewing, but it also has a matching (and free) app for the iPad that presents your saved websites in an eye-catching format that might remind you of a catalog or a magazine. Even better—it doesn't even require an Internet connection to access your saved websites. Let me show you how Pocket works.

Pocket works in three ways:

- Save websites from a web browser.
- Save websites from a supported app (on iPhone or iPad).
- Email a link to a special Pocket email address.

Before you can begin using Pocket, however, you need to create a free account. So open a web browser, point it www.getpocket.com, shown in Figure 11.1, and click the Sign Up Now button.

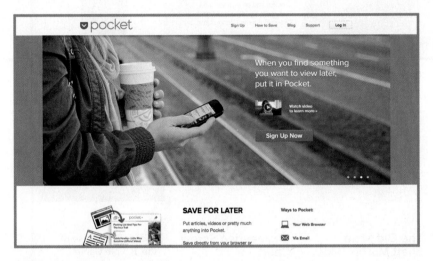

FIGURE 11.1 Create a free account on Pocket.com to get started.

After creating an account, a new window appears to immediately let you install the free Pocket app for your iPad.

Before you learn how to use Pocket, take a look at Figure 11.2 and you'll see an example of how the Pocket app looks when running on the iPad. (It will work in Portrait or Landscape mode.) This is the Pocket home page.

Websites that you save with Pocket will appear with a text header along with some text or image or both. Beneath the text or image will be a shorter version of the URL so you'll know which website it belongs to. To open and read a saved item, just tap it. The item will open full screen and present you with a few options at the top, as shown in Figure 11.3.

Main
Menu
button

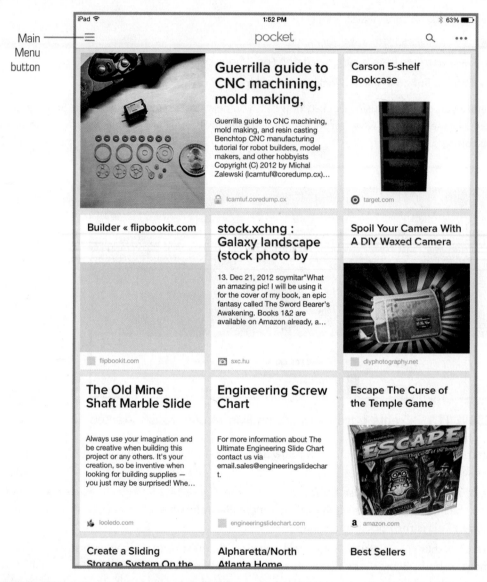

FIGURE 11.2 The Pocket app for iPad.

FIGURE 11.3 Tap a saved website or article in Pocket to open full screen.

Running from left to right across the top of the screen are the Pocket controls:

- **Back**—Takes you back to the previous page. The Pocket app works like a web browser, so tapping a link in the currently viewed page will open that page just as if you were using a browser. The Back button can take you all the way back to the original page—one more tap will return you to the Pocket home page.

- **Read/Archive**—Tap the checkmark if you wish to acknowledge that you've read a website or article. The item will be removed from the Pocket home page, so only tap this button if you're ready to dismiss a saved URL and have it removed from the home page. (You can always view archived URLs by tapping the Main Menu button on Pocket's home page and tapping the Archive option.)

- **Star**—Tapping this button while a saved page is opened will place a star icon in the lower-right corner of the item's box on the Pocket home page.

- **Article View**—Tapping the Article View button will attempt to remove banner ads, menus, and other items, leaving behind only the page's main content. It doesn't always work 100%, but when it does it will remove a large amount of distraction and leave behind only the text and imagery that make up the main focus of the page.

- **Web View**—Tapping the Web View button provides you with exactly what you would see if browsing the page on a standard web browser. Buttons, menus, advertisements, and other features will all appear.

- **Refresh**—If the page contains content that is constantly being updated (such as a weather website that updates the temperature every 30 seconds), the Refresh button can reload the page to display the updated material.

- **Adjust Display**—This button will allow you to increase or decrease the brightness of the screen. If you are using the Content Only button, additional controls will let you increase or decrease the size of the text displayed as well as switch between serif and sans-serif font.

- **Share**—The Share button will allow you to send the URL and page's content to a variety of final destinations that include box.com, Twitter, Facebook, Evernote, Safari, and more.

While on the Pocket home page, you can press and hold an item for two seconds until it's highlighted yellow. Tap and hold additional items and those will be selected (in yellow) as well; you can also tap a highlighted item to turn off the highlight if necessary. Figure 11.4 shows two items selected.

By selecting multiple items at once, you enter the Bulk Edit stage and can perform tasks such as tapping the Checkmark icon to archive all selected items at once or "Star" all selected items. (You can also enter the Bulk Edit stage by tapping the three dots in the upper-right corner of the screen; a menu appears that offers Bulk Edit plus the ability to switch between List View and Tile View.)

Two additional icons shown in Figure 11.4 are the Delete button (to delete all selected items; this cannot be undone) and the Add Tags button, which will let you select from keywords found on the pages. Click the New button shown in Figure 11.5 to create a new keyword.

Delete button   Add Tags button

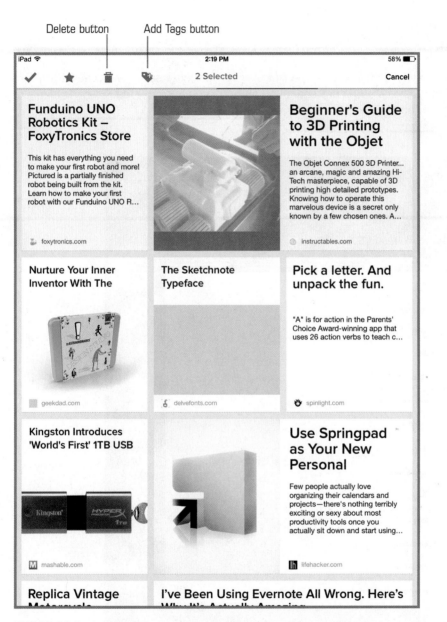

FIGURE 11.4 Bulk select items from the Pocket home page.

NOTE

When in Tile View, you can also swipe from left to right on a saved webpage to gain access to some of the same buttons found elsewhere in Pocket—Tag, Star, Read/Archive, Trash, and Share.

iPad 🔋   2:23 PM   57% 🔋

✓   ★   🗑   🎴   2 Selected   Cancel

Funduino UNO Robotics Kit – FoxyTronics Store

This kit has everything you need to make your first robot and more! Pictured is a p...
robot being bu...
Learn how to r...
robot with our ...

foxytronics....

Beginner's Guide to 3D Printing with the Objet

The Objet Connex 500 3D Printer...
...amazing Hi-
...pable of 3D
...prototypes.
...ate this
...secret only
...en ones. A...

Close	Add Tags	New

ALL TAGS

3d printing

3dp

123d

extraordinaires

fonts

games

ibooks author

inventor

lego book

macsparky

publisher

robot summer camp

Nurture Yo... r. And Inventor V... fun.

...e Parents'
...ng app that
...s to teach c...

geekdad.co...

Kingston ... ...jpad 'World's Fi... ...w

...ove
...dars and
projects—there's nothing terribly
exciting or sexy about most
productivity tools once you
actually sit down and start using...

Ⓜ mashable.com   lifehacker.com

Replica Vintage   **I've Been Using Evernote All Wrong. Here's**

FIGURE 11.5   Add keyword tags to your saved URLs for easier searches.

Using tags/keywords, you can use the Search button on the Pocket home page to filter the saved pages to display only those that match up to your keyword(s). It's a very helpful feature when your Pocket collection of saved websites and articles starts to reach into the hundreds or even thousands—you won't have to scroll down the page looking for that one particular URL you can't remember but you know you flagged it with the "painting" tag.

TIP

Pocket works almost the same on a computer's web browser in terms of opening/viewing, sorting, and adding tags, but each individual URL block has its own Checkmark (to archive), Star, Delete, and Share buttons.

But how do you get a web page or article into Pocket in the first place? There are a lot of ways to do this, so let's start with adding a URL while you're using your iPad. There are two methods to do this.

Copy a URL to the Clipboard

If you have an open browser on your iPad, simply tap the URL (typically at the top of the browser screen) to select it, and then tap again and choose the Copy option. (To copy a link embedded in a webpage, simply tap and hold the link—a window appears with a Copy option.)

Next, open up the Pocket app and look near the bottom right of the screen. You'll see an Add button like the one in Figure 11.6—tap the button if you wish to add the URL to Pocket+.

Email the URL to Pocket

If you have an email account created and set up to use the Mail app on your iPad, all you have to do is paste the URL into the body of an email. In the TO: field, enter add@getpocket.com. No subject is required. This method does require that the email address you are using match the address you provided when creating your Pocket account.

NOTE

There is a third option to add URLs to Pocket from your iPad, but it uses the Safari Mobile app and requires a few steps to install. Tap the Pocket Main Menu button, then Help, and then the How to Save option. Scroll down and read the "From Mobile Safari" section to enable this feature.

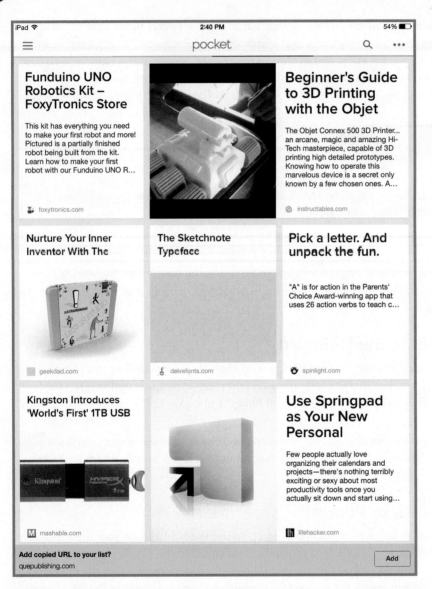

FIGURE 11.6 Save a URL to the iPad's clipboard and let Pocket import it.

I'm not always finding URLs that I wish to save while using my iPad; most often, I'm on a computer. For computer web browsers, there are two methods that Pocket offers to users to save URLs; you can use one or both, it doesn't matter because they are identical in how they work. Point your web browser to https://getpocket.com/add/, shown in Figure 11.7, and follow the instructions, which will vary depending on your choice of web browser.

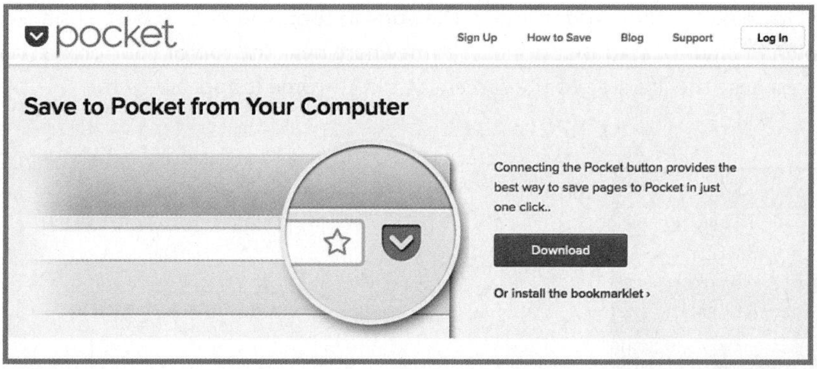

FIGURE 11.7 Install a special add-on or toolbar button to save URLs to Pocket.

If you choose to add the bookmarklet, a button similar to the one shown in Figure 11.8 will appear on the toolbar running along the top edge of the screen when your browser is open.

FIGURE 11.8 The bookmarklet lets you quickly add a page to Pocket.

When viewing a page in the browser window that you wish to save, click the bookmarklet button and you'll see a pop-up window appear like the one in Figure 11.9—add tags if you like by clicking the Add Tags button.

FIGURE 11.9 Add tags to a saved page by clicking the bookmarklet button.

If you clicked the Download button and installed the add-on tool, you'll see a button similar to the one shown in Figure 11.10 that appears somewhere near the top of your browser. (In Safari, it's placed near the left side of the screen, but in Chrome it appears to the far right.)

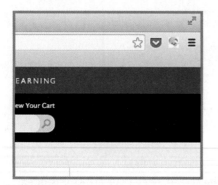

FIGURE 11.10   The Pocket button also lets you save a URL with one click.

The Add-On button works identically to the bookmarklet, briefly flashing a message on the screen to let you know the URL is saved and offering you an "Add Tags" button, if you like, as shown previously in Figure 11.9.

In addition to these methods, there are over 300 apps that can save directly to Pocket—consult the Help option in the iPad app for more details.

TIP

Keep in mind that any app that has a Share button that lists the Mail app among the options can be used to send a link to Pocket. Just use the add@getpocket.com address and you're in business.

With Pocket running on your computer's web browser and the Pocket app on your iPad, you'll have an eye-catching and easy-to-use tool for catching up on your saved web pages and online articles. The Pocket app will synch with your Pocket account every time it is opened, downloading the latest saved URLs so you can even read them when an Internet connection isn't available.

CAUTION

Videos will not be available when offline, only text and images. Also, you can use your iPad's Settings app to configure whether the Pocket app can download using cellular data or Wi-Fi only.

After you review a website or read an article of interest, a single tap will easily archive a saved item, removing it from your reading list. But what if you'd like to save the content of a web page or article long term? With the Internet, you honestly never know if something will be there next year (or even next week).

You've probably experienced the dreaded 404 Error (missing web page) you get when you click a bookmark or return to a web page you haven't visited in some time. Websites change, information gets moved around or archived, and entire articles can disappear without any notice. Fortunately, there are tools available for ensuring any information you find online can be kept long term.

Convert Online Content to PDF

Have you ever found an interesting recipe on the Internet that you bookmarked so you could return later to try it out? If not a recipe, maybe a set of instructions for a hobby you enjoy? Or maybe just an inspirational article that you wanted to keep for a child or to maybe use later in a speech? How would you feel if you returned later—a week, a month, maybe even a year or more—only to find that web page gone?

It's happened to me more than I care to remember, and a few years back I made it a point to find a solution that would guarantee I never lost something from a website again.

Pocket is useful for storing web content that you wish to revisit later, but even Pocket can't guarantee your saved websites will be there for you when you choose to read them; even its ability to store offline content is susceptible because Pocket synchronizes occasionally with all the URLs it saves. If a page is deleted or replaced with other information, it will eventually be deleted or replaced within Pocket.

So, what's the solution? The answer is to grab the content immediately and save it offline so that you know you'll be able to access for years. And there are a couple of ways to do this.

Most web browsers have the ability to save an entire web page for offline viewing, but this solution typically saves all the text and images and links and such as an HTML file in a folder on your computer. When you double-click the HTML file, it opens up in your browser and presents it just as if you were looking at the original web page. It's not a bad solution, but it's not perfect.

Software exists that can download an entire website's content in one swoop. The problem here is that you often get a lot of stuff you don't need. And although some applications will let you specify a single page to grab, you also tend to get all the extras with it—banners, advertisements, menus, logos, sidebars, and other items. Again, it's a solution, but not perfect.

What's the perfect solution, then? A perfect solution would be one that would allow you to select exactly what content you wish to pull from a website and nothing more. Furthermore, that solution would allow you to save it in a format that you could read on your Ultimate iPad whenever you need it.

In the section, you'll find examples of two services that are as close to the perfect solution for saving online content to an offline format. Use one or both of these, and you'll never have to worry about losing access to something important you found online again.

PrintFriendly.com

I browse websites from both my computer and my iPad (and sometimes my phone). Let's say for the moment that I'm browsing on my iPad and I find an interesting article that I really want to keep but I'm not wanting to keep all the other "stuff" floating around the article. Figure 11.11 shows an article I wish to keep, but notice that it's surrounded by a logo and menus at the top and a sidebar with some books for sale on the right.

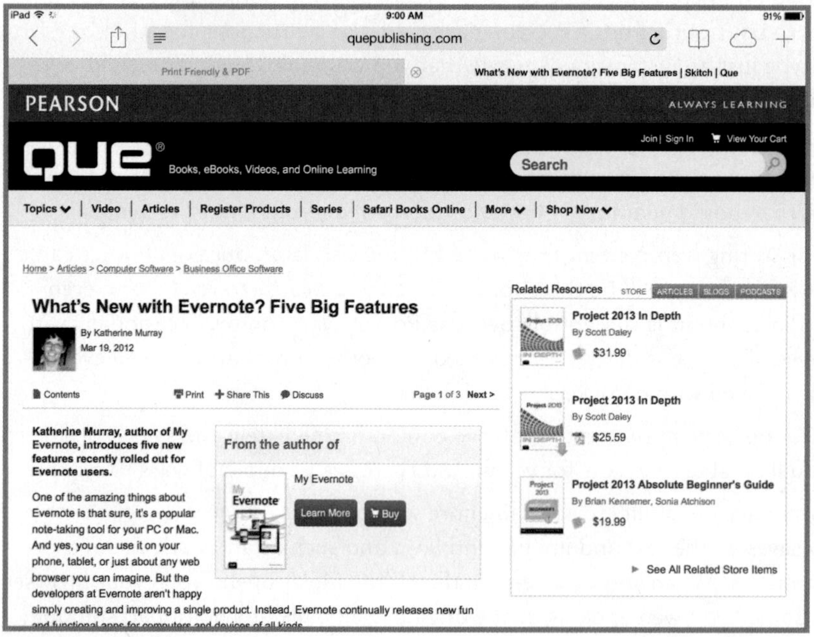

FIGURE 11.11 I want to save this article minus all the other "stuff."

When I find an article like this (or some other online content) that I wish to keep, I immediately open up a new browser tab and point it to www.printfriendly.com, shown in Figure 11.12.

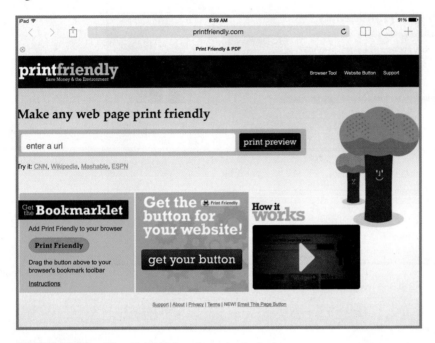

FIGURE 11.12 The PrintFriendly.com website.

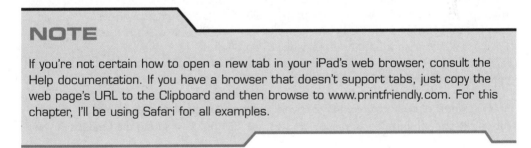

NOTE

If you're not certain how to open a new tab in your iPad's web browser, consult the Help documentation. If you have a browser that doesn't support tabs, just copy the web page's URL to the Clipboard and then browse to www.printfriendly.com. For this chapter, I'll be using Safari for all examples.

PrintFriendly.com has this nice, big box where you can copy and paste the URL, as I've done in Figure 11.13.

FIGURE 11.13 Paste a web page's URL into the text box.

TIP

To copy an entire URL in Safari, all you have to do is tap inside the URL box near the top. The entire URL will be highlighted (selected). Simply tap once more on the selected URL and tap Copy to put the URL in the Clipboard. Then return to PrintFriendly.com and tap in the box labeled "enter a url" and select Paste.

Tap the Print Preview button and PrintFriendly.com will attempt to pull out the main content on the page (minus logos, menus, and so on). Figure 11.14 shows the final result. Not bad.

Print button   PDF button   Email button   Text Size menu   Undo button

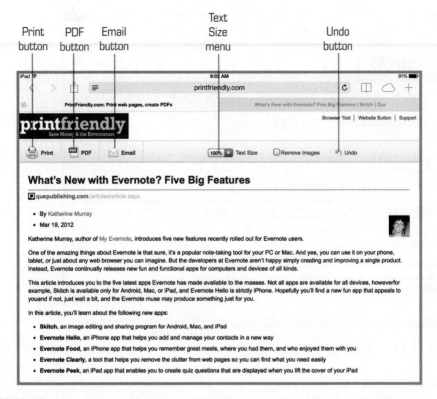

FIGURE 11.14 The web page is simplified to just text and a few images.

Sometimes PrintFriendly.com gets it right the first time. Other times, you may have some stragglers (such as a menu or an advertisement). This is not a problem. By tapping near the start of any line of text or on an image, you can delete the tapped item. If you make a mistake, simply tap the Undo button once and try again. Notice in Figure 11.15 that I've deleted the two bullet items (the By line and the date) as well as the single image to the right. You can also place a checkmark in the Remove Images check box to immediately remove all images. And, finally, you can adjust the font size using the Text Size drop-down menu.

After cleaning up the page, it's time to save it. If you have a printer that supports the Apple AirPrint service, you can tap the Print button to get a paper copy. You can also email yourself a copy by tapping the Email button. But I'm wanting to save this to a PDF file, so I'll click the PDF button. A screen appears like the one in Figure 11.16. Tap the Download Your PDF button.

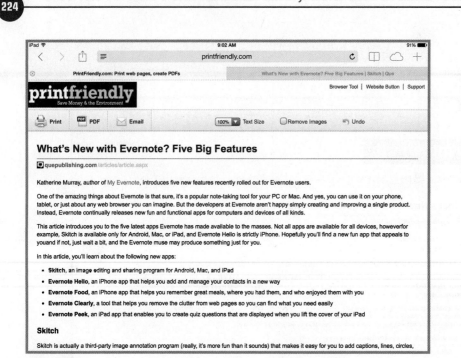

FIGURE 11.15 Clean up the web page by deleting any unwanted text or images.

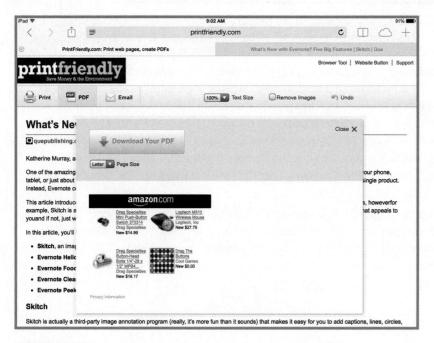

FIGURE 11.16 Convert your saved web page to a PDF.

After you tap Download Your PDF, your saved PDF will open in the Safari app, as shown in Figure 11.17.

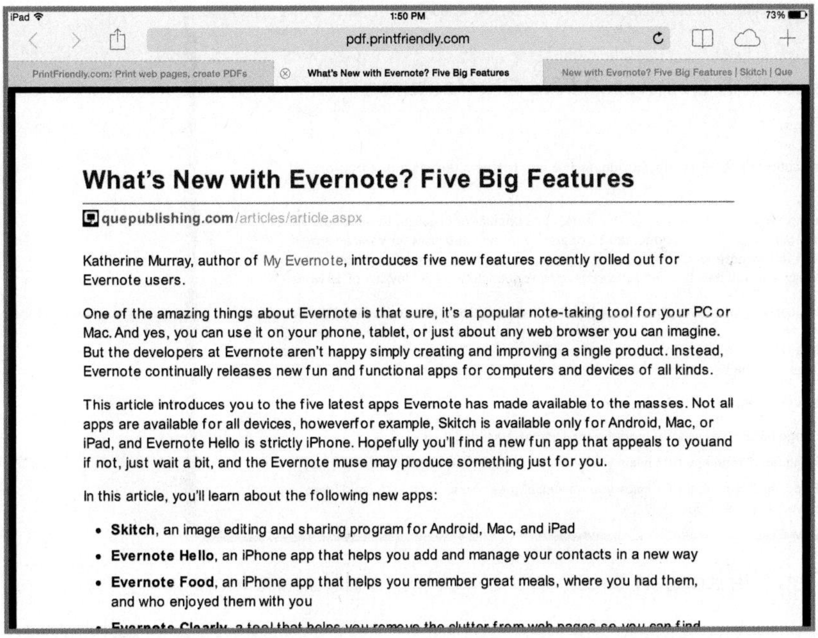

FIGURE 11.17 Your saved PDF will be displayed within Safari.

While viewing the saved PDF, tap anywhere on the open page and a small menu will appear near the top, as shown in Figure 11.18.

CAUTION

If you're using a browser other than Safari, the steps to save the PDF to another app or to a service such as Dropbox may be different. Consult your browser's Help documentation for instructions on how and where downloads are saved by the browser.

Tap the "Open in" option (shown in Figure 11.18) and a side-scrolling list of apps will appear, as shown in Figure 11.19. I like to save to Dropbox, but you could just as easily send the saved PDF to Evernote, GoodReader, or any other app you prefer.

FIGURE 11.18   Tap the screen to save the PDF to a different location.

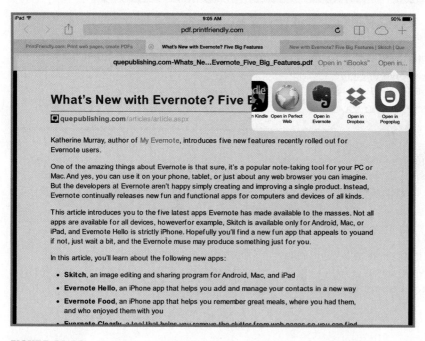

FIGURE 11.19   Select an app that will receive the saved PDF.

As you can see in Figure 11.20, the PDF is now safe in my Dropbox folder and can even be viewed and read by selecting it. (I'll move it to a more specific folder later.)

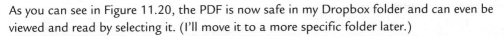

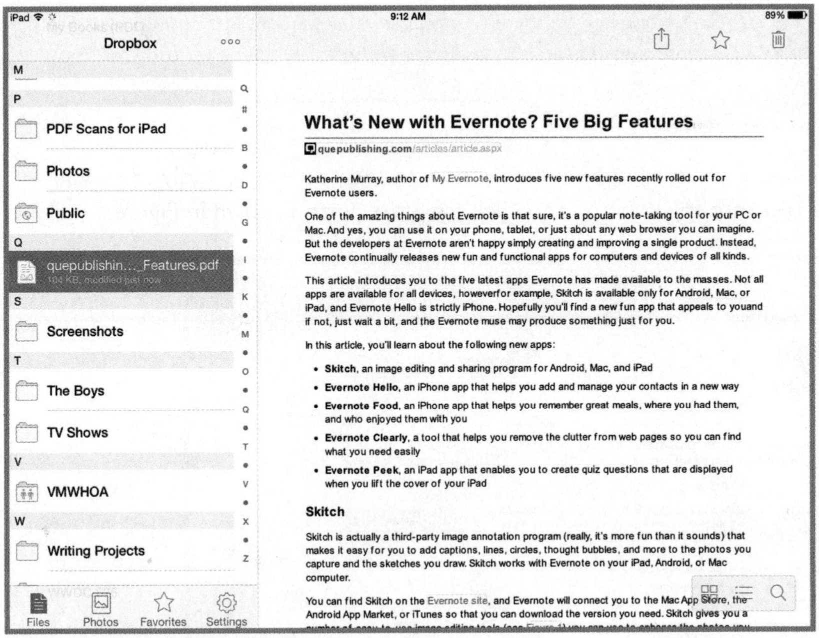

FIGURE 11.20   View your saved PDF from within Dropbox.

PrintFriendly.com is a great way to immediately save online content you discover while browsing with your iPad, but it does have some limitations. It's not always accurate in what it chooses to keep and discard, so you'll always want to read over the content to make certain nothing has been deleted.

For those times when I need a bit more fine control over the final look and layout of the saved PDF, I turn to a slightly more advanced tool called PrintWhatYouLike.com.

PrintWhatYouLike.com

Both the PrintFriendly.com and PrintWhatYouLike.com websites were designed as a way for people to use less paper when printing out content from an website. It's a great idea, and by eliminating advertisements and menus and banners and such, users can certainly save paper by printing only what they need from a web page. Fortunately, both of these websites support saving to PDF files, so Ultimate iPad owners can benefit from these tools, too.

NOTE

PrintWhatYouLike.com doesn't work well on the iPad because it uses a series of pop-up windows for editing a web page, and these pop-ups aren't supported by Safari or any other browser that I've found.

The PrintWhatYouLike.com tool works in much the same way as PrintFriendly.com—you copy and paste a URL into the text box and click the Start button shown in Figure 11.21.

FIGURE 11.21   Use PrintWhatYouLike.com for more fine-tuning of a web page edit.

Unlike PrintFriendly.com, the PrintWhatYouLike.com service doesn't try to guess what you will and won't want in the final cleaned-up page. Figure 11.22 shows that the article I'm wanting to save has been opened and includes all the extra stuff—menus, logos, search bar, and so on. The only difference is the toolbar running down the left side of the screen.

The PrintWhatYouLike.com service has more features than I have room to cover in this chapter, but I am going to show you how to do the basic editing of a web page so you can save it to a PDF. I encourage you to play around with all the buttons and click the Help link for assistance if you need it.

PrintWhatYouLike.com treats just about anything you see on the screen as an editable object. If you move your mouse pointer over something as small as the Next button indicated in Figure 11.23, you'll see a red box appear around it.

FIGURE 11.22   Your URL opens looking identical to the original.

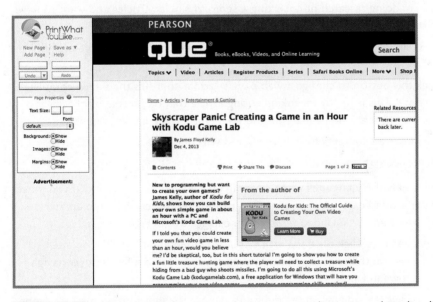

FIGURE 11.23   Hover your mouse pointer over an item to select it with a red box.

After an item is surrounded by a red box, left-click and a small menu will appear, like the one in Figure 11.24.

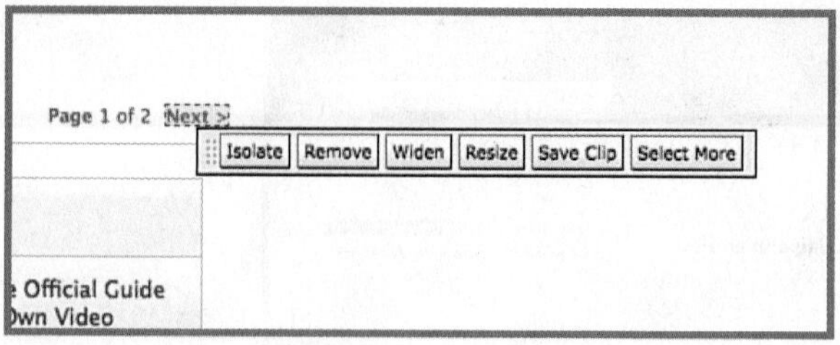

FIGURE 11.24 Use the pop-up menu to edit the item.

Moving from right to left, the buttons work as follows:

- **Select More**—This will slightly enlarge the red box surrounding an object. Once you click the Select More button, a matching Select Less button will appear to let you shrink the box. This is useful for fine-tuning the removal of items such as menu buttons, icons, and more.

- **Save Clip**—Clicking this button will save the selected item (anything inside the red box) for later use. You can collect clips and then save them to a single PDF; this is a useful feature if you're doing research or collecting a series of similar articles and want to have them all in one document.

- **Resize**—Select an icon or photo or other image and you'll be able to enlarge or shrink the item.

- **Widen**—Click this button to change a web page's format so it fills the screen completely from left to right. This is handy for taking a long article that requires a lot of scrolling down due to large left and right margins and forcing it to take up fewer pages.

- **Remove**—Removes all contents from within a red selection box.

- **Isolate**—Deletes everything outside of the red selection box.

The Isolate tool is one of my favorites when cleaning up web articles for saving. If you move the mouse pointer around carefully, you can often cause a red selection box to appear around just the article and its included figures. You can see this in Figure 11.25.

Now all that's needed is to click once the article is surrounded and then click Isolate. Almost everything else on the page is gone except for my article and a few leftover navigation controls, as shown in Figure 11.26.

All that's left is to click the sidebar on the right and remove the individual components one at a time.

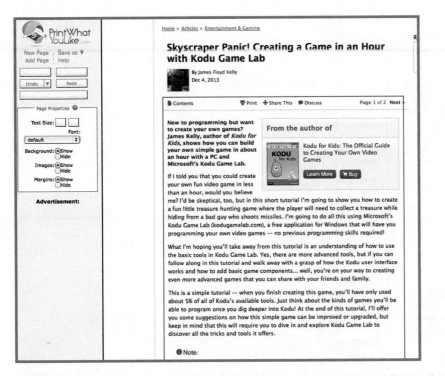

FIGURE 11.25 Try to get a red selection box to surround only what you wish to keep.

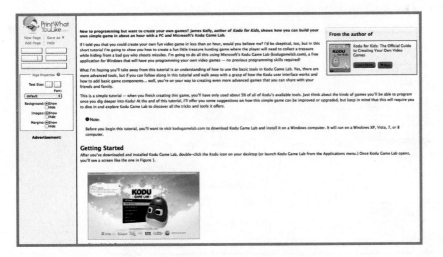

FIGURE 11.26 Use the Isolate tool to remove everything else.

Once you're satisfied with the content's final look and layout, it's time to save it as a PDF. Click the Print button on the left-side toolbar shown in Figure 11.27.

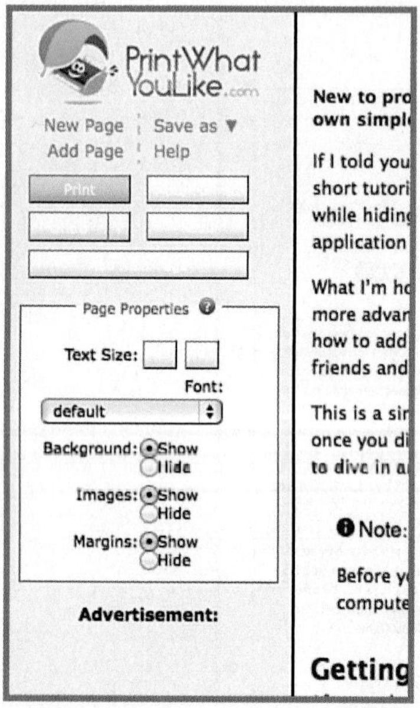

FIGURE 11.27 Click the Print button to save the content.

If you're using a Mac, click the PDF button that appears in Figure 11.28. Select the Save as PDF option, name the document, select its destination, and you're done.

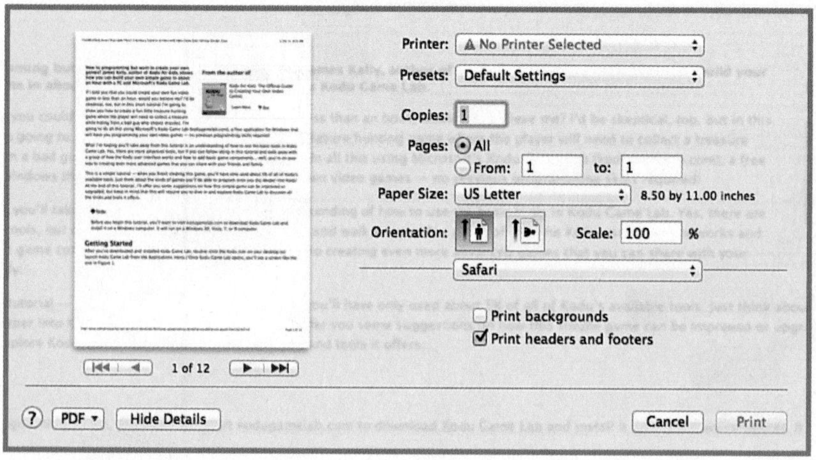

FIGURE 11.28 Select the PDF option.

For Windows users, unfortunately, saving to PDF will require downloading a free add-on such as PDFCreator (www.pdfforge.org) or a similar service that will allow Windows to save print jobs as PDF files.

PrintFriendly.com and PrintWhatYouLike.com are two services I cannot do without. I save a lot of content off of the Internet, and I prefer that it be as clean and clutter free as possible. These two tools allow me to remove advertisements, menus, and so much more, leaving behind only the text and the images that I want to include in my final saved PDF file.

After I create my PDF files, all that's left to do is save them to Dropbox or my Pogoplug-connected hard drive, and they'll always be there should I need them. (And if I save them to my paid Evernote account, the PDFs are also scanned and become keyword searchable.)

Between my desktop scanner, the Pocket app, PrintFriendly.com, and PrintWhatYouLike. com, you'd think that I would have covered just about every aspect of getting content into my Ultimate iPad...but not quite. What's left? Let me show you.

Notes and Sketches Straight into Evernote

With a camera or a scanner, it's easy to just take a photo of a hand sketch or a written note and send it to Dropbox or Evernote. As a matter of fact, I do this quite a bit—I do a bit of woodworking here and there, and I also tend to collect and modify schematics for electronic circuits. Both of these hobbies often have me sketching or drawing items on paper along with measurements and other values. I used to do these sketches on plain paper, but not anymore. A couple of years ago I discovered Evernote's Notebook system, shown in Figure 11.29, and now everything has changed.

FIGURE 11.29 Evernote's Notebook system.

NOTE

An Evernote Notebook can be purchased from the Evernote Market by visiting http://bit.ly/ QLaBhO. Notebooks run between $11.95 and $32.95 depending on the size and format. Notebook sizes are small to large, blank or ruled pages, and paper or hardback covers. All notebooks come with a code for three months of Evernote Premium service; existing Premium customers will have their subscription extended by three months.

In a nutshell, anything you write or draw in an Evernote Notebook can be photographed using your iPhone or iPad's camera and the free Evernote app. The Evernote app scans the page and converts any text it finds to searchable text. Also, special colored stickers that come with the notebooks can be configured to send the scans directly into certain notebooks. I use the green stickers to send photo-scans directly into a Woodworking notebook in Evernote and yellow stickers to send photo-scans into an Electronics notebook.

NOTE

To assign a custom notebook to a particular sticker, open the Evernote app on your iPad to the home screen, tap your name in the upper-left corner to open the Settings screen, and then tap the General option. Under General, tap Camera, followed by Moleskine Notebook, and then tap an icon (each icon has a unique color) and pick the notebook you wish to link to that sticker. Now, any time you stick one of the colored stickers on a page and take a photo with the Evernote app, the photo-scan will automatically drop into its matching notebook.

In Figure 11.30, you'll notice that I've opened the Evernote app and the toolbar appears along the top left of the screen.

Tap the Camera icon to start the photo-scan process. Evernote's camera tool will open (it differs slightly from the standard iPad Camera app) and you must select from one of the four options at the bottom that include Post-It Note, Photo, Document, and Business Card.

Here's the really cool thing about Evernote—it will scan a Post-It Note, a document (text or even handwriting), or a business card and make all text it discovers searchable. Based on your selection, a box will appear on the screen to help guide you in properly fitting an item for scanning.

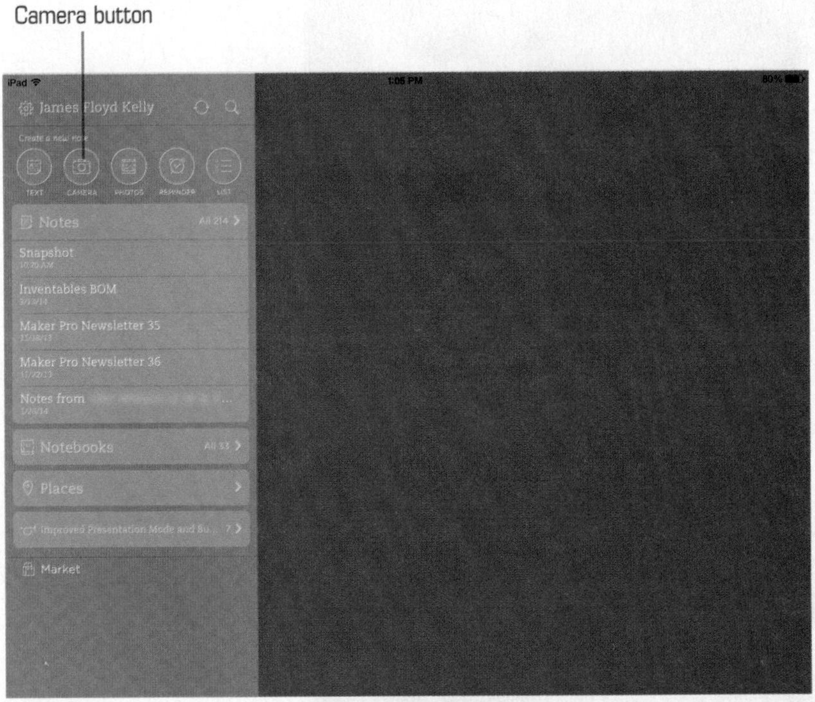

Camera button

FIGURE 11.30 The Evernote app toolbar.

For example, if you're scanning a Post-It Note, tap the Post-It Note option and the screen will display a perfectly square area, as shown in Figure 11.31.

After taking the photo, tap the checkmark in the lower-right corner (to indicate you're done taking photos) and the note will appear in your default notebook, as shown in Figure 11.32. Notice that even though the text was written on a blue Post-It Note, the Evernote app scanned only the text and then placed it on a yellow Post-It Note background!

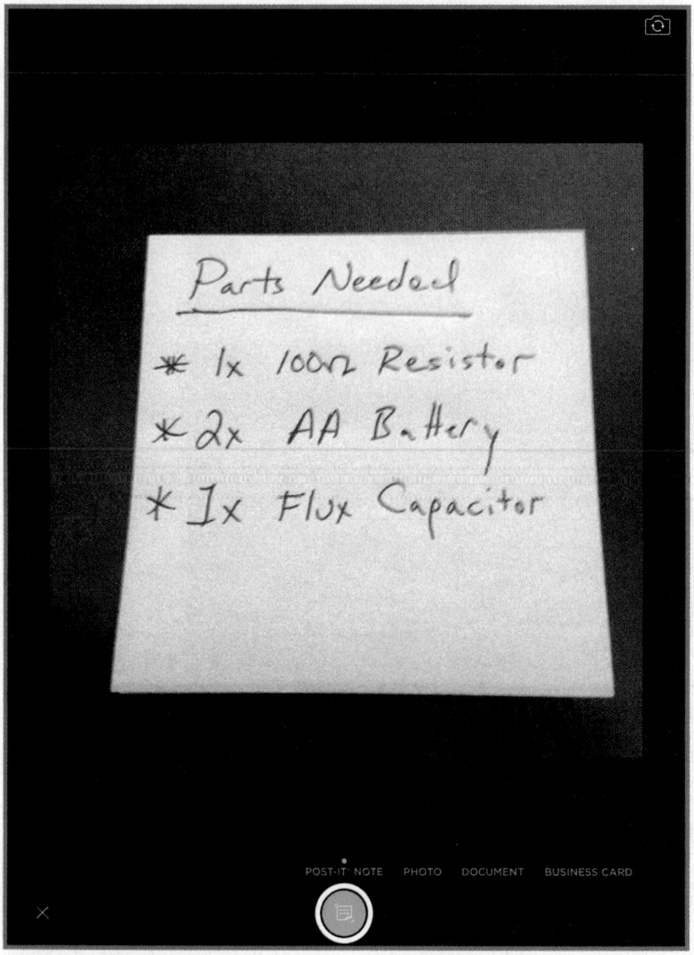

FIGURE 11.31 Evernote can convert Post-It Notes to a searchable note.

Using the Evernote Notebook system, the process is almost identical. Figure 11.33 shows that I'm preparing to take a photo of a sketch I made for some furniture placement along with dimensions. I've also placed a green sticker on the page that tells Evernote to file this photo-scan into my Woodworking notebook.

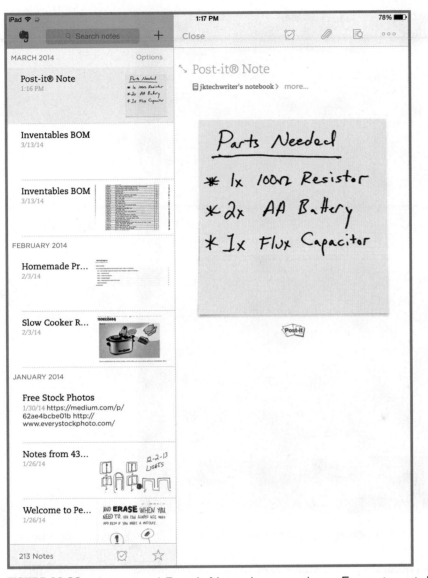

FIGURE 11.32 A scanned Post-It Note shows up in an Evernote notebook.

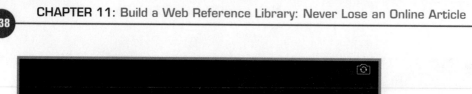
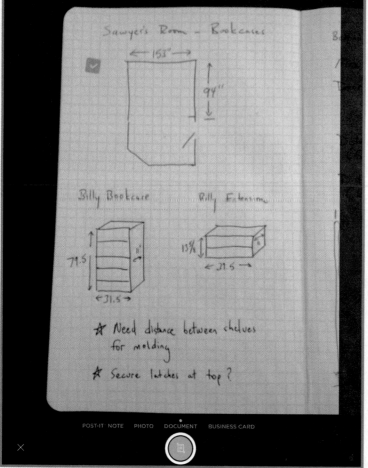

FIGURE 11.33   Take a photo of a sketch or text written in an Evernote notebook.

After I take the photo, the page is scanned, converted, and displayed in the Evernote app, as shown in Figure 11.34.

There are a few things you should take note of in Figure 11.34. First, notice that I used the Search box in the upper-left corner of the app to search for all documents containing the word "Bookcase." On the left side of the screen will be a list of all notes in my Evernote account that contain that word. If I tap one, the note will appear on the right side of the screen with the keyword(s) highlighted. Finally, notice that this particular note is stored in the Woodworking notebook, just as I expected it to be because I used the green Smart Sticker.

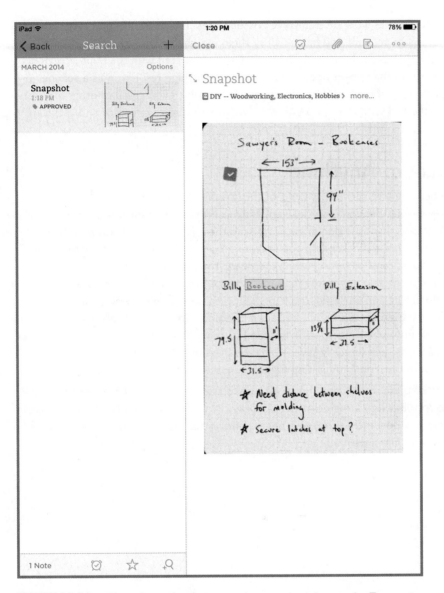

FIGURE 11.34 The photo is converted to a saved note in Evernote.

As you can see, using the Evernote app offers up a variety of methods for storing and accessing your important documents. You could create a notebook called "Tax Documents" and assign that notebook to the purple Smart Sticker. From that point forward, all you have to do is stick a purple Smart Sticker on the document, take a photo of it with the Evernote app, and know that your bill is being backed up to Evernote. What's more, you'll be able to search the Tax Documents notebook using keywords any time you like.

Brainstorming sessions at work often involve Post-It Notes. Imagine collecting every Post-It Note in your Evernote account and having all of them searchable with keywords. And if you lack a personal or desktop scanner, Evernote has you covered with the built-in scanning capabilities from the app—it doesn't support the same high resolution as a scanner, and it can't do front and back at the same time, but in a pinch you could photograph every document you like and send them straight into Evernote for future reference and archiving purposes.

Never. Lose. Anything.

I hope you're beginning to see that any mix of the various tools covered in this book can be used to help ensure that you never lose anything important. A scanner is a great and powerful way to take any loose documents and scan them in and make them searchable via keywords. Services such as Pocket help you save and store away web pages for later reading, and also support tags for finding what you need. Tools such as PrintFriendly.com and PrintWhatYouLike.com help guarantee that anything you find online that you absolutely must have in the future can be saved and kept safe, even if the original web content goes away. And with the Evernote app, you can use an Evernote Notebook to capture your notes and file them instantly away into specific notebooks using Smart Stickers. And Post-It Notes and business cards are just as easily saved using the Evernote app's camera scanner feature that can make both text and handwriting fully searchable.

Using any or all of these tools, combined with a solid backup plan (refer back to Chapter 9, "Don't Forget Your Backup: Long-Term Deep Storage"), will give you peace of mind because you'll know that any documentation, web page, handwritten note, or anything else will be accessible from your Ultimate iPad.

12

"Plays Well with Others": Remote Control and an Extra Screen

In This Chapter

- Control remote computers easily with your iPad
- Get some additional screen space for your laptop or desktop computer

The iPad continues to develop as a product, with new features and tools added with each new version. There are many iPad owners who use their iPad almost exclusively; these folks have very little need (or no need) for a laptop or desktop computer. As a matter of fact, many believe Apple has a desire to reduce the number of non-iPad computers it sells and to develop the iPad as an all-in-one solution. If anything, I'm hoping this book has convinced you that you can do a lot of things with an iPad that you would have done traditionally on a laptop or desktop computer.

People still use laptops and desktop computers, however, and that's not looking like it's going to change any time soon. I still use a laptop to write my chapters—the version of Microsoft Word I use offers me more tools and features than any word processing app I've found yet, and I keep a Windows desktop computer handy for games and the occasional book I write that covers software only available for Windows. In a nutshell, my Ultimate iPad can do a lot of things—but not *everything*. Yet.

Your Ultimate iPad brings so many things right to you on that screen—books, movies, music, games, email, Internet, and much more. But interestingly enough, your iPad can also bring access to your other computers as well. You're about to learn about some special software that will let you take control of any or all of your other computers using your iPad's touchscreen. And should you find yourself needing to use a laptop or desktop computer, you're also about to see just how easy it is to use your iPad for additional screen space.

Remotely Control Computers and Laptops

A few months ago, I got a call from my wife who was at home with my oldest son. I had installed *Minecraft* on my Windows computer for him to play, and he was having difficulty getting the game to open. It's a bit finicky to open and log in, and I tried to walk her through the few steps to get it working. But if you've ever tried to offer tech support over a phone, you know it's not so easy when you're not seeing what the other person sees on the screen.

I wasn't home, but I did have my iPad with me and an Internet connection. I also had a very special piece of software installed on my desktop computer called TeamViewer and a matching TeamViewer app installed on my iPad.

Using the TeamViewer app, I was able to connect to the desktop computer and see the Windows desktop screen. My son watched as the mouse cursor on the screen magically moved on its own, opening the Minecraft app, clicking the right set of buttons, logging in with a username and password, and finally launching the right saved game. Call me Super-Dad.

NOTE

I continue to find new and interesting uses for TeamViewer, and the most recent need for it was editing a photo that was stored on my 3TB hard drive. I could access and view that photo with the Pogoplug app on my iPad, but in this instance I needed to open the photo with a specialty app and perform some special cropping and editing on it that I couldn't do with any of my iPad apps. I was able to make the needed edits and then, as you'll see shortly, grab the edited photo and email it from my iPad.

TeamViewer is amazing. First, it's free for noncommercial use. (If you're just using it for personal needs, both the computer software and the iPad app are free to use as much as you like.) Second, it works on both Windows and Mac. And, third, it has a high level of built-in security that will help guard against anyone trying to access your computer(s) without permission.

To download the free version to your computer, open a web browser to www.teamviewer.com and click the big green Download button shown in Figure 12.1.

The installation of the software is different for Windows and Macs, so just follow the instructions carefully to install. For Windows computers, at one point you'll see a screen like the one in Figure 12.2.

FIGURE 12.1 Grab the free TeamViewer software for your computer.

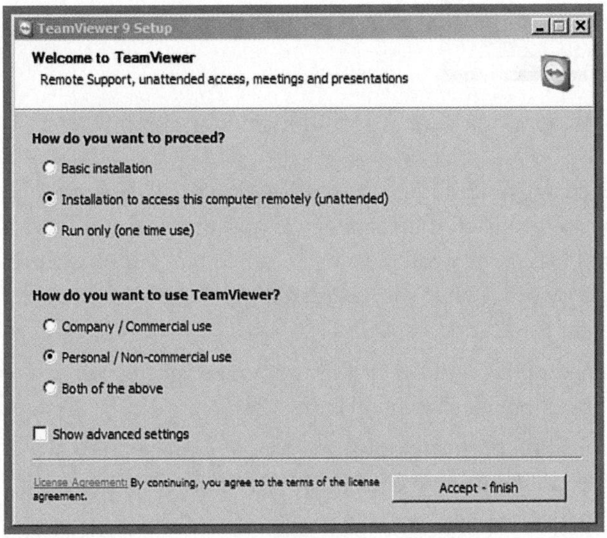

FIGURE 12.2 TeamViewer setup menu.

Notice in Figure 12.2 that the first section asks "How do you want to proceed?" followed by three options. You're going to want to select the second option labeled "Installation to access this computer remotely (unattended)" and also select the Personal/Non-Commercial Use option for the section asking "How do you want to use TeamViewer?"

For Mac users, you won't be asked this question; instead, the software simply installs and configures itself for unattended access automatically.

In both instances, you'll reach a point in the software installation where you'll be asked to provide a password, as shown in Figure 12.3.

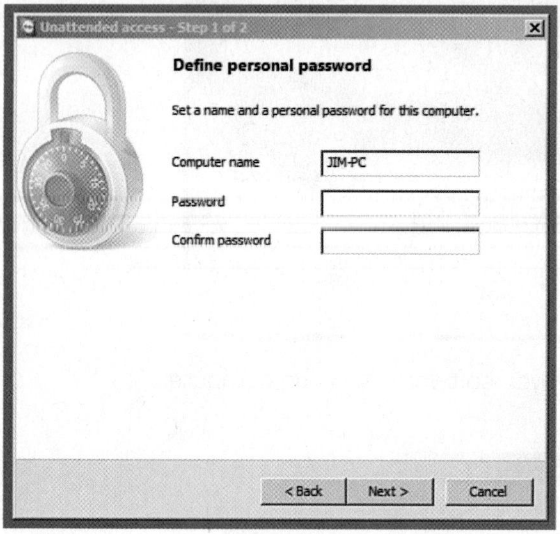

FIGURE 12.3   Create a strong password for your TeamViewer installation.

You'll want to make this password as strong and unique as possible; don't risk using an easy password that might allow someone to install the TeamViewer app on their own iPad and then use it to access your personal files. When you're using TeamViewer, this password will be referred to as your "Personal Password." After you've created the Personal Password, the software will finish installing.

The TeamViewer software can be opened on a Windows or Mac computer, giving you access to the TeamViewer Remote Control panel, shown in Figure 12.4.

The Remote Control panel looks identical on both Windows and Mac computers. For accessing a computer with your iPad, you'll be using the information displayed in the Your ID and Password sections, indicated in Figure 12.4.

Your ID

Password

Personal
Password

FIGURE 12.4   The TeamViewer Remote Control panel.

NOTE

You can use the Personal Password you created as well, but I don't recommend it. The User ID and Password sections include information that can be provided to anyone with an iPad and the TeamViewer app; this means a spouse could be given access or a work colleague. There's simply no need to use your Personal Password when accessing a computer via iPad; save this Personal Password for logging in to the Team Viewer application and making changes to settings.

You'll want to consult the TeamViewer documentation for information on the other sections of the Remote Control panel. You'll find details relating to accessing other computers (instead of from your iPad) as well as a database of contacts that can be used to hold access information for other TeamViewer users and their computers. For the purposes of this chapter, however, we're only interested in the Your ID and Password information that will be used by the matching iPad app.

The information in the Your ID section contains a nine-digit number that is unique to the computer the TeamViewer software is installed on. The nine-digit number I see when opening the TeamViewer Remote Control panel on my Windows desktop is different from the one I see on my Mac laptop. The same goes for the Password.

On a Mac, if you two-finger tap (or right-click) on the Password, you'll see a small menu appear, as shown in Figure 12.5. For Windows users, hover your mouse over the Password section and you'll see a small Refresh symbol appear to the left of the Password—click it to see the same small menu shown in Figure 12.5.

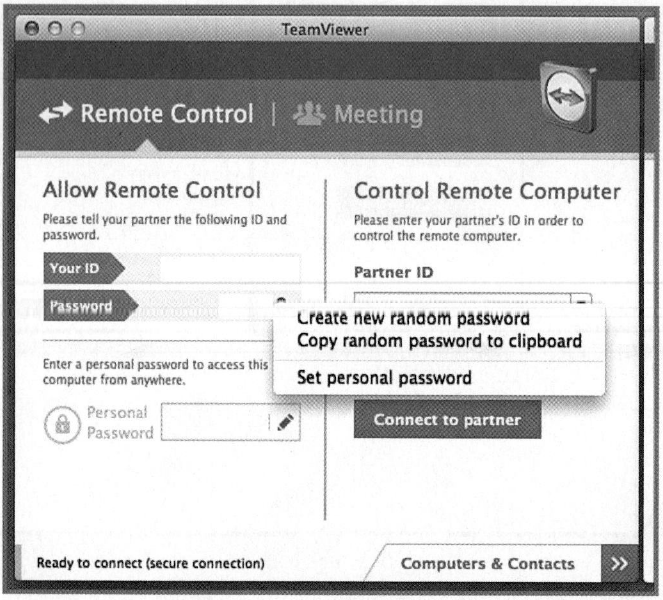

FIGURE 12.5 Options for the Your ID Password are available.

From this small menu, you can click "Create new random password" to change the current password or click "Copy random password to clipboard" to both change the password and place a copy of the text on the Clipboard. The "Set personal password" option allows you to replace the random password with the Personal Password you created during the installation of the software. (You can also change the Personal Password by typing in a new one in the Personal Password text box.)

TIP

If you wish to give someone access to your desktop (for troubleshooting purposes, for example), creating a new random password would give them one-time access from an iPad running the TeamViewer app or a computer running the TeamViewer application. You'll need to remember to go back into TeamViewer and create a new random password if you wish to block an individual from using the Remote Control access again.

Once you've got the Your ID and Password information handy, it's time to install the iPad app. Browse the App Store for the app TeamViewer: Remote Control, shown in Figure 12.6.

FIGURE 12.6   Install the free TeamViewer: Remote Control app.

After installing the app, you'll see a screen like the one in Figure 12.7.

Type in the "Your ID" information found on either a Windows or Mac Remote Control panel and click the Remote Control button. Enter the Password when requested.

TIP

The first time you use the TeamViewer app, the connection will be made, but instead of seeing the Windows or Mac screen, you'll first be given a page of instructions for using the app that show you how to tap to click, how to tap and hold to emulate a right-click, and how to double-tap to emulate selecting a group of files. Click the Continue button to proceed to the remote control of your desktop.

Figure 12.8 shows what I see on my iPad's screen when accessing my Windows desktop computer. (Yes, I keep a tidy Windows desktop.)

FIGURE 12.7 Enter the "Your ID" information in the box.

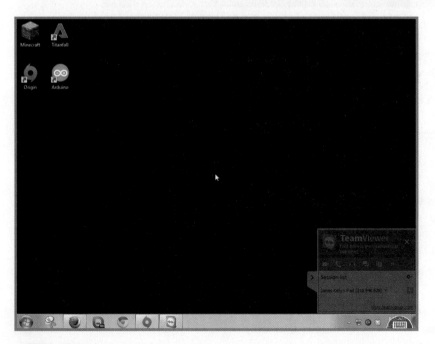

FIGURE 12.8 Accessing a Windows desktop from the iPad.

It takes a minute or so to get used to the interface. You're probably used to dragging a mouse so that the mouse pointer moves across the screen to an icon. But with TeamViewer: Remote Control, you simply tap an icon to move the mouse pointer to that icon; dragging your finger over the iPad's touchscreen will cause a selection box to appear on both screens (iPad and Windows), as shown in Figure 12.9.

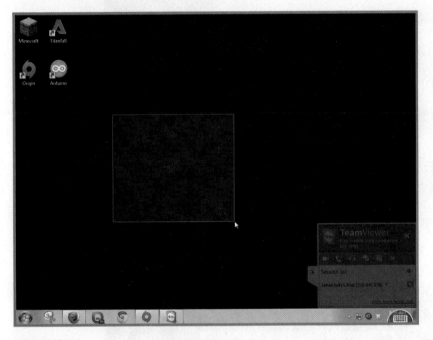

FIGURE 12.9 Dragging a finger on the iPad's screen performs a selection.

To open an application on a Windows desktop or laptop computer, tap the icon on the desktop to move the mouse pointer on top of the icon. Likewise, to click the Start button on a Windows computer, you must first tap the Start button (from your iPad) to move the mouse cursor to that location. A double-tap is then needed to open an application. (A single tap is needed to open the Start button.) I've opened an application on my desktop computer by double-tapping its icon, and that application is now displayed on my iPad's screen (see Figure 12.10).

Dragging a window around the screen is as easy as tapping and holding on the open window or application and moving it to the desired location. Menus, buttons, and more can be used, as shown in Figure 12.11.

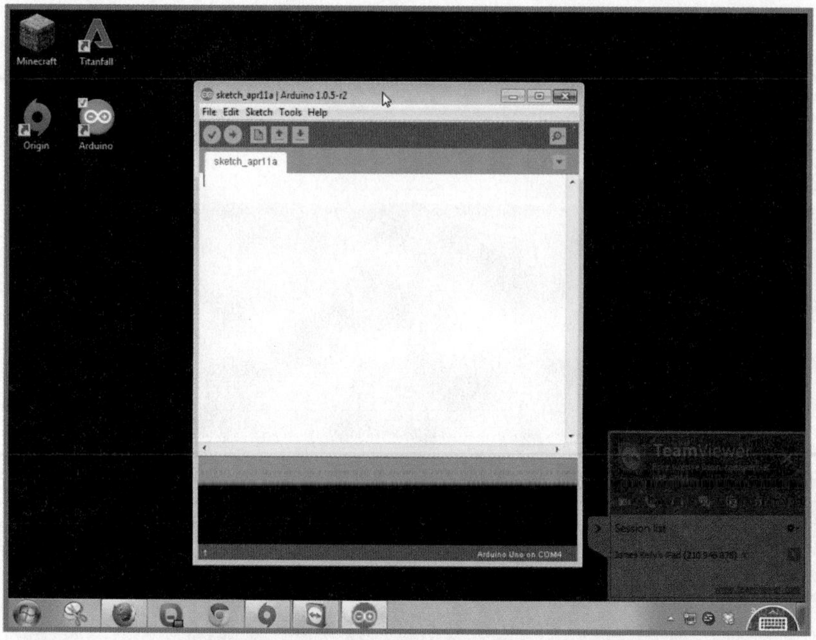

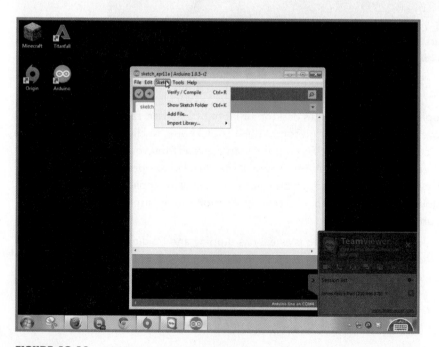

FIGURE 12.10 Applications open on the iPad's screen.

FIGURE 12.11 Menus and other features can be accessed by tapping.

TIP

If someone is sitting at the computer (while an iPad user is using TeamViewer to remotely control that computer), that person will see the mouse pointer move quickly and windows will open on the screen as if by magic. If that same person was to use a mouse or touch pad to close the app, the iPad user would see the app closing on the iPad's screen. The TeamViewer app does not prevent anyone from actually using the computer it is remotely controlling.

Should you find you need to enter text in a text box or an application, tap the small keyboard icon located in the lower-right corner of the TeamViewer app, and a set of buttons will appear along the bottom edge of the screen, as shown in Figure 12.12.

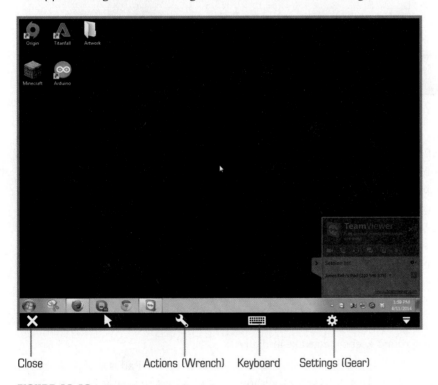

Close   Actions (Wrench)   Keyboard   Settings (Gear)

FIGURE 12.12 Other control options appear on this menu.

You'll see that there's a keyboard icon that provides you with the iPad's onscreen keyboard, as shown in Figure 12.13.

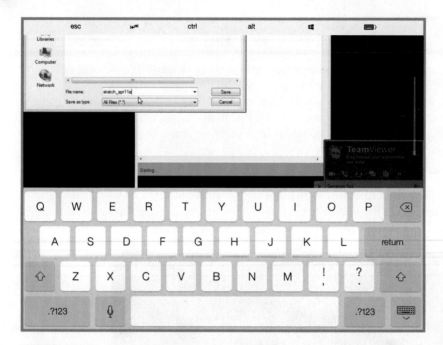

FIGURE 12.13 You can use the iPad's keyboard to enter text.

The menu also provides additional TeamViewer controls:

- **Close**—The big X will cut your connection to the remote computer. Use this to cut the connection but leave the TeamViewer: Remote Control app open and running.

- **Actions**—The Wrench icon allows you to remotely lock the computer and even reboot it. Choose the "Disable remote input" option, and anyone sitting at the computer won't be able to use the mouse or keyboard. (Tapping the Wrench icon again will offer a "Enable remote input" option to once again allow someone to control the computer.)

- **Settings**—The Gear icon provides you with customizable options while using your iPad to remotely control a computer.

As you can see in Figure 12.14, I also use the TeamViewer app to access my Mac laptop. (That orange background keeps me awake and alert.)

Although controlling the applications on my laptop and desktop via iPad is useful, that's not the only way I use the TeamViewer app. Although I do my best to keep my files stored either in Dropbox or on my 3TB hard drive that's available via the Pogoplug app, that's not always the case. Sometimes I forget to move a file from my laptop's hard drive to Dropbox. Sometimes my wife transfers photos to my desktop computer. There are a dozen reasons why a file might be sitting on my laptop or desktop and not in Dropbox where I can easily access it. When that happens, TeamViewer comes to the rescue.

FIGURE 12.14   Controlling my Mac laptop from my iPad.

Take a look back at Figure 12.12 and you'll see that I have a folder on the Windows desktop labeled Artwork.

Inside that folder is a drawing my oldest son made for me. I double-tap the folder to open it, and there's the drawing that I'd really like to copy to my iPad, as shown in Figure 12.15.

All I have to do is tap-and-hold on the file—this is interpreted as a right-click, which offers me the pop-up menu shown in Figure 12.16.

TIP

When dealing with TeamViewer's access to my desktop or laptop computer, I always copy a file and paste it into Dropbox rather than drag and drop the original. Once I determine the file is in Dropbox and is safe, only then do I delete the original from the computer. If you're the trusting type, however, there's nothing to prevent you from tapping a file to select it and then tapping and dragging that file to Dropbox or another location. This is a Move operation, not a Copy and Paste operation, so the original file will be placed when you lift your finger to drop it into its final destination.

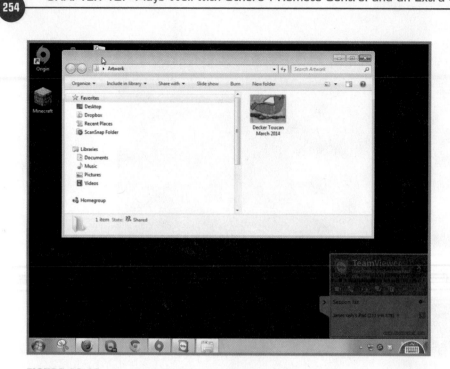

FIGURE 12.15   Tap a file once to select it.

FIGURE 12.16   Tap-and-holding a file or folder is the same as right-clicking.

I'm interested in the fifth option from the bottom—Copy. A single tap there and the file is copied to the Clipboard. Next, I simply tap the Dropbox link shown in Figure 12.17 and then tap-and-hold again and select the Paste option.

FIGURE 12.17 Copy files from a computer's hard drive to Dropbox.

As you can see, the TeamViewer: Remote Control app brings your desktop or laptop to your iPad. There are some limitations (such as the smaller viewing screen), but in a pinch you can use your iPad to remotely launch an application and save yourself a drive home (or a walk up a flight of stairs...don't judge me). And file transfers from a computer to an iPad are a cinch if you have a cloud service configured on both your computer and your iPad.

In so many ways, your Ultimate iPad can replace a traditional desktop or laptop. Using an application like TeamViewer, you need only ensure that the remote computer is turned on, has an Internet connection, and that you know the Your ID and Password information; with those three items checked off, you may very well discover another reason to refer to your tablet as an Ultimate iPad.

Get Some Extra Screen Space

Not everyone is ready to give up their desktop or laptop computer. I'll admit it...I'm not. There are simply some things I prefer doing on the larger screen that comes with a laptop or desktop computer. I enjoy playing some advanced games on my Windows desktop computer that require a bit more memory and processing power to handle all those explosions and detailed graphics. My MacBook Air is where I do 90% of my writing, and I prefer its keyboard over the iPad's onscreen keyboard or the optional Bluetooth version.

As I write, I often find myself needing to refer to an application or a website or some other bit of information. Most of the time, this involves flipping back and forth between screens. My MacBook Air is running the OS X Mavericks operating system, and I'm very fast at using the touchpad and a three-finger swipe to move between screens. (Windows users click the tabs running along the bottom of the screen to move between apps and web pages and such.)

Most of the time, the occasional swiping back and forth to change between a website, for example, and a Word document I'm writing isn't a big deal. But there are times that I'll be writing on my laptop while sitting in front of my desktop just so I can have two screens.

A few years ago I was sitting in the coffee shop, swiping back and forth, back and forth, and not getting a lot of writing done. On one screen was the open Word application and on another screen was an application I was using and needing to click here, click there, drag this, and drop that. Very annoying. I looked over at my sleeping iPad and silently wished that it could run the application I needed. (This was before I had discovered TeamViewer and had the ability to run the other app on my desktop computer.)

I have a friend who has two flat panel LCD screens hooked up to his home computer, and a thought popped into my head—"I wonder if there's an app that would let me use my iPad as a second screen?" It took less than two minutes for me to find my answer.

The solution comes in two parts, just like the TeamViewer application. First, you'll need to install the iDisplay application on your Windows or Mac computer. Just point a web browser to www.getidisplay.com and click one of the buttons shown in Figure 12.18 for your computer's operating system. The computer's application is free to download and install.

After installing the iDisplay application, you'll open the application. The iDisplay application appears as a tiny icon near the top of the screen (on a Mac), as shown in Figure 12.19. You can right-click it to see a submenu with various options.

Windows users may encounter a screen like the one in Figure 12.20; click the Allow Access button if you wish to proceed; otherwise, the iDisplay application won't allow your iPad to function as a second display.

For Windows users, the iDisplay application will run in the background; a small icon will appear in the notification bar in the lower-right corner of the screen.

FIGURE 12.18 The iDisplay application must be installed on your computer.

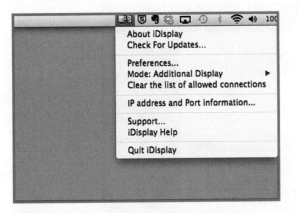

FIGURE 12.19 The iDisplay application running on a Mac.

Once iDisplay is running on your Windows or Mac computer, it's time to install the iDisplay app for your iPad. This app is $2.99 from the App Store, so read ahead and see how it works before deciding if the app is for you. I think you'll agree, however, that it's a small price for the added screen space it provides.

Figure 12.21 shows the iDisplay information screen in the App Store. After purchasing, click the Open button to launch the app.

FIGURE 12.20   Some Windows computers require permission for iDisplay to work.

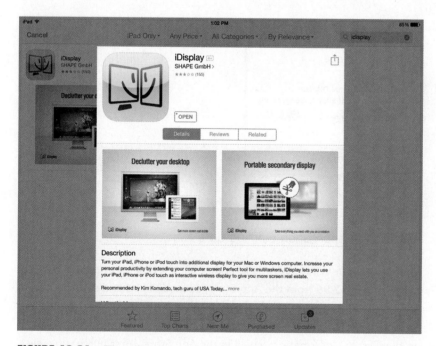

FIGURE 12.21   The iDisplay app information page.

When the iDisplay app opens, it will list any computers it finds that are sharing a Wi-Fi network with your iPad. As you can see in Figure 12.22, my MacBook Air is listed.

FIGURE 12.22 Find the computer running the iDisplay application.

Tap a computer, and your iPad will change to a completely empty screen (but having the background color or wallpaper), as shown in Figure 12.23.

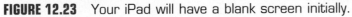

FIGURE 12.23 Your iPad will have a blank screen initially.

To use your iPad as a second screen, all that's needed is for you to drag an open application to the right of your computer's screen—it will instantly appear on the iPad's screen. Figure 12.24 shows half of an application on my MacBook Air's screen and the other half on the iPad's screen. Cool!

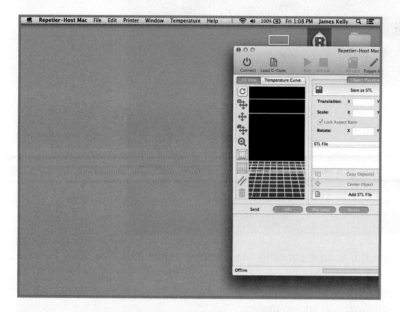

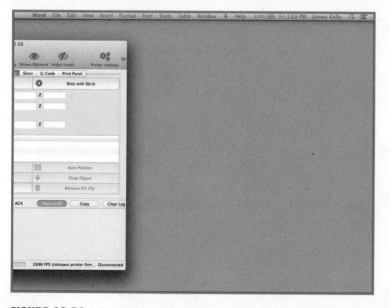

FIGURE 12.24   Drag an application to the right so it appears on the iPad's screen.

Once you drop an application on the iPad, it stays in place, as shown in Figure 12.25.

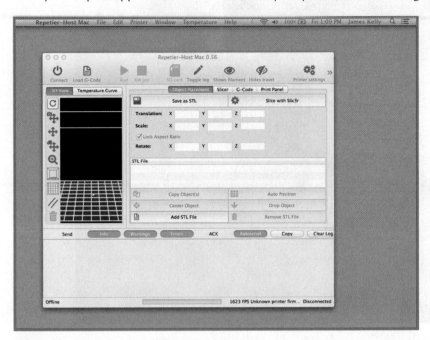

FIGURE 12.25 A dropped application holds its place on the iPad screen.

To interact with that application, all that's needed is to move the mouse pointer to the right until it appears on the iPad's screen. Then, it works just as if you were viewing that screen on your laptop or desktop—you can click, double-click, open menus, save files, and everything else you would normally be able to do from your laptop or desktop's screen. The only difference here is that you have two screens now!

Move the mouse pointer to the left and keep going, and it will appear once again on your laptop or desktop computer's screen.

Using iDisplay while I'm writing, I am able to move a web browser or other application to my iPad's screen while maintaining the open Word document on my MacBook Air's screen. As you can see in Figure 12.26, I place my iPad to the right of my MacBook to make it easier to keep eyes on both screens.

Rather than drag the mouse to the right, you can also immediately tap the iPad's screen and the mouse pointer will jump to that location.

One nice feature found in the Mac's version of iDisplay is its mirroring feature. What this does is simply place a copy of whatever's on your laptop or desktop screen on your iPad's screen. Imagine handing a friend or work colleague your iPad, turning on the mirror feature, and then showing them how to use a piece of software; they see what you see!

FIGURE 12.26 Working and writing—laptop on the left, iPad on the right.

Enabling the mirror feature is done from the computer running the iDisplay software. Click the iDisplay icon and choose Preferences. Figure 12.27 shows the iDisplay Preferences window.

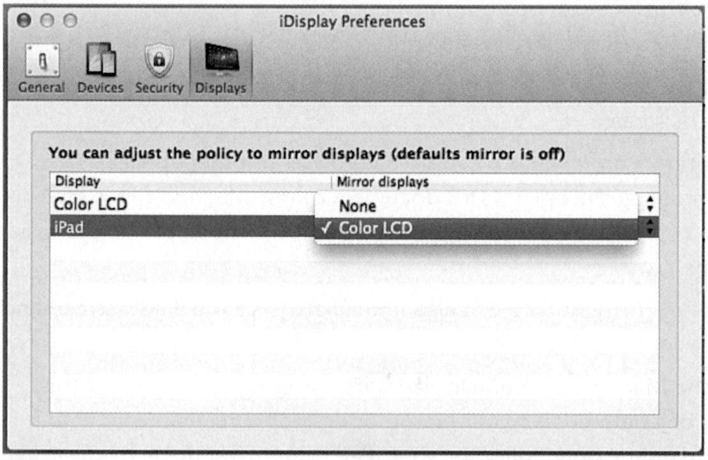

FIGURE 12.27 Use iDisplay Preferences to specify mirroring or second screen.

The iDisplay app on your Ultimate iPad and the iDisplay application running on your computer are so useful for those times when you're doing two or more things on a computer. Simply side-load an application or web browser to your iPad's screen, and there it will stay until you close it or shut down iDisplay.

I've had more people come up to me at the coffee shop and make a comment about my amazing multitasking because they see a laptop and an iPad open at the same time. When I tell them I'm simply using my iPad as a second screen, most of the time I hear, "I didn't know you could do that!"

My son likes to watch me play a few games as well, but sometimes he's almost sitting in my lap because he scoots in so close. Not anymore. Now I mirror my screen to the iPad, hand him the iPad, and he can relax on the couch and watch his cool Dad win a race or save the world.

Your tablet is not only able to provide additional screen space while you're working on a laptop or desktop, but as you saw earlier it's also able to take control of your computer(s) with the TeamViewer: Remote Control app and extra screen space...only with an Ultimate iPad.

13

Scan and Use Again: Activity Books and More

In This Chapter

- The problem with one-time-use activity books
- The solution offered by PDFpen
- Create your digital signature
- Other reuse ideas

This won't be the lengthiest chapter in the book, but it does contain some tips and tricks that have saved me not only hours of time and frustration but also hundreds of dollars. Back in Chapter 5, "Cut the Clutter: Scan Everything," you learned all about the different types of scanners; in this chapter, you'll learn how one of those $200 to $500 scanners can (and should) end up paying for itself in many situations.

At this point in the book, it's my hope that your iPad is really starting to behave like an Ultimate iPad, providing you access to all sorts of files and tasks that you might not ever have considered possible with a tablet. Whether it's books and magazines, TV shows and movies, or documentation such as medical records, financial data, and receipts, your goal should be to recover the expense of your iPad by having it save you time—which for most of us does equate to a dollar amount of some sort.

I don't know anything about your home or work life, so all I can do is present you with some examples of ways my Ultimate iPad has saved me money (and time) and hope that these examples spark a few ideas of your own. Not every suggestion in this chapter is likely to be relevant to you, but if just one of them can start saving you money then you're off to a good start.

Kids Activity Books

I have two boys, three years apart. If I had to sit down and add up the dollar value of all the coloring books, mazes, and workbooks that my wife and I have purchased over the years, it'd probably bring a few tears to my eyes, and not for sentimental reasons.

> **NOTE**
>
> My boys have spent hours upon hours coloring and drawing and connecting dots and filling in details in so many workbooks, and I've kept so much of it for scanning and long-term storage so that I can present them each a disc (or whatever the future technology is called) in the future with a good collection of artwork, homework, report cards, photos, and so much more—all scanned in and kept as a record of their childhood. When possible, I write in pen (prior to scanning) the date, the age, and (when necessary) a brief description of what's on the page. ("Yes, that solid blue line looks just like a giraffe!")

My sons love all kinds of activity books, but not me. Why? Let me count the reasons:

- **They're not cheap**—A plain coloring book might cost $2 or $3, but the ones your child is going to want are the ones that typically feature a favorite TV show or well-known cartoon characters—and they're usually $5–$8 and sometimes higher. Dot-to-dot, mazes, and word searches also fall into this category. (My oldest son's favorite maze books are $5 each.)

- **They're printed on paper**—There are some activity books that come with a special pen that can be wiped off the special plastic pages, but they're rare. Most activity books are not designed to be reused. That fun maze your son just finished and now wants to do again...out of luck.

- **Kids prefer clean pages**—If my oldest son made so much as a single orange checkmark on a coloring book page, my youngest thinks it's ruined and should be burned immediately. This seems to be a universal kid-reaction to pages that are not pristine.

- **They run out**—For math and writing activity sheets, there often aren't enough of one kind of practice sheet. If your child uses up all three subtraction pages that offered a unique method of teaching, you're again out of luck. For coloring books, your child's favorite superhero might only be on six of the 20 pages—and when they're gone, you might be left with 14 pages of that other superhero and a child with no interest in showing the sidekick some love.

I'm not a fan of activity books overall, as you can tell. Over the years there have been a few standout activity books that my wife and I gladly repurchased so the youngest son could have his own copy, but most of the activity books that we've purchased have just grown into a sad stack—unfinished coloring books, workbooks with half of the pages torn out, and maze books with the first 10–20 mazes easily solved and the remaining 30–40 pages of more difficult challenges left for the recycle bin. Sad.

But you already know where this is going. I had a scanner, and I was a man with a plan. I can't put my finger on the exact "Eureka" moment, but I do remember thinking to myself, "Just try it and see what happens." I took both sons to the bookstore and asked them to each pick out an activity book, telling them that I had something special planned and would need their help; my oldest picked up a maze book (and he's still into mazes), and my youngest picked up a coloring book.

At the house, they watched in horror as I removed the staples, cut apart the two-page spreads, and reorganized both books into two stacks. Out came the scanner and in went the pages. I scanned in both books and saved them as PDF files. (I'll explain in the next section why I chose to save them as PDF and not JPEG files.)

After saving them, I did a test print from the laser printer. The coloring pages came out looking almost identical to the original black-and-white pages. The maze book was in color, so my black-and-white printer didn't do such a great job, but I could tell that it would have been a perfect match (but an expensive match given the cost of color ink these days) if I chose to print maze pages out on a color printer. Now I could reproduce activity book pages at will...

...but creating paper copies wasn't my ultimate goal.

Creating and Using Digital Activity Books

Having activity books in PDF format was great, but the real question was if I could find a way for my boys to open and use the pages on my iPad (of course, only one boy can use the iPad at a time). The short answer is yes, there are plenty of solutions, and I'm going to show you two here. One solution uses PDF files and the other uses JPEG files.

Back in Chapter 1, "The Ultimate iPad," I recommended that you purchase the PDFpen app ($14.99) because it's one of the more useful apps for creating and editing PDF files on your iPad. Now you're about to see how it works with scanned activity book sheets. (You can also purchase a slightly less expensive version of PDFpen for your iPhone at $4.99 but the smaller screen might not be the best solution for larger items such as coloring sheets and mazes.)

After scanning in an activity book and storing it in Dropbox, I'll open up PDFpen, as shown in Figure 13.1.

I've organized PDFs into a small number of folders that include Business Forms (such as W-9 and other tax documents I tend to need again and again), Contracts, and Archive.

Let's see how easy it is to pull in a scanned activity book. First, tap the Add menu (+ sign in the upper-left corner) and you'll see a menu appear like the one in Figure 13.2.

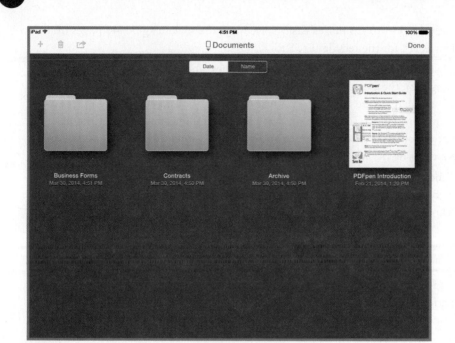

FIGURE 13.1 PDFpen can create and edit PDF files.

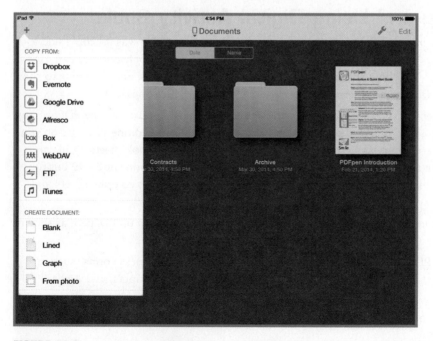

FIGURE 13.2 Import documents using the Add menu.

Near the bottom of the pop-up menu, you can see how PDFpen allows you to create new PDF files that include blank, lined, and graph paper and even photo backgrounds.

Skip those options and look at the list of services to which PDFpen is capable of connecting. Dropbox is the one I'm interested in. When I click it, I'm able to browse the folder structure of my Dropbox account. Figure 13.3 shows that I've browsed to the folder where I've stored a number of maze books I've scanned in for my oldest son.

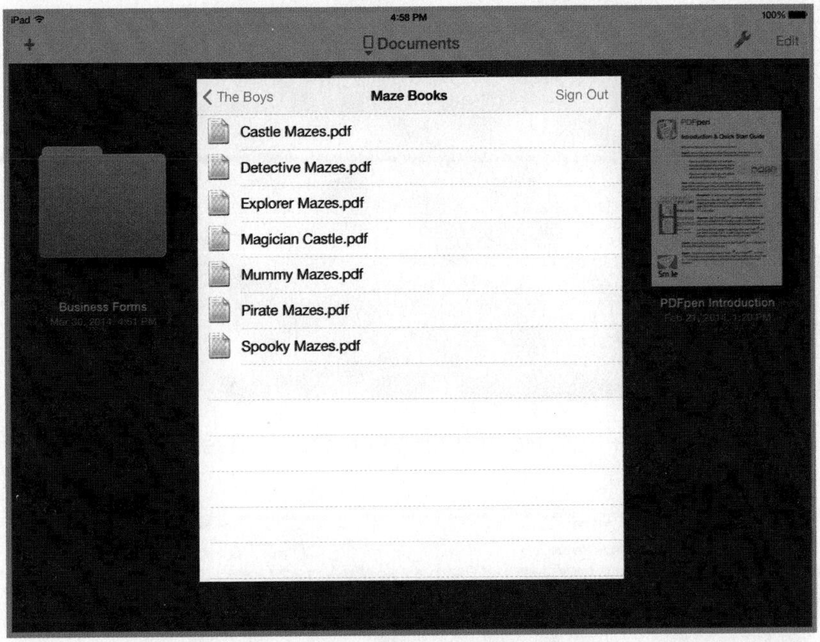

FIGURE 13.3 Find the folder holding the PDF file you wish to import into PDFpen.

Tap a PDF file and it's added to PDFpen's desktop, as shown in Figure 13.4.

Using this method, you could easily import a PDF book or a single PDF page. PDFpen offers a variety of editing tools, such as a highlight tool and the ability to add text and other images to an opened PDF. One of those tools is a digital pen, and you can choose both the color and the thickness of the mark made on the screen.

To access this tool, my son will first open the maze book by tapping the book's cover on the desktop. The book opens as shown in Figure 13.5.

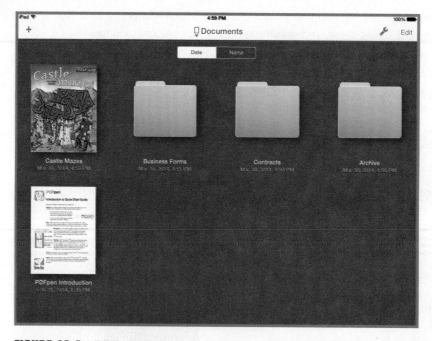

FIGURE 13.4   PDFpen imports a PDF file and places it on the desktop.

FIGURE 13.5   Open a PDF file by tapping its icon on the desktop.

PDFpen can open a PDF in Portrait or Landscape view, but it works best if you open the file in the original scanned book's native format. The maze book was taller than it was wider, so Portrait view will work best. That will require rotating the iPad. The page adjusts and can now be viewed properly, as shown in Figure 13.6.

FIGURE 13.6 Rotate the iPad to view an opened PDF properly.

Turning pages in a digital PDF book works just like any other digital book—swipe from right to left to turn a page and move forward in a book, and swipe left to right to turn to the previous page.

As you can see in Figure 13.7, my son has chosen the first maze in the book and is anxious to solve it.

FIGURE 13.7   Turn pages by swiping left or right.

Note also in Figure 13.7 that the toolbar appears running along the top of the page. A single tap anywhere on the page will cause the toolbar to disappear. Another tap brings the toolbar back.

Now, for my son to actually "write" on the maze, all he needs to do is tap the Pen tool, which opens the Markup menu shown in Figure 13.8.

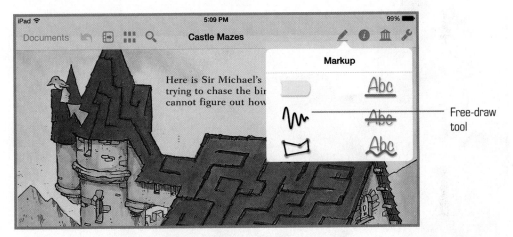

Free-draw tool

FIGURE 13.8 Choose a Markup tool from the menu.

The yellow rectangle is the Highlight tool, and the other options include Underline, Strikethrough, and a few others. The one my son needs to tap is the Free-draw tool (the squiggly line). When he taps the Free-draw tool, another toolbar appears near the bottom of the screen, as shown in Figure 13.9.

FIGURE 13.9 Select a color and thickness for the Pen tool.

TIP

Your child may need to experiment with both color and thickness, depending on the type of activity book they are using in PDFpen. In general, the thicker the Pen selection, the better. Color is best chosen based on the background color of the displayed PDF file.

My son taps the color green and then taps the next-to-last thickness button and goes to work on the maze. As you can see in Figure 13.10, he's pretty good at solving mazes.

Done button

FIGURE 13.10 One solved maze and then on to the next one.

What I really like about the PDFpen app is its Undo feature. If one of my sons makes a mistake on a digital activity book page, he can tap the Undo button and try again.

TIP

The Undo button will undo any actions made on the screen up to when a finger was last touched, and multiple Undo actions can be made. So if you press your finger and draw a short line, remove your finger and then touch again and draw another short line and remove your finger, the Undo button will only take away the last short line. Another tap of Undo will remove the first short line.

If my son is happy with his work and wishes to save it and show it to one of us later, all he has to do is tap the Done button in the upper-right corner of the screen. After he taps Done, the PDFpen app will completely surround any added elements (such as the line from the Pen tool) and allow him to cut or copy it, as shown in Figure 13.11.

If my son would like to redo a maze, he can tap Cut and his previous work goes away. (This beats tapping Undo over and over again.)

If he wants to save his work, it's really not a problem because he (or I) can always go back into PDFpen and delete anything that has been added to a PDF file, essentially wiping it clean of previous work. To save the work, ignore the Cut and Paste options (shown in Figure 13.11) and simply swipe to the next page or tap the Documents button to return to PDFpen's desktop and choose another digital activity book. (Another option is to press the iPad's Home and Power buttons simultaneously to take a screenshot and save it to the Photos app.)

If my younger son should happen to open a maze book and find it already solved, all I have to do is tap near or on the squiggly line and once again the Cut and Paste buttons will appear, allowing me to clean the page.

As for my younger son, coloring book pages work just as great in PDFpen. You may have to show your child how to change between colors and pen thickness, but once he or she gets the hang of it, you'll start seeing little masterpieces like the one in Figure 13.12.

As with the maze book, a coloring book can be restored to pristine glory with a few taps of the Cut button. It works great—no more melted crayons on the floor of the car or lost down in the seats, and definitely no more fussing because a favorite page was colored on by a sibling.

FIGURE 13.11 You can cut or copy the added elements to a PDF file.

FIGURE 13.12 Open digital coloring books in PDFpen.

Before I close out this section, let me touch on one situation that sometimes comes up with activity books—two-page spreads. Look at Figure 13.13 and you'll see a maze that was spread out over two pages of the maze book.

FIGURE 13.13   Two-page spreads are easily handled by PDFpen.

TIP

Not all scanners support the ability to "stitch" together two pages, side by side. Consult a scanner's software description to find out if it offers this feature. The ScanSnap iX500 comes with a special clear folder where you place one half of the spread facing up in the folder and the other half facing down (behind the face up sheet). The special folder is fed into the scanner and the software automatically combines the two pages into one.

For this maze, my son has to rotate the iPad to Landscape view, and the text and path appear a bit smaller, but I've yet to hear a complaint.

Maze books and coloring books are just two of the many types of books that can be scanned in and accessed with the PDFpen app. Other options that my wife and I are now discovering are math and spelling worksheets, although the spelling and handwriting sheets are obviously best done with a real pencil. Still, for fast "quizzes," it's easy to scan in a homework sheet sent home by the teacher and drop it on my son a few days later to see if he's retaining what he's learning.

PDFpen is a great little app that kids can pick up and understand quickly. If you keep a folder on PDFpen that holds a mix of activity books, your Ultimate iPad will always have a nice selection of activities to occupy any child.

Adults will find PDFpen just as useful, however. In the next section, I'm going to introduce you to a few features that PDFpen offers for both work and home.

NOTE

Why not save scans as JPEG files? You can certainly do that, but you'll end up saving each page as a separate JPEG file; a 50-page coloring book will create 50 JPEG files—a lot to sift through! Although PDFpen will open JPEG files, that's not really its strength. If you're looking for a free app for kids to open JPEG files that offers a similar Pen tool with color selection and more, search for Doodle Buddy for iPad in the App Store.

PDFpen for Filling Out Digital Documents

The paperless home/office has been talked about and talked about for decades, yet it's still not here. But that's not for lack of trying. For some reason, so much paperwork required of adults still requires just that...paper. But with tools such as PDFpen, you might be able to make a dent in some of it.

For example, do you receive documents in the mail that must be signed and sent back? Think about that for a moment—it required postage to get to you and postage to get back. And what about those documents that someone emails to you as attachments with instructions to print out, sign, and then mail back? Crazy! They saved some postage, but now you have to take the time to print out the document and then spend some money on postage to send it back.

Whenever this happens to me, I typically email back (or call the sender) and ask them if they can accept a digital version of the document along with a digital signature. Over the last few years, in almost every instance I've asked the response has been yes. (Where the answer has been no, I usually didn't get a good explanation.)

If the document has been emailed to you as an attachment, you're halfway home. Even if it's a Word document, Word has the ability to open a document and save it as a PDF file. Do that, save the file in Dropbox or other location so you can get it into PDFpen and you're almost done.

If you get a printed document that can be returned as a signed, digital document, all you have to do is scan it, save it as a PDF, and again get it into Dropbox or box.com or some other service that PDFpen can access and import from.

Once the PDF file is imported and sitting on PDFpen's desktop, you'll typically have two things that must be done with the document:

1. Fill in areas such as address, date, and other details requiring text.

2. Sign it with your signature.

PDFpen can handle both. Let's use a sample W-9 PDF file downloaded from the Internal Revenue Service website and see how all this is done. We'll start with adding simple text.

Adding Text to a PDF Form

Take a look at Figure 13.14 and you'll see that I've imported a W-9 into PDFpen.

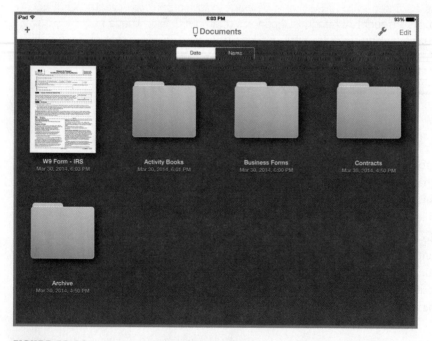

FIGURE 13.14 A blank PDF W-9 form on the PDFpen desktop.

Tapping the PDF form opens it—you can see in Figure 13.15 that the form is blank and has quite a few fields that may or may not need to be filled in.

To enter text in a field, you first need to type the text and then drag and drop it where needed. Let's start with creating the text. Tap the Object tool (it looks like a small building) and a small menu opens like the one in Figure 13.16.

iPad 🔋   6:12 PM   ✳ 93% ◼

Documents ↰ ⬅ ⦙⦙⦙ 🔍   **W9 Form - IRS**   ✎ ⓘ 🏛 🔧 ——— Object tool

---

| Form **W-9**
(Rev. October 2007)
Department of the Treasury
Internal Revenue Service | **Request for Taxpayer**
Identification Number and Certification | Give form to the
requester. Do not
send to the IRS. |

Name (as shown on your income tax return)

Business name, if different from above

Check appropriate box: ☐ Individual/Sole proprietor   ☐ Corporation   ☐ Partnership
☐ Limited liability company. Enter the tax classification (D=disregarded entity, C=corporation, P=partnership) ▶ ....
☐ Other (see instructions) ▶   ☐ Exempt
payee

Address (number, street, and apt. or suite no.)   Requester's name and address (optional)

City, state, and ZIP code

List account number(s) here (optional)

Print or type
See Specific Instructions on page 2.

Part I   **Taxpayer Identification Number (TIN)**

Enter your TIN in the appropriate box. The TIN provided must match the name given on Line 1 to avoid backup withholding. For individuals, this is your social security number (SSN). However, for a resident alien, sole proprietor, or disregarded entity, see the Part I instructions on page 3. For other entities, it is your employer identification number (EIN). If you do not have a number, see *How to get a TIN* on page 3.

Note. If the account is in more than one name, see the chart on page 4 for guidelines on whose number to enter.

Social security number

or

Employer identification number

Part II   **Certification**

Under penalties of perjury, I certify that:

1. The number shown on this form is my correct taxpayer identification number (or I am waiting for a number to be issued to me), and
2. I am not subject to backup withholding because: (a) I am exempt from backup withholding, or (b) I have not been notified by the Internal Revenue Service (IRS) that I am subject to backup withholding as a result of a failure to report all interest or dividends, or (c) the IRS has notified me that I am no longer subject to backup withholding, and
3. I am a U.S. citizen or other U.S. person (defined below).

Certification instructions. You must cross out item 2 above if you have been notified by the IRS that you are currently subject to backup withholding because you have failed to report all interest and dividends on your tax return. For real estate transactions, item 2 does not apply. For mortgage interest paid, acquisition or abandonment of secured property, cancellation of debt, contributions to an individual retirement arrangement (IRA), and generally, payments other than interest and dividends, you are not required to sign the Certification, but you must provide your correct TIN. See the instructions on page 4.

Sign
Here | Signature of
U.S. person ▶   Date ▶

General Instructions

Section references are to the Internal Revenue Code unless otherwise noted.

Purpose of Form

A person who is required to file an information return with the IRS must obtain your correct taxpayer identification number (TIN) to report, for example, income paid to you, real estate transactions, mortgage interest you paid, acquisition or abandonment of secured property, cancellation of debt, or contributions you made to an IRA.

Use Form W-9 only if you are a U.S. person (including a resident alien), to provide your correct TIN to the person requesting it (the requester) and, when applicable, to:

1. Certify that the TIN you are giving is correct (or you are waiting for a number to be issued),

2. Certify that you are not subject to backup withholding, or

3. Claim exemption from backup withholding if you are a U.S. exempt payee. If applicable, you are also certifying that as a U.S. person, your allocable share of any partnership income from a U.S. trade or business is not subject to the withholding tax on foreign partners' share of effectively connected income.

Note. If a requester gives you a form other than Form W-9 to request your TIN, you must use the requester's form if it is substantially similar to this Form W-9.

Definition of a U.S. person. For federal tax purposes, you are considered a U.S. person if you are:

• An individual who is a U.S. citizen or U.S. resident alien,
• A partnership, corporation, company, or association created or organized in the United States or under the laws of the United States,
• An estate (other than a foreign estate), or
• A domestic trust (as defined in Regulations section 301.7701-7).

Special rules for partnerships. Partnerships that conduct a trade or business in the United States are generally required to pay a withholding tax on any foreign partners' share of income from such business. Further, in certain cases where a Form W-9 has not been received, a partnership is required to presume that a partner is a foreign person, and pay the withholding tax. Therefore, if you are a U.S. person that is a partner in a partnership conducting a trade or business in the United States, provide Form W-9 to the partnership to establish your U.S. status and avoid withholding on your share of partnership income.

The person who gives Form W-9 to the partnership for purposes of establishing its U.S. status and avoiding withholding on its allocable share of net income from the partnership conducting a trade or business in the United States is in the following cases:

• The U.S. owner of a disregarded entity and not the entity,

Cat. No. 10231X   Form **W-9** (Rev. 10-2007)

FIGURE 13.15 The open PDF form has a number of areas where text is required.

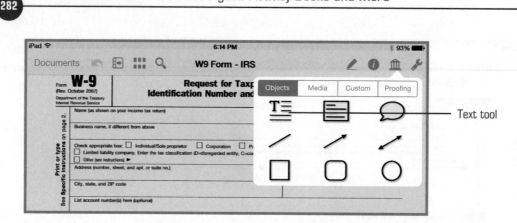

Text tool

FIGURE 13.16   The Object menu offers you the ability to add to the form.

There are a few tools in this menu such as the text balloon, the arrow, and the box, but it's the Text tool (upper-left corner) that will let you type text for your form. Tap that tool, and a blank text box appears in the center of the page, as shown in Figure 13.17.

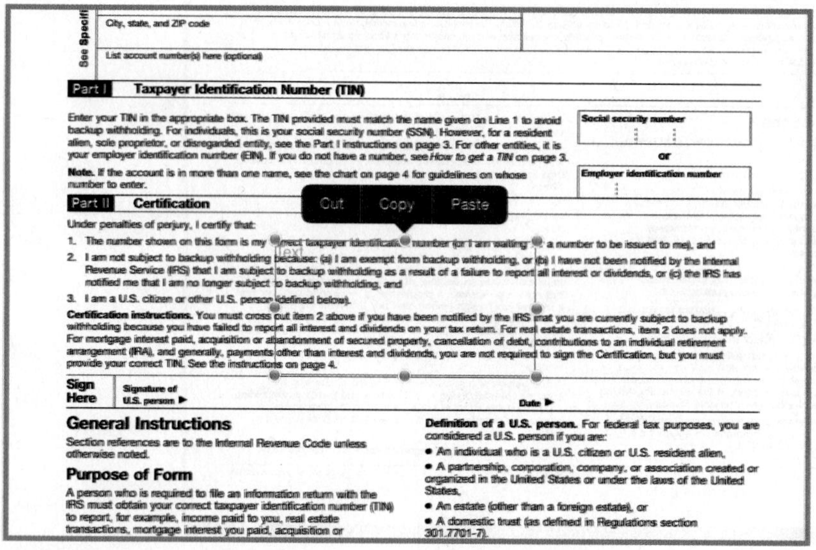

FIGURE 13.17   A blank text box appears onscreen.

Tap anywhere inside the text box and drag the box so that the top-left corner of the box is near the start of a blank line where you wish to add some text. Tap and hold on the blue dots surrounding the text box to lengthen and increase the width of the text box. You can see this in Figure 13.18.

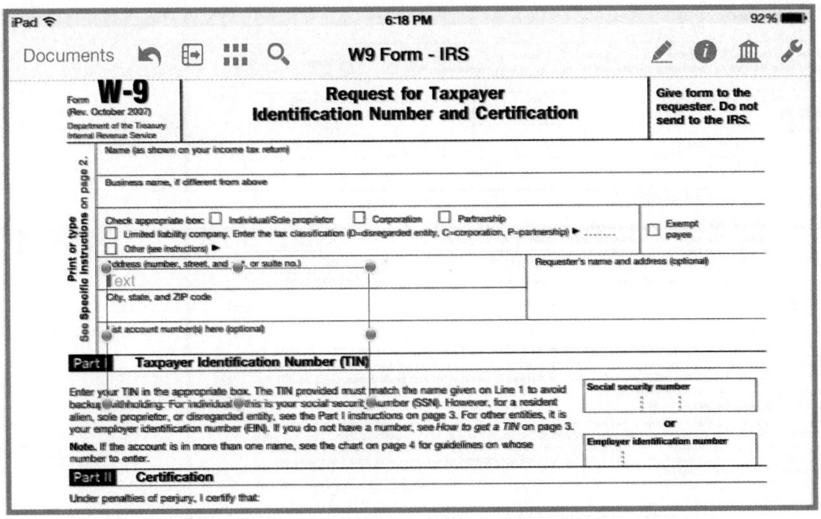

FIGURE 13.18 Drag the text box close to its final destination.

Type in your text and continue to tap and drag the text box until you are satisfied with the placement of the text. Figure 13.19 shows that I've added the address to the blank Address line.

You can type multiple lines in the text box (text will carry over to the next line when it reaches the end of the box), but text entered this way won't always line up perfectly. Figure 13.20 shows what happens when I tapped the Return key to move to the next line and tried to enter the city, state, and Zip code.

For this reason, you'll find that using a text box to add a single line of text works best. As you can see in Figure 13.21, I've tapped the Object button again and added a new Text box and dragged it to the City, State, and ZIP code line.

iPad 🛜　　　　　　　　　　6:19 PM　　　　　　　　　92% ▬

Documents　↰　▣　⋮⋮⋮　Q　　**W9 Form - IRS**　　　　✎　ⓘ　🏛　🔧

Form **W-9**
(Rev. October 2007)
Department of the Treasury
Internal Revenue Service

**Request for Taxpayer
Identification Number and Certification**

Give form to the
requester. Do not
send to the IRS.

Name (as shown on your income tax return)

Business name, if different from above

Check appropriate box: ☐ Individual/Sole proprietor　☐ Corporation　☐ Partnership
☐ Limited liability company. Enter the tax classification (D=disregarded entity, C=corporation, P=partnership) ▶ ....
☐ Other (see instructions) ▶

☐ Exempt
payee

Address (number, street, and apt. or suite no.)

123 Main Street

City, state, and ZIP code

Requester's name and address (optional)

List account number(s) here (optional)

Print or type
See Specific Instructions on page 2.

Part I　　**Taxpayer Identification Number (TIN)**

Enter your TIN in the appropriate box. The TIN provided must match the name given on Line 1 to avoid backup withholding. For individuals, this is your social security number (SSN). However, for a resident alien, sole proprietor, or disregarded entity, see the Part I instructions on page 3. For other entities, it is your employer identification number (EIN). If you do not have a number, see How to get a TIN on page 3.

Note. If the account is in more than one name, see the chart on page 4 for guidelines on whose number to enter.

Social security number

or

Employer identification number

Part II　　**Certification**

Under penalties of perjury, I certify that:

1. The number shown on this form is my correct taxpayer identification number (or I am waiting for a number to be issued to me), and
2. I am not subject to backup withholding because: (a) I am exempt from backup withholding, or (b) I have not been notified by the Internal Revenue Service (IRS) that I am subject to backup withholding as a result of a failure to report all interest or dividends, or (c) the IRS has notified me that I am no longer subject to backup withholding, and
3. I am a U.S. citizen or other U.S. person (defined below).

Certification instructions. You must cross out item 2 above if you have been notified by the IRS that you are currently subject to backup withholding because you have failed to report all interest and dividends on your tax return. For real estate transactions, item 2 does not apply. For mortgage interest paid, acquisition or abandonment of secured property, cancellation of debt, contributions to an individual retirement arrangement (IRA), and generally, payments other than interest and dividends, you are not required to sign the Certification, but you must provide your correct TIN. See the instructions on page 4.

**Sign
Here**　Signature of
U.S. person ▶　　　　　　　　　　　Date ▶

General Instructions

Section references are to the Internal Revenue Code unless otherwise noted.

Purpose of Form

A person who is required to file an information return with the IRS must obtain your correct taxpayer identification number (TIN) to report, for example, income paid to you, real estate transactions, mortgage interest you paid, acquisition or abandonment of secured property, cancellation of debt, or contributions you made to an IRA.

Definition of a U.S. person. For federal tax purposes, you are considered a U.S. person if you are:
● An individual who is a U.S. citizen or U.S. resident alien,
● A partnership, corporation, company, or association created or organized in the United States or under the laws of the United States,
● An estate (other than a foreign estate), or
● A domestic trust (as defined in Regulations section 301.7701-7).

Special rules for partnerships. Partnerships that conduct a

Q W E R T Y U I O P ⌫

A S D F G H J K L return

⇧ Z X C V B N M ! , ? . ⇧

.?123 🎤 　　　　　　　.?123 ⌨

FIGURE 13.19 Add a single line of text at a time.

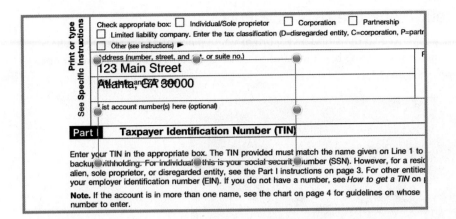

FIGURE 13.20 Additional text lines don't always line up perfectly.

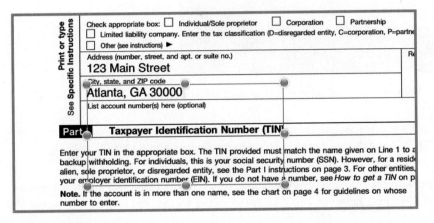

FIGURE 13.21 Use additional text lines for good text placement.

Using this method, you can fill in as many blank lines as necessary on a form (and, of course, you can use the Undo button for mistakes or simply cut out incorrect objects you've inserted into a PDF). Well, all but one. If a form requires your signature, you'll need to perform a few additional steps.

Adding Your Signature to a PDF Form

The first thing you'll need to do is find a very bright white piece of paper and sign your name in a normal manner using black ink and then use the iPad's camera to take a photo of it, as shown in Figure 13.22.

FIGURE 13.22   Sign a piece of white paper and then take its picture.

The photo of your signature will be saved to the Photos app, and, no surprise, PDFpen can easily access your photo galleries. Feel free to open the Photos app and verify your signature's photo is inside and isn't blurry.

If you're satisfied with the photo of your signature, return to the PDF form and tap again on the Object tool. This time, however, you'll want to tap the Media tab, as shown in Figure 13.23.

Tap the Camera Roll and scroll through the list of images until you find the photo of your signature. Tap it, and the signature will be added to the PDF form, as shown in Figure 13.24.

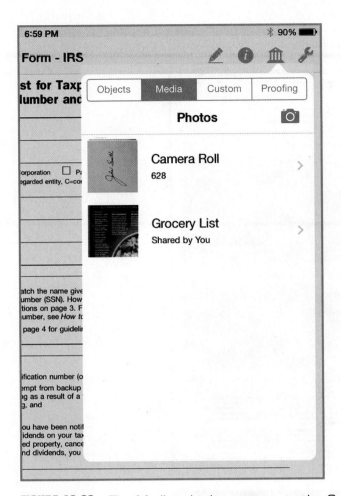

FIGURE 13.23 The Media tab gives access to the Camera Roll.

You need to perform two edits to the signature:

- Shrink it down to a reasonable size.
- Make the image transparent so only the black ink is visible.

To shrink the signature, simply tap the image and you'll see a selection box surround the signature, with blue dots in the corners. Tap the blue dot in the lower-right corner and drag it toward the blue dot in the upper-left corner; the signature should start to shrink, as shown in Figure 13.25.

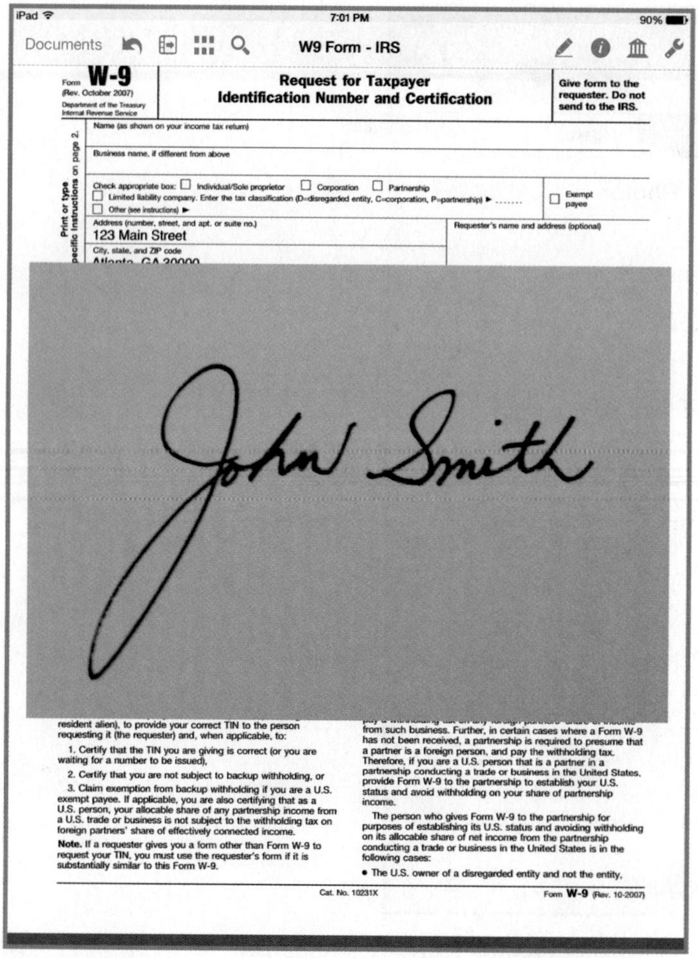

FIGURE 13.24 The photo of your signature is added to the PDF form.

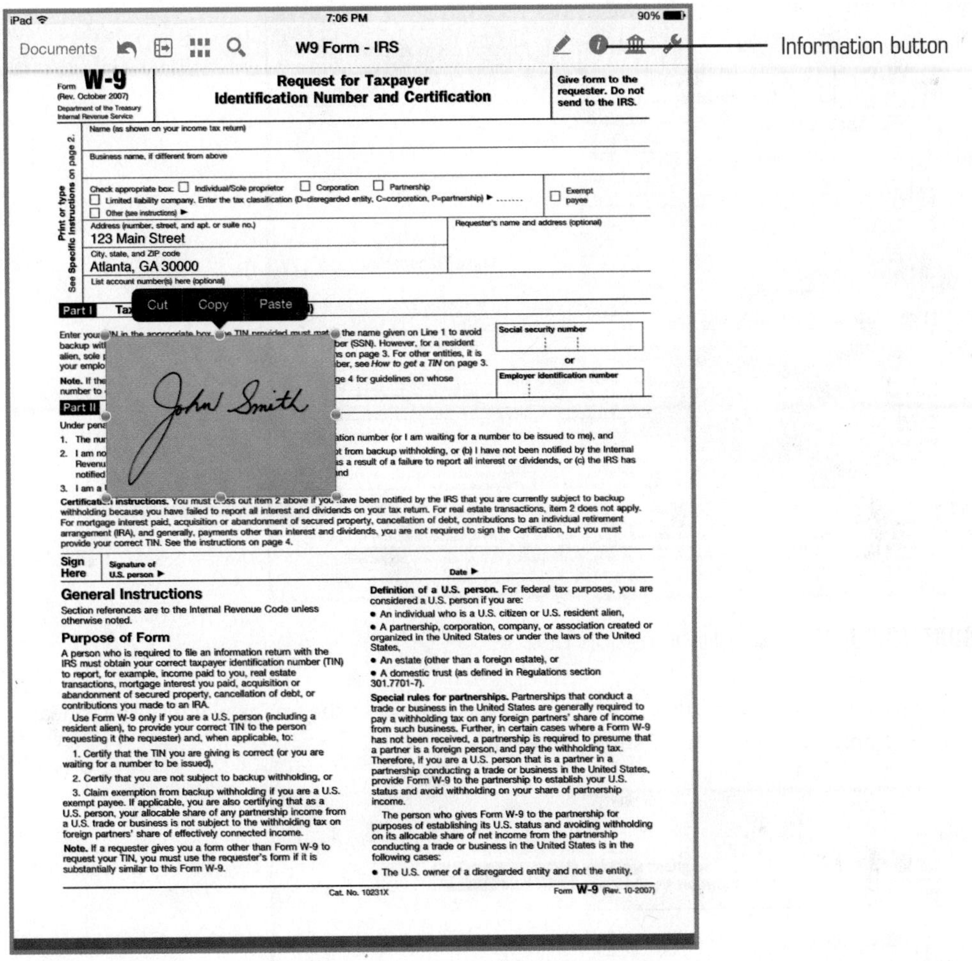

FIGURE 13.25 Shrink the signature using the blue dots.

To turn the image transparent, make certain the signature is still selected and tap the Information button—it's the blue dot with the "i" to the right of the Pen tool. A control appears like the one in Figure 13.26.

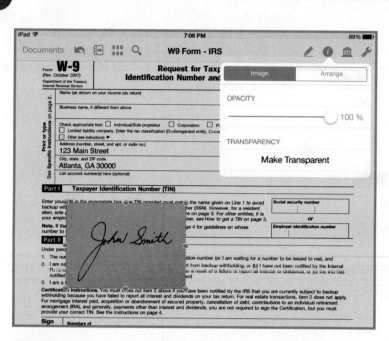

FIGURE 13.26 Tap the Information button.

Tap the Make Transparent button. The white background in the image will disappear, leaving behind only the signature, as shown in Figure 13.27.

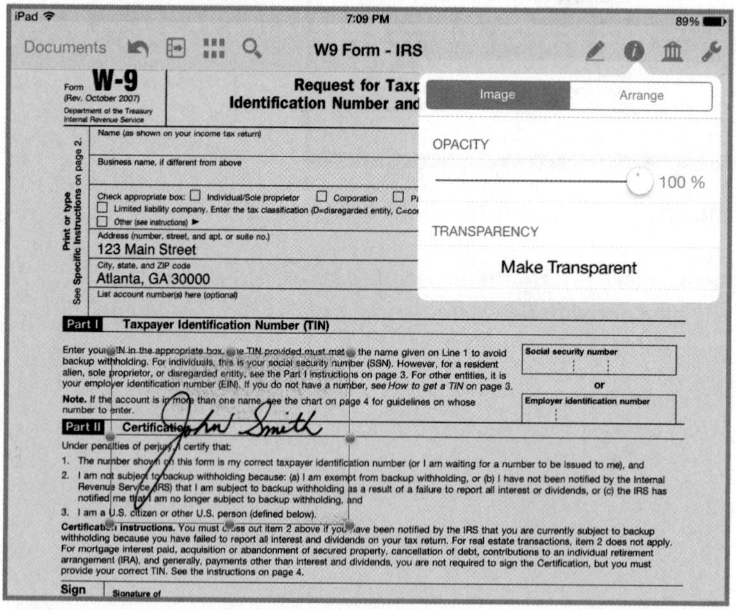

FIGURE 13.27 Turn the signature transparent.

Continue to resize the signature as needed until it fits in the blank Signature line. Tap outside the signature box when you're satisfied, and the signature is done, as shown in Figure 13.28. (Don't forget to use a text box to add the date to the blank Date line!)

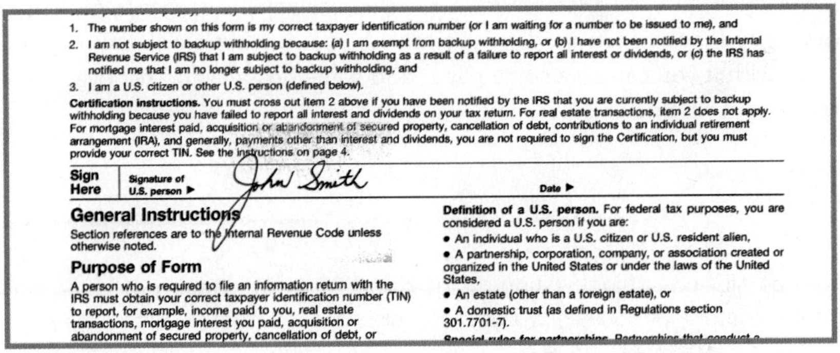

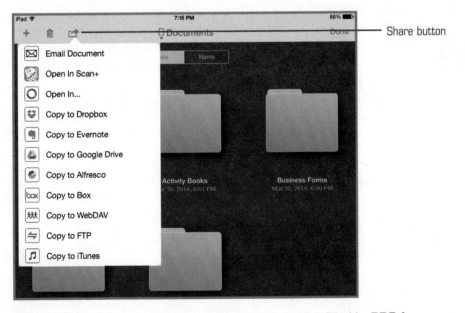

FIGURE 13.28 Drag and drop the signature where desired.

After adding all the required text and/or signature to a form, it's time to save your work. Tap the Documents button in the upper-left corner of the screen to save the changes and return to the desktop.

From the desktop, tap and hold on the PDF form until it is selected. (A quick tap will open it—press and hold for slightly more than a second and a yellow box will appear around the form.) When the document is selected, tap the Share button indicated in Figure 13.29.

FIGURE 13.29 Use the Share button to export the filled-in PDF form.

From the drop-down list, select a location where you wish to send the filled-in form. You can tap the Email Document option and email the form as an attachment or send it to Dropbox, Evernote, or another option.

As you can see, PDFpen can save you a lot of time and headache when it comes to forms. It's probably always a good idea to ask if a digital form with your signature will suffice, but if the recipient is okay with it you can save some paper and some postage and remove one more bit of clutter from your home or office.

NOTE

PDFpen will let you do all kinds of interesting things to a PDF it has imported. You can add text and a signature of course, but you can also drop in photos, insert proof-reader characters (for editors), print the document (to any printer supporting Apple's AirPrint), reorder pages, delete pages, rotate pages, and much more.

Other Areas for Reuse

You've seen how PDFpen can be used to reuse activity books and how it can be used to fill in digital forms, but what else might you be able to do with a mix of scanner, iPad, and PDFpen?

Do you have some sort of form that you use every week or every month that also requires you to fill in the same information? Something like a weekly time sheet or expense report is a great example. Pull in a blank expense report, for example, and fill out the details that will remain constant from week to week—your name and signature are likely candidates. Close this document down when you're done to save your work.

Back on the desktop, tap and hold the expense report document to select it. (It will be outlined with a yellow box.) Once it's selected, tap the name twice and edit the name as shown in Figure 13.30.

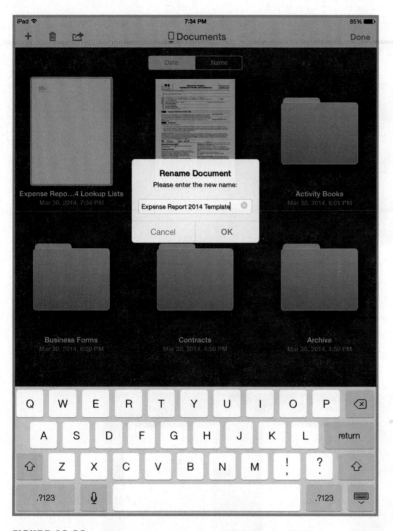

FIGURE 13.30 Edit the name of a PDF file in PDFpen.

After saving the template file, all that's needed is to create a copy of it each time you wish to create a new expense report. Once again, tap and hold on a document to select it and then tap the Main Menu button (+ sign) and select the Duplicate Document button shown in Figure 13.31.

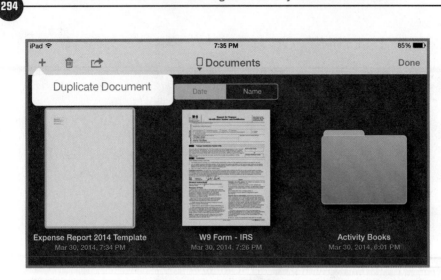

FIGURE 13.31 Make a copy of any PDF file.

The copy will be placed on the desktop, as shown in Figure 13.32. Change its name, add your details (but not your name and signature because you added those in the template, right?), and email that document off to Accounting!

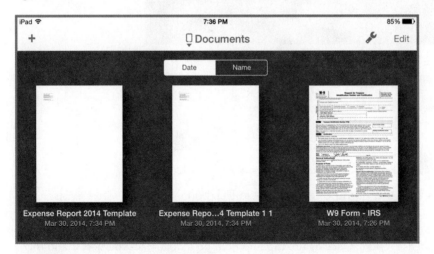

FIGURE 13.32 Your copy appears on the desktop next to the original.

What if you find a form on a company's website (in PDF format) while web browsing and wish to edit it in PDFpen? Thankfully, you don't have to download the file from the website into Dropbox and then import it back into PDFpen. Most web browsers, including Safari, will let you select PDFpen (if it's installed, of course) as the final destination for a PDF link you select. Notice in Figure 13.33 that after I tapped a PDF file link to open it, I get the

"Open in" button near the top that allows me to select a destination from a variety of apps that includes PDFpen.

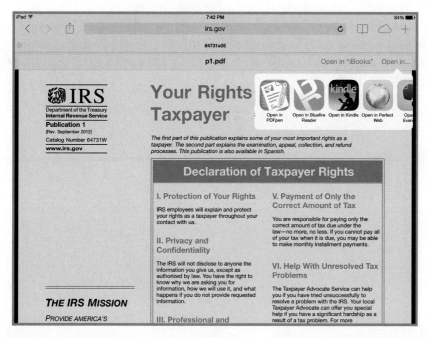

FIGURE 13.33 Open a PDF in a web browser and then "Open in PDFpen."

As you can see, PDFpen is also a great way to directly store PDF forms you find online, bypassing saving them to Dropbox, Pogoplug, or Evernote.

Your Ultimate iPad

An Ultimate iPad is in your hands right now; it's just waiting for you to push it to its limits by taking advantage of the many apps, services, and techniques you've read about in this book.

Rest assured, there are even more useful tips and tricks out there that will turn your Ultimate iPad into a Super-Ultimate iPad. You're likely to discover some of them on your own, too—what's the phrase, "Necessity is the mother of invention"?

If there's something you wish your iPad could do, some task or some trick that would make your life easier, don't take no for an answer just because you can't find it in the documentation. I was told there was no way to save a video directly from the Pogoplug app to my iPad for offline (no Internet) viewing, but the GoodReader app sure proved that wrong!

As each new generation of iPad adds more memory, more power, and more apps and features, it's likely that some or all of the tricks you learned in this book might no longer be necessary. Some might stop working. But that shouldn't stop you from being on the lookout for new and interesting ways to use your iPad. (And if you find a new or useful trick or app, please share by emailing me at feedback@quepublishing.com.)

Enjoy your new Ultimate iPad. Show off those new tricks you've learned. Impress a friend or family member with some task they had no clue could be done. Share something you've learned with a fellow iPad owner. Spread the word that the iPad can do so much more than people ever imagined.

And have fun.

Tips and Tricks

There are a number of tasks I perform with my iPad that just don't quite fit into any particular chapter of this book. These are typically little tricks or timesavers I've just picked up over the years from others or by creating my own solution to a small problem.

In no particular order, I'd like to share with you a few additional tasks you might find useful. These can be modified, of course, so be creative and twist and tweak any or all of these small how-to items to fit your own needs.

Online Instruction Manuals

If you end up purchasing an electronic device or tool or some other object that comes with a printed instruction manual, you might be pleasantly surprised to find just how often companies are now putting these same manuals online. (In some instances, there is *no* manual and only a small slip of paper telling you to access the manual online.)

Take advantage of this! If you can visit a company's website and locate a PDF of the instruction manual, simply download it to Dropbox or Evernote and toss the print version. Obviously, if a manual isn't available in digital format, you can always go the scanning route, but you can save a few minutes or more of your time by going online first. Often you don't even have to go hunting—just Google "Product Name user manual" or "Product Part # user guide" and you'll get a link that will take you straight to the download page.

Should you find the instructions online but not in a PDF format, just use the PrintFriendly.com or PrintWhatYouLike.com website (covered in Chapter 11, "Build a Web Reference Library: Never Lose an Online Article") to grab the text for yourself and convert it to a PDF. It might take you an additional few minutes, but, again, you'll be freeing yourself from a printed manual.

There's even one super-comprehensive website that seeks to make every manual ever printed available in digital form, allowing you to skip scanning your printed manuals. Check it out at www.manualsonline.com—they currently have over 700,000 manuals in their database, so chances are you'll find what you're looking for there.

LEGO Building Instructions

If you have a child who loves LEGO building blocks, then you know that the LEGO sets frequently come with a poster or small book that provides a colorful set of visual steps to build a car, airplane, or other creation. The more advanced LEGO sets also tend to come with enough parts to build numerous objects that are displayed on the box's front and back.

Kids loves these multiproject sets, but they tend to forget that they can often build only one object at a time. This means your child will need to break down the model in order to build a different object. And should they lose the little building instruction booklet, they'll probably have a difficult time building a new object from a single picture on the box.

Thankfully, LEGO is well aware that building instructions often disappear and they've made the instructions for their sets available for download as PDF files. Just point your web browser to http://service.lego.com/en us/buildinginstructions/ and enter in the set number, as shown in Figure A.1.

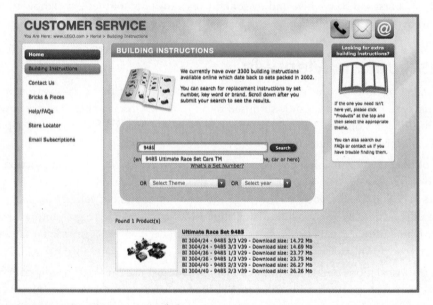

FIGURE A.1 Download LEGO building instructions to replace lost booklets.

As you can see from Figure A.1, after typing in the set number (most often a four- or five-digit number placed prominently on the cover in big numerals), you'll be given a number of download options. For U.S. printers that use standard 8.5×11 paper, you'll want to download the V39 version of any files. And be certain to look for multiple booklets (they'll often be designated as 1/2 and 2/2, for example), so be sure to grab both. Simply right-click the filename and choose to save the PDF to your choice of final destination. (I keep all mine stored in Dropbox.)

TIP

Be on the lookout for bonus instructions! You'll often find a section labeled "Extra Building Instructions" below the basic PDF files that don't come with the printed instructions in the box; these usually contain additional models that can be built with that set's parts—awesome!

Backup Driving Directions

Whenever I need to drive to an unfamiliar address or location, I tend to reach for my phone and use the Google Maps app. Ninety percent of the time, the instructions are accurate and get me to my destination.

But every now and then, Google Maps is either completely off target or stops working. I've had instances where the app (as well as Apple's own Maps app) just wouldn't work due to bad signal or some other technical difficulty.

I hate getting lost—I'm a stickler for knowing how to get from A to B, so years ago I began to get written directions by visiting maps.google.com by entering in the starting point and ending point of my trip. I would then take a screenshot of the step-by-step instructions, as you can see in Figure A.2.

I created a folder in Dropbox called "Directions and Hours" and I store these little snippet screenshots in that folder. Should I find that my driving app isn't working properly, I can simply open the Dropbox app on my iPhone and access the screenshot for the instructions. These little screenshots are also great for emailing to friends and family when they need the same driving instructions. I like accessing them on my iPad because of the larger screen.

TIP

The folder in Dropbox is titled "Directions and Hours" because I also grab screenshots of companies' business hours from their websites (not counting holidays, so be sure to call ahead to be certain they will be open). It saves me time by not having to go online or calling a business over and over again to ask them their hours for a particular day.

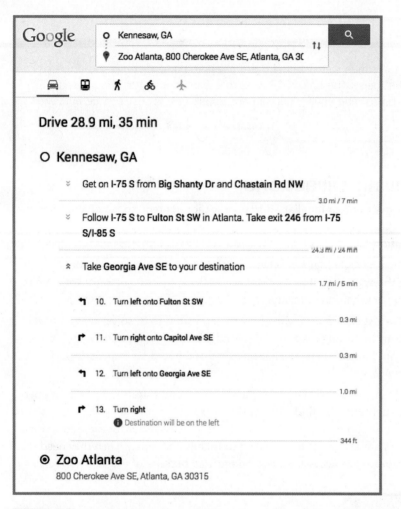

FIGURE A.2   Step-by-step instructions from Google's online map tool.

Cheap Password Manager

If you've followed the instructions in this book, you've probably created a handful of new user accounts. And hopefully you created a strong and unique password for each account. If you're like me, though, you probably don't have a photographic memory, so trying to remember all those passwords is a little unrealistic.

There are dozens and dozens of password manager applications out there, all offering you the ability to store passwords in the application and protecting them all with one super password. Open the app, enter the password, and the app then unlocks access to all your usernames and passwords. You can find these apps by searching the App Store for "password manager," and you'll find plenty with prices from free to $30 or more.

Password management apps are a great resource, but if you don't trust an app with your passwords, you can try this little trick that combines Dropbox and a password-protected PDF file.

You'll need a copy of Word that can save a file as a PDF or an application that can create new PDF files and let you add password protection. All you need to do is create a document that contains a list using the following format:

Website/Service:

Username:

Password:

As you create accounts, simply enter the information into the PDF document. If you assign the PDF with a sufficiently strong password and store the file in Dropbox (or other cloud service), you'll always be able to access your usernames and passwords from a mobile device or computer that can access your cloud service. You'll always have to enter the password to unlock the PDF file, but, again, if the password is strong enough, you shouldn't ever have to worry about someone obtaining the PDF file and breaking in to access your passwords.

Index

Numbers

1DollarScan.com, 126-127

A

accessing
  Dropbox files, 42-46
  Pogoplug files, 49-56
accounts
  Dropbox, 41-46
    accessing files in, 42-46
    limitations, 45
    subscription plans, 41-42
  Evernote
    cleanup, 74
    creating notes in, 68-71
    explained, 59-60
    navigating, 63-67
    offline notebook access, 67
    overview, 61-63
    Premium accounts, 70-71
    requirements, 62
    sending emails to notebooks, 72
    Web Clipper, 72-73
  Pocket, 209
  Pogoplug, 46-56, 242
    accessing files in, 49-56
    cloud hosting option, 47
    configuring, 48-51
    downloading files to GoodReader, 55-56
    passwords, 47
    Pogoplug hardware device, 46
    software solution, 46
Actions (IFTTT)
  associating with Recipes, 198
  creating, 202-203
  explained, 192
activity books, scanning and reusing
  advantages, 266-267
  with PDFpen, 267-279
additional screens, using iPad as, 256-263
Add Tags button (Pocket), 212
Add to Stack button (Evernote), 70
Adjust Display button (Pocket), 212
AirPlay, 55
Alert system (Dropcam), 184-185
Amazon Glacier, 175-178
Amazon Prime, 147
American Express app, 108
AppleTV, 55
apps
  Amazon Prime, 147
  American Express, 108
  Backblaze, 168-174
  banking apps, 104-105
  Bank of America, 107-108
  credit card apps, 107-110

Dropbox, 41-46
  accessing files in, 42-46
  limitations, 45
  subscription plans, 41-42
DVDShrink 3.2, 149-154
Edward Jones, 108-110
Evernote
  cleanup, 74
  creating notes in, 68-71
  explained, 59-60
  navigating, 63-67
  offline notebook access, 67
  overview, 61-63
  Premium accounts, 70-71
  requirements, 62
  scanning notes/sketches into, 233-240
  scanning service, 82
  sending emails to notebooks, 72
  Web Clipper, 72-73
Genius Scan, 78, 82
GoodReader, 55-56, 124
HandBrake, 149, 157-160
Hulu Plus, 147
iBooks, 118-119
iDisplay, 256-263
investment apps, 107-110
Kindle, 118
MakeMKV, 149, 154-157
Mint.com app, 110-112
Netflix, 144-147
Newsstand, 119-120
NextIssue, 119
Nook, 118
password management apps, 300-301
PDFpen, 279-280
  adding signatures to PDF forms, 286-292
  adding text to PDF forms, 280-285
  digital activity books, creating, 267-279
  editing and copying documents, 292-295

PDFpen Scan+, 83-89
Pocket, 208
  accounts, creating, 209
  controls, 211-215
  copying URLs to Clipboard, 215
  emailing URLs to Pocket, 215-219
  home page, 209
Pogoplug, 46-56, 242
  accessing files in, 49-56
  cloud hosting option, 47
  configuring, 48-51
  downloading files to GoodReader, 55-56
  passwords, 47
  Pogoplug hardware device, 46
  software solution, 46
TeamViewer, 242-255
  downloading, 242
  installing, 242-244
  passwords, 246
  Remote Control panel, 244
  TeamViewer: Remote Control app, 247-255
Video, 147-148
WeMo, 186-191
Zinio, 119
app scanners
  Evernote scanning service, 82
  Genius Scan, 78, 82
  PDFpen Scan+, 83-89
Article View button (Pocket), 212
AUDIO_TS folder, 152-159
automating tasks with IFTTT (If This Then That), 191-205

B

Backblaze, 168-174
Back button (Pocket), 211
backup driving directions, 299

backups
of books, 121
importance of, 163-164, 178-179
to disc, 165
to Dropbox or other cloud services, 165
to hard drives, 165
with online storage services (OSS), 166
Backblaze, 168-174
Carbonite.com, 174
CrashPlan, 174
Glacier, 175-178
SOS Online Backup, 174
to tape drive, 165
what to backup, 164-165
bank accounts
banking apps, 104-105
tracking with Mint.com app, 110-112
banking apps, 104-105
Bank of America mobile app, 107-108
Belkin WeMo, 186-191
bill management, 103-104
banking apps, 104-105
credit card apps, 107-110
investment apps, 107-110
Mint.com app, 110-112
security, 113-115
Blu-ray discs
backing up data to, 165
ripping, 148-154
books, 117-118
backing up, 121
converting to digital
cut-and-scan method, 122-126
risks and legal issues, 140-141
scanning services, 126-129, 133-139
organizing with Evernote, 63
purchasing online, 118-122
browsing Channels (IFTTT), 195-196

buying tips
digital books/magazines, 118-122
Dropbox subscription plans, 41-42
hard drives, 41
movies/TV shows, 147-148

C

cameras, Dropcam, 181-186
Carbonite.com, 174
CDs, backing up data to, 165
Channels (IFTTT)
browsing, 195-196
explained, 192
cleanup (Evernote), 74
Clipboard, copying URLs to, 215
cloud
cloud services, 165
compared to local hosting, 40-41, 57
Dropbox, 41-46
accessing files in, 42-46
limitations, 45
subscription plans, 41-42
Pogoplug as cloud hosting device, 47
Cloud Video Recording (CVR) with Dropcam, 184
computers
additional screens, using iPad as, 256-263
controlling remotely with iPad, 242-255
configuring Pogoplug, 48-51
controls (Pocket), 211-215
converting
books/magazines to digital
cut-and-scan method, 122-126
risks and legal issues, 140-141
scanning services, 126-128
ScanSnap SV600 Contactless Scanner, 128-129, 133-139

DVD/Blue-ray discs to digital, 148-150
  legal issues, 161-162
  with DVDShrink 3.2, 150-154
  with HandBrake, 157-160
  with MakeMKV, 154-157
copying
  PDF forms, 292-295
  URLs to Clipboard, 215
copyright
  books/magazines, 140-141
  DVD/Blue-ray discs, 161-162
costs
  Dropbox subscription plans, 41-42
  Evernote, 60
  hard drives, 41
  Pogoplug, 46
CrashPlan, 174
credit card apps, 107-110
CVR (Cloud Video Recording) with Dropcam, 184

D

decluttering system, 33-36
Deep Storage, 168. *See also* backups
Delete button (Pocket), 212
desktop scanners, 93-101
digital books, 117-118
  backing up, 121
  converting printed books to
    cut-and-scan method, 122-126
    risks and legal issues, 140-141
    scanning services, 126-128
    ScanSnap SV600 Contactless Scanner, 128-139
  purchasing, 118-122

digital documents, filling out with PDFpen, 279-280
  adding signatures to PDF forms, 286, 290-292
  adding text to PDF forms, 280-285
  editing and copying documents, 292-295
digital magazines, 117-118
  converting print magazines to
    cut-and-scan method, 122-126
    risks and legal issues, 140-141
    scanning services, 126-128
    ScanSnap SV600 Contactless Scanner, 128-129, 133-139
  purchasing, 118-122
Digital Millennium Copyright Act, 161
digital movies
  legal issues, 161-162
  purchasing online, 147-148
  ripping, 148-150
    with DVDShrink 3.2, 150-154
    with HandBrake, 157-160
    with MakeMKV, 154-157
  streaming subscription services, 144-147
directions, downloading, 299
DMCA (Digital Millennium Copyright Act), 161
documents, filling out with PDFpen, 279-280
  adding signatures to PDF forms, 286-292
  adding text to PDF forms, 280-285
  editing and copying documents, 292-295
downloading
  driving directions, 299
  LEGO building instructions, 298
  online instruction manuals, 297
  Pogoplug files to GoodReader, 55-56
  TeamViewer app, 242

Doxie Go, 91-92

driving directions, 299

Dropbox, 8-10, 41-46, 165
  accessing files in, 42-46
  configure, 22-24, 27-33
  limitations, 45
  sign up, 18-20
  subscription plans, 41-42

Dropcam, 181-186

duplicating PDF forms, 292-295

DVDs
  backing up data to, 165
  ripping, 148-150
    legal issues, 161-162
    with DVDShrink 3.2, 150-154
    with HandBrake, 157-160
    with MakeMKV, 154-157

DVDShrink 3.2, 149-154

E

Edit button (Evernote), 69-70

editing PDF forms, 292-295

Edward Jones app, 108-110

email
  sending to notebooks, 72
  sending to Pocket, 215-219

Evernote, 10-12
  cleanup, 74
  configure, 21, 24-25
  creating notes in, 68-71
  explained, 59-60
  navigating, 63-67
  Notebook system, 233-240
  offline notebook access, 67
  overview, 61-63
  Premium accounts, 70-71
  requirements, 62

scanning notes/sketches into, 233-240

scanning service, 82

sending emails to notebooks, 72

sign up, 20-21

Web Clipper, 72-73

Exclusions tab (Backblaze), 172

External Hard Drive, 7-8

F

FedEx/Kinkos offices, 122-123

files
  Dropbox files, accessing, 42-46
  PDF files, converting online content to,
    219-233
  Pogoplug files
    accessing, 49-56
    downloading to GoodReader, 55-56

filling out documents with PDFpen,
  279-280
  adding signatures to PDF forms, 286,
    290-292
  adding text to PDF forms, 280-285
  editing and copying documents, 292-295

financial management, 103-104
  banking apps, 104-105
  credit card apps, 107-110
  investment apps, 107-110
  Mint.com app, 110-112
  security, 113-115

flatbed scanners, 76

folders
  AUDIO_TS, 152, 158-159
  VIDEO_TS, 152, 158-159

forms (PDF)
  adding signatures to, 286, 290-292
  adding text to, 280-285
  editing and copying documents, 292-295

Fujitsu ScanSnap SV600 Contactless
Scanner, 128-129, 133-139
Fujitsu ScanSnap iX500, 93-101

G

Genius Scan app, 78, 82
Glacier, 175-178
GoodReader, 13-14, 25-33, 55-56, 124
Google Maps, 299

H

HandBrake, 149, 157-160
hard drives
  backing up data to, 165
  Deep Storage hard drives, 166-168, 172
hardware, Pogoplug device, 46
home page (Pocket), 209
Hulu Plus, 147

I

iBooks, 118-119
iDisplay app, 256-263
IFTTT (If This Then That), 191-205
  Actions
    associating with Recipes, 198
    creating, 202-203
    explained, 192
  Channels
    browsing, 195-196
    explained, 192
    Gmail Channel, 193
  PINs, 203

Recipes
  creating, 195-205
  explained, 192
Triggers, 192
iPad, purchasing, 3-4
installing TeamViewer app, 242-244
instructables.com, 139
instruction manuals, downloading
  LEGO building instructions, 298
  online instruction manuals, 297
investment apps, 107-110
investments, tracking with Mint.com app,
  110-112
Isolate button (PrintWhatYouLike.com),
  230
iTunes, 147-148

J-K

kids' activity books, scanning and reusing
  advantages, 266-267
  with PDFpen, 267-279
Kindle app, 118

L

laptops
  additional screens, using iPad as, 256-263
  controlling remotely with iPad, 242-255
LED light bulbs (WeMo), 189-190
legal issues
  books/magazines, 140-141
  DVD/Blue-ray discs, 161-162
LEGO building instructions,
  downloading, 298
Light Switch (WeMo), 190
limitations of Dropbox, 45

local hosting
compared to cloud hosting, 40-41, 57
Pogoplug, 46-56
accessing files in, 49-56
cloud hosting option, 47
configuring, 48-51
downloading files to GoodReader, 55-56
passwords, 47
Pogoplug hardware device, 46
software solution, 46
locking iPad, 113-115

M

magazines, 117-118
converting to digital
cut-and-scan method, 122-126
risks and legal issues, 140-141
scanning services, 126-128
ScanSnap SV600 Contactless Scanner,
128-129, 133-139
purchasing online, 118-122
MakeMKV, 149, 154-157
managing passwords, 300-301
manuals
downloading
LEGO building instructions, 298
online instruction manuals, 297
organizing with Evernote, 63
manuals (instruction), downloading, 297
manualsonline.com, 297
Maps (Google), 299
Mint.com app, 110-112
motion sensor (WeMo), 189
movies
legal issues, 161-162
playing with Pogoplug, 55
purchasing online, 147-148

ripping, 148-150
with DVDShrink 3.2, 150-154
with HandBrake, 157-160
with MakeMKV, 154-157
streaming subscription services, 144-147

N

navigating Evernote, 63-67
Netflix, 144-147
New button (Pocket), 212
New Notebook button (Evernote), 69
Newsstand app, 119-120
NextIssue app, 119
Nook app, 118
notebooks (Evernote), 64
Notebooks section (Evernote), 64
Notebook system (Evernote), 233-240
notes
adding web content to, 72-73
creating in Evernote, 68-71
scanning into Evernote, 233-240
sending email to, 72
novels, organizing with Evernote, 63

O

offline notebook access (Evernote), 67
online content
converting to PDF, 219-220
with PrintFriendly.com, 220-227
with PrintWhatYouLike.com, 227-233
saving with Pocket app, 208
accounts, creating, 209
controls, 211-215
copying URLs to Clipboard, 215
emailing URLs to Pocket, 215-219
home page, 209

online instruction manuals, downloading, 297

online storage services (OSS), 166
Backblaze, 168-174
Carbonite.com, 174
CrashPlan, 174
Glacier, 175-178
SOS Online Backup, 174

On/Off button (WeMo), 187-188

O'Reilly, 121

organizing
with Dropbox, 41-46, 165
  accessing files in, 42-46
  limitations, 45
  subscription plans, 41-42
with Evernote
  cleanup, 74
  creating notes in, 68-71
  explained, 59-60
  navigating, 63-67
  offline notebook access, 67
  overview, 61-63
  Premium accounts, 70-71
  requirements, 62
  sending emails to notebooks, 72
  Web Clipper, 72-73

OSS (online storage services), 166
Backblaze, 168-174
Carbonite.com, 174
CrashPlan, 174
Glacier, 175-178
SOS Online Backup, 174

P

Passcode Lock option, 113-115
password management apps, 300-301

passwords
managing, 300-301
Passcode Lock option, 113-115
Pogoplug, 47
testing, 47

PDF forms
adding signatures to, 286-292
adding text to, 280-285
converting online content to, 219-220
  with PrintFriendly.com, 220-227
  with PrintWhatYouLike.com, 227-233
editing and copying, 292-295

PDFpen app, 12-13, 279-280
adding signatures to PDF forms, 286-292
adding text to PDF forms, 280-285
digital activity books, creating, 267-279
editing and copying documents, 292-295

PDFpen Scan+, 83-89

PINs, IFTTT PIN, 203

playing movies/videos with Pogoplug, 55

Pocket app, 208
accounts, creating, 209
controls, 211-215
copying URLs to Clipboard, 215
emailing URLs to Pocket, 215-219
home page, 209

Pogoplug, 46-56, 242
accessing files in, 49-56
cloud hosting option, 47
configuring, 48-51
downloading files to GoodReader, 55-56
passwords, 47
Pogoplug hardware device, 46
software solution, 46

pointing, 70

portable scanners, 91-93

Post-It Notes, scanning into Evernote, 233-240

Premium accounts (Evernote), 70-71

PrintFriendly.com, 220-227, 297

PrintWhatYouLike.com, 227-233, 297

purchasing

digital books/magazines, 118-122

Dropbox subscription plans, 41-42

hard drives, 41

movies/TV shows, 147-148

Q-R

Read/Archive button (Pocket), 212

Reading List feature (Safari), 208

receipts, organizing with Evernote, 63

recipes, organizing with Evernote, 63

Recipes (IFTTT)

creating, 195-205

explained, 192

Refresh button (Pocket), 212

remote control

of computers/laptops, 242-255

with WeMo, 186-191

Remove button (PrintWhatYouLike.com), 230

Resize button (PrintWhatYouLike.com), 230

ripping

DVD/Blue-ray discs, 148-150

HandBrake, 157-160

legal issues, 161-162

MakeMKV, 154-157

with DVDShrink 3.2, 150-154

S

Safari Reading List feature, 208

Save Clip button (PrintWhatYouLike.com), 230

saving. *See also* scanning

online content as PDFs, 219-220

with PrintFriendly.com, 220-227

with PrintWhatYouLike.com, 227-233

websites with Pocket app, 208

accounts, creating, 209

controls, 211-215

copying URLs to Clipboard, 215

emailing URLs to Pocket, 215-219

home page, 209

scanners. *See also* scanning

app scanners

Evernote, 82

Genius Scan, 78, 82

PDFpen Scan+, 83-89

desktop scanners, 93-101

explained, 4-7, 76-77

features, 77

flatbed scanners, 76

overview, 75

portable scanners, 91-93

ScanSnap SV600 Contactless Scanner, 128-139

scanning

books/magazines

cut-and-scan method, 122-126

risks and legal issues, 140-141

scanning services, 126-128

ScanSnap SV600 Contactless Scanner, 128-139

digital documents, 279-280

adding signatures to PDF forms, 286-292

adding text to PDF forms, 280-285

editing and copying documents, 292-295

notes/sketches into Evernote, 233-240

kids activity books

advantages, 266-267

with PDFpen, 267-279

scanning services, 126-128

ScanSnap iX500 (Fujitsu), 93-101
ScanSnap SV600 Contactless Scanner,
   128-139
scheduling Dropcam, 184
school records, organizing with
   Evernote, 63
screen, using iPad as, 256-263
Search button (Pocket), 215
security, 36-37
   Passcode Lock option, 113-115
   passwords, 47
   Pogoplug, 47
Select More button
   (PrintWhatYouLike.com), 230
sending
   email to notebooks, 72
   email to Pocket, 215-219
services
   IFTTT (If This Then That), 191-205
      Actions, 192, 198-203
      browsing, 195-196
      Channels, 192-193
      PINs, 203
      Recipes, 192, 195-205
      Triggers, 192
   PrintFriendly.com, 220-227
   PrintWhatYouLike.com, 227-233
   scanning services, 126-128
   streaming subscription services, 144-147
Settings button (Dropcam), 184
Share button (Pocket), 212
Share button (Pogoplug), 55
signatures, adding to PDF forms, 286,
   290-292
Sign In button (Pogoplug), 51
sketches, scanning into Evernote, 233-240
Smart LED light bulbs (WeMo), 189-190
SOS Online Backup, 174

Star button (Pocket), 212
storage
   cloud hosting compared to local hosting,
      40-41, 57
   Dropbox, 41-46
      accessing files in, 42-46
      limitations, 45
      subscription plans, 41-42
   overview, 39-40
   Pogoplug, 46-56
      accessing files in, 49-56
      cloud hosting option, 47
      configuring, 48
      downloading files to GoodReader, 55-56
      passwords, 47
      Pogoplug hardware device, 46
      software solution, 46
streaming subscription services, 144-147
subscription plans (Dropbox), 41-42
subscription services, 144-147

T

tape drives, backing up data to, 165
tasks, automating with IFTTT (If This
   Then That), 191-205
TeamViewer, 242-255
   downloading, 242
   installing, 242-244
   passwords, 246
   Remote Control panel, 244
   TeamViewer: Remote Control app,
      247-255
testing passwords, 47
text, adding to PDF forms, 280-285
tracking bank accounts/investments with
   Mint.com, 110-112
Triggers (IFTTT), 192

turning on/off passcode lock feature, 113-115

TV shows. *See also* video
  purchasing online, 147-148
  streaming subscription services, 144-147

U

unlimited backup services, 166
  Backblaze, 168-174
  Carbonite.com, 174
  CrashPlan, 174
  Glacier, 175-178
  SOS Online Backup, 174

URLs
  copying to Clipboard, 215
  emailing to Pocket, 215-219

user manuals, organizing with Evernote, 63

V

video
  legal issues, 161-162
  playing with Pogoplug, 55
  purchasing online, 147-148
  ripping, 148-150
    with DVDShrink 3.2, 150-154
    with HandBrake, 157-160
    with MakeMKV, 154-157
  streaming subscription services, 144-147

Video app, 147-148

video monitoring with Dropcam, 181-186

VIDEO_TS folder, 152-159

viewing
  Dropbox files, 42-46
  Pogoplug files, 49-56

W-X-Y-Z

Web Clipper, 72-73

web content, adding to notes, 72-73

websites
  converting to PDF, 219-220
    with PrintFriendly.com, 220-227
    with PrintWhatYouLike.com, 227-233
  LEGO building instructions, 298
  manualsonline.com, 297
  PrintFriendly.com, 297
  PrintWhatYouLike.com, 297
  saving with Pocket app, 208
    accounts, creating, 209
    controls, 211-215
    copying URLs to Clipboard, 215
    emailing URLs to Pocket, 215-219
    home page, 209

Web View button (Pocket), 212

WeMo, 186-191

Widen button (PrintWhatYouLike.com), 230

Wi-Fi cameras, 181-186

Zinio app, 119

Cajun Style Chicken Leg Quarters

Barbeque chicken with New Orleans flavor

	x3	x6	x9
4 chicken leg quarters	12	24	36
1–14.5 oz. can diced tomatoes, undrained	3	6	9
½ cup vegetable oil	1½c	3c	4½c
¼ cup onion, finely chopped	¾c	1½c	2¼c
¼ cup green bell pepper, finely chopped	¾c	1½c	2¼c
2 cloves garlic, minced	6	12	18
1 t. brown sugar	1T	2T	3T
½ t. hot pepper sauce	1½t	1T	4½t
½ t. dried basil	1½t	1T	4½t
½ t. dried oregano	1½t	1T	4½t
1 bay leaf, crumbled	3	6	9
¼ t. cayenne pepper	¾t	1½t	2¼t
½ t. black pepper	1½t	1T	4½t

Original Recipe Yield

4 large servings

Cooking Day

Combine all ingredients except chicken. Place chicken quarters in a freezer bag and pour marinade over chicken. Freeze, using freezer bag method.

Serving Day

Thaw completely. Brush chicken with marinade and grill over medium heat, until chicken is tender and cooked through.

Lighter Fare Nutritional Information (per serving): Calories 184; Total Fat 15g; Cholesterol 31mg; Sodium 143mg; Total Carbohydrates 4g; Dietary Fiber 1g; Protein 8g

Calypso Salmon

Serve with rice and an assortment of grilled vegetables

	x2	x4	x6
2 lbs. fresh salmon	4 lbs	8 lbs	12 lbs
6 oz. amber beer (not light beer)	12oz	24oz	36oz
1 T. fresh ginger, chopped	2T	¼c	¼c + 2T
4 large cloves of garlic, minced	8	16	24
½ cup soy sauce	1c	2c	3c
¾ cup finely chopped cilantro	1½c	3c	4½c

Original Recipe Yield

4–6 servings

Cooking Day

Place fish in a large freezer bag. Mix remaining ingredients and pour over salmon. Freeze, using freezer bag method.

Serving Day

Thaw salmon completely before cooking. Discard marinade. Grill salmon over medium heat on foil that has been sprayed with cooking spray. Salmon may also be grilled on an oiled stovetop griddle pan or broiled in the oven 4 inches from heat, 5 minutes per ½ inch thickness or until fish flakes.

Lighter Fare Nutritional Information (per serving): Calories 377; Total Fat 15.4g; Cholesterol 134mg; Sodium 904mg; Total Carbohydrates 4.5g; Fiber .03g; Protein 50.4g

Chicken Cordon Bleu

A traditional favorite with a delicious twist

	x3	x6	x9
4 large boneless, skinless chicken breasts	12	24	36
½ lb. shaved or thinly sliced ham	1½ lbs	3 lbs	4½ lbs
8 thin slices Swiss cheese	24	48	72
½ cup flour	1½c	3c	4½c
1 T. paprika	3T	¼c + 2T	½c + 1T
1 beaten egg	3	6	9
½ cup plain breadcrumbs	1½c	3c	4½c

Béchamel sauce

	x3	x6	x9
2 T. butter	¼c + 2T	¾c	1c + 2T
1½ cups milk	4½c	9c	13½c
2 T. flour	¼c + 2T	¾c	1c + 2T
2 slices Swiss cheese	6	12	18

Original Recipe Yield

4 servings

Cooking Day

Béchamel sauce: warm butter and milk in saucepan over medium heat until butter melts. Whisk in flour. Add cheese, stirring until cheese melts and sauce thickens.

Pound chicken breasts to uniform thickness (approx. ¼ inch thick). Top each breast with 1–2 slices of ham, two thin slices of Swiss cheese, and a dollop of béchamel sauce. Roll up each chicken breast, securing with a toothpick if necessary. In a bowl, mix together flour and paprika. Place beaten egg and breadcrumbs in two additional bowls. Dip each breast first in the flour mixture, then the egg, and finally the breadcrumbs, rolling to cover well. Brown the rolled chicken on all sides in an oiled skillet for about three minutes. Wrap cooled chicken breasts individually in plastic wrap, then place in freezer bag and freeze. Freeze extra béchamel sauce in a separate bag.

Serving Day

Thaw completely. Bake thawed chicken breasts in a 375 degree oven until done, approximately 20–30 minutes. Pour thawed béchamel sauce over chicken breasts for the last 5 minutes of cooking.

Hint

For less mess and easy cleanup, place each chicken breast inside a large freezer bag before pounding breast to desired thickness using the flat side of a meat mallet or rolling pin.

Chicken Marsala

Elegant fare you can make at home

	x3	x6	x9
6 boneless, skinless chicken breasts	18	36	54
1 cup butter, melted and divided	3c	6c	9c
½ cup flour	1½c	3c	4½c
1½ cups fresh mushrooms, finely sliced	4½c	9c	13½c
1¼ cups Marsala wine	3¾c	7½c	11¼c
1 cup chicken broth	3c	6c	9c
¾ t. salt	2¼t	4½t	2T + ¾t
¼ t. pepper	¾t	1½t	2¼t

Serving Day

1 cup shredded mozzarella cheese
1 cup fresh parmesan cheese, grated

Original Recipe Yield

6 servings

Cooking Day

Pound chicken to ¼ inch thickness. Dredge chicken in flour and then sauté in ½ cup melted butter, 3–4 minutes per side. Place chicken breasts in a lined 9 x 13 baking dish, overlapping edges. In separate saucepan, sauté mushrooms in remaining ½ cup butter until tender, then spoon over chicken. Stir wine and chicken broth into skillet containing chicken drippings. Simmer for 10 minutes. Add salt and pepper. Spoon sauce over chicken. Cool completely, then freeze using foil and plastic wrap method.

Serving Day

Place chicken in original baking dish and thaw completely. Bake chicken at 450 degrees for 12–15 minutes. Sprinkle parmesan and mozzarella cheeses over chicken and broil on high heat for 1–2 minutes, until cheese is lightly browned.

Hint

For less mess and easy cleanup, place each chicken breast inside a large freezer bag before pounding breast to desired thickness using the flat side of a meat mallet or rolling pin.

Chicken Oreganato

A complete one-dish meal you can take to a friend

	x3	x6	x9
3 lbs. cut up chicken pieces	9 lbs	18 lbs	27 lbs
4 medium potatoes, cut into medium chunks	12	24	36
4 Roma or plum tomatoes, quartered	12	24	36
1 large onion, cut into medium chunks	3	6	9
¼ cup olive oil	¾c	1½c	2¼c
¼ cup fresh oregano, coarsely chopped	¾c	1½c	2¼c
½ t. kosher salt	1½t	1T	4½t
½ t. freshly ground pepper	1½t	1T	4½t

Original Recipe Yield

6 servings

Cooking Day

In a large bowl, combine chicken and vegetables. Add olive oil, oregano, salt, and pepper. Stir until chicken and vegetables are evenly coated. Place chicken and vegetables in a freezer bag. Freeze, using freezer bag method.

Serving Day

Thaw completely. Preheat oven to 450 degrees. Place chicken and vegetables into a large roasting pan, making sure that the chicken is skin-side up and resting on top of the vegetables. Roast until chicken juices run clear, about 1–1½ hours.

Ginger Glazed Mahi Mahi

A grilled dish with an Asian flair

	x3	x6	x9
4 mahi mahi fillets (1½ lbs. total)	12	24	36
3 T. brown sugar	½c + 1T	1c + 2T	1½c + 3T
2 T. honey	¼c + 2T	¾c	1c + 2T
3 T. soy sauce	½c +1T	1c + 2T	1½c + 3T
3 T. balsamic vinegar	½c +1T	1c + 2T	1½c + 3T
¾ t. freshly grated ginger root	2¼t	4½t	2T + ¾t
or ¼ t. ground ginger	¾t	1½t	2¼t
1 clove garlic, crushed	3	6	9
2 t. olive oil	2T	¼c	¼c + 2T
¼ t. salt	¾t	1½t	2¼t
¼ t. pepper	¾t	1½t	2¼t

Original Recipe Yield

4 servings

Cooking Day

In a mixing bowl, stir together brown sugar, honey, soy sauce, balsamic vinegar, ginger, garlic, and olive oil. Season fish fillets with salt and pepper, and place them into a freezer bag. Pour ginger marinade over fish. Freeze, using freezer bag method.

Serving Day

Allow fillets to thaw completely—do not microwave to thaw. Reserve marinade. Grill fillets over medium heat for 4–6 minutes per side (depending on thickness), turning only once. Fish may also be fried in 1 T. vegetable oil over medium-high heat. Fish is done when it flakes easily with a fork. Remove fillets to serving platter and keep warm.

While fish is on the grill, pour marinade into a saucepan and bring to a boil over medium heat. Boil for 2 additional minutes, until the mixture reduces to a glaze consistency. Spoon the glaze over the cooked fish and serve immediately with rice and a green vegetable.

Hint

Quality mahi mahi is easy to recognize. Fresh mahi mahi never smells fishy, and when you press it with a finger, its flesh will give slightly and then spring back into shape.

Lighter Fare Nutritional Information (per serving): Calories 259; Total Fat 7g; Sodium 839mg; Cholesterol 124mg; Total Carbohydrates 16g; Fiber .2g; Protein 32g

Gourmet Salmon Burgers

Not your average salmon patty!

	x3	x6	x9
1 lb. fresh salmon	3 lbs	6 lbs	9 lbs
1 egg, beaten	3	6	9
3 T. chopped onion	½c + 1T	1c + 2T	1½c + 3T
3 T. soy sauce	½c + 1T	1c + 2T	1½c + 3T
1 T. sugar	3T	¼c + 2T	½c + 1T
¼ t. ground ginger	¾t	1½t	2¼t
¼ t. garlic powder	¾t	1½t	2¼t
1½ t. sesame oil	4½t	3T	¼c + 1½t
1½ t. sesame seeds	4½t	3T	¼c + 1½t
6 T. plain breadcrumbs	1c + 2T	2¼c	3¼c + 2T

Original Recipe Yield

6 large burgers

Cooking Day

Cut fresh salmon into very small pieces and place in mixing bowl. Add remaining ingredients to bowl. Mix well. Form salmon mixture into patties. Wrap each patty separately in plastic wrap and place in freezer bag. Freeze, using freezer bag method.

Serving Day

Allow salmon patties to thaw. Heat 1 T. oil in skillet and fry burgers until browned on both sides. Serve with rice and steamed vegetables.

Lighter Fare Nutritional Information (per serving): Calories 195.3; Total Fat 8.7g; Cholesterol 89.1mg; Sodium 536.9mg; Total Carbohydrates 6.4g; Fiber 4g

Grilled Coconut Lime Chicken Tenders

Tender morsels in wonderful coconut cream and lime marinade

	x3	x6	x9
1½ lbs. chicken tenders or boneless chicken breast, sliced	4½ lbs	9 lbs	13½ lbs
2 T. sugar	¼c + 2T	¾c	1c + 2T
2 small cloves garlic, minced	6	12	18
1 stalk lemongrass, minced*	3	6	9
1 small jalapeno pepper, seeded and minced	3	6	9
1½ t. ground coriander	4½t	3T	¼c + 1½t
½ t. turmeric	1½t	1T	1T + 1½t
½ t. black pepper	1½t	1T	1T + 1½t
¾ cup unsweetened coconut milk	2¼c	4½c	6¾c
1½ T. fish sauce (nam pla)**	3T	¼c + 2T	½c + 1T
1½ T. soy sauce	3T	¼c + 2T	½c + 1T
2 T. lime juice***	¼c	½c	¾c

Serving Day

chopped cilantro or sesame seeds, for garnish

Asian peanut sauce (purchased, or see Bangkok Chicken Satay, page 124)

*Lemongrass can be found in Asian specialty stores and in the produce section of larger grocery stores. It can also be found in a "tube," allowing you to squeeze out the portion you need and store the rest for later use. *Substitution: 2½ T. lemongrass from squeeze tube or 2 strips of lemon zest may be substituted for the lemongrass stalk in this recipe.*

**Nam pla, known as fish sauce, is an intensely flavored sauce, adding a wonderful depth to many dishes. A little goes a long way. It can be found in Asian markets or in the gourmet/ethnic food aisles of many grocery stores. It lasts a long time when stored in the refrigerator.

***This measurement, when multiplied, has been adjusted to accommodate the intensified flavor of acidic ingredients when recipes are made in quantity.

Original Recipe Yield

6–8 appetizers or 4–6 entrées

Cooking Day

Rinse chicken tenders under cold running water. Blot dry on paper towels. In a freezer bag, lay chicken strips flat in a single layer; place bag in refrigerator. In a glass bowl, place sugar, garlic, lemongrass, jalapeno pepper, coriander, turmeric, and pepper. Mix together with a wooden spoon to form a paste. While mixing, use the back of the spoon to press the ingredients together to release the spices and oils.

Stir in the coconut milk, fish sauce, soy sauce, and lime juice until smooth and blended. Pour marinade over chicken, seal the bag well, and let marinate in refrigerator for 20 minutes. Freeze, using freezer bag method.

Serving Day

Thaw chicken tenders, allowing chicken to marinate in sauce. If you are using a grill and wooden skewers, soak the skewers in water for 30–40 minutes to prevent burning. Thread the skewers with chicken tenders, discarding marinade. Spray outdoor grill surface with oil or cooking spray, or oil an indoor grill pan or broiler pan. Grill the tenders for only 1–2 minutes per side—they cook very quickly. The chicken will turn white and be firm when done; don't over-cook. Transfer to a platter, sprinkle with cilantro or sesame seeds, and serve with peanut sauce.

Grilled Honey Lime Chicken

Great for summer on the grill, with a southwestern flair!

	x3	x6	x9
4 boneless chicken breasts	12	24	36
½ cup fresh lime juice*	1¼c	2½c	3¾c
½ cup olive oil	1½c	3c	4½c
¼ cup honey	¾c	1½c	2¼c
¼ cup fresh cilantro, finely chopped	¾c	1½c	2¼c
2 garlic cloves, minced	6	12	18
2 t. chopped jalapeno pepper	2T	¼c	¼c + 2T

*This measurement, when multiplied, has been adjusted to accommodate the intensified flavor of acidic ingredients when recipes are made in quantity.

Original Recipe Yield

4 servings

Cooking Day

Mix together lime juice, olive oil, honey, cilantro, garlic, and jalapeno pepper. Place chicken breasts in freezer bag. Pour marinade over chicken breasts. Freeze, using freezer bag method.

Serving Day

Thaw chicken completely. Grill over medium heat until chicken is tender and juices run clear. This dish is delicious served as a whole chicken breast, or it can be cut into strips and served as a southwestern chicken wrap with your favorite toppings!

Hint

This marinade makes an absolutely wonderful salad dressing served over fresh salad, with or without the chicken.

Lighter Fare Nutritional Information (per serving): Calories 167; Total Fat 7.2g; Cholesterol 17mg; Sodium 21mg; Total Carbohydrates 21g; Dietary Fiber .2g; Protein 7g

Maui Grilled Chicken Sandwiches

Teriyaki sauce, cheese, and pineapple make this sandwich a delight!

	x3	x6	x9
4 boneless chicken breasts	12	24	36
½ t. garlic powder	1½t	1T	4½t
2 t. Worcestershire sauce	2T	¼c	¼c + 2T
1 T. brown sugar	3T	¼c + 2T	½c + 1T
¼ t. ground ginger	¾t	1½t	2¼t
½ t. black pepper	1½t	1T	4½t
1 T. cooking oil	3T	¼c + 2T	½c + 1T
2 T. water	¼c + 2T	¾c	1c + 2T
½ cup soy sauce	1½c	3c	4½c
4 fresh (or canned) pineapple slices	12	24	36

Serving Day

4 sandwich buns

4–8 slices of provolone or Swiss cheese

fresh pineapple slices

lettuce, sliced tomato, and mayonnaise

Original Recipe Yield

4 sandwiches

Cooking Day

In a mixing bowl, stir together garlic powder, Worcestershire sauce, brown sugar, ginger, pepper, oil, water, and soy sauce. Place chicken breasts and pineapple slices in freezer bag. Pour marinade over chicken and pineapple and freeze, using freezer bag method.

Serving Day

Allow chicken to thaw completely. Reserve marinade from freezer bag and pour it into a saucepan. Heat slowly to boiling, and continue boiling for 2 additional minutes. Grill chicken over medium heat until done, turning only once. During final minutes, place 1 or 2 slices of cheese on each chicken breast until just soft but not completely melted. Remove breasts from grill and place on toasted buns with fresh pineapple slices. (Pineapple slices may also be grilled, if desired.) Spoon desired amount of marinade over chicken and add your preferred toppings. Serve with fresh fruit salad.

Lighter Fare Nutritional Information (per serving): Calories 493.3; Total Fat 21.3g; Cholesterol 181.4mg; Sodium 456.7g; Total Carbohydrates 6.3g; Fiber 1g; Protein 64.3g

Monterey Jack Stuffed Chicken

Outstanding—you will be asking for more!

	x2	x4	x6
6 fresh, boneless chicken breasts	12	24	36
10 oz. Monterey jack cheese with jalapenos (not shredded)	20oz.	40oz.	60oz.
4 eggs, beaten	8	16	24
¼ cup bottled salsa (not chunky) or taco sauce (mild or medium)	½c	1c	1½c
¼ t. salt	½t	1t	1½t
2 cups panko breadcrumbs*	4c	8c	12c
2 t. chili powder	1T + 1t	2T + 2t	¼c
2 t. ground cumin	1T + 1t	2T + 2t	¼c
1½ t. garlic salt	1T	2T	3T
½ t. dried oregano	1t	2t	1T

Serving Day

¼ cup butter

sliced avocado, cherry tomatoes, sour cream, and salsa

*Japanese panko breadcrumbs can be found in the gourmet/ethnic section of larger grocery stores or in larger quantities in Asian markets. Panko crumbs are much lighter than regular breadcrumbs, and make a crunchier coating when baked or fried.

Original Recipe Yield

5–6 servings

Cooking Day

Cut Monterey jack cheese into 6 equal pieces measuring approximately ⅜ x 4 inches. Cut a horizontal slit or pocket into the side of each chicken breast—don't cut all the way through! Place one piece of cheese in the pocket of each chicken breast. To secure the cheese in the pocket, use 2–3 wooden toothpicks if needed.

In a shallow pan or pie plate, mix together eggs, salsa, and salt. In a separate pan, combine the panko breadcrumbs, chili powder, cumin, garlic salt, and oregano. Dip each chicken breast in the egg mixture to coat, then dip the breast in the panko crumb mixture. (See kitchen tip below.) Place coated breasts in a shallow baking dish. Freeze for 1 hour, then carefully wrap each chicken breast in plastic wrap and place in a freezer bag. Freeze using freezer bag method.

Serving Day

Carefully unwrap chicken breasts. Place ¼ cup butter in a 9 x 13 baking dish and put in oven while it is preheating to 375 degrees. As soon as the butter is melted, remove the pan from the oven. Place chicken in dish, turning to coat with butter. Bake uncovered about 35–40 minutes, or just until done. Serve immediately and garnish with a side of salsa, sour cream, avocado slices, and tomatoes.

Kitchen Tip

Use disposable gloves to dip and bread chicken breasts. As well as safeguarding the chicken, it makes for a quick cleanup. Disposable gloves are available at warehouse club stores and in some larger grocery stores.

Orange Braised Chicken Thighs with Green Olives

A wonderful blend of flavors

	x3	x6	x9
4 chicken thighs, with skin	12	24	36
2 t. olive oil	2T	¼c	¼c + 2T
3 large garlic cloves, minced	9	18	27
1 medium onion, sliced thin	3	6	9
½ t. ground cumin	1½t	1T	4½t
½ cup fresh orange juice	1½c	3c	4½c
1 T. fresh lemon juice*	2T	¼c	¼c + 2T
⅓ cup small pitted green olives	1c	2c	3c
salt and pepper to taste			

*This measurement, when multiplied, has been adjusted to accommodate the intensified flavor of acidic ingredients when recipes are made in quantity.

Original Recipe Yield

4 servings

Cooking Day

Rinse chicken and pat dry. Season chicken with salt and pepper. In a heavy skillet, heat oil over moderately high heat until hot but not smoking, and brown chicken. Transfer chicken to a plate.

Pour off all but about 1 T. oil from skillet. Reduce heat to moderate, and add garlic, cooking and stirring until it begins to turn golden. Add onion and cook, still stirring, until onion is pale golden. Stir in cumin, citrus juices, and salt and pepper to taste. Stir in chicken and olives. Cool completely and place chicken and sauce in freezer bag. Freeze, using freezer bag method.

Serving Day

Thaw chicken completely. Simmer in sauce, covered, for 25–35 minutes, until chicken is tender and no longer pink.

Orange Pine Nut Chicken

A light and simple but classy company meal

	x3	x6	x9
4 boneless chicken breasts	12	24	36
¼ cup orange juice	¾c	1½c	2¼c
¼ cup white cooking wine	¾c	1½c	2¼c
1 T. olive oil	3T	¼c + 2T	½c + 1T
1 T. fresh Italian parsley, chopped	3T	¼c + 2T	½c + 1T
1 t. garlic, minced	1T	2T	3T
1 t. grated orange peel	1T	2T	3T
1 t. dried thyme	1T	2T	3T
½ t. salt	1½t	1T	4½t

Serving Day

1 T. honey

⅓ cup pine nuts, toasted

Original Recipe Yield

4 servings

Cooking Day

Mix all ingredients except chicken together in a medium bowl. Place chicken breasts in a freezer bag, and pour marinade over chicken. Freeze, using freezer bag method.

Serving Day

Thaw completely. Remove chicken breasts from freezer bag, reserving marinade. Grill chicken over medium heat, until chicken is tender and no longer pink. While chicken is grilling, toast pine nuts on a cookie sheet in a 350 degree oven for about 15 minutes, until lightly browned. In a small saucepan, combine the reserved marinade and 1 T. honey. Bring to a full boil and continue boiling for 2 minutes. Place grilled chicken on a serving platter and pour sauce over chicken breasts. Top with toasted pine nuts to serve.

Lighter Fare Nutritional Information (per serving): Calories 208; Total Fat 13.2g; Cholesterol 40mg; Sodium 406mg; Total Carbohydrates 9g; Dietary Fiber 1g; Protein 14g

Parmesan Garlic Chicken

A quick, kid-friendly dinner

	x3	x6	x9
6 boneless chicken breasts	18	36	54
1 cup freshly grated parmesan cheese	3c	6c	9c
1 envelope Italian salad dressing mix	3	6	9
2 cloves garlic, minced	6	12	18
½ cup olive oil	1½c	3c	4½c

Original Recipe Yield

6 servings

Cooking Day

Mix together cheese, garlic, and Italian dressing mix. Dip chicken breasts in olive oil, then coat with cheese mixture. Wrap each coated chicken breast individually in plastic wrap, then place in a freezer bag. Freeze, using freezer bag method.

Serving Day

Thaw completely. Unwrap desired number of chicken breasts and place in a greased baking dish. Bake at 400 degrees for 45–60 minutes until chicken is tender and no longer pink.

Lighter Fare Nutritional Information (per serving): Calories 299; Total Fat 24g; Cholesterol 51mg; Sodium 560mg; Total Carbohydrates 2g; Dietary Fiber 0g; Protein 18g

Pineapple Lemon Chicken

A bone-in citrus chicken for the grill

	x3	x6	x9
4 bone-in chicken breasts	12	24	36
1–20 oz. can crushed pineapple	3	6	9
1 small lemon, very thinly sliced	3	6	9
⅓ cup ketchup	1c	2c	3c
⅓ cup honey	1c	2c	3c
1 T. Worcestershire sauce	3T	¼c + 2T	½c + 1T
2 cloves garlic, minced	6	12	18
1 t. salt	1T	2T	3T
¼ t. dried rosemary, crushed	¾t	1½t	2¼t

Serving Day

1 T. cornstarch

Original Recipe Yield

4 servings

Cooking Day

Place chicken breasts in freezer bag (set in a large bowl for stability). For marinade, drain pineapple, reserving ¼ cup juice. In a large bowl, combine reserved pineapple juice, ketchup, honey, Worcestershire sauce, garlic, salt, and rosemary. Stir in pineapple and lemon slices. Pour marinade over chicken; seal bag. Freeze, using freezer bag method.

Serving Day

Drain thawed chicken, reserving marinade. Place chicken, bone side down, on the grill. Cover and grill for 50–60 minutes, turning once and brushing with ¼ cup of the reserved marinade, until chicken reaches 170 degrees internal temperature and no pink remains.

In a saucepan, combine remaining reserved marinade and cornstarch. Cook and stir over medium heat until thickened and bubbly. Cook and stir 2 minutes more. Spoon sauce over chicken and serve with rice.

Lighter Fare Nutritional Information (per serving): Calories 182.9; Total Fat 1.5g; Cholesterol 68.4mg; Sodium 123.8mg; Total Carbohydrates 10.6g; Fiber .5g; Protein 27.6g

Savory Chicken Bundles

A favorite family meal or snack!

	x3	x6	x9
3 oz. low-fat cream cheese, softened	9oz	18oz	27oz
¼ cup butter, melted and divided	¾c	1½c	2¼c
2 cups chicken, cooked and cubed	6c	12c	18c
1 T. green onions, chopped	3T	¼c + 2T	½c + 1T
2 T. milk	¼c + 2T	¾c	1c + 2T
1 T. roasted red peppers (from jar)	3T	¼c + 2T	½c + 1T
¼ t. salt	¾t	1½t	2¼t
¼ t. pepper	¾t	1½t	2¼t
1 cup seasoned croutons, crushed	3c	6c	9c
2–8 oz. cans crescent rolls	6	12	18

Original Recipe Yield

4 large bundles, 6 snack-size bundles

Cooking Day

In a mixing bowl, blend softened cream cheese and 2 T. of the melted butter until smooth. Add chicken, green onions, milk, roasted red peppers, salt, and pepper, and mix well. Set aside. Pour crushed croutons into a shallow-sided pan or plate.

On a flat surface or large cutting board, lay the crescent roll dough out flat, firmly pressing the perforations together to form one large sheet of dough. Using a knife or pizza cutter, divide the dough into 4 rectangles (if you are making smaller chicken bundles, divide dough into 6 rectangles). Spoon approximately ½ cup of chicken mixture onto center of each rectangle (¼ cup for snack size). Pull all 4 corners of dough to top, crimping edges together with fingers and sealing all around chicken. Brush or dip all sides in remaining butter, and dip bundles in crushed croutons. Wrap individual bundles in plastic wrap and place inside a freezer bag. Freeze, using freezer bag method.

Serving Day

Let bundles thaw at room temperature for 15–20 minutes. Preheat oven to 350 degrees. Place chicken bundles on an ungreased cookie sheet, leaving 2–3 inches between each bundle, as bundles will spread during baking. Bake for 25–35 minutes or until heated through. If bundles are browning too quickly, place a sheet of foil loosely over top. Remove foil during the last 3–5 minutes of cooking time.

Sesame Salmon

The sesame oil in this recipe makes the salmon moist and tender

	x3	x6	x9
1 lb. salmon fillets	3 lbs	6 lbs	9 lbs
Sesame marinade			
½ cup soy sauce	1½c	3c	4½c
¼ cup sesame oil	¾c	1½c	2¼c
1 T. lemon juice*	2T	¼c	¼c + 2T
2 T. rice wine vinegar**	¼c	½c	¾c
1 T. sugar	3T	¼c + 2T	½c + 1T
1 T. hot chili oil	3T	¼c + 2T	½c + 1T
½ t. ground ginger	1½t	1T	4½t

*This measurement, when multiplied, has been adjusted to accommodate the intensified flavor of acidic ingredients when recipes are made in quantity.

**This can be found in Asian markets or in the gourmet/ethnic food aisles of many grocery stores. This measurement has also been adjusted to accommodate the intensified flavor of acidic ingredients.

Original Recipe Yield

6 servings

Cooking Day

Combine sesame marinade ingredients and place in freezer bag with salmon fillets. Freeze, using freezer bag method.

Serving Day

Allow salmon fillets to thaw completely. Discard marinade. Spray grill surface with oil or cooking spray, and preheat grill to medium-high. Grill salmon 4–5 minutes per side. Salmon may also be broiled.

Lighter Fare Nutritional Information (per serving): Calories 62.1; Total Fat 3.5g; Cholesterol 10.1mg; Sodium 607mg; Total Carbohydrates 3.6g; Fiber .1g; Protein 4.3g

South of the Border Chicken Enchiladas

A classic Mexican dish the whole family will enjoy!

	x3	x6	x9
4 boneless chicken breasts, cooked and cubed	12	24	36
2 T. butter	¼c + 2T	¾c	1c + 2T
½ cup onion, chopped	1½c	3c	4½c
1 clove garlic, minced	3	6	9
1–16 oz. can diced tomatoes, undrained	3	6	9
1–8 oz. can tomato sauce	3	6	9
1–4 oz. can diced green chiles, drained	3	6	9
1 t. sugar	1T	2T	3T
1 t. cumin	1T	2T	3T
½ t. salt	1½t	1T	4½t
½ t. dried oregano	1½t	1T	4½t
½ t. dried basil	1½t	1T	4½t
12 corn tortillas	36	72	108
1½ cups sour cream	4½c	9c	13½c
4 cups grated Monterey jack cheese	12c	24c	36c

Original Recipe Yield

12 servings

Cooking Day

Enchilada sauce: Melt butter in a medium saucepan, then sauté onion and garlic in butter until tender. Add tomatoes, tomato sauce, green chiles, sugar, cumin, salt, oregano, and basil. Simmer on stovetop about 20 minutes, until heated through and seasonings are well-blended.

To assemble enchiladas, soften tortillas in a warm skillet, then dip each side of tortilla in sauce. Fill enchiladas with ⅓ cup chicken and sprinkle with 2 T.

cheese, then roll up and place seam side down in a lined 9 x 13 baking dish. Blend sour cream into remaining enchilada sauce. Pour sauce over enchiladas and then sprinkle with remaining Monterey jack cheese. Freeze, using foil and plastic wrap method.

Serving Day

Return to original pan and thaw completely. Bake uncovered at 350 degrees for 40–50 minutes, until sauce is bubbly and cheese is melted.

Hint

Use disposable gloves to assemble enchiladas—it makes for a quick cleanup. Disposable gloves are available at warehouse club stores and in some larger grocery stores.

Spicy Peanut Chicken

Sure to be a favorite with the kids!

Contributed by Karen Schultz — Denver, Colorado

	x3	x6	x9
4–5 boneless chicken breasts, about 2 lbs.	14–15	28–30	42–45
¼ cup sesame oil	¾c	1½c	2¼c
¼ cup creamy peanut butter	¾c	1½c	2¼c
¼ cup soy sauce	¾c	1½c	2¼c
3 T. sugar	½c + 1T	1c + 2T	1½c + 3T
1 t. minced garlic	1T	2T	3T
1 t. crushed red pepper	1T	2T	3T

Original Recipe Yield

6 servings

Cooking Day

Slice chicken into bite-size pieces and sauté in sesame oil until chicken is no longer pink. Add peanut butter, soy sauce, sugar, garlic, and red pepper. Simmer until sauce is thickened and heated through, about 15 minutes. Cool completely. Freeze, using freezer bag method.

Serving Day

Thaw completely. Heat chicken and sauce on stove. This dish is wonderful topped with crushed peanuts and served over rice. It's also really good served with a side of stir-fried snow peas.

Teriyaki Chicken Veggie Stir-Fry

Serve with rice or stir-fry noodles

	x2	x4	x6
4 boneless chicken breasts	8	16	24
2 cups broccoli crowns, sliced	4c	8c	12c
1 medium onion, sliced or diced	2	4	6
8 oz. mushrooms, sliced	16oz	32oz	48oz
1 cup red bell pepper, chopped (optional)	2c	4c	6c
canola oil, for sautéing			

Teriyaki stir-fry sauce

	x2	x4	x6
1 cup soy sauce	2c	4c	6c
1 cup sugar	2c	4c	6c
½ cup Mirin (rice cooking wine)	1c	2c	3c
1 t. fresh ginger, grated	2t	1T + 1t	2T
1 t. garlic, minced	2t	1T + 1t	2T

Original Recipe Yield

4–6 servings

Cooking Day

Stir-fry sauce: In a medium saucepan, mix together all sauce ingredients and cook over medium heat, stirring constantly, until sugar is dissolved. Set aside to cool.

Chicken and vegetables: In a large skillet or wok, heat 1–2 T. of oil over medium heat. Stir-fry broccoli, onion, and red pepper for 2–3 minutes, adding more oil as needed. Add mushrooms and cook 1–2 minutes more. Remove from heat and set aside to cool slightly. Add about ½–¾ cup of the stir-fry sauce to the vegetables and stir gently to coat. In a separate skillet, heat 2–3 T. oil over medium-high heat; add chicken slices in separate batches and stir-fry just until chicken starts to lightly brown. The chicken will not be completely cooked through at this point. Add more oil as needed for each batch of chicken. Add another ½–¾ cup of stir-fry sauce to the cooked chicken, mixing well to coat. When food is cool, place chicken and vegetables in two separate freezer bags. Freeze, using freezer bag method. Any unused stir-fry sauce may be stored for approx. 1 week in the refrigerator in an air-tight container, then used on serving day. The sauce will also keep in the freezer for up to 6 months.

Serving Day

Thaw chicken and vegetables completely. To reheat, place 1–2 T. oil in a large skillet or wok and stir-fry chicken and vegetables just until heated through. Add more stir-fry sauce as needed. If you like your stir-fry with more broth, you can also add water or chicken stock (¼ cup or more as needed) to thin it out a little. Serve over rice or stir-fry noodles.

Succulent Beef and Pork

Asian Flank Steak

Barbeque Sandwiches

Beef Bourguignon

Beef Tacquitos

Belgian Creek Beef Goulash

Burgundy Slow Roasted Beef

Chuck Roast for the Grill

Creamy Chuck Roast with Mushrooms

Elegant Steak Dionne

Elliott's Gourmet Burgers

English Sirloin Pasties

Greek Meatballs with Mint (Keftethes)

Grilled Rib-Eye Steaks

Herb Crusted Pork Chops

Honey-Dijon Glazed Ham

Italian Stuffed Meatloaf

Oven Baked Pork Roast with Barbeque Sauce

Poppy Seed Ham and Cheese Melts

Pork Loin with Garlic Rub

Pulled Pork Sandwiches with White Barbeque
Sauce

Simple Salisbury Steak

Sliced Beef Brisket

Steak Kabobs with Orange Hoisin Glaze

Steak Soft Tacos

Stuffed Flank Steak

Tangy Chops with Honey Curry Sauce

Telluride Black Bean Tortilla Bake

Tender Beef on a Skewer

Top Sirloin with Red Wine Marinade

Asian Flank Steak

A wonderful grilled steak for entertaining

	x3	x6	x9
1½ lbs. flank steak	4½ lbs	9 lbs	13½ lbs
½ cup sherry cooking wine	1½c	3c	4½c
⅓ cup soy sauce	1c	2c	3c
2 T. ketchup	¼c + 2T	¾c	1c + 2T
2 garlic cloves, minced	6	12	18
2 T. fresh ginger, peeled and minced	¼c + 2T	¾c	1c + 2T
1 T. sesame oil	3T	¼c + 2T	½c + 1T

Original Recipe Yield

6 servings

Cooking Day

Mix all ingredients together, except steak, until well blended. Place steak in a freezer bag and pour marinade over steak. Freeze, using freezer bag method.

Serving Day

Thaw completely. Remove steak from marinade. Bring marinade to a boil in a medium saucepan, and continue boiling for two minutes over medium-high heat. Grill steak over medium heat to desired doneness. Place steak on a platter and cut crosswise into thin slices. Pour sauce over steak and serve.

Lighter Fare Nutritional Information (per serving): Calories 286; Total Fat 13.6g; Cholesterol 76mg; Sodium 972 mg; Total Carbohydrates 2g; Dietary Fiber 0g; Protein 32g

Barbeque Sandwiches

*A combination of beef, pork,
and pickling spice make this a favorite!*

Contributed by Marla White—Mason, Ohio

	x3	x6	x9
Meat			
1 medium onion, halved	3	6	9
1½ lbs. lean beef roast, cubed	4½ lbs	9 lbs	13½ lbs
½ lb. pork roast, cubed	1½ lbs	3 lbs	4½ lbs
Barbeque sauce			
1–26 oz. bottle ketchup	3	6	9
1 green bell pepper, chopped	3	6	9
2 T. dry mustard	¼c + 2T	¾c	1c + 2T
2 T. white vinegar	¼c + 2T	¾c	1c + 2T
2 T. sugar	¼c + 2T	¾c	1c + 2T
1 t. salt	1T	2T	3T
2 T. whole pickling spice, tied in a clean cloth bag*	¼c + 2T	¾c	1c + 2T
Serving Day			
buns or hard rolls			

*A piece of cheesecloth tied with kitchen string or a "tea ball" can be used to hold the pickling spices.

Original Recipe Yield

9–12 sandwiches

Cooking Day

Meat: Place onion halves, beef, and pork in a large stockpot. Cover with a generous amount of water. Simmer for approximately 2½ hours or until tender. Roast may also be cooked in a crockpot on low for 4–6 hours. Remove cooked meat from liquid and shred. Set aside.

Sauce: Combine all sauce ingredients in large saucepan; simmer for 30 minutes. Add shredded meat to sauce. Simmer an additional 20 minutes. Remove pickling spice bag. Cool completely and freeze, using freezer bag method.

Serving Day

Thaw barbeque to a slushy consistency and reheat in saucepan. Serve on warm rolls or buns. Thawed barbeque may also be placed in a crockpot on a low setting for approximately 4 hours prior to serving.

Beef Bourguignon

A delicious, classic French meal

Contributed by Peg McMillen—Golden, Colorado

	x3	x6	x9
2½ lbs. beef for stew	7½ lbs	15 lbs	22½ lbs
¼ cup + 3 T. butter, divided	1¼c + 1T	2½c + 2T	3¾c + 3T
1 T. oil	3T	¼c + 2T	½c + 1T
1 med. onion, coarsely chopped	3	6	9
6 small green onions, chopped	18	36	54
4 carrots, sliced	12	24	36
2 T. flour	¼c + 2T	¾c	1c + 2T
2 cloves garlic, mashed	6	12	18
1–14 oz. can beef broth	3	6	9
⅔ cup water	2c	4c	6c
2 T. tomato paste	¼c + 2T	¾c	1c + 2T
1 whole bay leaf	3	6	9
⅛ t. dried thyme	⅜t	¾t	1⅛t
1 t. salt	1T	2T	3T
2 sprigs parsley, coarsely chopped	6	12	18
1 T. Worcestershire sauce	3T	¼c + 2T	½c + 1T
2 cups Burgundy wine (not cooking wine)	6c	12c	18c
1 lb. fresh mushrooms, sliced	3 lbs	6 lbs	9 lbs
salt and pepper to taste			

Original Recipe Yield

10 servings

Cooking Day

Melt ¼ cup butter and oil together in heavy skillet. Brown beef, onion, and carrots slowly, about 15–20 minutes. Sprinkle mixture with flour and stir to coat. Add garlic and toss briefly. Stir in broth, water, tomato paste, bay leaf, thyme, salt, parsley, Worcestershire sauce, and wine. Simmer over very low heat, covered, for 2 hours. (The liquid should barely bubble while cooking.) In a separate pan, sauté mushrooms in remaining 3 T. butter until tender. Add to beef mixture. Season with salt and pepper to taste and simmer, covered, another half hour. Cool completely and freeze, using freezer bag method.

Serving Day

Thaw beef until slightly slushy. Place in stockpot and heat on low until simmering. Serve with French bread for dipping in sauce.

Beef Tacquitos

Really simple, really delicious!

	x3	x6	x9
2 lbs. beef chuck or arm roast	6 lbs	12 lbs	18 lbs
2 T. oil (more if needed)	¼c + 2T	¾c	1c + 2T
1 pkg. onion soup mix	3	6	9
1 medium onion, diced	3	6	9
7 oz. can chopped green chiles, undrained*	21oz	42oz	63oz
1 bay leaf	3	6	9
½ t. pepper	1½t	1T	4½t
1 cup water	3c	6c	9c
salt, to taste			
24 corn tortillas	72	144	216

Serving Day

cooking oil

salsa

sour cream

guacamole

*1 cup fresh roasted green chiles (mild or medium) may be substituted for canned.

Original Recipe Yield

6–8 servings (approx. 18–24 tacquitos)

Cooking Day

In a heavy Dutch oven or skillet, heat oil on medium to medium-high heat. Brown roast in hot oil on all sides, adding more oil if needed. Place roast in a crockpot along with onion soup mix, onion, green chiles, bay leaf, pepper, and water. Cover and cook for 4–6 hours on high or 6–8 hours on low, until beef is very tender. Cool beef and shred, adding any remaining juices back into beef. Add salt to taste, if needed.

To assemble: Between 2 paper towels, heat 3–4 corn tortillas at a time in the microwave for 15–20 seconds or until soft. Spread 2–3 T. of meat mixture on corn tortilla and roll up. Place seam side down on a piece of plastic wrap. If needed, temporarily secure tacquitos with toothpicks. Once you have made six tacquitos, wrap them securely in the plastic wrap and place inside a freezer bag. Repeat with remaining corn tortillas and meat mixture. Freeze, using freezer bag method.

Serving Day

Thaw tacquitos slightly. Heat 2–3 inches of oil on medium-high in a stockpot or Dutch oven. Fry tacquitos a few at a time for 2–3 minutes per side, or until golden brown and heated through. Use slotted spoon to remove tacquitos; drain them on paper towels. Serve immediately with salsa, sour cream, and guacamole.

Belgian Creek Beef Goulash

Wonderful comfort food!

	x2	x4	x6
2 lbs. beef chuck or arm roast, cut into bite-size pieces	4 lbs	8 lbs	12 lbs
2½ t. salt	1T + 2t	3T + 1t	¼c + 1T
½ t. pepper	1t	2t	1T
½ cup sifted flour	1c	2c	3c
½ cup canola or other cooking oil	1c	2c	3c
3 cups onion, sliced	6c	12c	18c
1 clove garlic, minced	2	4	6
1–12 oz. can beer	2	4	6
1 T. soy sauce	2T	¼c	¼c + 2T
1 T. Worcestershire sauce	2T	¼c	¼c + 2T
1 T. steak sauce	2T	¼c	¼c + 2T
2 bay leaves	4	8	12
½ t. dried thyme	1t	2t	1T
1½ t. brown sugar	1T	2T	3T

Serving Day

fresh parsley

buttered noodles, rice, or mashed potatoes

freshly grated parmesan cheese

Original Recipe Yield

4–6 servings

Cooking Day

Combine salt, pepper, and flour and mix well. Place flour mixture in gallon-size freezer bag with meat; gently roll or toss meat to coat well. Remove meat from bag and brown in cooking oil; separate into 2–3 batches so that meat can spread out in pan and not touch. In large crockpot or stockpot, stir together remaining ingredients. Add browned meat. Cover and simmer slowly until beef is very tender, stirring occasionally. Cook in crockpot on low for 3–4 hours, or on stovetop over low heat for 2–3 hours. Check meat for tenderness. Cool completely. Freeze, using freezer bag method.

Serving Day

Thaw goulash mixture. Prepare noodles, rice, or mashed potatoes. Over very low heat in saucepan, gently reheat goulash (do not boil), or reheat in microwave on low setting. If you prefer the goulash to be thinner in consistency, stir in a little water while reheating. Serve over buttered noodles, rice, or mashed potatoes, and garnish with fresh parsley and freshly grated parmesan cheese.

Hint

Other vegetables can be added to the goulash. For example, add carrots to other ingredients on cooking day; add peas to goulash during reheating phase on serving day.

Burgundy Slow Roasted Beef

An upscale variation of Mom's Pot Roast

	x3	x6	x9
4 lbs. chuck roast (tenderized by butcher) or round roast (boned and tied)	12 lbs	24 lbs	36 lbs
2 T. oil	¼c + 2T	¾c	1c + 2T
1 cup chopped onion	3c	6c	9c
1 clove garlic, minced	3	6	9
2 chopped carrots	6	12	18
1 T. peppercorns	3T	¼c + 2T	½c + 1T
1 cup Burgundy wine	3c	6c	9c
1 T. maple syrup	3T	¼c + 2T	½c + 1T
1–14 oz. can beef broth	3	6	9
1–6 oz. can tomato paste	3	6	9
¼ t. bay leaf, crumbled	¾t	1½t	2¼t
salt and pepper to taste			

Original Recipe Yield

8 servings

Cooking Day

Brown meat in Dutch oven in oil. Add onions and garlic and cook about 3 minutes longer. Add all other ingredients, cool completely, and place in freezer bag. Freeze, using freezer bag method.

Serving Day

Place contents of freezer bag in stockpot or crockpot. Allow to cook very slowly for about 4 hours in a covered stockpot. If cooking in crockpot, allow to cook for approximately 6 hours on low. Reserve the juice for serving as gravy over meat, if desired.

Chuck Roast for the Grill

This roast is prepared on the grill. Try it!

	x3	x6	x9
4 lbs. chuck roast, 2 inches thick (have meat tenderized by butcher)	12 lbs	24 lbs	36 lbs
Marinade			
½ cup salad oil	1½c	3c	4½c
½ cup ketchup	1½c	3c	4½c
¼ cup red wine	¾c	1½c	2¼c
2 T. red wine vinegar	¼c + 2T	¾c	1c + 2T
2 cloves garlic, minced	6	12	18
½ t. salt	1½t	1T	4½t
½ t. pepper	1½t	1T	4½t
½ t. dry mustard	1½t	1T	4½t
½ t. celery salt	1½t	1T	4½t
¾ t. chili powder	2¼t	4½t	2T + ¾t
dash Tabasco sauce			

Original Recipe Yield

4–6 servings

Cooking Day

Place chuck roast in freezer bag. Combine remaining ingredients and pour over meat. Freeze, using freezer bag method.

Serving Day

Allow roast to thaw. Pour marinade into saucepan and boil for 2 minutes. Place roast on grill on high heat and brown on both sides. Raise grill rack a little (or reduce heat) and cook roast 15 minutes on each side, depending on heat and desired degree of rareness. Baste frequently with marinade. Roast can also be broiled on low for approximately 17 minutes per side. Serve with potatoes or rice. Roast can also be shredded and served on buns or hard rolls.

Creamy Chuck Roast with Mushrooms

Stroganoff type flavor . . . very good!

	x3	x6	x9
1 beef chuck roast (3–4 pounds), tenderized*	3	6	9
1 T. oil	3T	¼c + 2T	½c + 1T
1 t. salt	1T	2T	3T
⅛ t. white pepper	⅜t	¾t	1⅛t
½ lb. fresh mushrooms, sliced	1½ lbs	3 lbs	4½ lbs
1 cup sliced onion	3c	6c	9c
3 whole cloves	9	18	27

Serving Day

1–14 oz. can beef broth

½ cup sour cream

2 T. flour

½ cup dry white wine—not cooking wine (optional)

*To save time and for better flavor, ask the butcher to run the roast through the meat tenderizing machine.

Original Recipe Yield

12 servings

Cooking Day

In heavy skillet or Dutch oven, heat oil and brown meat well on all sides. Sprinkle with salt and pepper. Combine remaining ingredients and place with meat in a freezer bag. Freeze, using freezer bag method.

Serving Day

Thaw completely. Place contents of freezer bag in Dutch oven or deep skillet; add beef broth. Cover and simmer for 2½–3 hours until tender. Transfer meat to heated platter. Mix flour with small amount of water; stir into drippings in skillet. Cook, stirring constantly, until thickened. Stir in sour cream and wine (if using); heat through but do not boil. Return meat to skillet and cover with sauce; heat through and serve.

Serving Suggestion

Serve with potatoes tossed with parsley or buttered noodles.

Elegant Steak Dionne

Wonderful for entertaining or anytime!

	x2	x4	x6
1½–2 lbs. sirloin (or beef tenderloin, fat trimmed)	3–4 lbs	7–8 lbs	11–12 lbs
2 cups fresh mushrooms, thinly sliced	4c	8c	12c
1 small white onion, chopped	2	4	6
3 cloves garlic, crushed	6	12	18
1½ t. lemon juice	1T	2T	3T
3 T. Worcestershire sauce	¼c + 2T	¾c	1c + 2T
¼ cup soy sauce	½c	1c	1½c
1 T. brown sugar or honey	2T	¼c	¼c + 2T
¼ cup butter, melted	½c	1c	1½c
¼ t. dried oregano	½t	1t	1½t
¾ cup red wine	1½c	3c	4½c

Original Recipe Yield

4–6 servings

Cooking Day

Place the meat in a large freezer bag. In a separate bowl, mix together remaining ingredients and pour over meat. Freeze, using freezer bag method.

Serving Day

Thaw steak. Place meat and marinade in crockpot. Simmer on low for about 5–6 hours or until tender. Remove meat and thinly slice. Place meat on a serving platter; pour juices from crockpot over meat and serve. This is great served over noodles, rice, or garlic mashed potatoes. The wine dissipates while cooking but gives the meat a wonderful, rich flavor.

Elliott's Gourmet Burgers

So delicious—keep them on hand for grilling all year long!

	x3	x6	x9
2 lbs. ground beef or buffalo	6 lbs	12 lbs	18 lbs
1 small onion, chopped	3	6	9
¼ cup fresh parsley, chopped	¾c	1½c	2¼c
2 T. Worcestershire sauce	¼c + 2T	¾c	1c + 2T
⅓ cup green chiles (mild or medium)	1c	2c	3c
2 oz. crumbled bleu cheese (or feta or asiago)	6oz	12oz	18oz
4 oz. fresh mushrooms, sliced (optional)	12oz	24oz	36oz
1 t. salt	1T	2T	3T
½ t. freshly ground pepper, or more to taste	1½t	1T	1T + 1½t
1 egg, beaten (more if needed)	3	6	9

Serving Day

hamburger buns, split and toasted

cheese slices: cheddar, American, Monterey jack

Spicy Ranch Style Sauce (see recipe below)

fresh tomato slices

lettuce

crisp bacon slices

avocado slices

caramelized onions

ketchup, mustard, or mayonnaise

Original Recipe Yield

8–10 servings, depending on size and thickness of patties

Cooking Day

Gently mix all ingredients together in a large bowl. Form meat mixture into 8–10 patties (½–¾ inch thick). Place patties on baking sheet; cover and chill for 1 hour. Individually wrap each patty with plastic wrap. Alternatively, place a piece of parchment or waxed paper between each patty and stack 2–4 patties together; wrap stack with plastic wrap. Place wrapped patties inside a large freezer bag. Freeze, using freezer bag method.

Serving Day

Thaw patties. Spray grill or frying pan with nonstick spray. Grill patties until brown, to desired doneness. In last minute of grilling, top burgers with cheese slices. Place on buns and top with a dollop of Spicy Ranch Style Sauce and your choice of serving day suggestions.

Spicy Ranch Style Sauce

Whisk together: 1 cup mayonnaise, 1 cup sour cream, ½ cup chopped fresh cilantro, 6 T. fresh lime juice, 4 finely chopped green onions, 1 T. minced, seeded jalapeno pepper (or more to taste), ¼–½ t. cayenne pepper (to taste), 1 T. sugar (or more to taste), and salt and pepper to taste. Refrigerate sauce until ready to serve. Makes approximately 2½ cups.

English Sirloin Pasties

A delicious sirloin mixture wrapped in a pastry crust

	x3	x6	x9
Filling			
12 oz. top sirloin steak, cut into 1 inch pieces	36oz	72oz	108oz
3 T. butter	½c + 1T	1c + 2T	1½c + 3T
1 cup russet potato, peeled and chopped	3c	6c	9c
¾ cup carrot, peeled and chopped	2¼c	4½c	6¾c
½ cup onion, chopped	1½c	3c	4½c
1 T. fresh parsley, chopped	3T	¼c + 2T	½c + 1T
1½ t. dried thyme	4½t	3T	¼c + 1½t
1 large clove garlic, chopped	3	6	9
½ cup whipping cream	1½c	3c	4½c
salt and pepper to taste			
Pastry dough			
2½ cups flour	7½c	15c	22½c
1 t. salt	1T	2T	3T
¾ cup shortening	2¼c	4½c	6¾c
7 T. cold water	1¼c + 1T	2½c + 2T	3¾c + 3T
Alternative to homemade pastry dough			
2–15 oz. pkgs. refrigerated pie crusts (2 crusts)	6	12	18

Original Recipe Yield

6 pasties

Cooking Day

Filling: Using the pulse setting, coarsely chop meat in food processor. Melt butter in large, heavy skillet over medium heat. Add potato, carrot, onion, parsley, thyme, and garlic. Sauté until vegetables are just tender, about 12 minutes. Add meat. Sauté until meat browns, about 10 additional minutes. Stir in cream. Season filling to taste with salt and pepper. Cool completely.

Dough: We recommend that you prepare the dough one batch at a time, even if you're preparing multiple batches. Mix flour and salt together in a large mixing bowl; cut in shortening with a pastry blender or 2 knives until mixture is the size of small peas. Stir in just enough cold water with fork, 1 T. at a time, until the flour mixture is just moistened and dough forms a ball. The pastry may also be mixed in a food processor. Divide dough into 6 pieces. Roll out into 6 inch pastry circles as you would a pie crust.

Pasties: Place pastry circle on work surface. Spoon ¼ cup filling onto one half of pastry. Fold other half of pastry over filling, forming a half circle. Seal edges with fork. Repeat with remaining pastry circles. Wrap each pasty individually with plastic wrap and place in freezer bag. Freeze, using freezer bag method.

Serving Day

Thaw pasties completely. Preheat oven to 425 degrees. Place thawed pasties on baking sheet. Bake about 20 minutes or until pastry is golden brown. Do not over-bake. May be served with gravy on the side, if desired.

Greek Meatballs with Mint (Keftethes)

These unique meatballs are crisp on the outside and soft on the inside!

An authentic family recipe, contributed by Mary Sares—Englewood, Colorado

	x2	x4	x6
1 lb. ground beef	2 lbs	4 lbs	6 lbs
4 slices white bread	8	16	24
1 medium onion, very finely chopped	2	4	6
½ cup dried parsley	1c	2c	3c
1 t. dried mint	2t	4t	2T
1 t. salt	2t	4t	2T
⅛ t. pepper	¼t	½t	¾t
1 clove garlic, minced	2	4	6
1 egg, beaten	2	4	6
½ cup flour	1c	2c	3c
½ cup vegetable oil	1c	2c	3c

Serving Day: Egg-Lemon Sauce

3 eggs

6 T. lemon juice

1 cup beef broth

Original Recipe Yield

18–24 meatballs

Cooking Day

Dip bread in a bowl of water and squeeze out excess water. In a large mixing bowl, crumble the moistened bread. Add ground beef, onion, parsley, mint, salt, pepper, garlic, and egg. Mix well. Place flour in a pie plate or dinner plate.

Using a teaspoon, scoop out small amounts of meat mixture and form into balls. Coat each meatball evenly with flour. Heat oil in skillet over medium-high heat and fry meatballs for 10–15 minutes. Outside should be crisp and brown on all sides; inside of meatballs should no longer be pink. Cool meatballs completely and then freeze, using freezer bag method.

Serving Day

Thaw meatballs completely. Place desired number of meatballs on an ungreased cookie sheet and cook in a preheated 350 degree oven approximately 15–20 minutes, until meatballs are heated through. Place meatballs in serving dish and pour warm Egg-Lemon Sauce over meatballs. Serve with rice and additional Egg-Lemon Sauce, according to taste.

Egg-Lemon Sauce: Beat 3 eggs in electric mixer on high, until eggs are thick and light yellow—at least 5 minutes. Reduce mixer speed to medium and gradually add 6 T. of lemon juice to eggs, continuing to beat until well mixed. Slowly add 1 cup of hot beef broth, being careful not to curdle the egg mixture. Transfer to saucepan on stove and continue heating on low, stirring constantly, until sauce is warm and slightly thickened, but do not allow sauce to boil.

Hint

Meatballs may be eaten either hot or cold. The mint really gives them a distinctive flavor. This recipe is a good use for the overgrown mint leaves in the garden—simply dry leaves and store them in a jar. When making these meatballs, take out several leaves and crumble them in your hand.

Grilled Rib-Eye Steaks

Great for entertaining on a summer evening

	x3	x6	x9
4 rib-eye steaks, approximately 1 inch thick	12	24	36
3 medium cloves garlic	9	18	27
½ t. kosher salt	1½t	1T	4½t
3 T. extra virgin olive oil	½c + 1T	1c + 2T	1½c + 3T
¼ t. celery seed	¾t	1½t	2¼t
⅛ t. cayenne pepper	⅜t	¾t	1⅛t
2 t. coarsely ground black pepper	2T	¼c	¼c + 2T
Sauce			
½ cup ketchup	1½c	3c	4½c
1 T. steak sauce	3T	¼c + 2T	½c + 1T
½ cup water	1½c	3c	4½c
1 T. dark brown sugar	3T	¼c + 2T	½c + 1T
2 t. Worcestershire sauce	2T	¼c	¼c + 2T
¼ t. garlic powder	¾t	1½t	2¼t
¼ t. kosher salt	¾t	1½t	2¼t
¼ t. ground black pepper	¾t	1½t	2¼t

Original Recipe Yield

4 servings

Cooking Day

Trim most of exterior fat from steaks. Roughly chop garlic, then sprinkle with salt. Using the sharp and flat sides of a knife, crush garlic and salt together into a paste. In a small bowl, mix the garlic paste with oil, celery seed, cayenne pepper, and black pepper. Spread mixture evenly over the steaks. Wrap each steak individually with plastic wrap, then place in freezer bag. Freeze, using freezer bag method.

Sauce: Whisk all sauce ingredients together in small saucepan. Bring to a boil over medium-high heat, then reduce heat and slowly simmer for 10 minutes, stirring occasionally. Cool completely. Freeze sauce using freezer bag method, and place in freezer with steaks.

Serving Day

Thaw steaks and sauce. Grill steaks over direct high heat until cooked to desired doneness (6–8 minutes per side for medium-rare). Turn steaks on grill only once. Remove steaks from grill and let rest for 3–5 minutes. Reheat sauce on stovetop. Serve steaks warm with sauce on the side.

Lighter Fare Nutritional Information (per serving): Calories 345.7; Total Fat 11.1g; Cholesterol 66.3mg; Sodium 568.7mg; Total Carbohydrates 12.5g; Dietary Fiber 2g; Protein 36.3g

Herb Crusted Pork Chops

The parsley and thyme are savory and pleasing to the palate

Contributed by Beverly Garrison—Highlands Ranch, Colorado

	x3	x6	x9
8 pork chops, bone-in	24	48	72
1½ cups breadcrumbs	4½c	9c	13½c
1 cup fresh parsley, chopped	3c	6c	9c
2 t. dried thyme	2T	¼c	¼c + 2T
½ cup olive oil	1½c	3c	4½c
salt and pepper to taste			

Original Recipe Yield

8 servings

Cooking Day

Mix together breadcrumbs, parsley, thyme, olive oil, salt, and pepper. Coat each pork chop with bread and herb mixture. Wrap each pork chop individually in plastic wrap and then place in a freezer bag. Freeze, using freezer bag method.

Serving Day

Thaw pork chops completely. Broil pork chops on high for 2–3 minutes each side. Lower oven temperature to 350 degrees and bake for 20 minutes, or until pork chops are tender.

Honey-Dijon Glazed Ham

May also be used to make kabobs with pineapple chunks

	x3	x6	x9
1 center cut ham steak, 1 inch thick	3	6	9

Glaze

	x3	x6	x9
1 T. honey	3T	¼c + 2T	½c +1T
1 T. Dijon mustard	3T	¼c + 2T	½c +1T
2 t. fresh lemon juice*	1T	2T	3T
2 green onions, chopped	6	12	18
2 T. olive oil	¼c + 2T	¾c	1c + 2T
1 t. lukewarm water	1T	2T	3T
½ t. kosher salt	1½t	1T	4½t
¼ t. cayenne pepper	¾t	1½t	2¼t

Serving Day

5 slices fresh pineapple

*This measurement, when multiplied, has been adjusted to accommodate the inten-sified flavor of acidic ingredients when recipes are made in quantity.

Original Recipe Yield

6 servings

Cooking Day

Glaze: Whisk honey, mustard, lemon juice, and green onions together in medium mixing bowl. In a steady stream, whisk in olive oil and lukewarm water. Sprinkle ham steak with salt and cayenne pepper and place in freezer bag. Pour glaze over ham and freeze, using freezer bag method.

Serving Day

Place ham steak on grill, basting occasionally with glaze, until steak is marked by grill and well warmed through. Pineapple slices may also be grilled before serving with ham. Ham can also be cut into chunks and threaded alternately on skewers with chunks of pineapple, then grilled.

Italian Stuffed Meatloaf

A really delicious variation . . . serve with pasta and our Garlic Herb Bread!

	x2	x4	x6
2 lbs. ground beef, turkey, or buffalo	4 lbs	8 lbs	12 lbs
1 cup breadcrumbs	2c	4c	6c
1 t. salt	2t	1T + 1t	2T
1 t. pepper	2t	1T + 1t	2T
3 cloves garlic, minced	6	12	18
½ cup onion, diced	1c	2c	3c
¼ cup celery, finely diced	½c	1c	1½c
1 t. Italian seasoning	2t	1T + 1t	2T
½ t. basil	1t	2t	1T
¼ cup parmesan or Italian cheese blend, shredded	½c	1c	1½c
2 eggs	4	8	12
¼ t. Worcestershire sauce	½t	1t	1½t
¼ t. hot pepper sauce	½t	1t	1½t
milk, if needed			

Filling

	x2	x4	x6
1 cup ricotta cheese (low fat)	2c	4c	6c
1 cup parmesan cheese or Italian cheese blend, shredded	2c	4c	6c
1 T. parsley	2T	¼c	¼c + 2T
1 cup mushrooms, sliced (optional)	2c	4c	6c
1–2 T. olive oil (optional)	2–4T	¼–½c	½–¾c
2 T. sun-dried tomatoes, rehydrated* (optional)	¼c	½c	¾c

Serving Day

1–2 cups of your favorite tomato sauce or spaghetti sauce

*To rehydrate sun-dried tomatoes, place desired amount of tomatoes in a small bowl filled with a little warm water. Let stand until tender, then drain tomatoes.

Original Recipe Yield

12–14 servings

Cooking Day

Meat mixture: In a small mixing bowl, mix breadcrumbs, salt, pepper, garlic, onion, celery, Italian seasoning, basil, and cheese. Set aside. In a large mixing bowl, break up beef and make an indentation in the center. Break the eggs into this well; add Worcestershire sauce and hot pepper sauce. With a fork, quickly beat the eggs and sauces together in the well. Using either your hands (see kitchen tip below) or a large spoon, mix eggs and meat together until well combined. Pour the breadcrumb mixture into the meat mixture in 2–3 installments, mixing each time until well incorporated. If mixture seems too dry, add a little milk—or one more beaten egg—to the meat mixture.

For filling: In a mixing bowl, combine ricotta cheese, shredded cheese, and parsley. Mix together and set aside. If using mushrooms: in a small pan, heat 1 T. of olive oil over medium heat. Pour sliced mushrooms into pan and sauté for 3–4 minutes, until tender. Remove from heat and cool.

To assemble: Divide meat mixture into 4 equal parts. Line two loaf pans; press ¼ of meat mixture into each loaf pan. Pressing down with your fingers or the back of a spoon, create a shallow "ditch" down the middle of the meat mixture. Spread ½ of the ricotta filling mixture into each ditch, leaving about a 1½ inch border of meat all around. If using sun-dried tomatoes and/or mushrooms, divide and layer over the ricotta filling. Press a second ¼ of meat mixture into each loaf pan, pushing down around the outside edges to help seal in the filling. Freeze, using foil and plastic wrap method.

Serving Day

Return meatloaf to original pan and thaw. Preheat oven to 350 degrees. Bake meatloaf for 30 minutes, then spoon off any excess grease, if necessary. Pour 1–2 cups of your favorite tomato or spaghetti sauce on top of the meatloaf and bake for an additional 25–30 minutes. Be careful not to over-bake. Serve with buttered noodles or pasta, a salad, and our Garlic Herb Bread (see page 78).

Kitchen Tip

Use disposable gloves to mix together all the meatloaf ingredients. It makes for a quick cleanup. Disposable gloves are available at warehouse club stores and some larger grocery stores.

Oven Baked Pork Roast with Barbeque Sauce

The apple jelly gives this roast a unique flavor

	x2	x4	x6
4 lbs. boneless pork loin roast, rolled and tied	8 lbs	16 lbs	24 lbs
1 t. salt	2t	4t	2T
1 t. garlic salt	2t	4t	2T
1 t. chili powder	2t	4t	2T
½ t. fresh ground pepper	1t	2t	1T
Barbeque Sauce			
1 cup apple jelly	2c	4c	6c
1 cup ketchup	2c	4c	6c
2 T. cider vinegar*	3T	⅓c	½c
2 t. chili powder	1T + 1t	2T + 2t	¼c

*This measurement, when multiplied, has been adjusted to accommodate the intensified flavor of acidic ingredients when recipes are made in quantity.

Original Recipe Yield

8 servings

Cooking Day

Mix together salt, garlic salt, chili powder, and fresh pepper in a small bowl. Rub onto pork roast until roast is well coated. Wrap roast in plastic wrap, then place in a freezer bag. Freeze, using freezer bag method.

Barbeque sauce: Mix all sauce ingredients together in a medium saucepan. Bring to boil on stove, then allow to simmer, uncovered, for 2 additional minutes. Cool sauce, then place in a separate freezer bag. Freeze, using freezer bag method, and store in freezer with roast.

Serving Day

Thaw roast and barbeque sauce. Place roast in a shallow roasting pan, fat side up, and bake in a 325 degree oven for approximately 2 hours, until an inserted meat thermometer reads 185 degrees. About 15 minutes before roast is done, brush with some of the barbeque sauce. Reheat remaining barbeque sauce until heated through. After removing roast from oven, carve into thin slices and serve with barbeque sauce.

Poppy Seed Ham and Cheese Melts

Keep these on hand for a quick on-the-run meal

	x3	x6	x9
1½ lbs. thinly sliced deli ham	4½ lbs	9 lbs	13½ lbs
1 lb. Swiss or cheddar cheese, sliced	3 lbs	6 lbs	9 lbs
½ cup butter	1½c	3c	4½c
2 T. prepared mustard	¼c + 2T	¾c	1c + 2T
3 T. poppy seeds	½c + 1T	1c + 2T	1½c + 3T
1 t. Worcestershire sauce	1T	2T	3T
18 hamburger buns	54	108	162

Original Recipe Yield

18 sandwiches

Cooking Day

Poppy seed sauce: Melt butter in a saucepan over low heat. Stir in mustard, poppy seeds, and Worcestershire sauce. To assemble sandwiches, layer 1–2 slices of ham, a slice of cheese, and then about 1 T. of sauce on bun. Wrap sandwiches in foil, then place in a freezer bag and freeze.

Serving Day

Remove desired number of sandwiches from freezer. Preheat oven to 350 degrees. Place foil-wrapped sandwiches directly on oven rack and warm in oven until cheese is melted and sandwiches are warm, about 20 minutes.

Pork Loin with Garlic Rub

A bit of a Spanish flair!

Contributed by Jan Barreth—Lone Tree, Colorado

	x3	x6	x9
3 lbs. boneless pork loin	9 lbs	18 lbs	27 lbs
6 garlic cloves, peeled	18	36	54
2 t. salt	2T	¼c	¼c + 2T
2 T. fresh parsley, chopped	¼c + 2T	¾c	1c + 2T
1 T. sweet Spanish paprika	3T	¼c + 2T	½c + 1T
½ t. dried oregano	1½t	1T	4½t
¼ cup olive oil	¾c	1½c	2¼c

Original Recipe Yield

12 servings

Cooking Day

Pound the garlic and salt together with a mortar and pestle to form a smooth paste, or use the flat and sharp sides of a knife (see Grilled Rib-Eye Steaks, page 184). Add parsley and mix well. Stir in paprika and oregano, then gradually stir in olive oil to form a thick, oily mixture. Rub all over pork loin, then place pork in freezer bag. Freeze, using freezer bag method.

Serving Day

Thaw pork loin by placing in refrigerator for up to 2 days (or defrost in microwave). Bring pork loin to room temperature before roasting. Preheat oven to 450 degrees. Place pork in roasting pan and pour over any extra marinade from the freezer bag. Roast pork for 15 minutes, then reduce oven to 350 degrees. Roast for an additional 45 minutes, until juices run clear. Transfer pork to a cutting board, cover loosely with foil, and let rest for 10 minutes prior to serving.

Lighter Fare Nutritional Information (per serving): Calories 237; Total Fat 11g; Cholesterol 89mg; Sodium 261mg; Total Carbohydrates 3g; Dietary Fiber 2g; Protein 32g

Pulled Pork Sandwiches with White Barbecue Sauce

Serve this to the marching band

	x3	x6	x9
1¼ lbs. pork tenderloin, trimmed	3¾ lbs	7½ lbs	11¼ lbs
½ cup apple cider vinegar*	1¼c	2½c	3¾c
¼ cup water	¾c	1½c	2¼c
3 T. brown sugar	½c + 1T	1c + 2T	1½c + 3T
2 t. kosher salt	2T	¼c	¼c + 2T
¾ t. freshly ground black pepper	2¼t	4½t	2T + ¾t
½ t. ground red pepper	1½t	1T	4½t
½ t. mild chili powder	1½t	1T	4½t
¼ t. garlic powder	¾t	1½t	2¼t

Serving Day: White Barbeque Sauce

½ cup reduced-fat mayonnaise

1 T. white vinegar

1 t. coarsely ground fresh pepper

1 t. fresh lemon juice

dash of salt

8 sandwich buns or rolls

*This measurement, when multiplied, has been adjusted to accommodate the intensified flavor of acidic ingredients when recipes are made in quantity.

Original Recipe Yield

8 servings

Cooking Day

To prepare pork: Slice in half lengthwise, then cut crosswise into 2½ inch pieces. Combine remaining ingredients in a medium saucepan; bring to a boil. Add pork to pan. Cover, reduce heat, and simmer 1–1½ hours or until tender. Also may be cooked on low in a crockpot for 4–6 hours. Remove pork from juices;

shred with 2 forks. Pour desired amount of juices over pork. Cool completely. Freeze, using freezer bag method.

Serving Day

White barbeque sauce: Combine all ingredients in a small bowl, mixing thoroughly. Cover and chill. Heat pork through and serve on rolls with white barbecue sauce. *Alternately, skip the white sauce, heat pork through, and serve on rolls with bottled barbecue sauce and cheddar cheese slices.*

Simple Salisbury Steak

A great meal for life on the go

	x3	x6	x9
1½ lbs. ground beef	4½ lbs	9 lbs	13½ lbs
3–10 oz. cans cream of mushroom soup, divided	9	18	27
½ cup dry breadcrumbs	1½c	3c	4½c
1 egg, beaten	3	6	9
¼ cup finely chopped onion	¾c	1½c	2¼c
½ t. salt	1½t	1T	4½t
¼ t. pepper	¾t	1½t	2¼t
1½ cups sliced mushrooms	4½c	9c	13½c

Original Recipe Yield

6 servings

Cooking Day

In a medium bowl, mix together ground beef, ¼ cup mushroom soup, bread-crumbs, egg, onion, salt, and pepper. Shape *firmly* into 6 patties. Wrap patties individually in plastic wrap and place in freezer bag. Freeze, using freezer bag method.

Mix together remaining soup and sliced mushrooms; place in quart-sized freezer bag. Attach to bag containing steak patties and freeze.

Serving Day

Thaw patties and sauce completely. Place patties in skillet and cook until browned on both sides and cooked through. Spoon off any excess fat. Add mushroom sauce to skillet and reduce heat to low. Cover and simmer for 20 minutes or until sauce is heated through, turning patties occasionally.

Sliced Beef Brisket

Great with baked potatoes and a salad

	x3	x6	x9
3 lbs. beef brisket	9 lbs	18 lbs	27 lbs
2 T. cooking oil	¼c + 2T	¾c	1c + 2T
1 cup water	3c	6c	9c
4 stalks celery, chopped	12	24	36
1 medium onion, chopped	3	6	9
1 green bell pepper, chopped	3	6	9
⅔ cup ketchup	2c	4c	6c
2 T. barbecue sauce	¼c + 2T	¾c	1c + 2T
2 T. Worcestershire sauce	¼c + 2T	¾c	1c + 2T
2 t. salt	2T	¼c	¼c + 2T
1 t. chili powder	1T	2T	3T
1 t. pepper	1T	2T	3T

Original Recipe Yield

14 servings

Cooking Day

Heat oil in skillet; brown brisket. Mix remaining ingredients in a large bowl to form sauce. Place cooled brisket along with sauce in freezer bag. Freeze, using freezer bag method.

Serving Day

Place brisket and sauce in crockpot. Cover and cook on low for 6 hours. More water may be added during cooking if brisket seems dry. Remove meat and slice to serve, pouring crockpot juices over meat if desired.

Steak Kabobs with Orange Hoisin Glaze

A terrific blend of flavors!

Contributed by Amy Sunahara—Highlands Ranch, Colorado

	x3	x6	x9
1½ lbs. tenderloin steaks, cut into 1 inch cubes	4½ lbs	9 lbs	13½ lbs
½ cup orange juice concentrate, thawed	1½c	3c	4½c
½ cup hoisin sauce	1½c	3c	4½c
2 T. chili powder	¼c + 2T	¾c	1c + 2T
2 T. olive oil	¼c + 2T	¾c	1c + 2T
2 t. grated orange peel	2T	¼c	¼c + 2T
salt and pepper to taste			

Serving Day

| green onions, chopped |
| 2 oranges, cut into wedges |
| 1 onion, cut into chunks |
| skewers |

Original Recipe Yield

6 servings

Cooking Day

Whisk orange juice concentrate, hoisin sauce, chili powder, olive oil, and orange peel in medium bowl; season with salt and pepper. Place beef cubes in large bowl. Sprinkle meat with salt and pepper; toss to coat. Add ¼ cup orange hoisin sauce; toss well. Place in freezer bag and freeze, using freezer bag method. Pour remaining sauce into separate freezer bag and freeze.

Serving Day

Allow meat and sauce to thaw completely. Place steak on kabob skewers alternately with onion chunks and orange wedges. Grill kabobs to desired doneness (about 10 minutes for medium-rare), basting with orange hoisin sauce and turning occasionally. Garnish with green onions before serving.

Hint

To prevent wooden skewers from burning, soak skewers in water for 30–40 minutes before use.

Lighter Fare Nutritional Information (per serving): Calories 386.5; Total Fat 25.2g; Cholesterol 77.8mg; Sodium 401.9mg; Total Carbohydrates 5.7g; Dietary Fiber 3.1g; Protein 23.2g

Steak Soft Tacos

Not your average soft taco!

	x3	x6	x9
1½ lbs. flank steak	4½ lbs	9 lbs	13½ lbs
3 T. olive oil	½c + 1T	1c + 2T	1½c + 3T
1 T. chili powder	3T	¼c + 2T	½c + 1T
1 T. ground cumin	3T	¼c + 2T	½c + 1T
2 t. freshly ground pepper	2T	¼c	¼c + 2T
½ t. garlic powder	1½t	1T	4½t
1 t. dried oregano	1T	2T	3T

Serving Day

8 flour tortillas, fajita-size
lettuce, chopped
tomatoes, finely chopped
cheddar cheese, grated
sour cream
avocado

Original Recipe Yield

8 servings

Cooking Day

In a small bowl, mix together olive oil, chili powder, cumin, pepper, garlic powder, and oregano to form a paste. Coat both sides of steak with olive oil paste. Wrap steak in plastic wrap and then place in freezer bag. Freeze, using freezer bag method.

Serving Day

Thaw steak completely. Let sit at room temperature for 20–30 minutes before grilling. Grill over direct medium heat until steak is desired doneness. Let rest for a few minutes, then slice steak across the grain into thin strips. Assemble soft tacos using warmed flour tortillas and desired toppings.

Lighter Fare Nutritional Information (per serving): Calories 254; Total Fat 16.5g; Cholesterol 60mg; Sodium 72mg; Total Carbohydrates 1g; Dietary Fiber 0g; Protein 24g

Stuffed Flank Steak

So easy and so good—a perfect entertaining entrée!

	x3	x6	x9
1½ lbs. flank steak	4½ lbs	9 lbs	13½ lbs
¼ cup butter	¾c	1½c	2¼c
8 oz. mushrooms, sliced	24oz	48oz	72oz
1 cup packaged bread stuffing	3c	6c	9c
3 T. grated parmesan cheese	½c + 1T	1c + 2T	1½c + 3T

Serving Day

3 T. cooking oil

1 pkg. brown gravy mix

¼ cup dry red wine

¼ cup minced green onions

⅓ cup currant or berry jelly

Original Recipe Yield

4–6 servings

Cooking Day

In large saucepan, melt butter over medium-high heat. Add mushrooms and sauté until tender. Remove from heat and add stuffing mix and cheese. Mix well. Spread onto one side of flank steak. Roll up flank steak jellyroll-style. Secure with toothpicks or string. Wrap steak in plastic wrap and then place in freezer bag. Freeze, using freezer bag method.

Serving Day

Thaw steak completely. Pour 3 T. oil in crockpot. Place steak in crockpot, rolling to coat all sides in oil. Prepare gravy mix according to package directions. Pour gravy, wine, and green onions over meat. Cover and cook on low for 8–10 hours. Remove meat from crockpot. Add jelly to sauce and stir until dissolved. Slice meat into 1 inch slices and arrange on serving platter. Pour half of the sauce over meat. Serve remaining sauce at the table.

Tangy Chops with Honey Curry Sauce

An unlikely blend of flavors makes these chops irresistible

	x3	x6	x9
6 pork loin chops, approx. 1 inch thick	18	36	54
3 slices bacon, diced	9	18	27
1 cup onion, chopped	3c	6c	9c
2 cloves garlic, minced	6	12	18
½ cup soy sauce	1½c	3c	4½c
⅓ cup lemon juice*	¾c	1½c	2¼c
2 T. honey	¼c + 2T	¾c	1c + 2T
1 T. curry powder	3T	¼c + 2T	½c + 1T
2 t. chili powder	2T	¼c	¼c + 2T
¼ t. salt	¾t	1½t	2¼t

*This measurement, when multiplied, has been adjusted to accommodate the intensified flavor of acidic ingredients when recipes are made in quantity.

Original Recipe Yield

6 servings

Cooking Day

Cook bacon in skillet until lightly browned. Add onion and garlic; sauté until tender. Stir in soy sauce, lemon juice, honey, curry powder, chili powder, and salt. Simmer for 2–3 minutes. Remove from heat. Allow sauce to stand for 1 hour until flavors are blended. Place pork chops in freezer bag and add sauce. Freeze, using freezer bag method.

Serving Day

Thaw completely. Drain pork chops and save marinade. Place chops on broiling pan and place in oven, 4 inches from heat. Broil 12–15 minutes; flip chops and broil 10–15 minutes more. Brush chops frequently with marinade. Pork chops may also be grilled.

Telluride Black Bean Tortilla Bake

A great dish for a casual get-together with friends

	x3	x6	x9
1 lb. ground beef*	3 lbs	6 lbs	9 lbs
½ cup chopped onion	1½c	3c	4½c
1–15 oz. can black beans, drained and rinsed	3	6	9
1–16 oz. can stewed tomatoes (Mexican style)	3	6	9
½ cup enchilada sauce (mild or medium)	1½c	3c	4½c
1 t. chili powder	1T	2T	3T
1 t. cumin	1T	2T	3T
¼ t. pepper	¾t	1½t	2¼t
6 flour tortillas, fajita-size	18	36	54
3 oz. low-fat cream cheese, softened	9oz	18oz	27oz
1–4 oz. can diced green chiles, drained	3	6	9

Serving Day

½–1 cup shredded Monterey jack or cheddar cheese

*Ground turkey or buffalo meat can be substituted for ground beef.

Original Recipe Yield

4–6 servings

Cooking Day

Brown ground beef and onion in a large skillet; drain fat. Put stewed tomatoes into a blender (or food processor) and blend just long enough to break up large tomato pieces. Add to skillet with meat. Stir in black beans, enchilada sauce, chili powder, cumin, and pepper. Bring to a boil, cover, and simmer about 10 minutes. Remove from heat and let cool.

Spread one side of tortillas with cream cheese, topping with green chiles. Fold tortillas in half over cream cheese. Pour half of the cooled meat sauce into the bottom of a lined 7 x 11 baking dish. Arrange the folded tortillas over the sauce, overlapping if necessary. Pour the remaining sauce over the tortillas. Freeze, using foil and plastic wrap method.

Serving Day

Return the unwrapped meal to original baking dish and thaw to a slushy state. Cover dish with foil and bake in 350 degree oven for 20–30 minutes, until heated through. Uncover and sprinkle cheese on top; bake for 5 more minutes or until bubbly.

Tender Beef on a Skewer

These grill up very quickly—
and are nice to have on hand year round!

	x2	x4	x6
1½ lbs. flank steak (can also use sirloin steak)	3 lbs	6 lbs	9 lbs
2–3 stalks lemongrass*, trimmed and finely chopped	4–6	10–12	16–18
3 T. brown sugar	¼c + 2T	¾c	1c + 2T
3 cloves garlic, coarsely chopped	6	12	18
1–2 Thai chile or jalapeno peppers, seeded and chopped	3–4	6–8	10–12
¼ cup chopped fresh cilantro	½c	1c	1½ c
2 t. ground coriander	4t	2T + 2t	¼c
¼ cup lime juice**	¼c + 2T	¾c	1c + 2T
2½ T. soy sauce	¼c + 1T	½c + 2T	¾c + 3T
2½ T. fish sauce*** (nam pla)	¼c + 1T	½c + 2T	¾c + 3T
¼ cup vegetable oil	½c	1c	1½c

*Lemongrass can be found in Asian specialty stores and in the produce section of larger grocery stores. It can also be found in a "tube," allowing you to squeeze out the portion you need and store the rest for later use. *Substitution*: 2½ T. lemongrass from squeeze tube or 2 strips of lemon zest may be substituted for the lemongrass stalk in this recipe.

**This measurement, when multiplied, has been adjusted to accommodate the intensified flavor of acidic ingredients when recipes are made in quantity.

***Nam pla*, also known as fish sauce, is an intensely flavored sauce that adds a wonderful depth to many dishes. A little goes a long way. It can be found in Asian markets or in the gourmet/ethnic food aisles of many grocery stores. It lasts a long time when stored in the refrigerator.

Original Recipe Yield

36 skewers

Cooking Day

Marinade: Combine lemongrass, brown sugar, garlic, peppers, and cilantro in a food processor or blender and process to a coarse paste. With machine running, slowly add coriander, lime juice, soy sauce, fish sauce, and vegetable oil.

Slice the flank steak across the grain into long, thin strips, holding knife at an angle while cutting. Place in freezer bag and pour marinade over meat. Freeze, using freezer bag method.

Serving Day

Thaw meat slices and thread onto soaked bamboo skewers. Skewers can be grilled on an outdoor grill, on a stovetop grill pan, or under the broiler. Coat grill surface, grill pan, or broiler pan with cooking spray or oil, adding more oil as needed to avoid sticking/burning. Grill/broil each skewer for 1–2 minutes per side or until cooked through.

Serve with rice, grilled vegetables, or peanut sauce for dipping.

Hint

This marinade is also good for marinating pork, lamb, or chicken.

Top Sirloin with Red Wine Marinade

Outstanding!!

	x3	x6	x9
2 lbs. top sirloin steak*	6 lbs	12 lbs	18 lbs
¾ cup vegetable oil	2¼c	4½c	6¾c
⅓ cup soy sauce	1c	2c	3c
2 T. Worcestershire sauce	¼c + 2T	¾c	1c + 2T
1 T. dry mustard	3T	¼c + 2T	½c + 1T
1½ t. black pepper	4½t	3T	¼c + 1½t
¼ cup red wine	¾c	1½c	2¼c
¼ t. dried parsley	¾t	1½t	2¼t
3 T. lemon juice**	½c	1c	1½c
1 clove garlic, minced	3	6	9

*Steak may also be cubed for kabobs.

**This measurement, when multiplied, has been adjusted to accommodate the intensified flavor of acidic ingredients when recipes are made in quantity.

Original Recipe Yield

6 servings

Cooking Day

Place sirloin, whole or cubed, in freezer bag. Mix remaining ingredients together to form marinade and pour over steak. Freeze, using freezer bag method.

Serving Day

Thaw steak completely. Discard marinade. Grill over medium heat until cooked according to preference. If steak is cubed, grill on skewers with your favorite fresh vegetables.

Lighter Fare Nutritional Information (per serving): Calories 468; Total Fat 27.4g; Cholesterol 138mg; Sodium 1221mg; Total Carbohydrates 2g; Dietary Fiber 0g; Protein 49g

Tempting Pizza and Pasta

Baked Penne with Sausage, Tomatoes, and Cheese

Beef Pasta Bake

Butternut Squash Lasagna

Donna's Stromboli

Four Cheese White Pizza

Mediterranean Lasagna

Mexican Manicotti

Quick Cheese Ravioli with Two Different Fillings

Veggie Pizza

Wes's Roasted Red Pepper Pasta Sauce

White Chicken Lasagna with Spinach

Baked Penne with Sausage, Tomatoes, and Cheese

Serve at your next get-together
with Caesar salad and French bread!

	x3	x6	x9
1 lb. uncooked penne pasta	3 lbs	6 lbs	9 lbs
1 lb. hot Italian sausage	3 lbs	6 lbs	9 lbs
1 cup chopped onion	3c	6c	9c
2 garlic cloves, minced	6	12	18
8 oz. tomato paste	24oz	48oz	72oz
8 oz. tomato sauce	24oz	48oz	72oz
¼ t. salt	¾t	1½t	2¼t
¼ t. black pepper	¾t	1½t	2¼t
2–14 oz. cans diced tomatoes, undrained	6	12	18
¼ cup fresh basil, chopped	¾c	1½c	2¼c
1 cup fresh mozzarella cheese, shredded	3c	6c	9c
1 cup fresh parmesan cheese, grated	3c	6c	9c
1 cup Italian fontal cheese, grated	3c	6c	9c

Original Recipe Yield

12 servings

Cooking Day

Cook pasta according to package directions, omitting salt and oil. Drain pasta and set aside. Remove casings from sausage. Cook sausage, onion, and garlic in a large, nonstick skillet over medium heat until browned, stirring to crumble. Drain. Add tomato paste, tomato sauce, salt, pepper, and tomatoes; bring to a boil. Cover, reduce heat, and simmer 10 minutes, stirring occasionally.

Combine cooked pasta, sausage mixture, and basil. Place half of the pasta mixture in a lined 9 x 13 baking dish. Top with half of each cheese. Repeat layers. Freeze, using foil and plastic wrap method.

Serving Day

Returned unwrapped meal to original baking dish. Thaw slightly. Bake in a preheated 350 degree oven for 25 minutes or until bubbly.

Beef Pasta Bake

Serve with a side salad and our Cheesy Breadsticks

Contributed by Jenny Mills—Lakewood, Colorado

	x3	x6	x9
2 cups bowtie pasta, uncooked	6c	12c	18c
1 lb. ground beef	3 lbs	6 lbs	9 lbs
1 onion	3	6	9
2 cloves garlic, chopped	6	12	18
½ t. garlic salt	1½t	1T	4½t
3 cups spaghetti sauce	9c	18c	27c
6 oz. cream cheese, cubed	18oz	36oz	54oz
⅔ cup milk	2c	4c	6c
½ cup sour cream	1½c	3c	4½c
1 green bell pepper, chopped	3	6	9
¾ cup grated parmesan cheese, divided	2¼c	4½c	6¾c

Original Recipe Yield

12 servings

Cooking Day

Cook bowtie pasta according to package directions; drain and set aside. Brown beef, onion, and garlic until beef is no longer pink; drain. Add spaghetti sauce and garlic salt; simmer for 10 minutes. In a separate bowl, combine cream cheese and milk. Microwave 1–2 minutes on high, stirring once. Stir with whisk until blended. Stir in sour cream, green pepper, and ½ cup parmesan cheese. Place cream cheese mixture in lined 9 x 9 casserole dish. Spread cooked pasta on top of cream cheese mixture. Top with beef mixture and remaining ¼ cup parmesan cheese. Freeze, using foil and plastic wrap method.

Serving Day

Return unwrapped meal to original baking dish and allow to thaw to a slushy state. Preheat oven to 350 degrees and bake for 25–30 minutes, covered. Uncover and bake 5–10 more minutes, until bubbly.

Butternut Squash Lasagna

A vegetarian dish—delicious!

Contributed by Terri Bisio—Denver, Colorado

	x3	x6	x9
2 lbs. whole butternut squash	6 lbs	12 lbs	18 lbs
Béchamel sauce			
½ cup butter	1½c	3c	4½c
¼ cup flour	¾c	1½c	2¼c
3½ cups whole milk	½gal + 2½c	1gal + 5c	1½gal + 7½c
⅛ t. nutmeg	⅜t	¾t	1⅛t
¾ cup fresh basil, chopped	2¼c	4½c	6¾c
12 lasagna noodles	36	72	108
2½ cups shredded mozzarella cheese	7½c	15c	22½c
⅓ cup parmesan cheese, grated	1c	2c	3c

Original Recipe Yield

12 servings

Cooking Day

Slice squash in half lengthwise. Scoop out seeds. In a 9 x 13 baking dish, place squash facedown in 1 inch of water. Bake at 350 degrees for 45–60 minutes, or until squash is soft enough to scoop out with a spoon. Scoop squash into bowl; mash with a fork.

Béchamel sauce: Warm butter and milk in saucepan over medium heat. Whisk in flour and nutmeg and cook, stirring constantly, until it begins to thicken. Pour sauce into blender, add basil, and blend until thoroughly combined.

Cook lasagna noodles until slightly firm, according to package directions. Drain noodles. In a lined 9 x 13 pan, layer ¾ cup béchamel sauce, followed by a layer of noodles, squash, and finally mozzarella cheese. Repeat three times. Top with parmesan cheese. Freeze, using foil and plastic wrap method.

Serving Day

Return unwrapped lasagna to original pan and thaw to a slushy state. Bake uncovered at 350 degrees for one hour, or until completely heated through and bubbly.

Donna's Stromboli

Assemble these as a family night activity!

	x3	x6	x9
1 loaf frozen bread dough, thawed and slightly risen	3	6	9
4 cups shredded mozzarella cheese	12c	24c	36c
½ t. dried oregano	1½t	1T	4½t
½ t. dried basil	1½t	1T	4½t
½ t. garlic powder	1½t	1T	4½t
1 egg, beaten slightly	3	6	9

Pizza toppings of your choice, such as:

pepperoni

Italian sausage, cooked

pastrami

black olives

frozen spinach, thawed and drained

ham

mushrooms

red onion, diced

Serving Day

marinara sauce

Original Recipe Yield

4–6 servings

Cooking Day

After bread dough has been thawed and is easy to manage, roll out into a 14 x 12 inch rectangle. Add any or all of the suggested pizza toppings. Sprinkle cheese over toppings, then sprinkle with oregano, basil, and garlic powder. Roll dough into a log and seal all edges. Place seam-side down on a greased cookie sheet. Brush with beaten egg. Bake in a 350 degree oven for 20–25 minutes.

Remove from oven and cool completely on wire rack. Wrap in plastic wrap, then foil, and freeze.

Serving Day

Thaw completely (about 2 hours). Place on a greased cookie sheet and bake at 350 degrees for 15–20 minutes or until golden brown. Slice and serve with warmed marinara sauce.

Four Cheese White Pizza

A Sunday night tradition at Susie's house

	x3	x6	x9
Dough			
¼ cup warm water	¾c	1½c	2¼c
1 t. yeast	1T	2T	3T
4 cups bread flour	12c	24c	36c
1 T. olive oil	3T	¼c + 2T	½c + 1T
1 t. honey	1T	2T	3T
½ t. salt	1½t	1T	4½t
1 cup ice water, divided	3c	6c	9c
Pizza			
2 T. extra virgin olive oil	¼c + 2T	¾c	1c + 2T
1 clove garlic, minced	3	6	9
¼ cup mozzarella cheese, shredded	¾c	1½c	2¼c
¼ cup ricotta cheese	¾c	1½c	2¼c
¼ cup gouda cheese, shredded	¾c	1½c	2¼c
¼ cup parmesan cheese, shredded	¾c	1½c	2¼c
2 Roma tomatoes, cut into slices	6	12	18
3 T. fresh basil, thinly sliced	½c + 1T	1c + 2T	1½c + 3T
2 cardboard rounds*	6	12	18
cornmeal, for dusting cardboard rounds			

*Cardboard rounds can be found at hobby/craft stores or party/paper goods stores, usually in the cake decorating aisle.

Original Recipe Yield

2 pizzas

Cooking Day

Dough: For best results, pizza dough should be prepared in single batches. Dissolve yeast in ¼ cup warm water. Place in bowl for electric mixer with dough hook. Add flour, olive oil, honey, salt, and ¾ cup ice water. Turn mixer on low and mix until ingredients begin to combine. As the mixture starts to resemble dough, slowly pour in remaining ¼ cup of cold water. Mix for 2 more minutes on low. Lightly dust counter with flour. Remove dough from mixer and knead for 1 minute. Place dough back in mixer, change mixer speed to medium, and knead with the dough hook for another 6 minutes. Dough will not be completely smooth. Note: dough may also be mixed and kneaded by hand.

Spritz counter with a little water. Divide dough into two pieces and roll each half into a smooth ball. Place into individual bowls, cover lightly with plastic wrap, and let rest and rise for at least 2 hours.

At this point, the whole pizza can be assembled, or pizza dough may be frozen in dough balls after rising by wrapping each half of dough in plastic wrap and placing in a freezer bag. To assemble pizzas on serving day, thaw pizza dough and roll to desired thickness. Assemble pizza and bake as described below.

To assemble pizza: Roll out pizza dough onto 2 cornmeal-dusted cardboard rounds. Mix extra virgin olive oil and garlic in small bowl. Brush crusts lightly with garlic mixture. Top crusts with mozzarella and gouda cheeses, leaving ½ inch border of dough. Crumble ricotta cheese over top, then sprinkle with parmesan. Place sliced tomatoes on the pizzas and sprinkle with fresh basil. Wrap each pizza with plastic wrap and foil and place in freezer.

Serving Day

Position rack in center of oven and preheat oven to 450 degrees. Sprinkle cornmeal on 2 pizza stones or greased baking sheets. Remove cardboard rounds and place frozen pizzas on pizza stones or baking sheets. Bake pizzas until crusts are golden brown and cheese melts, about 18 minutes. Let stand 3 minutes before slicing. Serve.

Mediterranean Lasagna

Included is Amy's amazing salad for you to try with this dish!

Contributed by Amy Sunahara—Highlands Ranch, Colorado

	x3	x6	x9
1 T. oil	3T	¼c + 2T	½c + 1T
2 garlic cloves, diced	6	12	18
¼ cup fresh parsley, chopped	¾c	1½c	2¼c
2 t. fresh basil, chopped	2T	¼c	¼c + 2T
1 t. dried rosemary	1T	2T	3T
1 t. salt	1T	2T	3T
1 t. pepper	1T	2T	3T
⅛ t. cayenne pepper	⅜t	¾t	1⅛t
1–28 oz. can crushed Italian tomatoes	3	6	9
2–6 oz. cans tomato paste	6	12	18
1 cup water	3c	6c	9c
¼ cup sugar	¾c	1½c	2¼c
⅓ cup red wine	1c	2c	3c
1 lb. ground beef	3 lbs	6 lbs	9 lbs
½ lb. Italian sausage	1½ lbs	3 lbs	4½ lbs
8 wide lasagna noodles, cooked al dente	24	48	72
1½ lbs. sour cream	4½ lbs	9 lbs	13½ lbs
3 cups grated mozzarella cheese	9c	18c	27c
1 cup freshly grated parmesan cheese	3c	6c	9c

Original Recipe Yield

6–8 servings

Cooking Day

Sauce: Heat 1 T. olive oil in bottom of a large, heavy saucepan over medium heat. Add garlic, parsley, basil, rosemary, salt, pepper, and cayenne pepper.

Cook and stir until garlic is golden brown and herbs are fragrant. Add crushed tomatoes, tomato paste, and water. Let mixture come to a boil, then add sugar. When mixture boils again, add red wine. Reduce heat and simmer for 2 hours over low heat, stirring occasionally.

Meat: Brown ground beef with Italian sausage, breaking into very small pieces. Drain off fat. Add meat to sauce. Layer sauce, then noodles, sour cream, and mozzarella cheese in a lined 9 x 13 baking dish. Repeat layers, ending with another layer of sauce. Sprinkle parmesan cheese on top. Freeze, using foil and plastic wrap method.

Serving Day

Unwrap lasagna, return to original baking pan, and thaw to a slushy state. Bake at 350 degrees until bubbly, about 45 minutes. Serve with Bacon and Garlic Salad.

Bacon and Garlic Salad
1 bunch Bibb (or butter) lettuce
1 bunch romaine lettuce
bleu cheese crumbles
½ lb. bacon, fried and crumbled
sunflower seeds (optional)

Toss lettuce, bleu cheese, bacon, and sunflower seeds together. Right before serving, pour dressing over salad. Toss thoroughly.

Salad Dressing
¾ cup salad oil
½ cup garlic wine vinegar
5½ T. sugar
1½ t. salt
3–4 cloves garlic, minced

Whisk all dressing ingredients together until sugar dissolves; refrigerate prior to pouring over salad.

Mexican Manicotti

A Mexican twist on an Italian favorite—
and one of the group's favorites!

Contributed by Beth Doll's Cooking Co-op—Sterling, Colorado

	x3	x6	x9
1–8 oz. package manicotti shells	3	6	9
1 t. salt	1T	2T	3T
1 lb. ground beef	3 lbs	6 lbs	9 lbs
½ cup onion, diced	1½c	3c	4½c
2 cups cottage cheese (small curd)	6c	12c	18c
2 cups cheddar or cheddar/jack cheese, shredded and divided	6c	12c	18c
1 t. chili powder	1T	2T	3T
1 t. garlic powder (or 1 clove garlic, minced)	1T	2T	3T
1 t. cumin (more if desired)	1T	2T	3T
2–15 oz. cans tomato sauce	6	12	18
1–4 oz. can green chiles, chopped	3	6	9
½ cup water	1½c	3c	4½c
¼ t. cayenne pepper (optional)	¾t	1½t	2¼t
salt and pepper to taste			

Original Recipe Yield

6–8 servings

Cooking Day

Fill a large, deep pan or stockpot ⅔ full with water; add salt and bring to a boil on stovetop. Add manicotti shells and cook for *half* of the recommended time on package directions. Drain manicotti; cool and set aside. *Skip this step when using "no-boil" manicotti shells.*

In a skillet, brown ground beef and onion. Drain excess grease and cool slightly.

In a large mixing bowl, combine cottage cheese, 1 cup of the shredded cheese, chili powder, garlic powder, and cumin. Add the meat mixture. Mix well. In another bowl, mix together tomato sauce, green chiles, water, cayenne pepper, and salt and pepper to taste.

Place approximately half of the tomato sauce mixture in the bottom of a lined 9 x 13 pan.

Stuff parboiled manicotti shells with beef/cheese mixture, and place stuffed shells over a layer of sauce. Pour the remaining half of sauce over the shells. Top with the remaining 1 cup shredded cheese. Freeze, using foil and plastic wrap method.

Serving Day

Return unwrapped manicotti to original baking dish and thaw overnight in refrigerator. In a preheated 350 degree oven, bake for 45–50 minutes or until hot. If the manicotti is still icy when starting to bake, tent dish with foil for 30 minutes, then remove foil and bake for another 20–30 minutes.

Hint

To stuff shells more easily, place some of the beef/cheese mixture into a large freezer bag. Press out air and seal. Cut off a corner of the freezer bag and use as a pastry bag to squeeze filling into manicotti shells.

Quick Cheese Ravioli with Two Different Fillings

Delicious as an appetizer, side dish, or main course!

	x2	x4	x6
24 square wonton wrappers (3½ inch size)	48	96	144
6 oz. goat cheese (feta, chevre, etc.) or Italian blend cheese, grated*	12oz	24oz	36oz
½ cup part-skim ricotta cheese	1c	2c	3c
1 large clove garlic, pressed	2	4	6
⅛ t. ground nutmeg	¼t	½t	¾t
⅛ t. pepper, or to taste	¼t	½t	¾t
⅛ t. salt, or to taste	¼t	½t	¾t

*Italian blend cheese is a blend of parmesan, asiago, Romano, and mozzarella cheeses, and is found among the packaged, refrigerated cheeses in your local grocery store.

Original Recipe Yield

4 main-dish servings

Cooking Day

In a small bowl, mash together the goat cheese (or Italian blend cheese), ricotta cheese, garlic, and nutmeg. Add salt and pepper to taste.

To assemble ravioli, place a sheet of waxed paper on a baking sheet or other flat surface. Arrange 6 wonton wrappers on this work surface. (Keep the remaining wrappers covered with a damp paper towel.) Spoon 1 T. of cheese filling into center of each wonton wrapper. Wet the edges of the wrappers with water. Fold the corner of each wrapper over the filling to form a triangle. Flatten the area around the cheese filling to eliminate any air pockets, pressing the edges to seal. Repeat with remaining filling and wrappers. Freeze ravioli on a flat tray for 1 hour. Wrap ravioli in bundles of 6–8 in plastic wrap, then place in a freezer bag. Freeze, using freezer bag method.

Serving Day

Bring a large pot of water to boil. Add ¼ t. salt to water. Drop desired number of frozen ravioli into water, one at a time. Stir gently and cook for 5–7 minutes, until al dente (just done). Using a slotted spoon, remove the raviolis and drain them very quickly on a plate lined with paper towels. Serve immediately with Parsley-Basil Butter Drizzle or your favorite marinara or meat sauce.

Parsley-Basil Butter Drizzle

1 T. chopped fresh parsley

1 T. chopped fresh basil

2 T. butter, melted

1 T. parmesan cheese, grated

salt, pepper, and garlic salt to taste

In a small bowl, stir together parsley and basil. Add butter, parmesan cheese, salt, pepper, and garlic salt (optional). Microwave for 30 seconds or until heated to liquid consistency. Drizzle over ravioli.

Veggie Pizza

With a wonderful homemade pizza sauce!

Pizza sauce contributed by Flo Kitashima—Denver, Colorado

	x3	x6	x9
Pizza Dough (see page 215)			
Pizza sauce			
2 cups tomatoes, canned (whole or diced)	6c	12c	18c
2 T. onion, minced	¼c + 2T	¾c	1c + 2T
1 large clove of garlic, pressed	3	6	9
1–6 oz. can tomato paste	3	6	9
½ T. dried oregano (or more to taste)	1½T	3T	4½T
1 T. dried basil	3T	¼c + 2T	½c + 1T
¼ t. pepper	¾t	1½t	2¼t
½ t. dried thyme	1½t	1T	4½t
⅛ t. red pepper (optional)	⅜t	¾t	1⅛t
1 T. brown sugar, packed	3T	¼c + 2T	½c + 1T
salt, to taste			
Toppings (or add other favorite veggies)			
2 T. olive oil, divided	¼c + 2T	¾c	1c + 2T
1 cup red onion, diced	3c	6c	9c
1 red or green bell pepper, diced or strips	3	6	9
2 cups mushrooms, sliced	6	12	18
¼ cup black olives, sliced (or to taste)	¾c	1½c	2¼c
2 cups mozzarella cheese, shredded (or more)	6c	12c	18c
1 cup parmesan or Romano cheese, shredded	3c	6c	9c
2 cardboard rounds*	6	12	18
Serving Day			
cornmeal, for dusting pizza dough			
olive oil			

*Cardboard rounds can be found at hobby/craft stores or party/paper goods stores, usually in the cake decorating aisle.

Original Recipe Yield

2 pizzas (6–8 servings per pizza)

Cooking Day

Pizza dough: Prepare the dough, using cooking day instructions for Four Cheese Pizza found on page 215.

Pizza sauce: Drain canned tomatoes and blend in a food processor or blender to desired consistency. Combine tomatoes with remaining sauce ingredients in a medium saucepan and bring to a boil over medium heat. Reduce heat to low, cover, and simmer for 10–15 minutes more. Cool completely. (Pizza sauce can also be frozen at this point, using the freezer bag method.)

Pizza toppings: In a large skillet, heat 1 T. of olive oil over medium-high heat. Add onions and sauté for 1–2 minutes. Add green and/or red bell peppers and continue to sauté for 1–2 minutes more, until crisp tender. If needed, add more oil to the pan. Stir in mushrooms and sauté for 1 more minute, then add black olives. Remove from heat and cool.

To assemble pizzas: Roll out prepared dough and place on cardboard rounds that have been sprinkled with cornmeal. Spoon pizza sauce on top of crusts, leaving a ½ inch border. Top sauce with cheeses and then the veggie mixture. Cover and wrap each pizza tightly with plastic wrap and then a layer of heavy-duty foil. Freeze.

Serving Day

Position rack in center of oven and preheat oven to 450 degrees. Sprinkle cornmeal on 2 pizza stones or 2 greased baking sheets. Remove pizzas from cardboard rounds and place on prepared stones or baking sheets. Brush pizza dough border with olive oil. Bake pizzas until crust is golden brown and cheese is melted, about 18–21 minutes. Let stand 3 minutes. Serve.

Hint

Extra sauce is great to keep on hand as a dipping sauce for our Hot Soft Pretzels (page 46) or Cheesy Breadsticks (page 70).

Wes's Roasted Red Pepper Pasta Sauce

A delicious red sauce to use on your favorite pasta

	x3	x6	x9
1 lb. Italian sausage	3 lbs	6 lbs	9 lbs
1–28 oz. can whole tomatoes, undrained	3	6	9
4 large red bell peppers, seeded and cut into chunks	12	24	36
1 T. fresh rosemary, coarsely chopped	3T	¼c + 2T	½c + 1T
1 T. fresh sage, coarsely chopped	3T	¼c + 2T	½c + 1T
¼ cup olive oil	¾c	1½c	2¼c
¼ cup balsamic vinegar	¾c	1½c	2¼c
4 oz. tomato paste	12oz	24oz	36oz
½ cup fresh parmesan cheese, grated	1½c	3c	4½c
½ cup fresh Romano cheese, grated	1½c	3c	4½c

Serving Day

pasta of your choice, prepared according to package directions

Original Recipe Yield

8 servings

Cooking Day

In a large skillet, brown Italian sausage on stovetop. Drain and set aside. In a large bowl, mix whole tomatoes, red peppers, rosemary, sage, and olive oil. Pour into a jellyroll pan with raised edges. Drizzle balsamic vinegar over tomato mixture. Preheat oven on broil and place jellyroll pan in oven 6 inches from heat. Broil for 30 minutes, stirring occasionally. Peppers will begin to roast and sauce will begin to caramelize. Remove mixture from oven and purée in blender, adding tomato paste to thicken sauce. Place pasta sauce in a large skillet and stir in cheeses and sausage. Heat sauce on medium low on stovetop, until cheese is

▶

melted and sauce is heated through, but do not boil. Cool completely. Freeze, using freezer bag method.

Serving Day

Thaw completely. Warm sauce in skillet on stovetop until heated through, but do not boil. Serve over cooked pasta.

White Chicken Lasagna with Spinach

This creamy white sauce gives a whole new meaning to lasagna

	x3	x6	x9
½ cup butter, melted	1½c	3c	4½c
½ cup flour	1½c	3c	4½c
¾ t. salt	2¼t	4½t	2T + ¾t
¼ t. black pepper	¾t	1½t	2¼t
½ t. dried basil	1½t	1T	4½t
3 cups chicken broth	9c	18c	27c
3 cups cooked chicken, diced	9c	18c	27c
8 oz. lasagna noodles	24oz	48oz	72oz
2 cups cottage cheese	6c	12c	18c
1 egg, slightly beaten	3	6	9
1–10 oz. pkg. frozen chopped spinach, cooked and drained	3	6	9
½ lb. mozzarella cheese, thinly sliced	1½ lbs	3 lbs	4½ lbs
8 oz. fresh parmesan cheese, grated	24oz	48oz	72oz

Original Recipe Yield

10–12 servings

Cooking Day

Melt butter in a large saucepan; blend in flour, salt, pepper, and basil. Stir in chicken broth. Bring to boil, stirring constantly, until mixture is thickened. Remove from heat and add chicken. Cook and drain noodles according to package directions. Mix cottage cheese with beaten egg and set aside. Place one third of the chicken mixture into a lined 9 x 13 baking dish. Top with half the noodles, half the cottage cheese mixture, half the spinach, and half the mozzarella cheese.

Repeat. Top with the last third of the chicken mixture. Sprinkle with parmesan cheese. Freeze, using foil and plastic wrap method.

Serving Day

Unwrap lasagna, return to original baking dish, and thaw completely. Bake 45 minutes at 375 degrees until bubbly. Remove from oven and let stand for 10 minutes prior to serving.

Adding a Side Dish

Broccoli Rice Casserole

Four Corners Refried Beans

Glazed Carrots

Green Beans with Pine Nuts

Grilled Vegetable Medley

Harvest Sweet Potato Cranberry Casserole

Homemade Baked Beans

Marvelous Mashed Potatoes

Rice for Any Meal

Southwestern Green Chile Rice Bake

Twice Baked Potatoes

Broccoli Rice Casserole

Use your leftover rice for this traditional favorite

	x3	x6	x9
4 cups fresh broccoli florets	12c	24c	36c
½ cup butter, melted	1½c	3c	4½c
¼ cup onion, chopped	¾c	1½c	2¼c
1–10 oz. can cream of mushroom soup	3	6	9
8 oz. Velveeta cheese, cubed	24oz	48oz	72oz
1 cup cooked rice	3c	6c	9c

Original Recipe Yield

8–10 servings

Cooking Day

In a large, covered saucepan, cook broccoli in a small amount of boiling water for 6–8 minutes, until crisp tender. Drain well. In a large skillet, sauté onion in melted butter over medium heat for 2–3 minutes. Add soup, then cheese, stirring until cheese is melted and well blended. Add broccoli and rice to soup mixture. Place in a lined 9 x 13 baking dish and freeze, using foil and plastic wrap method.

Serving Day

Unwrap, return to original baking dish, and thaw completely. Bake uncovered at 350 degrees for 25–30 minutes or until heated through.

Four Corners Refried Beans

Oh—so good!

	x2
1 lb. bacon (optional; can also use turkey bacon)	2 lbs
3 cups uncooked pinto beans	6c
7 cups water	14c
1½ cups chopped onion	3c
4 cloves garlic	8
1 T. salt (to start)	2T
1–2 cups fresh or canned green chiles, diced (optional)	2–4c

Original Recipe Yield

24–36 servings

Cooking Day

Fry bacon in heavy pan until crisp. Crumble and drain, reserving half of the bacon grease. Place bacon, remainder of ingredients, and reserved bacon grease into the crockpot and cover. *Green chiles can either be added along with all the ingredients into the crockpot, or they can be added after the beans have been cooked. If the chiles are added at the beginning, they will cook down in size. If you prefer to have more visible, "diced" chunks of green chiles, add them after the beans have cooked, right before mashing.*

Cook beans on high for 1 hour, then reduce heat to low and cook overnight (10 hours). Beans may also be cooked on high for 6–7 hours. Cool slightly and then mash pinto beans, in batches, using a potato masher (or electric mixer). Add more salt to taste, if needed.

Cool mashed beans completely, measure desired serving size into freezer bags. Freeze, using freezer bag method.

Serving Day

Thaw beans. Refried beans can be reheated either on the stovetop or in the microwave on medium-low heat. If you prefer a creamier consistency, add a small amount of water and stir until smooth. Top with cheese if serving as a side dish, or use in your favorite Mexican dishes.

Glazed Carrots

Serve with your favorite roast or chicken recipe

---

	x3	x6	x9
2 lbs. of pre-peeled baby carrots, or regular carrots cut in 2 inch pieces and halved lengthwise	6 lbs	12 lbs	18 lbs
3 T. butter	½c + 1T	1c + 2T	1½c + 3T
⅓ cup apricot preserves (optional)	1c	2c	3c
¼ cup brown sugar, packed	¾c	1½c	2¼c
⅛ t. ground nutmeg	⅜t	¾t	1⅛t
¼ t. salt	¾t	1½t	2¼t
1 t. freshly grated orange zest (optional)	1T	2T	3T
2 t. fresh lemon juice*	1½T	3T	¼c + ½T

Serving Day

parsley, chopped (fresh or dried)

*This measurement, when multiplied, has been adjusted to accommodate the intensified flavor of acidic ingredients when recipes are made in quantity.

Original Recipe Yield

4–6 servings

Cooking Day

In a large pot of boiling water, cook the carrots just until tender crisp, about 20–25 minutes. Drain; immediately immerse carrots in cold water 2–3 times, until carrots are cooled. (This will stop the carrots from cooking any further.)

While the carrots are cooking, melt butter in a saucepan over medium-low heat and add remaining ingredients; stir until well blended. Remove from heat.

Toss carrots with the butter mixture until well coated; cool completely. Freeze, using the freezer bag method.

Serving Day

Thaw slightly or defrost carrots in microwave. Heat carrots on stovetop or in microwave, on low heat, stirring occasionally, until heated through. Garnish with parsley just before serving.

Green Beans with Pine Nuts

Easy and delicious!

	x2	x4	x6
1½ lbs. green beans, trimmed and cut diagonally into ½ inch pieces	3 lbs	6 lbs	9 lbs
1 t. salt	2t	1T + 1t	2T
¼ cup olive oil (or butter), more if needed	½c	1c	1½c
⅓ cup red onion, finely chopped	⅔c	1⅓c	2c
1½ t. fresh lemon juice	1T	2T	3T
salt and pepper, to taste			
¼ cup pine nuts, toasted*	½c	1c	1½c

Serving Day

2 T. fresh parsley (or mint), finely chopped

*Slivered or chopped almonds may be substituted for the pine nuts. To toast nuts: Heat skillet over medium low heat; add nuts, stir or toss until light golden brown. Watch closely, as nuts will burn quickly. Remove from heat and cool.

Original Recipe Yield

6–8 servings

Cooking Day

Add salt and green beans to a medium saucepan of boiling water. Cook 5–10 minutes, or until beans are crisp tender. Drain; immediately immerse green beans in cold water 2–3 times, or until beans are cooled. (This will stop green beans from cooking any further.) Drain beans well and return to pan.

In a small saucepan, cook onion in olive oil over medium heat just until tender. Add lemon juice, salt, and pepper. Toss green beans with the olive oil mixture until well coated; cool completely and place in freezer bag. In a separate, smaller freezer bag, place the toasted pine nuts. Freeze green beans and pine nuts, using freezer bag method.

Serving Day

Thaw slightly, or defrost green beans in microwave. Let pine nuts come to room temperature. Heat beans on stovetop or in microwave on low heat, stirring occasionally, until heated through. Garnish with parsley (or mint) and pine nuts just before serving.

Lighter Fare Nutritional Information (per serving): Calories 134; Total Fat 11g; Cholesterol 0mg; Sodium 20mg; Total Carbohydrates 8.4g; Dietary Fiber 3.6g; Protein 2.5g

Grilled Vegetable Medley

Veggies become delicious!

	x3	x6	x9
1 green bell pepper	3	6	9
1 red bell pepper	3	6	9
1 medium onion	3	6	9
1 zucchini squash	3	6	9
1 cup mushrooms, quartered	3c	6c	9c
1 garlic clove, pressed	3	6	9
1 cup Italian dressing	3c	6c	9c

Original Recipe Yield

12 servings

Cooking Day

Cut bell peppers, onion, and zucchini into 1 inch chunks; place in medium bowl. Add mushrooms to bowl, along with garlic. Pour Italian dressing over vegetables, stir, and place in freezer bag. Freeze, using freezer bag method.

Serving Day

Place vegetables in grilling basket and grill over medium heat, stirring frequently, just until heated through (approx. 5–8 minutes). Serve as a complement to almost any meal.

Lighter Fare Nutritional Information (per serving): Calories 110; Total Fat 9.6g; Cholesterol 0mg; Sodium 226mg; Total Carbohydrates 6.3g; Fiber .7g; Protein .9g

Harvest Sweet Potato Cranberry Casserole

Great complement to any holiday meal!

	x3	x6	x9
3½ lbs. sweet potatoes or yams, peeled and cut into ¾ inch cubes	10½ lbs	21 lbs	31½ lbs
1 large onion, diced	3	6	9
olive oil or vegetable oil cooking spray			
1½ cups fresh cranberries or frozen cranberries (do not thaw if using frozen cranberries)	4½c	9c	13½c
⅔ cup light brown sugar	2c	4c	6c
2 T. butter or margarine, melted	¼c + 2T	¾c	1c + 2T
¼ cup orange juice	¾c	1½c	2¼c
¾ t. salt	2¼t	4½t	2T + ¾t
1 t. nutmeg	1T	2T	3T
½ t. ground ginger	1½t	1T	4½t
¾ t. cinnamon	2¼t	4½t	2T + ¾t
1 cup chopped pecans	3c	6c	9c

Original Recipe Yield

12 servings

Cooking Day

Preheat oven to 450 degrees. Spray two shallow baking dishes (about 9 x 13 each) with oil. Mix sweet potatoes and onions, and place half in each prepared baking dish. Spray lightly with oil and bake until sweet potatoes are just tender (a bit underdone), about 20–25 minutes. In a large bowl, combine remaining ingredients and mix well. Stir in sweet potato mixture. Place mixture in two freezer bags. Freeze, using freezer bag method.

Serving Day

Slightly defrost or thaw to slushy state. Preheat oven to 350 degrees. Place potato/cranberry mixture in two 9 x 13 baking dishes. Bake uncovered about 30–40 minutes or until tender and slightly sticky. Stir once during cooking.

Homemade Baked Beans

Great for a picnic in the mountains

	x3	x6	x9
2–15 oz cans white beans (navy or great northern)	6	12	18
1–15 oz. can pinto beans	3	6	9
1–15 oz. can butter beans	3	6	9
1 cup ketchup	3c	6c	9c
1 cup brown sugar	3c	6c	9c
1 T. dry mustard	3T	¼c + 2T	½c + 1T
½ t. garlic powder	1½t	1T	4½t
1 t. Worcestershire sauce	1T	2T	3T
¼ cup chopped onion	¾c	1½c	2¼c
1 lb. bacon, cooked and crumbled	3 lbs	6 lbs	9 lbs

Original Recipe Yield

6–8 servings

Cooking Day

Mix all ingredients together in a large bowl. Place in a freezer bag and freeze, using freezer bag method.

Serving Day

Thaw completely. Place beans in a greased 2 quart baking dish. Bake in 250 degree oven for 4 hours or until bubbly and thickened. May also be placed in a crockpot and cooked on low for 4–5 hours.

Marvelous Mashed Potatoes

A medley of potato variations sure to please!

Variation #4 contributed by Paula McGuire — Sterling, Colorado

	x3	x6	x9
Basic mashed potatoes			
4 lbs. russet potatoes (approx. 6–8 medium)	12 lbs	24 lbs	36 lbs
1 T. salt	3T	¼c + 2T	½c + 1T
1½ cups milk (more or less if needed)*	4½c	9c	13½c
½ cup butter, cubed*	1½c	3c	4½c
salt and pepper, to taste			
Serving Day			
Milk and/or butter, if needed			
Chopped parsley for garnish			

*See recipe variations for changes to these ingredients.

Variation #1: Garlic Mashed Potatoes

Add:

	x3	x6	x9
1 head garlic, peeled (12–15 small cloves)	3	6	9

Variation #2: Buttermilk Mashed Potatoes

Add:

	x3	x6	x9
1½ cups buttermilk (instead of milk)	4½c	9c	13½c
Reduce the following			
6 T. butter, cubed	1c + 2T	2¼c	3¼c + 2T

Variation #3: Cheesy Mashed Potatoes

Add:

	x3	x6	x9
2 cups grated cheddar or parmesan cheese	6c	12c	18c

½ cup onion, finely chopped and sautéed (optional)	1½c	3c	4½c

Serving Day
8 pieces of bacon, fried crisp and crumbled

Variation #4: Green Chiles and Cheese Mashed Potatoes

Add:

1 head garlic, peeled (12–15 small cloves)	3	6	9
6 oz. cream cheese, softened	18oz	36oz	54oz
1 cup sour cream	3c	6c	9c
1 cup green chiles, chopped (canned or fresh)	3c	6c	9c

Reduce the following

⅔ cup milk (more or less if needed)	2c	4c	6c
¼ cup butter, cubed	¾c	1½c	2¼c

Original Recipe Yield
8–10 servings

Cooking Day

Peel potatoes and cut into quarters. Place potatoes in a large stockpot. Add enough water to cover potatoes plus 1 inch more. Stir in salt. Bring potatoes to a boil; reduce heat and simmer until potatoes are fork-tender, about 25–30 minutes.

Drain potatoes immediately and return to pan; cover to keep warm. (For best freezing results, *do not* let potatoes sit in water, as they will absorb too much water and become mushy.) Heat milk in saucepan until boiling. Mash potatoes with a potato masher or an electric mixer on low speed. Add butter, salt, pepper, and enough hot milk to make potatoes smooth and creamy. Cool completely. Freeze, using freezer bag method.

Mashed Potato Variations

Variation #1: Garlic Mashed Potatoes
Add whole garlic cloves to the quartered potatoes and water. Cook as directed.

Variation #2: Buttermilk Mashed Potatoes
Follow cooking day directions above, replacing hot milk with room-temperature buttermilk (do not boil). Butter is reduced; note the quantity difference.

Variation #3: Cheesy Mashed Potatoes
Follow cooking day directions above; add cheese and sautéed onion to potatoes when hot milk is added. On serving day, gently mix in crumbled bacon right before serving.

Variation #4: Green Chiles and Cheese Mashed Potatoes
Follow cooking day directions above, but add whole garlic cloves to the quartered potatoes and water. Add softened cream cheese and sour cream when mashing potatoes. Hot milk and butter are reduced; note the quantity differences. Add only as much milk as is needed to make potatoes creamy. Gently stir in green chiles.

Serving Day

Thaw potatoes completely. To reheat in the oven, place potatoes in an oven-proof dish and reheat at 350 degrees for 25 minutes or until heated through. Cover if necessary. Stir halfway through cooking time. To reheat in the microwave, place potatoes in a microwave-safe baking dish and reheat, covered, for 10–12 minutes or until heated through, stirring occasionally. For either method, you may add just enough milk and/or butter to bring potatoes back to a smooth, creamy consistency, if necessary. Serve with suggested garnishes, if applicable.

Rice for Any Meal

Yes, you can freeze rice for a side dish.

	x3	x6	x9
2 cups rice (long grain, short grain, jasmine, or basmati)	6c	12c	18c
water			
1 t. salt (optional)	1T	2T	3T
1 T. oil or butter (optional)	3T	¼c + 2T	½c + 1T
cooking spray or oil			

Serving Day

Depending on the type of rice and what it is being served with, garnish rice with any of the following items:

parsley, chopped

cilantro, chopped

lemon or lime zest

toasted sesame seeds

garlic butter drizzle

Original Recipe Yield

6–8 servings, depending on the type of rice

Cooking Day

In a large bowl, rinse rice in cold water, using a sieve to drain. Continue rinsing rice until water runs clear.

For short grain, jasmine, or basmati rice: soak rice in cold water for 30 minutes. Long grain rice does not need to be soaked.

In a 2–3 quart saucepan, add rice and enough water to cover rice plus ½ inch more. Bring the water to a boil, stirring occasionally; boil for 5 minutes. Add salt and oil, if using. Reduce heat to a low boil. Cover saucepan tightly with lid and simmer: 12–15 minutes for jasmine or short grain rice, 15–18 minutes for

▶

long grain or basmati rice. Remove rice from heat and let stand 10–15 minutes before removing lid.

Cool rice completely. Gently spread rice onto a jellyroll pan or baking sheet and fluff with fork to separate grains. Very lightly spray or drizzle oil over rice grains to coat; gently toss. Package rice flat in freezer bags. Freeze, using the freezer bag method.

Serving Day

Thaw rice slightly. For stovetop: Place rice in saucepan on medium-low heat with 1–2 T. of water and cover. Heat through. Toss gently. For microwave: Place rice in microwaveable dish with 1–2 T. of water and cover tightly. Cook on medium-high for 3–4 minutes or until heated through. Check rice halfway through and toss gently with fork.

Lighter Fare Nutritional Information (per 1 cup serving): Calories 156; Total Fat 0g; Cholesterol 13mg; Sodium 82 mg; Total Carbohydrates 35g; Dietary Fiber 3g; Protein 3g

Southwestern Green Chile Rice Bake

Perfect complement to Steak Soft Tacos

	x2	x4	x6
2 cups long grain rice, cooked	4c	8c	12c
1 cup sour cream	2c	4c	6c
7 oz. green chiles, canned or fresh	14oz	28oz	42oz
10–12 oz. Monterey jack and/or cheddar cheese, shredded	20–24oz	40–48oz	60–72oz
¼ t. salt	½t	1t	1½t

Original Recipe Yield

6–8 servings

Cooking Day

Combine rice, sour cream, chiles, cheese, and salt. Spread mixture evenly in a lined 2 quart baking dish. Freeze, using foil and plastic wrap method.

Serving Day

Return unwrapped rice bake to original baking dish and thaw slightly. Preheat oven to 350 degrees. Bake for 25–30 minutes or until rice is heated through and bubbly.

Twice Baked Potatoes

Great to have on hand for any meal

	x3	x6	x9
6 medium baking potatoes	18	36	54
butter, softened (for greasing)	6T	¾c	1c + 2T
salt, to taste	1T	2T	3T
8 oz. cream cheese, softened	24oz	48oz	72oz
½ cup hot milk	1½c	3c	4½c
1 t. onion salt	1T	2T	3T
2 T. butter	¼c + 2T	¾c	1c + 2T
½ t. fresh ground pepper	1½t	1T	4½t
¼ cup fresh parsley, chopped	¾c	1½c	2¼c
paprika, for garnish			

Original Recipe Yield

12 servings

Cooking Day

Clean potatoes and dry. Grease potatoes with butter and salt the skins. Bake potatoes at 350 degrees for 1 hour. Remove from oven and cool until you are able to handle them. Cut potatoes in half lengthwise and scoop cooked potato out into mixing bowl, being careful to keep the skins whole. Mash potatoes with cream cheese, hot milk, onion salt, butter, and pepper. Pile potato mixture back into skins. Sprinkle with paprika and parsley. Wrap potatoes individually in plastic wrap and freeze, using freezer bag method.

Serving Day

Thaw potatoes completely. Place in 350 degree oven and bake for 20 minutes or until heated through.

Hint

A melon baller makes quick work of scooping out the cooked potato.

Delightful Desserts

Almond Cheesecake with Chocolate Glaze
Apple Cake with Warm Caramel Sauce
Butterscotch Chocolate Chip Cookies
Caramel Brownies
Cherry Crisp
Chocolate and Vanilla Striped Cookies
Chocolate Lava Cakes
Crispy Chocolate Log
Decadent Chocolate Strawberry Shortcakes
Frozen Caramel Dream Dessert
Frozen Lemon Pie
Giant Chocolate Toffee Cookies
Gooey Dark Chocolate Hot Fudge
Key Lime Pie
Lime Snowball Cookies
Mint Chip Ice Cream Dessert
Old Fashioned Peach Pie
Orange Almond Shortbread Slices
Pumpkin Cake Roll
Summer Strawberry Crunch
Texas Sheet Cake

Almond Cheesecake with Chocolate Glaze

A creamy, delicious finish to a wonderful meal

	x2	x4	x6
Crust			
2½ cups gingersnap cookie crumbs	5c	10c	15c
⅓ cup butter, melted	⅔c	1⅓c	2c
Filling			
24 oz. cream cheese, softened	48oz	96oz	144oz
1 cup sugar	2c	4c	6c
3 large eggs, room temperature	6	12	18
2½ t. vanilla extract	1T + 2t	3T + 1t	¼c + 1T
2½ t. pure almond extract	1T + 2t	3T + 1t	¼c + 1T
Chocolate glaze			
1 cup heavy cream	2c	4c	6c
1⅓ cups semisweet chocolate chips	2⅔c	5⅓c	8c
1 t. vanilla extract	2t	4t	2T
Serving Day			
mint leaves or fresh fruit (optional)			

Original Recipe Yield

10–12 servings

Cooking Day

Crust: Crush gingersnap cookies into fine crumbs by placing in a freezer bag and pounding with rolling pin or meat mallet. Combine crumbs with melted butter; press into bottom of a buttered 9 inch springform pan and push as far up sides as crumbs allow.

Filling: In food processor or large mixing bowl, beat cream cheese until smooth. Blend in sugar, eggs, vanilla, and almond extract. Pour into crust. Bake at 350 degrees for 45 minutes. Turn off oven and allow cheesecake to cool in oven with door open. Cool to room temperature. If serving that day, refrigerate at least 3 hours before cutting.

Glaze: In a small saucepan, scald cream. Add chocolate, stirring until melted. Add vanilla and stir until glaze is smooth. Cool to room temperature. Pour glaze over top of cooled cheesecake and refrigerate until set. Cover springform pan with plastic wrap and then a layer of heavy duty foil. Freeze.

Serving Day

Remove cheesecake from freezer and thaw for 30 minutes at room temperature. Run knife along inside of pan to loosen cake from sides of pan. Remove outer ring of springform pan. Allow cheesecake to continue thawing on countertop for 20–30 minutes more; if serving later, place cheesecake in refrigerator. Garnish with mint leaves or fresh fruit if desired.

Apple Cake with Warm Caramel Sauce

A scrumptious autumn dessert

	x2	x4	x6
3 eggs	6	12	18
1 cup vegetable oil	2c	4c	6c
2 cups sugar	4c	8c	12c
1 T. vanilla	2T	¼c	¼c + 2T
2½ cups flour	5c	10c	15c
1 t. salt	2t	1T + 1t	2T
1 t. baking soda	2t	1T + 1t	2T
2 t. baking powder	1T + 1t	2T + 2t	¼c
1 t. cinnamon	2t	1T + 1t	2T
1 t. nutmeg	2t	1T + 1t	2T
3 cups golden delicious apples, peeled and chopped	6c	12c	18c
1 cup pecans, chopped	2c	4c	6c

Serving Day

whipped cream

Caramel sauce

½ cup butter

1 cup brown sugar

¼ cup half-and-half

Original Recipe Yield

10–12 servings

Cooking Day

In a large mixing bowl, beat eggs with an electric mixer until light yellow. Add oil and sugar; beat on medium speed until well mixed. Add vanilla. In a separate bowl, sift together flour, salt, baking powder, baking soda, cinnamon, and nutmeg. Blend into egg mixture. Fold in apples and pecans with a wooden spoon. Pour batter into greased and floured Bundt pan. Bake in a 350 degree oven for 50–60 minutes, until toothpick inserted in the center comes out clean. Remove from Bundt pan immediately, inverting cake onto a wire rack. Cool cake completely. Wrap in plastic wrap, then foil, and freeze.

Serving Day

Thaw cake completely. Warm cake slightly in microwave. Serve immediately with dollop of whipped cream and warm caramel sauce.

Caramel sauce: Melt butter in a medium saucepan. Add brown sugar and half-and-half, stirring constantly. Bring to a gentle boil, then continue cooking for an additional 5 minutes, stirring frequently, until sauce reaches desired consistency.

Butterscotch Chocolate Chip Cookies

Johnny Garcia's favorite cookie—he makes them by himself!

	x2	x4	x6
2½ cups flour	5c	10c	15c
1 t. salt	2t	1T + 1t	2T
½ t. baking soda	1t	2t	1T
¾ cup + 2 T. unsalted butter, softened	1¾c	3½c	5¼c
½ cup granulated sugar	1c	2c	3c
½ cup brown sugar	1c	2c	3c
2 large eggs, room temperature	4	8	12
2 t. vanilla	1T + 1t	2T + 2t	¼c
6 T. sour cream	¾c	1½c	2¼c
1½ cups semisweet chocolate chips	3c	6c	9c
1½ cups butterscotch chips	3c	6c	9c

Original Recipe Yield

4 dozen cookies

Cooking Day

Mix together flour, salt, and soda in medium sized bowl. Set aside. In a large mixing bowl, beat butter and both sugars with an electric mixer on medium speed until fluffy, about 3–5 minutes. Add eggs and vanilla, mixing well. Add flour mixture in two batches, alternating with sour cream. Beat until combined. Stir in butterscotch and chocolate chips. Cover and refrigerate until dough is chilled, about one hour. Using an ice cream or cookie scoop, drop 1½ inch balls of dough onto cookie sheets lined with parchment paper. Bake at 350 degrees for 12–14 minutes, until cookies are golden brown. Freeze, using instructions for baked goods.

Serving Day

Thaw completely and serve. For fresh-baked cookies, cookie dough balls may be flash frozen on cooking day and placed in a freezer bag, then thawed and baked on serving day.

Caramel Brownies

A perfect blend of caramel and chocolate!

	x3	x6	x9
4–1 oz. squares unsweetened chocolate	12	24	36
¾ cup butter	2¼c	4½c	6¾c
2 cups sugar	6c	12c	18c
4 eggs	12	24	36
1 cup flour	3c	6c	9c
14 oz. bag caramels, unwrapped	42oz	84oz	126oz
⅓ cup heavy cream	1c	2c	3c
2 cups pecans, chopped	6c	12c	18c
12 oz. chocolate chips	36oz	72oz	108oz

Original Recipe Yield

4 dozen brownies

Cooking Day

Melt butter and chocolate in microwave or in a double boiler on stovetop. In a mixing bowl, combine sugar with melted chocolate and butter. Add eggs one at a time, beating well after each addition. Add flour and blend until well mixed. Spread half of the batter into a greased 9 x 13 baking pan or disposable foil pan. Bake in a 350 degree oven for 25 minutes. While first layer is baking, melt caramels and cream in microwave on high for 3 minutes. Blend with a spoon and add 1 cup of pecans. Once brownies are removed from oven, immediately spread caramel mixture on top of brownie layer. Sprinkle chocolate chips over caramel layer. Pour rest of batter on top of chocolate chip layer. Sprinkle with remaining pecans. Return brownies to oven and bake 30 more minutes. Cool brownies completely in pan. Cover with a layer of plastic wrap, then foil, and freeze.

Serving Day

Thaw completely. Enjoy!!

Cherry Crisp

Always a favorite!

	x3
Crisp topping	
⅔ cup packed brown sugar	2c
½ cup all-purpose flour	1½c
½ cup quick-cooking oats	1½c
½ t. ground cinnamon	1½t
¼ t. salt	¾t
6 T. butter, cubed and chilled	1c + 2T
Cherry filling	
4 cups fresh pie cherries (sour cherries)*	12c
¾ cup sugar	2¼c
1 T. quick-cooking tapioca	3T
⅓ cup water	1c
1 T. butter	3T
Serving Day	
vanilla ice cream	

*Canned sour cherries may also be used when fresh cherries are not available.

Original Recipe Yield

6–8 servings

Cooking Day

Topping: Combine brown sugar, flour, oats, cinnamon, and salt. Cut in butter until mixture resembles coarse crumbs. Freeze, using freezer bag method.

Filling: In a medium saucepan, combine cherries, sugar, tapioca, and water. Let mixture stand on the countertop 5 minutes, stirring occasionally. Transfer to stovetop, and cook and stir over medium heat until slightly thickened and bubbly. Add butter and stir to combine. Set aside to cool. Freeze, using freezer bag method.

Serving Day

Thaw filling and topping. Place filling in a 1½ quart baking dish. Sprinkle topping over filling. Bake in a 350 degree oven for 40–45 minutes or until bubbly. Serve with ice cream.

Hint

Make the crisp topping ahead in larger quantities and freeze in 2-cup portions. It will be ready to go for whatever fresh seasonal fruit you want to top with it. The original recipe makes about 2 cups of topping, which is what most fruit crisp recipes use.

Chocolate and Vanilla Striped Cookies

These cookies take a bit of work—but they are worth it!

	x3	x6	x9
Vanilla dough			
1¼ cups all-purpose flour	3¾c	7½c	11¼c
⅛ t. salt	⅜t	¾t	1⅛t
½ cup powdered sugar	1½c	3c	4½c
¼ cup butter, softened	¾c	1½c	2¼c
1 large egg yolk	3	6	9
1½ t. vanilla extract	4½t	3T	¼c + 1½t
2 T. ice water	¼c + 2T	¾c	1c + 2T
Chocolate dough			
¾ cup all-purpose flour	2¼c	4½c	6¾c
⅓ cup unsweetened cocoa	1c	2c	3c
⅛ t. salt	⅜t	¾t	1⅛t
1 cup powdered sugar	3c	6c	9c
¼ cup butter, softened	¾c	1½c	2¼c
1 large egg yolk	3	6	9
½ t. vanilla extract	1½t	1T	4½t
2 T. ice water	¼c + 2T	¾c	1c + 2T

Original Recipe Yield

36 cookies

Cooking Day

Vanilla dough: Combine flour and salt; set aside. Place powdered sugar, butter, and egg yolk in a medium bowl and beat with a mixer at medium speed until smooth. Beat in vanilla. Gradually add flour mixture to butter mixture, beating at low speed, just until combined. Sprinkle ice water over surface of dough; beat just until moist. Dough will be slightly crumbly. Press dough into a 4 inch disk and wrap in plastic wrap; cover and chill 1 hour or until firm.

Chocolate dough: Combine flour, cocoa, and salt, stirring well with a whisk; set aside. Place powdered sugar, butter, and egg yolk in a medium bowl; beat with a mixer at medium speed until smooth. Beat in vanilla. Gradually add cocoa mixture to butter mixture, beating at low speed, just until combined. Sprinkle ice water over surface of dough; beat just until moist. Press dough into a 4 inch disk and wrap in plastic wrap; cover and chill 1 hour or until firm.

Unwrap chilled vanilla dough and place on a sheet of plastic wrap. Cover dough with 2 additional sheets of overlapping plastic wrap. Roll covered dough into a 12 x 8 inch rectangle. Repeat process with chocolate dough. Remove top layers of plastic wrap and place chocolate dough on top of vanilla dough rectangle. Roll up dough into a 12 inch cylinder as if you are making cinnamon rolls. Cover with plastic wrap. Place in freezer bag and freeze.

Serving Day

Preheat oven to 375 degrees. Slice frozen cookie dough roll into ¼ inch slices. Place slices 2 inches apart on baking sheets lined with parchment paper. Bake for 12 minutes or until set but not yet golden brown. Cool on baking sheets for 5 minutes. Remove cookies from pans; cool completely on wire racks.

Lighter Fare Nutritional Value (per 2 cookie serving): Calories 73; Total Fat 3g; Sodium 35 mg; Total Carbohydrates 10g

Chocolate Lava Cakes

An impressive restaurant dessert you can make at home!

	x 2	x4	x6
butter or nonstick cooking spray			
½ cup unsalted butter, room temperature	1c	2c	3c
⅓ cup sugar	⅔c	1⅓c	2c
3 large eggs	6	12	18
⅓ cup flour	⅔c	1⅓c	2c
½ t. salt	1t	2t	3t
1½ cups bittersweet chocolate pieces, melted*	3c	6c	9c

Serving Day

vanilla or coffee ice cream
powdered sugar

*8 oz. of a 60–70% bittersweet chocolate bar (coarsely chopped) or 1½ cups semisweet chocolate pieces may be substituted for the bittersweet chocolate pieces. To melt chocolate: Place chopped or chocolate pieces in a bowl that has been set over a pan of simmering water. Stir occasionally until chocolate is smooth and melted.

Original Recipe Yield

10–12 individual cakes

Cooking Day

Generously butter or spray 10–12 muffin cups (or 6 oz. ramekins). In a medium mixing bowl, cream butter and sugar together with an electric mixer until fluffy. Add eggs one at a time, mixing well after each addition. On low speed, mix in flour and salt until just combined. Add melted chocolate, being careful not to over-mix. Divide the batter evenly into prepared muffin cups or ramekins.

Cover and freeze lava cakes for 1–3 hours or until firm. Carefully pop out the frozen cakes (using a small paring knife to loosen sides, if needed). Wrap each individual cake in plastic wrap and place inside a freezer bag. Freeze, using freezer bag method.

▶

Serving Day Instructions

Unwrap desired number of lava cakes and place in buttered or sprayed muffin cups or ramekins. Allow the cakes to come to room temperature before baking. Preheat oven to 400 degrees. Place the muffin cups or ramekins on a baking sheet and bake 10–15 minutes or just until tops of cakes no longer jiggle when shaken. (The centers will still be soft to the touch.) Remove from oven and let stand for 5–7 minutes.

Run a paring knife around the edges of each cake to loosen. Place each cake right side up on individual serving plates. Dust each cake with powdered sugar and add a scoop of ice cream; serve immediately.

Crispy Chocolate Log

A new spin on the Rice Krispies treat—kids love them

Contributed by Joanne Decker—Aurora, Colorado

	x2	x4	x6
1–10 oz. pkg. large marshmallows	2	4	6
¼ cup butter	½c	1c	1½c
¼ cup peanut butter	½c	1c	1½c
5½ cups Rice Krispies cereal	11c	22c	33c
1⅓ cups semisweet chocolate chips	2⅔c	5⅓c	8c
¾ cup butterscotch chips	1½c	3c	4½c

Original Recipe Yield

12–15 servings

Cooking Day

Line a 10 x 15 jellyroll pan with waxed paper. Grease paper with butter and set aside. In a large microwave-safe bowl, combine marshmallows, butter, and peanut butter. Cover and microwave on high for 2 minutes. Stir until well blended. Stir in cereal until well coated: spread in prepared pan, pressing mixture into pan.

In a microwave-safe bowl, combine chocolate and butterscotch chips. Microwave on high for 2 minutes. Stir and spread over cereal mixture. Roll up jellyroll style, starting with the long side, peeling waxed paper away while rolling. Place seam side down on serving plate and refrigerate for 1 hour or until set. Wrap log in plastic wrap, then place in freezer bag and freeze.

Serving Day

Thaw completely; slice and serve.

Decadent Chocolate Strawberry Shortcakes

Great for entertaining in the summer or winter

	x3	x6	x9
Chocolate shortcakes			
1¼ cups all-purpose flour	3¾c	7½c	11¼c
½ cup unsweetened cocoa powder	1½c	3c	4½c
½ cup sugar	1½c	3c	4½c
1 T. baking powder	3T	¼c + 2T	½c + 1T
⅛ t. salt	⅜t	¾t	1⅛t
1 cup chilled whipping cream	3c	6c	9c
1 t. vanilla extract	1T	2T	3T
Strawberries*			
2 lbs. small strawberries, hulled and quartered (about 3½ cups)	6 lbs	12 lbs	18 lbs
½ cup powdered sugar	1½c	3c	4½c
¼ cup fresh orange juice	¾c	1½c	2¼c
2 T. Grand Marnier (optional)	¼c + 2T	¾c	1c + 2T
½ t. finely grated orange peel (optional)	1½t	1T	4½t
⅛ t. salt	⅜t	¾t	1⅛t

Serving Day

½ cup chilled whipping cream

½ cup chilled sour cream (light may be used)

2 T. powdered sugar

*We love strawberries at the height of their season, but when fresh strawberries aren't available, you can pull this from the freezer, which is the next best thing.

Original Recipe Yield

6 servings

Cooking Day

Shortcakes: Preheat oven to 400 degrees. Line baking sheet with parchment paper or grease lightly with shortening. Whisk flour, cocoa, sugar, baking powder, and salt together in a large bowl. In a medium bowl, beat cream and vanilla, using an electric mixer, until firm peaks form. Stir cream into flour mixture until moist clumps form. Transfer the mixture to a lightly floured surface and knead gently until dough forms a ball, about 10 strokes. Pat dough out to ¾ inch thickness. Cut into shortcakes using a 3 inch biscuit cutter. Place on prepared baking sheet. Bake until toothpick inserted into center comes out almost clean, approximately 12–15 minutes. Do not over-bake. Cool shortcakes on cooling rack. Wrap individually in plastic wrap, then place in a freezer bag and freeze, using freezer bag method.

Strawberries: Stir together strawberries, powdered sugar, and next 4 ingredients. Freeze, using freezer bag method.

Serving Day

Thaw shortcakes and strawberries. Using electric mixer, beat chilled whipping cream, sour cream, and powdered sugar until soft peaks form. Place 1 shortcake on each plate; top with one large spoonful of berries with juices. Finish with a dollop of whipped cream mixture.

Frozen Caramel Dream Dessert

This will become a favorite!

	x3	x6	x9
1 cup vanilla wafer crumbs (about 25 wafers)*	3c	6c	9c
¼ cup brown sugar (firmly packed)	¾c	1½c	2¼c
¼ cup butter, melted	¾c	1½c	2¼c
½ cup chopped pecans	1½c	3c	4½c
1 cup caramel ice cream topping	3c	6c	9c
1 quart praline ice cream, softened	3qts	6qts	9qts

*To make vanilla wafer crumbs, place the wafers inside a freezer bag and use a rolling pin or the flat side of a meat mallet to crush.

Original Recipe Yield

6–8 servings

Cooking Day

Preheat oven to 350 degrees. In a medium mixing bowl, combine vanilla wafer crumbs and brown sugar; pour melted butter over mixture and mix well. Spread the crumbs onto a baking sheet and bake for 15 minutes or until browned. Put chopped pecans in a separate oven-proof dish and place in the same oven with crumb mixture. After 7 minutes, remove toasted pecans. Check and stir the crumb mixture. When the crumb mixture is done, remove from oven and cool.

In an 8 x 8 baking pan or disposable foil pan, sprinkle ¾ of the crumb mixture on bottom of pan. Sprinkle ¾ of toasted pecans on top of crumb mixture. Drizzle caramel sauce over pecans. Spread ice cream on top of sauce and then top with the remaining crumbs and pecans. Cover with plastic wrap, then foil, and freeze.

Serving Day

Remove from freezer a few minutes prior to serving to ease cutting. Cut into squares and serve. Additional caramel (or chocolate) topping can be drizzled on top.

Frozen Lemon Pie

Very light dessert; complements a summer barbeque

Contributed by Kaye Matthews—Denver, Colorado

	x3	x6	x9
¾ cup sugar	2¼c	4½c	6¾c
1 whole egg	3	6	9
2 egg yolks	6	12	18
½ t. salt	1½t	1T	4½t
¼ cup lemon juice	¾c	1½c	2¼c
½ t. lemon zest	1½t	1T	4½t
1⅓ cups whipping cream	4c	8c	12c
2 egg whites	6	12	18
graham cracker crust for 9 inch pie (see Key Lime Pie, page 269)	3	6	9

Serving Day

whipped cream

Original Recipe Yield

6–8 servings

Cooking Day

In a double boiler, mix together sugar, whole egg, egg yolks, salt, lemon juice, and lemon zest. Cook mixture over medium heat until thickened; remove from heat and allow to cool.

In a separate bowl, beat egg whites until stiff peaks form. In a second mixing bowl, beat whipping cream until it forms soft peaks. Fold egg whites and whipping cream into lemon filling mixture. Spread mixture into prepared graham cracker pie crust. Cover pie with plastic wrap, then foil, and freeze.

Serving Day

Allow pie to thaw slightly, slice, and serve with dollop of whipped cream on top.

Giant Chocolate Toffee Cookies

Make them once . . . you'll make them again!

	x3	x6	x9
½ cup all-purpose flour	1½c	3c	4½c
1 t. baking powder	1T	2T	3T
¼ t. salt	¾t	1½t	2¼t
1 lb. bittersweet or semisweet chocolate, chopped	3 lbs	6 lbs	9 lbs
¼ cup unsalted butter	¾c	1½c	2¼c
1¾ cups packed brown sugar	5¼c	10½c	15¾c
4 large eggs	12	24	36
1 T. vanilla extract	3T	¼c + 2T	½c + 1T
5–1.4 ounce chocolate-covered English toffee bars (i.e. Heath Bars), coarsely chopped	15	30	45
1 cup walnuts, toasted and chopped	3c	6c	9c

Original Recipe Yield

18 cookies

Cooking Day

Combine flour, baking powder, and salt in a small bowl; whisk to blend and set aside. Place chocolate and butter in top of double boiler and set over simmering water, stirring occasionally, until melted and smooth. Remove from heat; cool to lukewarm.

Using an electric mixer, beat sugar and eggs in a large mixing bowl until thick, about 5 minutes. Beat in chocolate mixture and vanilla. Stir in flour mixture, then toffee and nuts. Chill batter until firm, about 45 minutes. Cookie dough may be formed into cookie balls (¼ cup of dough each) at this point, flash frozen, and placed in a freezer bag. Cookies may also be baked, cooled, wrapped in plastic wrap, placed in a freezer bag, and frozen.

Serving Day

Preheat oven to 350 degrees. Line 2 large baking sheets with parchment or waxed paper. Place dough balls onto sheets, spacing 2½ inches apart. Bake just until tops are dry and cracked but cookies are still soft to touch, about 15 minutes. Cool on sheets.

Gooey Dark Chocolate Hot Fudge

Sinfully delicious!

	x2	x4
⅔ cup heavy cream	1⅓c	2⅔c
¾ cup brown sugar	1½c	3c
2–1 oz. unsweetened chocolate squares	4	8
2 T. butter	¼c	½c
2 T. light corn syrup	¼c	½c
1½ t. vanilla	1T	2T
¼ t. salt	½t	1t

Original Recipe Yield

1 cup sauce

Cooking Day

Heat cream and brown sugar in saucepan over medium-low heat until sugar is dissolved. Add chocolate squares, butter, and corn syrup to saucepan. Bring to a boil, stirring constantly. Boil for 6–7 minutes. Remove from heat and stir in vanilla and salt. Cool completely. Freeze in a plastic container with layer of plastic wrap over top of sauce.

Serving Day

Thaw sauce in microwave slowly, stirring every 30 seconds, until sauce just begins to boil. Pour over ice cream.

This hot fudge will thicken when placed on ice cream and have a chewy consistency. Delicious!

Key Lime Pie

Just like in Key West . . . Wonderful!!

Contributed by Cassie Martinez—Lakewood, Colorado

	x2	x4	x6
Crust			
1 cup graham cracker crumbs	2c	4c	6c
¼ cup + 1 T. melted butter	½c + 2T	1¼c	1¾c + 2T
⅓ cup sugar	⅔c	1⅓c	2c
Filling			
3 egg yolks	6	12	18
1½ t. grated lime zest	1T	2T	3T
1–14 oz. can sweetened condensed milk	2	4	6
½ cup key lime juice	1c	2c	3c
Serving Day			
1 cup heavy cream, chilled			
1 T. powdered sugar			

Original Recipe Yield

6–8 servings

Cooking Day

Crust: Preheat oven to 350 degrees. Butter a 9 inch pie pan. Break up graham crackers; place in a food processor and process to crumbs. (You may also place crackers in a large plastic bag; seal bag and then crush crackers with a rolling pin.) Add melted butter and sugar to cracker crumbs and stir until combined. Press the mixture into the bottom and sides of pie plate or disposable pie pan, forming a neat border around the edge. Bake the crust until set and golden, about 8 minutes. Set aside on a wire rack; leave the oven on.

▶

Filling: Using an electric mixer with a wire whisk attachment, beat egg yolks and lime zest at high speed until very fluffy, about 5 minutes. Gradually add condensed milk and continue to beat until thick, 3–4 minutes longer. Change mixer speed to low and slowly add lime juice, mixing just until combined. Pour mixture into the crust. Bake for 10 minutes or until filling has just set. Cool on a wire rack. Cover pie with plastic wrap and then foil. Freeze.

Serving Day

Remove pie from freezer approximately 30 minutes prior to serving. Whip the cream and powdered sugar until nearly stiff. Cut pie in wedges and serve very cold, topping each wedge with a large dollop of whipped cream.

Lime Snowball Cookies

Addicting!

	x3	x6	x9
1½ cups flour	4½c	9	13½c
½ cup cornstarch	1½c	3c	4½c
1 cup butter, softened	3c	6c	9c
½ cup powdered sugar	1½c	3c	4½c
2 T. fresh lime juice	¼c + 2T	¾c	1c + 2T
1 t. finely grated lime peel	1T	2T	3T
½ t. lime oil*	1½t	1T	4½t

Serving Day

powdered sugar, for dusting

*Lime oil is what gives this cookie such tremendous flavor. It can be found in gourmet grocery stores and specialty kitchen and spice stores.

Original Recipe Yield

3 dozen cookies

Cooking Day

Whisk flour and cornstarch to blend; set aside. In a large bowl, use electric mixer to beat butter and sugar until light and fluffy. Mix in lime juice, lime peel, and lime oil. Beat in flour mixture. Refrigerate dough until firm, about 45 minutes. Form dough into balls, using a scant 1 T. of dough per ball. Cookie dough balls may be flash frozen and placed in a freezer bag, or cookies may also be baked and then frozen for up to 2 months.

Serving Day

Preheat oven to 350 degrees. Line cookie sheets with parchment paper. Place cookie dough balls 1 inch apart on cookie sheets. Bake until pale golden on top and browned on bottom, approximately 20–23 minutes. Immediately sift generous amounts of powdered sugar over cookies. Cool completely on sheets, or cookies will fall apart.

Store cookies wrapped in plastic wrap in an airtight container for up to 5 days at room temperature. Dust with more powdered sugar right before serving.

Mint Chip Ice Cream Dessert

If you love mint and chocolate, this dessert is for you

	x3	x6	x9
½ lb. Oreo cookies, crushed (approx. 23 cookies)	1½ lbs	3 lbs	4½ lbs
¼ cup butter, melted	¾c	1½c	2¼c
½ gallon mint chip ice cream, softened	1½gals	3gals	4½gals

Fudge sauce

	x3	x6	x9
1–13 oz. can evaporated milk	3	6	9
1 cup sugar	3c	6c	9c
½ cup butter	1½c	3c	4½c
2–1 oz. squares semisweet chocolate	6oz	12oz	18oz
1–8 oz. carton Cool Whip	3	6	9
½ cup crushed Oreo cookies	1½c	3c	4½c

Original Recipe Yield

12 servings

Cooking Day

Mix crushed cookies and melted butter together. Press into 9 x 13 pan or disposable foil pan and chill until set. Spoon softened ice cream on top of cookie layer and freeze. Prepare sauce by mixing evaporated milk, sugar, butter, and chocolate squares in a saucepan over medium heat. Bring to a slow boil; boil for 15 minutes. Cool. Spread cooled sauce over ice cream layer and freeze until set. Spread Cool Whip on top of fudge sauce. Garnish with additional ½ cup Oreo cookie crumbs. Cover with plastic wrap, then foil, and freeze.

Serving Day

Allow to soften at room temperature 15 minutes prior to serving.

Old Fashioned Peach Pie

*Having this filling made ahead takes
the prep work out of homemade pie!*

	x3	x6	x9
3 lbs. fresh, ripe peaches (approx. 3¾ cups sliced)	9 lbs	18 lbs	27 lbs
¼ cup brown sugar	¾c	1½c	2¼c
¾ cup granulated sugar	2¼c	4½c	6¾c
¼ cup cornstarch	¾c	1½c	2¼c
¼ t. nutmeg	¾t	1½t	2¼t
¾ t. cinnamon	2¼t	4½t	2T + ¾t

Serving Day

1 double pie crust

Original Recipe Yield

One 9 inch pie

Cooking Day

Peel, pit, and slice fresh peaches into a medium mixing bowl. In a separate small bowl, mix together brown sugar, granulated sugar, cornstarch, and spices. Pour mixture over peaches and stir until well coated. Place peach mixture in a freezer bag and freeze.

Serving Day

Thaw completely. Place bottom layer of pie crust in a 9 inch pie pan. Spoon peaches into pie pan. Cut top crust into ¼ inch wide strips, then form a lattice top in a crisscross pattern for top crust. Bake at 350 degrees for 45–60 minutes, until crust is golden brown and juices are bubbly.

Hint

To make peach peeling quick and easy, drop peaches into boiling water for 1–1½ minutes, then dip immediately into cold water. Drain. The loosened skins will practically slip off!

Orange Almond Shortbread Slices

Try these scrumptious shortbreads!

	x3	x6	x9
1 cup butter, room temperature	3c	6c	9c
1 cup powdered sugar	3c	6c	9c
½ t. almond extract	1½t	1T	4½t
½ t. salt	1½t	1T	4½t
2 cups all-purpose flour	6c	12c	18c
2 t. orange zest	2T	¼c	¼c + 2T
½ t. orange oil* (optional)	1½t	1T	4½t
¾ cup sliced almonds	2¼c	4½c	6¾c

*Orange oil is found in specialty kitchen or spice stores. It gives these cookies a more intense orange flavor.

Original Recipe Yield

about 40 slices

Cooking Day

In a medium mixing bowl, mix together butter, sugar, almond extract, and salt until smooth. With mixer on low speed, add flour, orange zest, and orange oil, mixing until dough forms. Gently fold in almonds with a spoon or spatula. On a piece of wax paper or plastic wrap, form dough into a rectangular log, about 12 inches long, 2 inches wide, and 1 inch thick. Wrap log in plastic wrap and place in a freezer bag. Freeze.

Serving Day

Remove dough from freezer and allow to sit for 30 minutes at room temperature. Preheat oven to 325 degrees. On a cutting board, cut dough with a sharp knife into ¼ inch thick slices. Lay slices on an ungreased baking sheet about 1 inch apart. Bake just until edges begin to turn golden, about 20–25 minutes. Cool on wire rack. Store in an airtight container at room temperature for up to 3 days—if they last that long!

Pumpkin Cake Roll

A fall dessert with beautiful presentation

Contributed by Donna Mayberry—Denver, Colorado

	x3	x6	x9
Cake roll			
3 eggs, separated	9	18	27
1 cup sugar, divided	3c	6c	9c
⅔ cup canned pumpkin	2c	4c	6c
¾ cup all-purpose flour	2¼c	4½c	6¾c
1 t. baking soda	1T	2T	3T
½ t. ground cinnamon	1½t	1T	4½t
⅛ t. salt	⅜t	¾t	1⅛t
Filling			
8 oz. cream cheese, softened	24oz	48oz	72oz
2 T. butter, softened	¼c + 2T	¾c	1c + 2T
1 cup confectioners sugar	3c	6c	9c
¾ t. vanilla extract	2¼t	4½t	2T + ¾t
Serving Day			
confectioners sugar, for dusting			

Original Recipe Yield

10 servings

Cooking Day

Cake: Preheat oven to 375 degrees. Line a 15 x 10 baking pan with waxed paper; grease the paper and set pan aside. In a large bowl, beat egg yolks on high speed until thick and lemon-colored. Gradually add ½ cup sugar and pumpkin, beating on high until sugar is almost dissolved.

In a small mixing bowl, beat egg whites until soft peaks form. Gradually add remaining ½ cup sugar and beat until stiff peaks form. Fold into pumpkin mixture. Combine flour, baking soda, cinnamon, and salt; gently fold into pumpkin mixture. Spread batter into prepared pan. Bake for 12–15 minutes or until the cake springs back when lightly touched. Cool for 5 minutes. Turn cake onto a clean kitchen towel dusted with confectioners sugar. Gently peel off waxed paper. Roll up cake in the towel jellyroll-style, starting with a long side. Cool completely on a wire rack.

Filling: In a mixing bowl, combine cream cheese, butter, confectioners sugar, and vanilla; beat until smooth. Unroll cake and remove from towel. Spread filling evenly to within ½ inch of cake edges. Roll up again. Wrap in layer of plastic wrap and then foil. Freeze. Cake roll may be frozen for up to 3 months.

Serving Day
Remove from freezer 15 minutes before slicing. Dust with confectioners sugar, if desired, and serve.

Summer Strawberry Crunch

A light and refreshing summer dessert

	x3	x6	x9
½ cup butter, melted	1½c	3c	4½c
1 cup flour	3c	6c	9c
⅓ cup brown sugar	1c	2c	3c
½ cup pecans, chopped	1½c	3c	4½c
2 egg whites	6	12	18
⅔ cup sugar	2c	4c	6c
1–16 oz. pkg. frozen strawberries, thawed	3	6	9
1–8 oz. carton Cool Whip Lite	3	6	9

Serving Day

fresh strawberries and mint leaves for garnish

Original Recipe Yield

12 servings

Cooking Day

In a medium bowl, add flour, brown sugar, and pecans to melted butter. Mix thoroughly with a fork. Crumble mixture and spread out on a baking sheet. Bake at 350 degrees for 20 minutes, stirring occasionally to break into smaller pieces. Cool. Pour half of crumbs into a 9 x 9 baking pan or disposable foil pan. For filling, beat egg whites until foamy. Gradually add sugar, beating until mixture forms soft peaks. Fold in strawberries and Cool Whip. Spoon filling into baking dish. Top dessert with remaining crumbs. Cover with a layer of plastic wrap, then foil, and freeze.

Serving Day

Remove from freezer about 10 minutes before serving. Garnish each piece with a sliced fresh strawberry and a fresh mint leaf.

Texas Sheet Cake

Oh my goodness—this cake is amazing!

	x3	x6	x9
1 cup butter	3c	6c	9c
¼ cup cocoa powder	¾c	1½c	2¼c
1 cup water	3c	6c	9c
2 cups flour	6c	12c	18c
2 cups sugar	6c	12c	18c
1 t. baking soda	1T	2T	3T
½ t. salt	1½t	1T	4½t
½ cup sour cream	1½c	3c	4½c
2 eggs, beaten	6	12	18

Frosting

	x3	x6	x9
½ cup butter	1½c	3c	4½c
¼ cup + 2 T. milk	1c + 2T	2¼c	3¼c + 2T
1 lb. powdered sugar	3 lbs	6 lbs	9 lbs
¼ cup cocoa	¾c	1½c	2¼c
1 t. vanilla	1T	2T	3T
1 cup pecan pieces (optional)	3c	6c	9c

Original Recipe Yield

20–24 servings

Cooking Day

Combine butter, cocoa, and water in a saucepan and bring to a boil. Remove from heat and cool slightly. Combine flour, sugar, baking soda, and salt in a mixing bowl. Add sour cream and beaten eggs. Add cocoa mixture and mix well. Pour into greased and floured 15 x 10 jellyroll pan. If you do not have this large-size pan, you can also use two 8 x 8 or 9 x 9 pans. (Do not make this cake in a 9 x 13 pan—it will not turn out as well.) Bake cake at 350 degrees for 20–25 minutes or until cake springs back when touched. Frost while still warm.

For frosting, place butter and milk in a medium saucepan and bring to a boil. Remove from heat and add powdered sugar, cocoa, vanilla, and nuts (if desired). Stir to mix well. Allow frosting to cool for approximately 5 minutes, stirring occasionally. Pour frosting evenly over warm cake and spread with knife. Allow to cool completely and cover cake with layer of plastic wrap and then heavy duty foil. Freeze.

Serving Day

Allow cake to thaw, and serve. This cake is delicious after freezing. It will be very moist!

Eliminating the Guesswork

Helpful Measurements, Equivalents, Weights, and Servings

Food Yield

Note: these equivalents are only **estimates** to aid you when purchasing ingredients.

Food Item	Food Amount (raw or prepared)
Apple (1 medium)	1 cup chopped
Avocado (1 medium)	1 cup, mashed or diced
Beans	
Dried (1 lb., 2½ cups)	6–7 cups cooked
Green/yellow, fresh (1 lb.)	2 cups cut
Breadcrumbs	
Dry (1 slice bread)	⅓ cup
Soft (1 slice bread)	¾ cup
Butter	
1 lb. (4 sticks)	2 cups
1 stick	½ cup or 8 T.
Carrots (2 medium)	1 cup diced or sliced
Celery (2 stalks)	1 cup diced or sliced
Cheese	
Cottage cheese (1 lb.)	2 cups
Cream cheese (8 oz.)	1 cup
Hard cheese (1 lb.)	4 cups grated
Soft cheese (1 lb.)	5 cups grated
Chicken breast, boneless	1½ cups cooked and diced
Chocolate (1 oz.)	1 square or 4 T.
Cilantro (1–4 oz. bunch)	2½ cups chopped
Garlic (1 medium clove)	½ teaspoon chopped or pressed
Green or red bell pepper (1 medium)	¾ cup diced
Green onions (2–3 stalks)	½–¾ cup chopped
Lemon (1 medium)	2–3 T. juice; 2–3 t. grated zest
Lime (1 medium)	1½–2 T. juice; 1–2 t. grated zest

Food Item	Food Amount (raw or prepared)
Milk	
Evaporated (5.33 oz. can)	⅔ cup
Evaporated (14.5 oz. can)	1⅔ cups
Sweetened condensed (14 oz. can)	1⅓ cups
Whipping or heavy cream (1 cup)	2 cups whipped
Mushrooms (3–4 oz.)	1 cup sliced
Nuts	
Almonds (8 oz.)	1 cup sliced or chopped
Cashews (6 oz.)	1 cup
Pecans (8 oz.)	2 cups whole or 1¾ cups chopped
Pine Nuts (3 oz.)	1 cup
Walnuts (6 oz.)	1 cup
Onion	
1 medium	1 cup diced
1 lb.	3–3½ cups diced
Orange (1 medium)	½ cup juice; 1½–2 T. grated zest
Parsley (1–4 oz. bunch)	3½ cups chopped
Pasta	
Macaroni (8 oz., 2 cups uncooked)	4 cups cooked
Egg noodles (8 oz., 3 cups uncooked)	6 cups cooked
Spaghetti (1 lb., uncooked)	7 cups cooked
Peaches	
1 lb.	1¼ cups sliced
1 medium	½–¾ cup sliced
Potatoes	
1 medium	½ cup diced or ¾ cup mashed
1 lb.	4 medium potatoes; 3½–4 cups diced or approximately 2 cups mashed
Raisins (5 oz.)	1 cup
Rice	
1 cup, raw	3–3½ cups cooked
1 lb.	2½ cups uncooked
Spinach (10 oz., fresh)	12 cups loose packed; 1 cup cooked
Strawberries (1 pint)	2 cups sliced
Sugar	
Brown sugar (1 lb.)	2¼ cups packed
Granulated (1 lb.)	2 cups
Powdered (1 lb.)	3¾ cups unsifted
Tomatoes	
1 medium	¾ cup diced; ½ cup puréed
1 lb.	3–4 medium; 2½ cups cooked
14 oz. canned	1½ cups with juice; ¾ cup drained

Baking Dish/Pan Equivalents

1 qt. dish	4 cup baking dish	9 inch pie plate	8 x 1½ inch round cake pan	7⅜ x 3⅝ x 2¼ inch loaf pan
1½ qt. dish	6 cup baking dish	10 inch pie plate	8 or 9 x 1½ inch round cake pan	8½ x 3⅝ x 2⅝ inch loaf pan
2 qt. dish	8 cup baking dish	8 x 8 x 2 inch square pan	11 x 7 x 1½ inch baking pan	9 x 5 x 3 inch loaf pan
2½ qt. dish	10 cup baking dish	9 x 9 x 2 inch square pan	11¾ x 7½ x 1¾ inch baking pan	9 x 5 x 3 inch loaf pan
3 qt. dish	12 cup baking dish	13 x 9 x 2 inch oblong pan		

Measurement Equivalents

Ounces	Tablespoon	Teaspoon	Cups
-	1	3	-
1	2	6	-
2	4	12	¼
-	5⅓	-	⅓
3	6	18	-
4	8	24	½
5	10	30	-
-	10⅔	-	⅔
6	12	36	¾
7	14	42	-
8	16	48	1

2 cups	1 pint
4 cups	1 quart
4 quarts	1 gallon
16 oz.	1 pound
32 oz.	1 quart

Metric Conversion Guide

VOLUME

U.S. Units	Metric
½ teaspoon	2 ml
1 teaspoon	5 ml
1 tablespoon	20 ml
¼ cup	60 ml
⅓ cup	80 ml
½ cup	125 ml
⅔ cup	170 ml
¾ cup	190 ml
1 cup	250 ml
1 quart	1 liter

LENGTH

Inches	Centimeters
1	2.5
2	5.0
3	7.5
4	10.0
5	12.5
6	15.0
7	17.5
8	20.5
9	23.0
10	25.5
11	28.0
12	30.5
13	33.0
14	35.5
15	38.0

TEMPERATURE

Fahrenheit	Celsius
250°	120°
275°	140°
300°	150°
325°	160°
350°	180°
375°	190°
400°	200°
425°	220°
450°	230°
475°	240°
500°	260°

WEIGHT

U.S. Units	Metric
1 ounce	30 grams
2 ounces	60 grams
3 ounces	90 grams
4 ounces (¼ pound)	125 grams
8 ounces (½ pound)	225 grams
16 ounces (1 pound)	500 grams

Note: The recipes in this cookbook have not been developed or tested using metric measures. When converting recipes to metric, some variations in quality may be noted.

Index of Recipes

Mouthwatering Appetizers

Bacon Roll-ups 38
Beijing Egg Rolls 39
Bleu Cheese Pine Nut Tart 41
Cocktail Meatballs with a Twist 43
Crab Cheese Wontons 45
Hot Soft Pretzels 46
Incredible Crab Cakes 48
Mushroom Cap Delights 51
Santa Fe Chicken Nachos 52
Spinach and Cheese in Puff
    Pastry 53
Tex Mex Chili Dip 55
Way Out West Wontons 57

Bountiful Breads and Brunch

Apricot-Pistachio Oat Bars 60
Bacon and Egg Strata 62
Baked Breakfast Blintz 63
Blueberry Sour Cream Pound
    Cake 65
Breakfast Sausage and Apples 67
Breakfast Strudel 68
Cheesy Breadsticks 70
Chicken and Broccoli Quiche 71
Cinnamon Bread Soufflé with Maple
    Butter Syrup 73
Double Dutch Cupcakes 75
Frozen Fruit Cups 77
Garlic Herb Bread 78
Heavenly Scones 80
Lake Powell Chile Relleno Bake 82

Old Fashioned Biscuits 84
Poppy Seed Bread with Orange
    Glaze 85
Savory Sausage Bread 86
Smothered Baked Breakfast
    Burritos 88
Sour Cream Coffee Cake 90
Steve's Chorizo and Egg Burritos 92

Savory Soups

Buffalo Chicken Soup 94
Chicken, Shrimp, and Sausage
    Stew 96
Chipotle-Chocolate Chili 98
Clam Chowder 100
Creamy Tomato Basil Soup 101
Crested Butte Chicken, Chile, and
    Corn Soup 103
Elegant Cream of Mushroom
    Soup 105
Four Cheese Italian Minestrone 106
Hearty Corn Chowder 108
Red Rocks Green Chili 109
Saucy Vegetable Beef Soup 111
Sausage with Cheese Tortellini
    Soup 113
Slow Cooker Split Pea Soup 114

Fabulous Poultry and Fish

All-Seasons Sesame Chicken 118
Baja Grilled Fish Tacos 120
Balsamic Roasted Chicken Thighs 122

Bangkok Chicken Satay   124
Basil Grilled Tuna Kabobs   126
Bombay Chicken Curry   128
Cajun Style Chicken Leg Quarters   129
Calypso Salmon   130
Chicken Cordon Bleu   131
Chicken Marsala   133
Chicken Oreganato   135
Ginger Glazed Mahi Mahi   136
Gourmet Salmon Burgers   138
Grilled Coconut Lime Chicken
  Tenders   139
Grilled Honey Lime Chicken   141
Maui Grilled Chicken
  Sandwiches   143
Monterey Jack Stuffed Chicken   145
Orange Braised Chicken Thighs with
  Green Olives   147
Orange Pine Nut Chicken   148
Parmesan Garlic Chicken   150
Pineapple Lemon Chicken   151
Savory Chicken Bundles   153
Sesame Salmon   155
South of the Border Chicken
  Enchiladas   156
Spicy Peanut Chicken   158
Teriyaki Chicken Veggie Stir-Fry   159

Succulent Beef and Pork

Asian Flank Steak   162
Barbeque Sandwiches   163
Beef Bourguignon   165
Beef Tacquitos   167
Belgian Creek Beef Goulash   169
Burgundy Slow Roasted Beef   171
Chuck Roast for the Grill   172
Creamy Chuck Roast with
Mushrooms   173
Elegant Steak Dionne   175
Elliott's Gourmet Burgers   176

English Sirloin Pasties   178
Greek Meatballs with Mint
  (Keftethes)   180
Grilled Rib-Eye Steaks   182
Herb Crusted Pork Chops   184
Honey-Dijon Glazed Ham   185
Italian Stuffed Meatloaf   186
Oven Baked Pork Roast with
  Barbeque Sauce   188
Poppy Seed Ham and Cheese
  Melts   190
Pork Loin with Garlic Rub   191
Pulled Pork Sandwiches with White
  Barbeque Sauce   192
Simple Salisbury Steak   194
Sliced Beef Brisket   195
Steak Kabobs with Orange Hoisin
  Glaze   196
Steak Soft Tacos   198
Stuffed Flank Steak   200
Tangy Chops with Honey Curry
  Sauce   201
Telluride Black Bean Tortilla
  Bake   202
Tender Beef on a Skewer   204
Top Sirloin with Red Wine
  Marinade   206

Tempting Pizza and Pasta

Baked Penne with Sausage, Tomatoes,
  and Cheese   208
Beef Pasta Bake   210
Butternut Squash Lasagna   211
Donna's Stromboli   213
Four Cheese White Pizza   215
Mediterranean Lasagna   217
Mexican Manicotti   219
Quick Cheese Ravioli with Two
  Different Fillings   221
Veggie Pizza   223

Wes's Roasted Red Pepper Pasta
    Sauce   225
White Chicken Lasagna with
    Spinach   227

Adding a Side Dish

Broccoli Rice Casserole   230
Four Corners Refried Beans   231
Glazed Carrots   233
Green Beans with Pine Nuts   235
Grilled Vegetable Medley   237
Harvest Sweet Potato Cranberry
    Casserole   238
Homemade Baked Beans   240
Marvelous Mashed Potatoes   241
Rice for Any Meal   244
Southwestern Green Chile Rice
    Bake   246
Twice Baked Potatoes   247

Delightful Desserts

Almond Cheesecake with Chocolate
    Glaze   250
Apple Cake with Warm Caramel
    Sauce   252

Butterscotch Chocolate Chip
    Cookies   254
Caramel Brownies   255
Cherry Crisp   256
Chocolate and Vanilla Striped
    Cookies   258
Chocolate Lava Cakes   260
Crispy Chocolate Log   262
Decadent Chocolate Strawberry
    Shortcakes   263
Frozen Caramel Dream Dessert   265
Frozen Lemon Pie   266
Giant Chocolate Toffee Cookies   267
Gooey Dark Chocolate Hot
    Fudge   268
Key Lime Pie   269
Lime Snowball Cookies   271
Mint Chip Ice Cream Dessert   272
Old Fashioned Peach Pie   273
Orange Almond Shortbread
    Slices   274
Pumpkin Cake Roll   275
Summer Strawberry Crunch   277
Texas Sheet Cake   278